ADVANCE PRAISE

"*Our Anxious Selves* masterfully distills the latest research in psychology and neuroscience, making it accessible to a wide audience. Ginot's book has deepened my understanding of the anxiety and trauma I see in my clients and has altered the ways we work together. It has helped me to process and heal my own family dynamics. This book should be read by every practitioner in psychology's allied fields—coaches, chaplains, clergy, spiritual directors, and healers."

—**Gretchen Martens**, ontological coach, spiritual companion, and Reiki master

"This is a book about the unconscious roots of fear and anxiety that reads like a novel! In her inimitable, engaging style, Ginot combines neuroscientific research with clinical material, illustrating how, while fear-reactions and anxiety are inevitable parts of life, we can live our lives to the fullest despite anxiety's presence. With rates of anxiety having risen dramatically across the globe during the COVID-19 pandemic, this is a tremendously timely and valuable book for therapists, educators, and anyone who wishes to successfully and adaptively ease the grip of anxiety."

—**Irit Felsen**, Professor, Columbia University and clinical psychologist, private practice

"In her latest book, Efrat Ginot continues her brilliant research building links between various psychoanalytic models, while investigating the neurobiological basis of emotions. Fear and anxiety become the crossroads of all this. The novelty is that the brain-wide system does not occur beforehand, but it is rather influenced and organized through a continuous dialogue with emotions. We discover that traumatic experiences, even when evolutionary and inevitable, are found in the intersubjective resonances of the consulting room. The book takes us into a psychoanalytic clinic that is enriched with complexity, but nonetheless remains light."

—**Giuseppe Riefolo**, training analyst, Italian Psychoanalytic Society, coauthor of *Enactment in Psychoanalysis*

Our Anxious Selves

THE NORTON SERIES ON INTERPERSONAL NEUROBIOLOGY

Louis Cozolino, PhD, Series Editor
Allan N. Schore, PhD, Series Editor, 2007–2014
Daniel J. Siegel, MD, Founding Editor

The field of mental health is in a tremendously exciting period of growth and conceptual reorganization. Independent findings from a variety of scientific endeavors are converging in an interdisciplinary view of the mind and mental well-being. An interpersonal neurobiology of human development enables us to understand that the structure and function of the mind and brain are shaped by experiences, especially those involving emotional relationships.

The Norton Series on Interpersonal Neurobiology provides cutting-edge, multidisciplinary views that further our understanding of the complex neurobiology of the human mind. By drawing on a wide range of traditionally independent fields of research—such as neurobiology, genetics, memory, attachment, complex systems, anthropology, and evolutionary psychology—these texts offer mental health professionals a review and synthesis of scientific findings often inaccessible to clinicians. The books advance our understanding of human experience by finding the unity of knowledge, or consilience, that emerges with the translation of findings from numerous domains of study into a common language and conceptual framework. The series integrates the best of modern science with the healing art of psychotherapy.

A Norton Professional Book

Our Anxious Selves

....

NEUROPSYCHOLOGICAL PROCESSES AND THEIR ENDURING INFLUENCE ON WHO WE ARE

EFRAT GINOT

W. W. NORTON & COMPANY
Independent Publishers Since 1923

This book is intended as a general information resource for professionals practicing in the field of psychotherapy and mental health. It is not a substitute for appropriate training or clinical supervision. Standards of clinical practice and protocol change over time. No technique or recommendation is guaranteed to be safe or effective in all circumstances, and neither the publisher nor the author can guarantee the accuracy, efficacy, or appropriateness of any particular recommendation in every respect.

The names and identifying details of clients, supervisees, and any other individuals referenced in clinical sessions have been changed, quotations have been fictionalized, and some client cases are composites. Any URLs displayed in this book link or refer to websites that existed as of press time. The publisher is not responsible for, and should not be deemed to endorse or recommend, any website, app, or other content that it did not create. The author, also, is not responsible for any third-party material.

For information about permission to reproduce selections from this book, write to Permissions, W. W. Norton & Company, Inc., 500 Fifth Avenue, New York, NY 10110

For information about special discounts for bulk purchases, please contact W. W. Norton Special Sales at specialsales@wwnorton.com or 800-233-4830

Manufacturing by Versa Press
Production manager: Gwen Cullen

Library of Congress Cataloging-in-Publication Data

Names: Ginot, Efrat, author.
Title: Our anxious selves : neuropsychological processes and their enduring
    influences on who we are / Efrat Ginot.
Description: First edition. | New York : W. W. Norton & Company, 2022. |
    Series: A norton professional book | Includes bibliographical references and index.
Identifiers: LCCN 2021050917 | ISBN 9780393714531 (hardcover) |
    ISBN 9780393714548 (epub)
Subjects: LCSH: Self-confidence. | Fear. | Anxiety. | Neuropsychology.
Classification: LCC BF575.S39 G526 2022 | DDC 158.1—dc23/eng/20211217
LC record available at https://lccn.loc.gov/2021050917

W. W. Norton & Company, Inc., 500 Fifth Avenue, New York, N.Y. 10110
www.wwnorton.com

W. W. Norton & Company Ltd., 15 Carlisle Street, London W1D 3BS

1 2 3 4 5 6 7 8 9 0

To my expanding family and to all my patients,
past, present, and future.

CONTENTS

ACKNOWLEDGMENTS

There are many people I want to thank for helping me during the process of researching and writing this book.

This is the second book I have written, and like the first, it could not have become a reality without having all my patients and their human struggles in mind. To all of them I owe a great deal of gratitude for placing their trust in me and letting me into their anxious and vulnerable selves. These encounters have given me the motivation to further research and better understand the oversized role of fear and anxiety in our psychological development.

First and foremost, I want to thank the dedicated staff at Norton Professional Books. I would like to start by thanking Deborah Malmud, Publishing Director, for trusting this project as well as for her patience, helpful guidance, and wise suggestions. A great deal of appreciation goes to all the Norton team members who provided enormous and indispensable editorial and production help: Mariah Eppes, Senior Project Editor; Sara McBride Tuohy, Editorial Assistant; Olivia Guarnieri, Editorial and Production Assistant; Gwen Cullen, Production Manager; Kevin Olsen, Associate Director; and Emma Paolini, Marketing and Publicity Assistant.

I would like to extend special thanks to Gretchen Martens who, with much warmth and many insights, believed in what I tried to convey in these chapters. As a well-rounded reader, she provided valuable editorial suggestions, helping me clarify my ideas and improve my writing. Her ongoing encouragement was invaluable.

And then there is my wonderful family. Both my daughters, Ariel Ramchandani-Pizzi and Talya Ramchandani, listened to my anxieties and complaints and countered with wise and helpful reality checks. I want to thank Nolan Wanecke and Andrew Pizzi for their indispensable technical help. I never once felt judged by them for my lack of computer proficiency. Even my grandchildren Isla and

Jordan deserve thanks for their patience when seeing their Amma so busy on her computer for long stretches of time.

Although living far away, my sister Bilha Neufeld has always been a strong and supportive presence, providing needed humor, as well as a steady common sense perspective. Thank you, Gera Neufeld, for all the scientific input throughout the years. I also want to thank my aunt Betty Daror, whose lively curiosity, wisdom, and wide knowledge in philosophy and psychology have greatly contributed to my own intellectual development. My cousin Serena Wieder also deserves special mention for her important role in my personal and professional life.

Adding to the inevitable difficulties involved in writing a book, this one was written and completed during the terrible months of the COVID-19 pandemic. In the face of social isolation, the frequent communications with my friends provided the strength and encouragement I needed when I felt anxious and overwhelmed both by the vastness of the book's subject matter and by the ongoing catastrophe happening outside. My friend Judy Kottick in particular did not let up on her weekly requests to find out about the "status" of the writing and the book's progress. Her ongoing support and belief in this book did not waver in the face of my occasional doubts.

My good friend Leanne Domash provided steady support and encouragement, as well as a deep understanding of what it means to see such a project to its end. She was always there with much needed inspiration on the one hand and down-to-earth perspective on the other. Similarly, the encouragement offered by Irit Felsen and John Parsons was important and appreciated, as well as the support expressed by Shelly Rosen and Abe Givner. I am also grateful to other friends who understood my dedication to this project even as it came at the expense of time spent with them. They were encouraging and cheered me on. Sara Lavner, Meryl Messineo, Henia Adoulami, Eve Eisenstadt, and Joshua Schreier; thank you all.

Last but not least, I wish to thank my very patient and Zen husband Prem Ramchandani. His unwavering support has been both emotional and practical. He was the one I turned to any time I was on the brink of panic because of some potential, often imagined, computer-related disaster. I knew I could always rely on him to retrieve "lost" or (more accurately) misplaced documents or fix the occasional formatting hiccups. I greatly appreciate your loving support.

INTRODUCTION

The Pervasive Effects of Fear and Anxiety: A New and Expanded Exploration

This book explores the outsized role that fear, anxiety, and other distressing emotions play in forming fundamental aspects of who we are. In other words, this book tells the story of the human condition. It examines how inevitable and commonplace adverse experiences during our development create predictable emotional effects that shape how we think, feel, and act. This undertaking results from my many years of psychotherapeutic practice and my attempts to understand the roots of the many personal difficulties and struggles I have witnessed in my clients, others, and myself.

We are all unique in our individuality and greatly differ in the ways we see ourselves, in how we feel about others, and in how we cope with the inevitable emotional injuries and painful turmoil that are part of life. We all come from extremely diverse and singular backgrounds and are raised by people distinctive in their personalities and behavioral tendencies. And yet, most of us share the complex emotional consequences of fear and anxiety, and the other painful feelings and behaviors they cause. In effect, when trying to help patients identify, understand, and alter emotional and behavioral patterns that do not enhance their lives but actually hurt them, I saw a commonality in their painful conditions, interpersonal problems, and professional difficulties: old anxieties and irrational fears, paralyzing self-doubts, convincing worries, fear of failing and being exposed as a fraud, negative self-narratives, and an extreme sensitivity to what others may say or think about them, to name just a few examples.

Furthermore, many of these fears, anxieties, sensitivities, and worries do not match people's current reality or the facts on the ground. Often, despite being productive and involved in a range of relationships, we may still experience persistent vulnerabilities and insecurities, often expressed through anxieties and worries about what may go wrong. When feeling particularly vulnerable, we may be filled with self-doubts and pay special attention to perceived, or more accurately projected, criticism from others whose approval we seek. Being too afraid of failure and fearing exposure, we avoid taking risks, thus failing to fully use our skills and talents. We can also find ourselves ruminating on past disappointments, both real and imagined, or unfavorably comparing ourselves to others.

When steeped in a negative mood, we can perceive ourselves as wounded victims of life, struggling to experience our more robust and resilient self. When threatened, we may feel as if we can only exist in the shadows of more powerful or knowledgeable people, following their lead and deriving our sense of self from the acceptance and validation of others. And finally, at times, we find ourselves with a cluttered and anxious mind, with incessant worries about lists that need to be checked and tasks that seem to be urgent, demanding, and yet overwhelming. At those times, when anxious feelings and distracting thoughts take over, we tend to lose connection to the details of the present moment, thus depriving ourselves of the joys and satisfaction of experiencing ourselves in the here and now.

As we will see in the research presented in the following chapters and in the various case descriptions, the repeated features behind the many internal difficulties and interpersonal entanglements we experience are the multilayered effects of the fear system. This consistent element is present in us all, leading to the familiar psychological difficulties rooted in fear and anxiety. As a matter of fact, a deeper understanding of human suffering, bouts of low self-esteem, negative ruminations, and incessant worries all seem to reveal the damaging effects of fear and anxiety. Over time, I have come to view our internal and interpersonal difficulties as largely driven and shaped by the underlying forces of the fear system.

However, what I am looking to accomplish in these chapters is not to focus on the broad categories of fear, anxiety, and trauma as they relate to the more familiar categories of symptoms. One can confidently state that there is a vast professional and popular body of writings on fear and anxiety symptoms and how to successfully cope with them. Rather, my purpose is to go beyond what is already known and explore the myriad unconscious effects that early dysregulation states have on various aspects of our lifelong personality traits and behaviors.

THE FEAR SYSTEM AND ITS TENTACLES

What leads to the prominence of fear and anxiety in our psychic life is what I call, throughout the book, the "fear system." However, the story of fear and anxiety is not limited to these emotions alone. From early on, fear and anxiety become entwined with other emotions and thoughts, giving rise to vulnerable and self-conscious feelings such as shame, low self-esteem, and self-doubt. Often, intense anxieties about how others see or judge us form the basis for recurrent states of negative rumination and preoccupation. In turn, anxieties about our self-worth lead us to frame failure as proof of our inferiority and to an entrenched defensive avoidance when it comes to taking chances. Anxieties about being accepted and understood often impede our ability to trust the intentions of others and may lead to feelings of being betrayed by their ill intentions. This, of course, is especially problematic in intimate relationships.

The innate fear system is only one among other innate emotion states that have all acquired essential survival functions throughout evolution (Chapter 2). The fear system, however, is the one most powerfully connected to the actual survival of all living creatures, whose very existence has depended on their ability to detect threat and react to it adaptively. Over eons, our successful ancestors indeed developed the most efficient threat detectors, brain circuits, that guaranteed their continual thriving. It is no surprise, then, that today, fear, anxiety, panic—emotions connected to the fear system—are behind many of our psychological difficulties. Their pervasive influence often leads to the distorted beliefs we possess about ourselves, others, and the world.

For complex negative feelings and convictions to take hold, our brain/minds and our bodies need to be especially susceptible to the neuropsychological consequences of the upsetting and therefore dysregulating emotions of fear and anxiety. Indeed, our brain/mind/bodies are extremely sensitive to innate fear circuits and in particular, the amygdala—the brain region responsible for detecting and generating fears. In addition, the extensive interconnectedness among brain regions and circuits, and an overlapping of functions, further contributes to the vulnerability of our brain/minds to fear and anxiety (Chapter 3).

This interconnectedness enables the brain-wide influence of stress, fear, and anxiety on all other mental and behavioral functions: attention, perceptions, memories, learning, defenses, and emotion regulation—the capacity to adaptively respond to potentially overwhelming emotions (Chapter 4). In addition, this interconnectedness also leads to the unconscious influence of fear and anxiety on other feeling states, becoming entwined with and intensifying feelings of shame, for example, or interfering with the quality of one's attachment (Chapter 5).

As described in Chapter 1, most of these processes are unconscious. We are not aware of what early interactions, memory traces, and learned experiences were encoded and stored throughout various brain circuits, forming the basis for how we come to experience ourselves and others. The unique malleability of our brain/minds during early development determines the nature of our unconscious emotional, cognitive, and response patterns. We can, however, learn a great deal about these unconscious patterns through our conscious experiences: our feelings, thoughts, and behaviors (Chapter 1).

The amygdala's influence on our thought processes is particularly significant. As a result of the wide interconnection among neural circuits, amygdala-driven emotions influence the tenor of our thoughts, beliefs, and convictions. Most significantly, the inextricable mixture of emotions and cognitions explains how during our early years such neuropsychological processes shape and establish our narratives about the self and others (Chapter 11).

CHILDHOOD FEARS AND ADULT ANXIETY

The still developing neuropsychological field indeed indicates that many of the aspects that determine who we are psychologically and even physiologically start in infancy. Early, innate needs for attachment, attunement, and physical and emotional comfort make us vulnerable to states of frustration, discomfort, or hyperarousal. In addition, we are also exquisitely sensitive to our caregivers' emotion states as well, internalizing their fears and anxieties as our own (Chapter 6). Unfortunately, these effects are extremely devastating when children are subjected to sexual, physical, or emotional abuse or severe neglect. Such traumatic experiences often cause enduring internal and interpersonal difficulties rooted in a pervasive state of vigilance and fear. As more research uncovers the neuropsychological underpinnings of post-traumatic stress disorder (PTSD) responses, it also highlights the short- and long-term effects of childhood trauma (Chapter 7).

But as the fear system and the amygdala and its related circuits are active even prior to birth, we are also vulnerable to emotional insults from a wide range of normative, run-of-the-mill events and experiences that may seem benign to parents but are still injurious to infants, children, and adolescents. From infancy on, children are at the mercy of disturbing emotions and then thoughts that can harm their sense of well-being and confidence. An accumulation of hurtful experiences strengthens and reinforces the development of anxious and injured self-states. Indeed, pockets of anxiety and negative self-narratives develop even with good parenting and within a loving and supportive environment. The lagging development of the prefrontal cortex, which is the region involved with a more reasoned understanding of our environment, results in emotional and often distorted conclusions about ourselves and others. Consequently, unbeknownst to parents and other adults in their lives, children will react internally to many events and interactions with limited perspective and understanding. This results in increased anxiety and irrational interpretations as to the source and meaning of upsetting interpersonal situations with parents and peers. In child-centered ways, children's understanding of dysregulating interactions tends to focus on their own erroneously perceived shameful behaviors and assumed shortcomings (Chapter 8).

In addition, this chapter also explores the role of epigenetics, the complex interactions between genes and the environment. From the very beginning of life, temperament and environment become enmeshed, and together influence who we become. Because of the prominence of fear from early childhood, this epigenetic interaction is particularly significant to the prevalence of our anxious states. A stronger tendency to experience fear renders the environment scarier and less safe in a child's experience. Conversely, an abusive environment will most often increase sensitivity to fear and anxiety disorders.

At the same time, and from the very beginning, in attempts to restore the sense of well-being, we automatically recruit and employ coping mechanisms and various defenses. As development progresses, early defenses become well-established patterns of automatic response to perceived threats. But defense mechanisms often outgrow their adaptability; what worked in early childhood and adolescence may not be helpful to us as adults (Chapter 9).

When the levels of the emotional injuries suffered during childhood are experienced as particularly dysregulating, the unconscious defenses utilized against them tend to be extreme as well. As avoiding the pain of reexperiencing one's dreaded injury and insecurity becomes the most urgent unconscious motivation, individuals can develop narcissistic traits. We remember, however, that from infancy on, inevitable and normative anxious states are inextricably entwined with insults and injuries to our sense of self. In this light, we can state that, in effect, we all have enduring smidgens of injury and defense; in this respect, we are all narcissists (Chapter 10).

As neuroscience supports the conclusion that fear and anxiety are at the heart of our psychological dynamics, it highlights the role these emotions have in the thoughts, views, and beliefs we develop about ourselves and others—our self-narratives (Chapter 11). These narratives are the many automatic and repetitive ways by which we give meaning to events and express entrenched ways of feeling and thinking about ourselves and judging others. As such a central expression of how we relate to ourselves and others, self-narratives are the essential building blocks of our identity and sense of self. They give voice to both the negative and the positive elements of our worldviews and, importantly, communicate the wide range of conscious and unconscious self-states (Chapter 1).

But in growing up, many more forces aside from our immediate family can influence our emotional stress. For example, I have written this book during the stressful year of the global COVID-19 pandemic. During that time, my attention often oscillated between the vast amount of research and information regarding fear and anxiety and the inevitable confusion, unpredictability, and fears caused by the pandemic. Consequently, although this book originally set out to explore the lasting effects of early fear systems on our development, I also examine the inevitable and very relevant interactions between the pandemic and our sensitive fear system. In particular, I focus on the anxiety-inducing consequences of events in 2020 and their effects on parenting and children (Chapter 12).

Other external circumstances that have been shown to contribute to elevated levels of anxiety are socially determined conditions such as poverty and racial discrimination. Growing psychological and neuropsychological data increasingly provide important knowledge about the pernicious effects of such conditions on generations of growing children (Chapter 13). It seems to me that, especially in this context, knowledge is power—the power of clarity about the role of socio-economic factors and the power to change them.

Chapter 14 examines another potential outside influence on children's levels of anxiety: violent media content and violent games. Although findings are still relatively sparse and their results controversial, an interesting picture already emerges of the negative effects that such violent images may have on children and adolescents. However, we are not doomed.

Although there is an (almost) universal pattern of negative feelings and narratives in our psyches, this is only a part of the story. Even in the face of automatically repeating and enacting difficult unconscious–conscious patterns, we still have the agency to modify their effects. Psychotherapy encourages us to observe, identify, and understand our harmful internal and interpersonal patterns with the goal of working to change their negative effects in our lives. In the process, we also strengthen our resilient and adaptive perceptions and response patterns. We learn to tolerate and live well with occasional and inevitable anxiety (Chapter 15).

But psychotherapy is not the only approach that can expand our capacity to understand and tackle the internal dynamics brought on by dysregulating emotions. Contemporary approaches based on mindfulness training and conscious breathing increasingly show their effectiveness in dealing with anxious and distractible states of mind. Mindfulness is especially crucial to good-enough parenting. More mindful parents, for example, can minimize the occurrences of upsetting emotional interactions by paying attention to their own tendencies to "lose it," to be impatient or dismissive. Apologizing to a hurt or angry child and accepting responsibility when appropriate goes a long way to reduce the child's anxiety about being wrong and losing a parent's love and approval. Mindful attitudes also enable caregivers to identify and respect the child's innate tendencies and preferences without imposing their own needs and entrenched patterns on them. And finally, a mindful parent can help a child under stress and anxiety mindfully process, accept, and understand difficult situations, thus presenting the child with a model of adaptive coping.

The greatest gift we can give ourselves and our children is the courage to become aware of our own anxious patterns and vulnerable states, understanding what triggers them, slowing down, and accepting them for what they are— inevitable parts of who we are. Accepting how we came to possess anxious and defensive self-states, understanding how they were formed before consciousness came online, can lead to genuine compassion for self and others. Therapy, in particular, can help us see that our negative perceptions, projections, interpretations, and defensive behaviors are the products of unavoidable developmental processes. The more we understand the power of the fear system in our early development, the better we'll accept our human frailties and learn to live and thrive with them (see the epilogue).

UNCONSCIOUS PROCESSES

In order to better understand how the fear system shapes our personality, we need to begin by addressing the foundation of who we are—our unconscious. In effect, unconscious processes guide and determine all facets of our development, our eventual traits, and our behavioral tendencies. Our experiences during early development leave no explicit or accessible memories. But implicit memories do not disappear; they become a dynamic and influential part of the many brain/mind networks that together build the unconscious patterns that are behind all our feelings, thoughts, and actions (Chapter 1).

The cases discussed in these chapters are drawn from patients I have seen during the last few years. Their identities are entirely disguised. Over the years, my patient population has reflected a wide variety of socioeconomic and ethnic diversity. In particular, I have had a large concentration of first- and second-generation immigrants to the United States. Some have struggled with social stigmas regarding their countries of origin; others still carry the scars of their parents' struggles. But regardless of background and financial status, like most of us, they all have struggled with the effects of early fear and anxiety on their psychological being.

And finally, a few words on the structure of the book. Although the overriding theme of the book is the fear system and its many effects on our brain/mind/bodies, each chapter addresses the neuropsychological roots and the behavioral consequences of these effects. Consequently, each chapter can be read and understood as a separate exploration of this complex topic.

JERRY'S CASE: UNCONSCIOUS PROCESSES AND ENTRENCHED PATTERNS

Jerry started therapy when he was 36 years old. A few years prior to that, he terminated a three-times-weekly analysis that lasted about 6 years. He had recently moved to New York City for a new job and wanted to resume treatment.

Jerry had changed careers a few times, made and lost money, but still could not settle on what he wanted to do when he "grew up." He also complained about his ongoing difficulties in sustaining a romantic relationship. During his previous therapy, he understood some of these difficulties: he quickly fell in love, idealized the woman for a while, and just as quickly started to see flaws and "things that drove him crazy." When this happened, he wanted out, looking forward to the next connection, to the "relationship that might be the one." The fall from an idealized love always hurt and devastated him, and yet he couldn't stay. Friendships were easier for him, as they didn't raise the high expectation for connection that romantic encounters did. "Staying in love," as he put it, was still a challenge.

Jerry said that although he got to know himself in analysis, especially in terms of the complicated relationship with his overbearing mother, he still did not feel better about himself, "or know how to be less anxious and conflicted." As we started to talk, it became clear that he had little awareness of what he liked in a job or in a woman; in effect, he could not articulate specific goals or desires beyond wishing to find a fulfilling relationship and make a great deal of money. With time, a clearer picture of Jerry's relational difficulties emerged, and two conflicting attitudes toward women as well as toward any other commitments came to the forefront.

He would begin a relationship with a great deal of sexual attraction and high hopes for a good and harmonious connection. But after a short while, weeks or months, feelings of being trapped in "something that was not good enough" would start to bother him and fill him with ambivalence. What made these feelings even stronger was a nagging sense that he must please his girlfriend, read her mind, and, most importantly, make sure that his behaviors guaranteed her love for him. This internal conviction also extended to the sexual aspects of his relationships. The more we explored his feelings and behaviors, Jerry realized that as the need to successfully "read their minds and be sure of their emotional and sexual needs" took center stage in the relationship, he would "lose touch with what he himself wanted." He would become aware, however, of a vague sense of being burdened and trapped.

When these thoughts surfaced, Jerry became convinced that the woman "wanted more" from him, that she took the relationship "for granted" and expected, for example, that they meet more regularly or more often. Concerns about being pushed into something he was not ready for or didn't want made him cautious and distant. A loss of sexual interest would follow and, although not quite understanding what was taking place, "the relationship would become too complicated and too much for him." Thoughts about the woman's shortcomings would intensify and the relationship would end.

In some ways, Jerry's difficulties in sustaining relationships reflected his problems committing to a career. He seemed to float from project to project in disparate fields: from high-tech to nonprofit to taking part in a design team for a public relations firm. Once involved, he worked very hard and with great efficiency, but he was still not sure why he was doing what he was doing, and how he got there. He did not feel he made conscious choices because, as he said, he "does not know what he likes." When a project was done, he felt relief; he could now go on to the next, potentially more lucrative gig. Again, little thought was given to conscious choices of what engagement might truly interest him.

What in Jerry's relational and emotional background led to such ambivalence toward intimate relationships? How did this ambivalence become generalized to work choices as well? How did conflicting desires and the difficulties in knowing his own mind become such an enduring pattern? In effect, Jerry's infancy and childhood experiences provided the blueprint for this pattern of relating and retreat, losing himself in a new relationship or a new job and then withdrawing altogether. Unsurprisingly, not long after starting our work together, it became obvious that complex states of anxiety underlay much of Jerry's personal and relational difficulties.

Jerry and his family moved to the United States when he was 4 years old. At that time, he did not speak any English. His parents, on the other hand, were quite fluent in English but overwhelmed by the new culture they encountered in the big city where they settled. Jerry was immediately placed in a preschool near his new home; it was the first time he was forced to leave his parents and older sister. His memories from those days are of a confused and frightened boy, attempting to but unable to connect with other kids, feeling alone and lost. His mother was his translator, and he continually turned to her to make sense of things and to teach him how to behave in class. He remembers his utter dependence on her and his need for her to be close by.

Jerry's sister, 6 years older, seemed to have an easier time in those first months at school. As the family settled down, Jerry's parents worked hard to support their kids' interests and ensure their success. Jerry's father, described by Jerry as "much weaker" than his mother, related to his children with support and calm. His mother, however, was described as "volatile and unpredictable." Alongside "a great sense of humor and ability to be loving," Jerry described frequent emotional outbursts against his father for what seemed to be the smallest or nonexistent infractions. Angry accusations could be triggered by his father's perceived carelessness when he did food shopping; for example, buying food items that were past their expiration date, she screamed, "could put the whole family in danger."

These frequent fights deeply scared Jerry. He remembered being agitated, fearful that the family would break apart. He vividly imagined the calamities that were sure to occur; he was especially afraid that once divorced, his parents would abandon him as well. With time, as the frequent fights just continued with no dramatic consequences, Jerry began to realize that what drove his mother's erratic behavior was an intense level of anxiety. He saw that she was fearful about everything with even a remote chance of hurting anyone in her family.

Already as a child, Jerry increasingly realized that his mother was not like the other mothers he knew. But only as therapy went on did Jerry realize how disruptive and invasive his mother's actions were. In effect, he had not previously understood the degree to which his mother's high levels of fear and anxiety were a constant in his life. "To describe her as overprotective," he now said, "is an understatement." She was consumed with potential dangers, real and imagined, often anticipating the worst possible outcome for normal activities. Warnings about crossing the street safely were delivered with the same emotional intensity as warnings regarding the "real" dangers of being kidnapped.

With the stated goal of protecting him from "kids who wouldn't understand him and (potentially) make fun of him," she did not let him go on sleepovers and did not allow him to go on school trips. She expressed anxiety about the danger of being molested by parents she did not know well, but she also did not trust those parents she did get to know. As a result, he could not stay over with other families or join them for trips when invited. However, despite the many restrictions put on him, Jerry frequently felt a great deal of empathy toward his mother and, as he says, "instinctively understood her anxiety." In effect, he remembered that he actively tried to change her mood, to humor her in order to lessen her anxiety, to protect her from her own worries.

When Jerry's sister left for college early, he felt even more confined by his mother's shifting moods and anxieties. Before she had left, sensing his distress, Jerry's sister told him not to "be so influenced by their crazy mother." She added that Jerry should insist on doing his own thing. At the time, around the age of 10, Jerry already was far from being sure about what "his thing" might be, and he did not fully understand what his sister meant. He still trusted his mother to make decisions for him, buy his clothes, and supervise his friendships; frequently interrogating him about his whereabouts, and more.

As upset as Jerry felt about his mother's habit of instigating fights with his father, he was also convinced that it was his job to worry about her well-being, to calm her down, and avoid explosive conflicts with her. For as long as he could remember, Jerry actually believed that if he could reduce her worries, everything in their home would be ideal. His sense of security became entirely entwined with his mother's moods; he felt calm if she was okay. At the same time, he often wished that his "weak" father would be the one to stand up to her and protect both himself and his son. Mostly, this did not happen.

As Jerry became aware of the many conflicting feelings and thoughts toward his mother—dependence, trust, empathy, resentment, fear, and anger—he wondered why he "took on this difficult and, in actuality, impossible job of placating his mother." Often his memories took him back to the time when the family immigrated to this country, when he was utterly dependent on her to help him navigate the new and scary environment. But increasingly Jerry felt that this dependency on her for his own sense of well-being had always been there, since infancy. He became convinced that from the very beginning, sensing her unease and anxiety, he tried to be a "good boy" and avoid further upsetting her.

Talking about his habit and "ability" to sense what others need from him, he now saw that he indeed developed an exquisite sensitivity to his mother's moods and needs, learning to anticipate them and, when possible, deflect them through being acquiescent or funny. When he felt that he succeeded in influencing her mood, Jerry remembered feeling most connected to his mother; he had the vague sense that they both achieved a state of harmony. At those times he was sure, he recently said, that they could read each other's minds. Unsurprisingly, he did not rebel as a child or an adolescent. On the contrary, into young adulthood, until he left for college, Jerry sought his mother's approval and the harmonious experiences that resulted from what he saw as their mutual understanding.

From the very beginning, as his own peace of mind depended on gratifying his mother, Jerry unconsciously learned that intimacy and harmony meant pleasing the other. However, as these relational habits became reinforced and increasingly came at the expense of his freedom to express himself and contradict her, another unconscious piece in him felt trapped and suffocated. Dedicated to maintaining his good relationship with his mother, Jerry could not fully or consciously attend to feelings and thoughts of being burdened and trapped. Consequently, a self-state that contained many negative memories of how controlled and constricted he actually was could only develop under the radar. But it was there nonetheless. The confusing rage he started to be aware of became much clearer to him when he left for college; Jerry could not wait to get away from home, and in his freshman year, once his started psychoanalysis, he stopped talking to his parents altogether.

The realization that his impulse to please his mother and take on her internal states prevented him from developing his own independent sense of self was particularly disturbing and painful to Jerry. Becoming convinced, or "brain washed " as he now says, that he needed to depend on his parents and especially his mother for guidance, and as a result of being consumed with worries in the wake of their fighting, Jerry literally did not have the psychological opportunity to find out who he was and what was important to him outside of his parents' internal and marital struggles.

At the center of Jerry's difficulties was his conflict regarding closeness and feeling trapped, two states that occurred almost simultaneously. Parallel to this, two other needs unconsciously guided his behavior: the constant search for harmony with his girlfriends and the inevitable disappointment when he realized that this idealized "harmonious union" could not last. As much as he craved a harmonious connection with others, with a project, or with a job, sooner or later these situations aroused a great deal of anxiety about being entrapped and controlled. As a relationship took shape and developed, he would start feeling discomfort and stress; he did not dare express his fears but could only withdraw and break it up. The relief he felt when a project ended guaranteed his freedom to avoid the "trap of staying on one place."

Unsurprisingly, Jerry brought these complex dynamics into all his important relationships: his romantic relationships and career choices, as well as his attitudes toward therapy. Throughout his therapy, although he was very engaged and comforted by it, Jerry had also occasionally experienced and expressed ambivalence toward me and the process. He was worried about losing his own ideas and becoming controlled by mine. I could feel his conflicting needs; to be close to me and trust what we were achieving together and at the same time resisting what he perceived to be "attempts to influence" him. Indeed, I needed to be acutely aware, as much as I actually could, of this dynamic between us. I often reflected on what I said, and if indeed I was too direct or controlling. When Jerry would get upset at my directness or perceived attempts to convince him with an interpretation, we were always able to discuss what happened, our respective contribution to the entangled dynamic, and each time learned a bit more about his conflicts. Jerry's ability to discuss theses entanglements has been a major benefit in his therapeutic progress.

As Jerry's therapy continued, it became exceedingly clear to him how unconsciously stuck he was between these two patterns: an urgent motivation to seek harmonious closeness with a romantic partner or a perfect job on the one hand, and the inevitable creeping sense that he was being controlled and pushed around, losing his sense of individuality and autonomy on the other. As the initial fantasies of harmony and agreement inevitably gave way to anxious thoughts about being trapped, he defensively convinced himself that he had to save his independent sense of self. In sessions, feeling upset, angry, and determined to "find his own self," Jerry also realized that neither of these extreme patterns served him well. He needed to explore and enact new ways of relating to himself and to others.

Jerry's brain/mind learned to oscillate between dread and hope, between the desire for harmony (with his mother, peace between his parents) and deep anxiety about being controlled and erased. The anxiety became even more intense when the wished-for harmony was not sustained but in essence turned into a prison from which he needed to flee.

As Chapter 1 demonstrates, our unconscious patterns are unconscious mainly in regard to the vast number of implicit memories, learned emotional and relational habits, and thought processes embedded within them. Out of awareness, however, we continually and repeatedly enact our entrenched patterns in everything we do and experience; they are the basis for who we are and how we relate to ourselves and others. Jerry's feeling, thinking, and behavioral habits developed from a very early age. In his adult life, as a part of him was trying to establish meaningful relationships or become engaged with a project he valued and enjoyed, an anxiety-infused self-state overwhelmed him, convincing him that he was about to be trapped. As we'll see, within the context of unconscious processes, when such internal fearful reality wins, there is little opportunity to learn from reality. Unless one becomes aware, past experiential patterns will surely and unconsciously repeat themselves. Chapter 1 explains why this is so.

Until Jerry became mindful of his childhood experiences, until he allowed himself to experience some of his more disturbing memories, his behaviors were at the mercy of this pendulum: harmony and disruption, desire and escape. What is important in the new view of unconscious processes is the realization that the conscious and the unconscious realm are on a continuum; they are not separate but mutually connected brain/mind/body functions. As I will often reiterate, much of the content embedded within unconscious patterns remains out of explicit knowledge. Implicit memories, and emotional and relational learned habits, as well as the meaning and very idiosyncratic interpretations we gave to events as young children, are hidden from us. This is especially true about all the experiences we had before the ages of 3 to 5 years, before the memory system comes online. But what is present is the way we unconsciously and continuously enact the emotional, cognitive, and behavioral patterns that were formed by those early experiences and the child-centered interpretations we give them.

In Jerry's case, unconscious, anxiety-influenced conclusions repeatedly warned him that he'd better watch out for the costs involved in a committed approach to people close to him and to other engagements as well.

His early interactions at home taught him to focus on the important adults in his life at the expense of developing a trust in his own internal life. As a child and adolescent, being so attuned to his mother's moods, frequently fantasizing about how to placate her and stop his parents from fighting linked his sense of well-being to how well the adults around him felt.

Consequently, throughout his childhood to his adult life, Jerry's sense of self and calm could mostly be found in an idealized, wished for harmony with others, in a constant need to be with others and connect with them. As a result, he had a difficult time developing desires and motivations that were separate from others. But at the same time, these early experiences also taught him that the cost of a harmonious connections is too anxiety-inducing. Besides being short-lived and unsustainable, these connections threatened to rob him of his fragile sense of self, and caused an intense fear of losing his freedom.

While Jerry continued to face his difficulties and interpersonal struggles, he continued to become aware of how his internal conflicts about surrendering to a relationship or to the expected structures of a job had affected many aspects of his life. Indeed, something shifted in him; as his general anxiety level decreased, he became more able to engage with others and with projects at work, this time with a diminished sense of dread about being trapped.

Our Anxious Selves

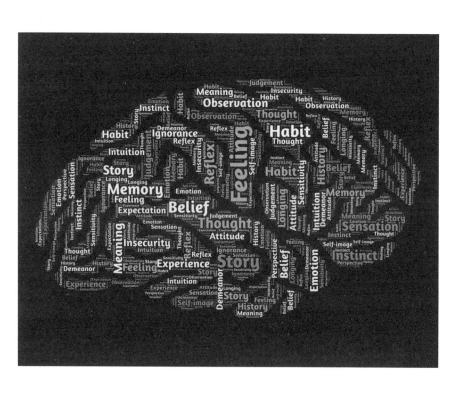

CHAPTER ONE

Unconscious Processes and Patterns

· ·

Examining the nature of the unconscious is the first and necessary step to the exploration of fear, anxiety, and the outsized influence of the fear system. This is critical because fear and anxiety influence how we feel and how we think about ourselves and the world. Without a better understanding of how our conscious traits and behaviors are fully rooted in unconscious processes, we cannot fully grasp the effects of these innate emotions on who we become as we mature from childhood to adulthood. We cannot see the full picture of how negative emotions such as fear and anxiety give rise to unconscious patterns of vulnerability, negative expectations, and self-defeating behaviors. Our vast, complex unconscious is the engine that continually operates outside our awareness but simultaneously generates everything we think, feel, and do.

Thus, a detailed examination of unconscious processes is essential when exploring the nature of psychological dynamics—what makes us who we are. All of our personality dynamics, those we are aware of as well as those outside our awareness, in essence express the inextricable integration of our all processes that connect our brains, minds, and bodies. In other words, all our mental and behavioral functions are the embodiments of this brain/mind/body unity.

Throughout this book I use the term *brain/mind/body* to emphasize the interconnected nature of all the processes underlying our human existence. Particularly in the West, we tend to think of our brains, minds, and bodies as separate entities. The brain is the hidden, unknown entity; although we know it is somehow "responsible for everything," we still don't appreciate the extent of its involvement. We consider the mind as the somewhat disembodied source of our thoughts, beliefs, values, and the like; and given our advanced cognitive functioning and intelligence, we believe we are in full control of them. Our bodies are the all-important physical structures that continuously perform our life-sustaining tasks, unencumbered by our emotions or our minds. In particular, the dichotomy between conscious and unconscious processes has hindered a fuller understanding of human functioning and well-being.

As you will see in this book, the elements that underlie our functioning as human beings are fully intertwined and integrated. All of us are a product and an expression of these integrated processes; brain, mind, and body, the conscious and the unconscious mingle together to underpin all facets of our personality. This reality sets the stage for our understanding of why internal states of fear and anxiety, as well as other emotions, have such an enduring effect. Our first step is to delineate the complex relationship between conscious and unconscious processes.

UNCONSCIOUS PROCESSES: THE HIDDEN AND CONTINUOUS ENGINE

Unconscious processes are the sum-total of the continuous neural activities that are involved in all aspects of our physiological, emotional, cognitive, and behavioral characteristics. They encode all of our experiences, retain our past, and predict the future. In short, they form the foundation for all that we remember, feel, know, and enact throughout our lives. When signals from the vast and intertwined brain circuits, in effect our unconscious patterns, reach awareness, they become conscious and give expression to what we recognize as our familiar attributes: internal monologues; thought processes; emotional sensitivities; typical ways of relating to others; habitual strategies for managing stress, anxiety, and challenges; and automatic ways of perceiving, interpreting, and responding to events around us.

These unconscious patterns, neural maps, or schemas are usually organized around specific emotions. For example, what we may recognize in somebody as an anxious and negative approach to life—one that often expects the worst possible outcome and ruminates about what can go wrong—is rooted in an entrenched and unconscious complex neural pattern. These neural patterns, hidden but always at the ready to become activated, are the essence of our unconscious processes (Damasio, 2010). Most significantly, these neural patterns unite within them brain, mind, body, and behavior, creating unconscious tendencies.

As we further recognize how unconscious brain/mind/body patterns are created and how actively and continually they are reenacted throughout our lives, we increasingly understand why we tend to automatically repeat patterns of behavior that essentially no longer work for us. Here, I am talking about unconscious patterns that are suffused with the emotions of fear, anxiety, and other negative feelings connected to fear and anxiety. For example, the tendency to perceive others as judgmental and critical, and the anxiety such perceptions bring, may lead to the avoidance of social interactions as a strategy of self-protection. Unconscious convictions about the inevitability of failure, and thereby being found out as incompetent, often results in automatic defenses that interfere with an active pursuit of one's conscious goals and desires.

Additionally, when under stress, we may drown in feelings of anxiety, becoming paralyzed and insecure; we may find ourselves scared of our own seemingly out-of-control physiological and emotional reactions. In such instances, we lack psychologically effective ways of regulating our emotions. As a result, we have a hard time tolerating the emotional and cognitive havoc they create. Other unconscious patterns may lead us to entrenched defenses against a host of cumulative childhood traumas that have created an enormous sense of vulnerability, which frequently remains unknown and unacknowledged. In our current reality as adults, such well-hidden but powerfully influential feelings of vulnerability often generate behaviors that may remain outside our awareness: automatic aggressive reactions against perceived slights; excessive preoccupation with negative thoughts or emotions; or prioritizing our own needs at the expense of other people's needs, even those we love. We may become argumentative because of an unconscious need to be right as a way to ward off vulnerability; we may not be good listeners because we are too anxious about expressing our own thoughts.

The discussion of unconscious processes and the unconscious patterns that we all possess is central to the topics explored in the following chapters. The extent and scope of all these complex processes that continually occur out of our awareness increase the need to understand how fear and anxiety so powerfully shape unconscious patterns as well as conscious experiences. First, we need to explore the biological and survival instincts that originated with our early human ancestors; these once-adaptive patterns that ensured the survival of our species have become an inseparable part of our emotional existence. Second, we must understand the interpersonal forces that may increase a child's vulnerability to fear, anxiety, and other negative feelings; this matters because we carry these patterns into adulthood, where they live in our unconscious and are invariably enacted throughout our lives. Third, we need to examine the many ways in which parents may unintentionally project and enact their own unconscious patterns onto their children, not realizing the potential harm embodied in words, unprocessed feelings, and unconscious hurtful behavior.

To begin our journey into the unconscious, the first chapter of this book examines some new neuropsychological insights into the characteristics of unconscious patterns: how they are created, maintained, and enacted.

THE ILLUSION OF CONSCIOUS CHOICE

In our daily lives, most of us take for granted the familiar sense of being in control. We believe our actions are entirely conscious. We are certain that we know why we do certain things and not others, why we pursue particular goals, and the reasons behind making important decisions. We are convinced that we are aware of all our feelings, thoughts, and desires and of our motivation for doing things, or conversely, refusing to do them. We are particularly adept at believing that our thought processes and feelings are rooted in the reality we encounter. In contrast, we think of the unconscious realm as a separate entity, a closed-off container of unacceptable and repressed conflicts, wishes, and traumatic experiences.

But this is far from being so. Unconscious processes are neurobiological functions that occur within our brain/mind/bodies. They are pervasive and ongoing, guiding each and every mental activity or action we take. For example, much of our perceptions and the processing of internal and environmental stimuli occur outside our awareness. Indeed, we are unaware of the massive unconscious scaffolding underneath each and every conscious feeling, thought, and action. We are not aware of what learned associations we attach to emotional memories during childhood, for example, or how a fear memory can become generalized by association and determine how we approach or avoid challenges. We may not be aware of the specific meaning given to experiences, especially those encoded preverbally in early childhood. We may not be aware of the automatic perceptions, defenses, and cognitive interpretations we employ. And, finally, we usually do not recognize our own expectations, automatic predictions, hidden triggers, and response tendencies. All these building blocks coalesce into what can be thought of as brain-wide unconscious maps (Damasio, 2010). When triggered by a familiar stimulus (which in itself can stay unconscious) a whole map or pattern becomes neurally activated, enacting all its particular and unique features: feelings, thoughts, sensations, and behaviors. This happens entirely out of awareness (Ginot, 2015).

We are often unaware of the stimuli to which we are reacting. Nor are we aware of the complex neural and chemical systems by which we perceive, categorize, and interpret the stimuli we encounter. Nevertheless, outside our awareness we constantly engage with our internal and external environments. In a parallel way, we are not aware of how we process nutrients like glucose, but we are aware that our body does in fact process them. In other words, a lot happens under the radar in our brain/mind/bodies that shapes virtually every aspect of our lives.

These unconscious processes are much more influential than we usually realize or acknowledge. In a departure from Freud's original concepts of the unconscious, we recognize today that unconscious processes are always working in the background, assessing the environment, and enacting appropriate reactions. In this way, unconscious processes are not isolated from our conscious forms of functioning. The two realms are intertwined, inseparable, and mutually influential. The unconscious gives rise to our conscious experiences, while our conscious, reality-bound experiences can add, modify, and change some of the neural connections that shape our unconscious patterns. The process of psychotherapy as well as a myriad of mindfulness and meditative approaches are good examples of how we can proactively influence and modify the unconscious.

Outside our awareness, the unconscious realm continually interacts with changes in the external environment and within our internal emotional and bodily states. An important aspect of this engagement is the continuous assessment of the valence (the perception of an experience as being good or bad) or the personal meaning of incoming stimuli. As we encounter an endless stream of stimuli, our unconscious processes decide what to perceive and register, and eventually react to and in what fashion. This is done through attention and perception biases, and entrenched patterns of interpreting our internal and external worlds. Our typical ways of assessing the world and our selective ways of reacting to it are based on these unconscious brain/mind/body processes that quickly and automatically enact already existing behavioral patterns. In effect, the automaticity of perception and reaction are major features of unconscious processes and, therefore, of our functioning as a whole (Bargh, 2014; Churchland, 2013; Damasio, 2010; Dixon et al., 2017; Koziol, 2014; Lewis & Todd, 2007; Pessoa, 2015; Todd & Manaligod, 2018; Tsuchiya & Adolphs, 2007).

MAJOR FEATURES OF UNCONSCIOUS PROCESSES AND NEURAL PROCESSES

What has emerged is an expanded picture of the scope of action and influence of our unconscious processes (Solms & Zellner, 2012ab). Numerous studies have showed that measured neural activity in the brain always precedes seemingly conscious decisions to take a particular action. For example, when subjects are instructed to raise their fingers at will, the area in the brain involved in movement fires before any action takes place. With the growing capacity to monitor brain activity with sophisticated functional magnetic resonance imaging (fMRI) scanning methods, it has become clear that unconscious neural processes guide our most complex decisions as well (Libet, 1985; Libet et al., 1967).

A few examples of enacted complex behaviors guided by unconscious patterns include choosing a particular type of partner each time, frequently changing romantic attachments because of perceived flaws or disappointments, or finding oneself yet again in the middle of complicated and volatile relationships that are doomed to fail. In our professional lives, we may repeatedly quit otherwise promising jobs, avoid challenging job situations altogether, or display such sensitivity to others' perceptions of us that we can't take any criticism. Throughout most of these long-term behavior patterns, we are convinced that we are fully aware of our motivations, that we understand our reasons, and that we know how and why we make our seemingly conscious choices. Indeed, we often feel justified in our reactions to others and our choice of behaviors. But these so-called conscious choices are seldom fully conscious. Often, and more so among those of us who tend to be less aware of our motivations, unconscious patterns guide our pursuits and the actions we take or neglect to take in order to fulfill our conscious goals and stated wishes (Bargh, 2007, 2014; Damasio, 2010; Wegner, 2007).

Unconscious patterns are based on memory traces, learning, and identification processes. In contrast to more traditional understandings, the unconscious is not a container for unconsciously rejected or repressed events. In effect, the brain's capacity to learn efficiently from the environment is at the heart of all unconscious and conscious patterns and, thus, at the center of our personality dynamics. From the very beginning of life, automatically and unconsciously, experiences are encoded and retained within brain-wide circuits. This is especially so during infancy and childhood. Early learning processes are by definition unconscious. Although we do not have access to our earliest memories and encoded experiences, as part of unconscious circuits, they still influence our emotional and behavioral patterns.

The neural networks that contain implicit memories and unconscious learning are spread throughout the brain regions, cortical areas such as the prefrontal cortex, and subcortical regions beneath the outer band of the cortex. All these brain regions are interconnected either by anatomical proximity or by functional connections when topographically remote areas resonate and thus relate through simultaneously firing in response to a stimulus or a situation. Numerous brain circuits activated in our unconscious patterns continually interact and form back-and-forth feedback loops. These include the limbic system (emotion processing), cortical sensory areas (sight, sound, and touch), the prefrontal cortex (higher-order cognitive processes such as deliberate planning and reflection), and areas such as the basal ganglia and the cerebellum (subcortical regions involved in habit formation and learning).

All learning processes, especially early in our development, are influenced by our immediate reactions to the external environment, basically our visceral and emotional states. We automatically assess the nature of the stimuli we encounter and our internal reactions to them (i.e., valence) as pleasant or unpleasant, threatening or safe, good or bad. The intensity of a stimulus or an event is determined by the triggered levels of visceral hyperarousal or calm within an individual. Generally, we experience hyperaroused states (i.e., emotionally intense feeling states) as dysregulating, fearful, volatile, and upsetting.

Memories, for example, are better remembered when encoded during hyperaroused emotion states. Similarly, all learning processes are influenced by the emotional quality under which they take place. Negative states tend to result in negative characteristics, unconsciously assigned to memories, early habits, and thoughts. In particular, elements of the fear system (e.g., fear, panic, and anxiety) cause memories, learning, and defenses that work to stick with us. As you will see later on, through epigenetics, we still carry with us the automatic defenses that helped to keep our human ancestors safe; unfortunately, some if not many of these unconscious programs are no longer adaptive or beneficial. The dopaminergic system that induces pleasant sensations and emotions, on the other hand, underlies reward learning and positive memories. While these unconscious memories are pleasant, they can have maladaptive aspects. For example, the comfort we found as infants in breastfeeding or taking a bottle is deeply embedded in us; while this is an outcome of positive caretaking, our unconscious association between food and comfort contributes to our tendency to eat more under stress. To be clear, both systems are effective teachers telling us what to avoid, approach, or repeat; however, both systems hold both adaptive and maladaptive potential. Understanding these unconscious patterns allows us to nurture the adaptive functioning and tame the maladaptive potential.

There has been an assumption that there is a self-agency that unconsciously determines what is allowed to stay conscious or, alternatively, what is not acceptable to one's sense of self and needs to be repressed (i.e., following Freud's original ideas, see Freud, 1926). This, however, has proven problematic (Horga & Maia, 2012; Lewis & Todd, 2007; Wegner, 2007). There is no single, central self-agency that intervenes or controls defensive activity. Rather, from the very beginning of life, widespread brain/mind/body processes are recruited for defensive purposes. Again, this concept is an additional rationale for this book. Therapy often approaches our dysfunctional, dysregulated patterns as if a central volitional self were in charge. In understanding that it is the complex web of interactions of the brain/mind/body that causes our defensive thoughts and actions, we can more effectively identify and change those automatic defenses that have long outlived their usefulness.

Patterns of avoidance are a good example, often becoming an inseparable part of our way of feeling, thinking, and acting. We often do not realize that we are avoiding something because we are not aware that rising anxiety has unconsciously activated the avoidance defense. More generally, defenses result from the automatic recruitment of all available physiological, mental, and action-oriented functions that can restore homeostasis. As we continue to develop from childhood through adulthood, our defenses become increasingly sophisticated, and those that work to restore well-being become entrenched and are automatically employed (see Chapter 9).

With continued development, new experiences are fitted into existing neural networks that integrate feelings, body sensations, thoughts, and actions. Speaking practically, an infinite number of associations with previous learning and experiences are continually generated and encoded. This is the beginning of our entrenched ways of seeing the world, and the basis for the distortions caused by childlike, immature ways of perceiving events and interactions. In turn, these ongoing unconscious processes underlie many of our repeated lifelong difficulties: perceptions, feelings, and reactions that are mainly based on internally encoded early interpretations rather than on current reality.

These processes can prevent effective adaptation to new situations. If we only identify and react to new experiences according to our existing patterns, we constrain our capacity to perceive them in fresh and more reality-bound ways. Rigid patterns that do not sufficiently perceive and consider the many nuanced qualities characterizing current situations tend to assess that reality according to internal knowledge only. This results in distorted perception and interpretations of what is actually occurring. When an anxious pattern, with its negative expectations and incessant worries is triggered, these distortions feel entirely real and convincing. Such internally guided habitual perceptions, automatic emotional reactions, and projections make it hard to learn from reality and approach new situations adaptively.

Thus, the two realms, the conscious and the unconscious, are intertwined and interdependent. Although we have no access to the content stored in the unconscious neural realm, we certainly can observe the myriad subjective experiences and behaviors they influence. In this way, the two realms produce a continuum of consciousness where most of our personality patterns incorporate both conscious and unconscious elements.

As developmental neuroscience increasingly indicates, dysregulating states of fear and anxiety go on to impact and shape other emotional, cognitive, and behavioral functions. Early memory traces, learning, interpersonal and relational patterns, defenses, and response tendencies are all affected by our early fears and anxieties. As these emotions become enmeshed with other mental functions, they create brain-wide neural maps or patterns that are organized around particular emotions (Damasio, 2010). Unconscious negative patterns become part of who we are, a facet of our personality. Based on the interactions between innate vulnerabilities and early environments, negative, anxiety-infused patterns may give expression to biased attention toward negative stimuli, pessimistic expectations, feelings of self-denigration, and recurrent negative self-narratives.

HOW HAVE CONSCIOUS AND
UNCONSCIOUS SYSTEMS EVOLVED?

As a result of the critical need to adapt, early humans faced an evolutionary pressure to develop a functioning survival system that could act quickly and efficiently without deliberation. As necessary learned skills became habitual, they proved effective in executing important survival tasks such as threat assessment, hunting, and defense. By not having to rely on time-consuming thought processes when confronting danger, unconscious processes led to the quick and automatic deployment of past learned and well-rehearsed abilities. Complex and repeated life challenges were well executed based on implicitly remembered and learned behaviors that successfully worked in the past.

With time, another system developed that was slower, more deliberate, reflective, and flexible. These processes led to thoughtful reasoning, planning, and higher-functioning capacities that depend on mindful thinking and attention (Dehaene & Changeux, 2011; Damasio, 2010; Lewis & Todd, 2007; and many others). What is becoming clear, however, is that despite the relatively recent development of conscious processes in human, the unconscious processes are still strongly influential and central to our overall functioning. Just as in our very distant past, these ways of reacting to the environment ensure fast and smooth functioning, a way of being whose value is as important today as it was throughout the long road of human evolution.

Being much better equipped to quickly respond to familiar situations, the unconscious realm has remained an essential mode of functioning. In fact, conscious awareness is not necessary for the execution of many of our emotional and interpersonal needs. There is ample evidence from social, psychological, and economic research that unconscious processes monitor, control, and guide the way we pursue goals or desires and make important decisions (Hassin et al., 2007).

This division in our modes of functioning make evolutionary sense. The prefrontal cortex alone (the seat of more deliberate and self-regulating functions) cannot fulfill all the demands of our daily life; doing so would prove too slow, making it difficult to accomplish our daily tasks. In other words, we had to retain the unconscious realm in order to function more efficiently, even if in retaining the unconscious we introduced new challenges in managing unconscious and automatic repetitions of patterns that remain out of our awareness. But despite the profound differences in how the two realms function, regions that underpin faster, automatic responses to stimuli have bidirectional connections to higher and newer brain areas. As a result, older, more unconscious regions still influence newer areas that mediate higher cognitive functions, such as planning and deliberate thinking. Similarly, the more flexible, thoughtful, and self-reflective qualities of the "more recent" brain regions can derail and modify the automaticity of entrenched old behavioral patterns (Ansermet & Magistrett, 2004).

More specifically, areas in the prefrontal cortex that mediate higher cognitive functions also affect and modulate more emotional and reactive response patterns. With an adaptive balance, these two realms function together in a way that equally promotes both instinctive and automatic behaviors as well as the more deliberate and consciously mindful ones. Lacking such a balance, one mode may be more prominent, claiming more neural space and greater influence over behavior. A mostly unconscious way of relating to other and the environment does not give enough space to a wider, flexible, and accurate assessment of stimuli; while a mode that mostly relies on reasoning and deliberation neglects the all-important emotional aspects that drive us. As we'll see in Chapter 15, increased mindfulness can establish this important, albeit only ideal, balance between the two realms.

THE CONSTRUCTION OF THE UNCONSCIOUS: MAP FORMING AND SELF-STATES

Many researchers conceptualize the vast unconscious as composed of many neural maps, organizations, or networks (Damasio, 2010; among many others). Such maps are metaphors for assembled neural networks that are spread throughout the brain. Each map is characterized by synchronized neural responses to internal and external stimuli. Clusters of neurons from diverse regions can fire together or stay quiet in response to incoming stimuli. As Hebb's (1964) famous observation declares, neurons that fire together wire together, thus forming a distinct neural hub or cluster that continues to perceive and react to specific events in the exact same way.

Neurons can be topographically or functionally connected, firing together in response to stimuli regardless of whether they are physically close or not. Repeated response patterns establish reinforced networks, giving rise to our conscious experiences and enacted behaviors. Brain/mind activities are mediated by electrical impulses, various neurotransmitters, and by the reward/punishment systems. These bioneurological systems guide us to assess what stimuli and situations are important and need special attention, and which are meaningful and need to be remembered and learned for future reference. Together these brain activities result in distinct, predictable, and repeated perceptual and response patterns.

Developmental Processes

Throughout our early development, constant neural activity connects, disconnects, and prunes out the massive neural networks we are born with. This process, which determines what kind of neural networks are formed and retained, is driven by epigenetic processes—the interaction between genes and environmental conditions. When neurons are firing in response to environmental stimuli, older hubs, clusters, or maps co-opt them into already existing circuits (Battalle et al., 2017; Kaiser et al., 2018). As a result, early networks win over later ones. They become increasingly stronger and more active, and achieve considerable influence over later perceptions, memories, learning, and behavioral tendencies. Furthermore, through real or perceived similarities among stimuli and the associations they evoke, new experiences attach to those already encoded. In this way, existing networks become even stronger and more prominent. For example, when a negative or an anxiety-infused pattern becomes prominent, it is triggered more frequently, easily, and intensely.

The process of pruning removes connections that are not neurally engaged (i.e., unused). Individuals who are understimulated in infancy and childhood have insufficient neural engagement of important emotional and cognitive functions. Misattuned attachment between a parent and baby will rob the infant's brain of healthy neural connections in the attachment circuit; another network may take over and become stronger, a circuit whose neurons are primarily embedded in circuits of fear and anxiety. The repeated activation of these dysregulating emotions, the inevitable result of compromised parental attunement, will determine the strength of the evolving fear system. The Hebbian principle that neurons firing together become wired together is part of the pruning process as well. At the same time, weak, unreinforced connections disappear. As brain, body, and environment are inextricably linked at all times, they create integrated networks or maps that reflect all of our physiological, emotional, perceptual, cognitive, and behavioral functions (Colombetti, 2010; Di Paolo et al., 2010).

It is important to remember that neural maps (i.e., our unconscious patterns) are an amalgam of all aspects of experience. Physio-affective and emotional memory traces fuse with our internal, mostly unconscious interpretations of what emotions mean and our unconscious learning and associations. We have more than one pattern, each activated in different contexts and under different situation and circumstances (Bromberg, 1998, 2006, 2011). Each pattern is suffused with a different emotional valence (e.g., negative or positive, threatening or safe) and many different feelings, thoughts, and beliefs.

The Expression of the Past Is Part of the Present

What makes these brain maps, self-systems, and eventually behavioral tendencies unconscious is not only the coalesced images, memory traces, and learned responses embedded in them but also the ongoing process of recreating them later on. Similar contexts and stimuli will unconsciously trigger old established response tendencies. Consequently, past-encoded self-systems are always being resurrected in the present time, blending the past and the present, the conscious and the unconscious (Chartrand et al., 2007; Damasio, 2010; Gendlin, 2012; Horga & Maia, 2012). Ideally, established patterns are flexible enough to let new input have an impact on current, reality-bound perceptions and behaviors. In the absence of such openness, rigidity and the automatic repetition of an unconscious pattern prevails (Churchland, 2013; Pollack et al., 2000).

This is relevant to our discussion of the conscious–unconscious continuum. More importantly, the previous sections explain why some individuals find it so difficult to change; their entrenched patterns are not open to new information and mostly enact old perceptual and response modes (Schaefer & Northoff, 2017). When triggered by familiar stimuli or merely by an imperceptible association to the past, we enact the only responses we know: emotional, cognitive, behavioral, and perceptual response patterns. The past and the present blend inextricably and seamlessly. Although the stimulating event is very much in the present, it nonetheless activates old perceptual and response patterns that may have no relevance to current events. To unconscious processes, however, the enacted old pattern is as relevant as it was when it was created early in life. For example, when triggered, a defensive pattern of avoiding risks is enacted by the unconscious as if it were as important to one's psychic survival as it was to the anxious child. In effect, this quality is one of the common threads of all the presented cases.

The Role of Subcortical Regions in Map Making

The role of subcortical regions emphasizes what we have always known: that emotions are the building blocks of all conscious and unconscious repeated patterns. Affect or emotions, as visceral bodily signals, are closely related to subcortical areas such as the brain stem, periaqueductal gray, the hippocampus, the basal ganglia, and the amygdala. Affect is always invoked as part of our approach to and way of being in the world. The basic emotions of good and bad, approach or avoidance, are an essential part of survival and functioning. As a basic mode of assessing our environment, emotions influence our cognition, behaviors, and conscious and unconscious patterns (Panksepp & Biven, 2012). The important subcortical areas (i.e., the basal ganglia, cerebellum, and amygdala) involved in many mechanisms of habit forming, learning, prediction, and expectation work closely together.

Together, the amygdala and the basal ganglia are involved in encoding memories, attention, perception, learning, and habits. We know now that habits are not confined to physical skills but also involve emotional, cognitive, and behavioral habits. Feelings and actions that led to favorable results, including successful defenses, coalesce into procedural knowledge. On the other hand, fearful feelings generated by the amygdala negatively tinge developing habits and important learning about the environment. Predominantly negative stimuli and the anxious reactions to a difficult environment teach the child's brain/mind/body to expect negative states and frustrating outcomes. Also guided by the amygdala, defenses that worked for the child, such as defensive withdrawal from others and overguardedness, teach the child's brain that these are the only ways to maintain one's well-being. Such avoidant and withdrawn behaviors are aided by the reward and fear systems, and the neurochemicals dopamine and cortisol, respectively (Bostan & Strick, 2018).

Additionally, the cerebellum is highly connected to the amygdala, the basal ganglia, and the prefrontal cortex. Together with the basal ganglia, it is involved in further establishing mental and behavioral patterns. Under the influence of the amygdala, the cerebellum encourages the development and execution of negative attention biases and anxious predictions and expectations. Both of these subcortical regions have a bidirectional loop with areas in the prefrontal cortex, influencing functions of the prefrontal cortex. A stronger influence from these subcortical areas will direct the prefrontal cortex toward the expression of older, more automatic patterns, even when they are no longer adaptive.

The cerebellum–basal ganglia–amygdala–prefrontal cortex loop also functions in coordination with the hippocampus, the memory center of the brain and an important region for learning. For example, as part of the learning circuit, the striatum, a part of the basal ganglia, is involved in Pavlovian conditioning; the orbitofrontal cortex encodes more flexible cognitive maps. Both types of learning are crucial for the automatic processing that associates fear to previously neutral stimuli and to the creation of enduring neural maps organized around fear and anxiety. Also, as part of these learning circuits, the cerebellum influences the release of learned behaviors and patterns mediated by the amygdala and the basal ganglia. Based on past experiences, the cerebellum unconsciously predicts what response will work best in specific situations (Andreasen & Pierson, 2008; Bostan & Strick, 2018; Habas & Manto, 2018; Koziol, 2014).

When taking the more flexible neural networks into account, areas in the prefrontal cortex also have input and influence the released response. A stronger influence from the prefrontal cortex reduces the automaticity of old patterns and regulates overly intense emotions. As we mature and develop, areas in the prefrontal cortex develop, mature, strengthen, and gain influence over subcortical areas. The increased interconnectivity of these circuits supports the increased complexity of motor, cognitive, and emotional functions, including our capacity for adaptive emotion regulation. This important function corresponds to our ability to bounce back from difficult, disturbing, and negative emotion states. It also influences our ability to take into account the wider perspectives of a situation, maintaining greater or lesser emotional stability. More important, an adaptive balance between subcortical and cortical regions will unconsciously attenuate our innate tendency to automatically act out unconscious patterns. This balance enables us to take into account actual, reality-bound events and to engage in new experiences and adaptive responses.

BORN TO ACT: THE CENTRALITY OF ENACTION TO BRAIN/MIND FUNCTIONING

Unless we work to increase our awareness, unconscious maps are continually and automatically enacted by our brain/mind/body. This happens in response to

triggers that activate neural networks. Situations reminiscent of original emotional experiences often trigger the same emotional and cognitive states we
experienced early on. The reason for such automatic enactments of unconscious
patterns is rooted in the brain's tendency to act; in fact, guidance of action is a
dominant function of the brain, a propensity that is facilitated by its motor functions (Gendlin, 2012; Koziol & Budding, 2010; Sheets-Johnstone, 2010; Stewart,
Gappenne, & DiPaolo, 2010). Motor circuits are intertwined with most other
brain networks and functions. Even our perceptions are intricately connected to
and dependent on the context of action. Upon perception, we often act quickly
and without reflection; we jump away from impending danger long before we
are aware of it. We habitually and automatically employ defenses before we
become aware of doing so.

This tendency to act is central to the expression of implicit patterns. We see
it in our tendency to enact responses and defenses that worked in the past, patterns that were encoded as part of a brain/mind map. Without awareness, slowing down, and reflecting on a response to a stressful situation, we are left with
automatic repetition of what we unconsciously know. However, this tendency
can also help us identify unconscious tendencies and patterns. As we continually
enact our typical response patterns, we reveal our deepest unconscious struggles
with fear, anxiety, guilt, and shame; we convey our painful and often distorted
ideas of who we are, our childlike understandings of our past, and our relational
difficulties. Because there is no access to early implicit memories from infancy,
and very few from early childhood, it is difficult to trace exactly how we were
affected by the fear system or how specific threatening events were experienced
and interpreted.

But what we can recognize is our unconscious/conscious self-state that is suffused with various forms of anxiety, vulnerabilities, shame, and self-denigration.
Such common states are the most visible manifestations of how, through the
amygdala, fears and anxieties co-opt and inform other emotions, thoughts, and
behaviors. Negative emotions such as fear and anxiety unconsciously insert
themselves into memories, learning, attention, perception, thinking, and beliefs
about our identity. Outside our awareness, they continue to influence how we
perceive and respond to new experiences as well as how we relate to our partners and children.

As I mentioned at the beginning of this chapter, unconscious patterns are the essence of who we are. Realizing and accepting this opens the door for deeper understanding of our own entrenched patterns, and those of family members, friends, colleagues, and clients. We can use this understanding to help parents become better aware of their own entrenched patterns so that they do not unconsciously and automatically project and direct hurtful behaviors onto their children; this helps to minimize the encoding of unhealthy, unproductive patterns in children, potentially ending generational cycles of abuse and trauma. As I observe in my own practice, parents are not exempt from being human, from possessing the same unconscious processes that all living humans have. As the following chapters show, a parent's awareness and self-reflection can mitigate many of the behaviors that elevate their children's fears and anxieties. While some anxiety is inevitable, even in the most of loving and caring families, with reflective awareness, parents can pay special attention to the innate vulnerability of their children, mitigating some of the effects of an easily activated fear system.

Now that we have a picture of how unconscious processes and patterns underlie our traits and behaviors, I think it is necessary to discuss the very first building blocks of our brain/mind/bodies and the foundation for our earliest impressions of life. This foundation is found in our initial intersubjective interactions with caregivers. The important aspects of intersubjective communications are the mutual and bidirectional verbal and nonverbal resonance between parents and infants. This emotional, verbal, and physical resonance is at the heart of parental attunement. In successful attunement, both baby and caregiver mutually communicate their internal states and coregulate distressed states. However, the intersubjective realm, like all other functions of our brain/minds, are very vulnerable to the disruptive states of fear and anxiety.

Furthermore, in exploring intersubjective communication, we must also examine the context of the wider, more complex picture of our psychological makeup. This is the duality of who we are: human beings suffused with fear and anxiety, but also possessing strength and resilience. At the end of this journey, this balance between these dualities will provide a much-needed hopeful note to our very interesting and complex search.

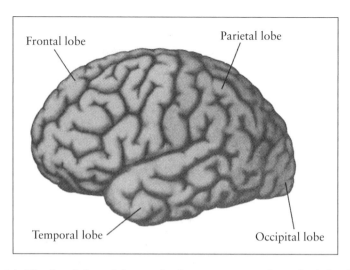

Frontal lobe

Parietal lobe

Temporal lobe

Occipital lobe

Figure 1.1: The four lobes of the cerebral cortex, as seen from the left side of the brain. *SOURCE*: "Figure 4.1, page 72," from THE NEUROSCIENCE OF PSYCHOTHERAPY: BUILDING AND REBUILDING THE HUMAN BRAIN by Louis Cozolino. Copyright © 2002 by Louis J. Cozolino. Used by permission of W. W. Norton & Company, Inc.

ANNA'S CASE: THE POWER OF THE FEAR SYSTEM

Anna's story exemplifies the power of the fear system to leave deep scars on one's self-confidence and consequently one's performance. Her struggles show how integrated brain/mind and body processes become entrenched self-states that are readily triggered and surface in anxiety-inducing situations. As we see in Chapter 3, these emotional, cognitive, and behavioral patterns are, in effect, the embodiment of unconscious neural activities that orchestrate all our brain/mind and body functions. When reaching consciousness, these patterns underpin the perceptions, feelings, thoughts, and behaviors we become aware of—in other words, our typical tendencies and personality traits.

Anna, a woman in her mid-30s, works as a computer system expert in the health care industry. She is married with two young children. Anna's initial complaints focused on the difficulties she experienced at work. She said that she had a hard time managing the daily stresses her managerial

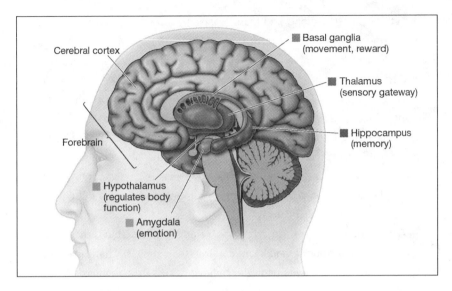

Figure 1.2: The forebrain and the subcortical regions. The subcortical regions are below the forebrain. They are responsible for many aspects of emotion and motivation. *SOURCE:* "Figure 3.24," from PSYCHOLOGICAL SCIENCE, FIFTH EDITION by Michael Gazzaniga and Todd Heatherton Diane Halpern. Copyright © 2016, 2013, 2010, 2006, 2003 by W. W. Norton & Company, Inc. Used by permission of W. W. Norton & Company, Inc.

position presented. What she continued to express in the following session was also a profound sense of insecurity and self-doubt about her performance. Although Anna had been at this job for a couple of years and received good reviews, she still felt as if she needed to prove to herself and to others that she was up to it. In her most anxious moments, she was convinced that she would eventually be found out as a fraud. She often compared herself to others in the office, especially those above her; she perceived herself as lacking qualities that are essential for achieving greater career success. As she said with the utmost earnestness: "I understand and appreciate what great qualities allowed my superiors to achieve their status and success."

Anna and her husband immigrated to this country as adults, looking to take part in the growing tech industry in New York City. Although her English language abilities were more than sufficient for her technical job, she still experienced nagging fears of lacking some essential skills that in her mind might hinder her performance. At work meetings, for example, Anna "read the room," and if she judged that others had "better ideas" or displayed the confidence she was lacking, she shut down and avoided active participation. Feeling anxious, her mind wandered, losing the thread of the conversation, making it yet harder to participate. It took a concerted effort for her to come back and reconnect with what was being discussed. When someone verbalized an idea or suggestion that she was also thinking about but was too anxious to express, she became both angry with herself and dejected. She described those moments as painfully debilitating, "making me wish I was far away."

Anna's recurring self-doubts kept reminding her that others were smarter, more eloquent, and more capable than she. This narrative made her feel "awful," in a vicious cycle; believing it to be true increased her anxious ruminations about her shortcomings. Anna's biggest dread was being criticized. She feared the confirmation of her belief that she was lacking the necessary talent to succeed. This is a common phenomenon known as imposter syndrome. In Anna's case, these severe self-doubts may have been exacerbated in her new chosen country, but they did not start then.

As we explored her internal states, Anna became aware of an unpleasant pressure in her chest and of racing negative thoughts that at times took over her consciousness. Avoidance, she clearly stated, was her refuge. She also found relief in being alone in the office, where she could take a break from potential judgments and thus do her work relatively free of anxiety. What was interesting for Anna to realize was that although intellectually she understood that her fears were not realistic, the anxious sensations and thoughts did not leave her. And in spite of performing her highly technical job consistently well, she still doubted her work, checking and rechecking it before she shared it with her colleagues and superiors.

Essentially, Anna was functioning on two tracks. Outwardly, she appeared to be an ambitious and high-achieving woman who worked hard to get ahead. Internally, however, she was besieged by anxieties about her abilities and fears of being exposed as less intelligent than she had presented herself to be. As therapy started, Anna expressed great distress and unhappiness with herself. In her words, "I could no longer tolerate my fear and my sensitivity to what others think of me." She realized that these painful experiences and debilitating fears, negative expectations, and ruminations stopped her from taking on more challenging roles at her company. Instead, to her own chagrin, she felt comfortable in the role she had carved out for herself, sticking with what felt protected and familiar. She desperately wanted to break out of the burden and constrictions that fears and anxiety placed on her.

Anna prided herself on being able to successfully read the room, scanning for potential threats. However, within a short time she gradually realized that these perceived threats and the negative narratives induced were more imaginary and internally generated than real. She also began to increasingly question why and how she became so "obsessed" with the judgment of others. As therapy continued, she oscillated between the belief that the opinions of others really defined her and a growing sense that others may not be as judgmental as she has imagined. Furthermore, she realized how exaggerated such fears were. "Even if others disapprove of me," she said, "Why is it so important to me? Also, I'm pretty sure they are not all focused on me, right?"

Anna actively struggled to anchor her perceptions and internal convictions in what was actually happening. Despite such efforts, she was still often affected by the overpowering force of her internal beliefs; threat perceptions still caused her to retreat from active participation in the meetings she attended. Anna's abilities to cope with her anxious states and the negative narratives that accompanied them improved when she was better able to pay close attention to her internal signals of anxiety. She began to notice that thoughts of incompetence and the automatic behavioral withdrawal always accompanied unpleasant visceral sensations that signaled the presence of old and familiar fears and anxieties. Initially, she was able to be aware of this only in hindsight, especially while discussing it in therapy. With time, however, Anna became increasingly able to pay attention to her internal processes as they were taking place in real time. Identifying a state of anxious hyperarousal, she learned to utilize calming strategies that eventually enabled her to feel and act less frozen. (Therapeutic approaches to anxious states are discussed in Chapter 15.)

What were the forces that led to Anna's distorted convictions about her abilities, and to her avoidant behaviors? Although her internal experiences of herself as an adult mostly did not reflect external reality, she still responded to them as if her projections were actual threats. When we try to understand such upsetting and convincing internal states and the roadblocks to better emotion regulation, we are confronted by questions surrounding the roots and persistence of such lingering fears, anxieties, and narratives. As we just learned, the automatic activation of the fear system and the circuits it affects explains Anna's persistent perceptions, feelings, thoughts, and behaviors. Equally important, we see how the powerful fear system prevented Anna from fully taking reality into account and creating a new, more reality-bound picture of her skills and abilities, as well as of the entirely exaggerated sensitivity to the projected judgment of others.

Looking at Anna's childhood for clues, we can appreciate how an enmeshment of her inborn tendencies and environmental factors combined to amplify the innate power of the fear system. Anna is the youngest of three children in what she initially described an "ideal loving family." All their neighbors, she said, looked up to them as a "model family." Closer investigation, however, revealed many cracks in the perfect picture she bought into. As she started to explore her childhood experiences, different memories of her parents' marriage began to emerge. A "cold truce" that hung up in the air, led to an unaffectionate and distant relationship between her parents. Yes, they rarely fought, she said, but they also did not engage in loving behaviors. They essentially led separate lives.

Even as a child, Anna remembered wondering about the true nature of her parents' marriage. Anna described her mother as a very strong and willful woman who dedicated her life to her job outside the house. In spite of her mother's busy schedule, and the need for the three siblings to take care of many of their own food and school needs, Anna felt loved, understood, and supported by her. She described her father as "a loving person as well." But he could also be severe and critical. He checked the children's schoolwork and showed clear disappointment when he thought they felt short. He often reminded the kids to work hard in school so they could "make something of themselves." He himself was a hard worker, Anna said: "As hard as he was on the kids, he was doubly hard on himself." There was not much room for mistakes or failure in his life vision. As Anna grew older, his emphasis on schoolwork, good grades, and extracurricular achievements increased as well. Anna envied her siblings: they did their best but did not take their father as seriously as she did. He would lecture and become upset with them, but her siblings did not seem to mind it as much as she did.

For her part, Anna's anxiety about how well she was doing intensified. She desperately wanted to receive her father's approval; she wanted to be the good girl who followed his directions. But Anna struggled with some of her schoolwork. She needed more time to read, comprehend what she read, and complete her assignments. From today's vantage point, it seems that Anna had difficulties in processing new information as quickly as was demanded, and consequently sensed that studying did not come as easy to her. But in spite of these hurdles, through sheer will and hard work Anna still was a good student. She wished, however, that she were a better one, that she was "as fast and intelligent" as some of the other kids in class. She harshly criticized herself for being different from them. She still remembers her anxiety around tests and grades. At those times, she felt like her whole existence depended on those test results. If she did not do well, she thought, she "literally wished not to exist."

Anna's mother did not seem to be concerned about Anna's difficulties and ensuing anxieties about school. She often told Anna to relax and not to worry so much about her performance. She tried to reassure her daughter that she would be okay even if she was not among the very best students. Her father, however, although recognizing her difficulties, kept pushing her to overcome them, to work harder and for longer hours. He was not exactly critical of her struggles, but he was not fully accepting of them either. The message that she could still be as good as the others if she tried hard enough, and that there were no good excuses for not doing well, became more powerful in Anna's psyche than her mother's relaxed attitude. Internally, Anna did not believe what her mother said—that she should be less judgmental of herself—and persistent anxious feelings that she was not as smart or capable as some of the other kids took total hold of her.

It is not difficult to draw a direct line between Anna's home life and her internalized entrenched ideas of herself. In addition to her father's constant demands and dissatisfaction with her performance, Anna was also affected by the strange dichotomy she experienced at home and outside it. In the tight-knit community where she grew up, keeping up a façade of a perfect existence was prized above all else. As a matter of fact, her parents themselves often expressed pride in how others saw the family and especially the marriage. But Anna and her older siblings often discussed what they saw as the "weird" cold relationship between their parents. These expressed impressions only increased Anna's general sense of anxiety; the projected importance of the judgment of others became all-consuming.

While her siblings found refuge in outside activities and many friends, Anna remained confused and worried. She wholeheartedly took to heart her parents' attitude about their projected ideal marriage and was always very careful never to divulge the other side of their home life. With time, the necessity to appear perfect took center stage and became part of an anxious self-state. Under her father's close supervision, it unconsciously intensified and generalized to her school and later work life as well.

Not surprisingly, Anna enacted this harsh, demanding, and critical pattern with her husband and children as well. Outside her awareness, she found herself pushing her children to do more and better, mindlessly yelling at them. She often found flaws with how her husband performed his household chores. At those moments, she felt entirely justified in her perceptions, feelings, and behaviors. Only upon further reflection did she become very upset with herself and decide to work hard not to repeat her father's behaviors. With me, Anna's criticalness surfaced as well. In those sessions, she would become critical of my interventions, questioning if they were the best possible ones. But as we continued to explore her unconscious perceptions, interpretations, and actions, she was able to see them in action with me as well.

As therapy continued, Anna began to feel compassion for the little girl she had been, and her painful struggles both at home and at school. It took time, but she also started to appreciate some things she never fully considered, including her grit, hard work, and persistence. What amazed her now was how she had learned to live with such a high level of anxiety, and how despite her fears and self-doubts, she "did not fall apart."

The pandemic proved to be a blessing in disguise for Anna. She enjoyed her work away from the stressful meetings, and that reprieve allowed us to further explore, develop, and practice new strategies to deal with her anxious states as they were happening. These new ways of becoming aware of her internal states and automatic behaviors helped her both at work and at home. Whenever she caught herself comparing herself to others, she reframed what was taking place. A growing ability to slow down and reflect on her inner state in real time allowed her to more consciously derail the older entrenched patterns.

· ·

CHAPTER TWO

Emotions

· ·

As a prelude to examining the significant place that fear and anxiety occupy in our nature and behaviors, we need to start with an abridged discussion of the very complex topic of emotions. Here, as in the chapters that follow, neuropsychological findings combined with clinical observations elucidate and guide our discussion. Even this brief discussion of the nature of emotions highlights their unique place in human existence (Kragel & LaBar, 2016). Whether we fully know it or not, we often sense that our emotions shape and guide our identity and behaviors. Consciously and unconsciously, we are frequently tuned into the ongoing physiological sensations and feelings created by our different emotion states. Even when we are not feeling emotional or when we feel nothing, emotional processes, the memories they carry, and the defensive behaviors they generate are still operating outside our awareness.

For millennia, people have tried to decipher the nature of emotional experiences. By paying special attention to how things feel, we have tried again and again to capture and fully comprehend what constitutes an emotion; we have tried to grasp those visceral sensations and put them into words. The countless expressions and the intensely personal meaning of emotional states have consistently preoccupied us in literature, poetry, psychology, and, perhaps most importantly, in our imagination. Unsurprisingly, an endless number of metaphors have been used to capture the elusive but powerful qualities embedded within emotions.

THE EARLY STUDY OF EMOTIONS

Following Darwin's seminal conceptualizations of emotions and the evolving psychological theories that followed, most notably those of Sigmund Freud and William James, the importance of emotions in the study of human nature became established. Within the fields of psychology and psychoanalysis, for example, emotions have always been central to our understanding of our unconscious motivations as well as our emotional and interpersonal difficulties. Emotions form the foundation in formulating a comprehensive psychodynamic diagnosis. More recently, the importance of emotion regulation—how we manage dysregulated, disturbing states—has been recognized. Consequently, therapeutic techniques to enhance emotional regulation using approaches such as cognitive–behavioral therapy have become established. At the same time, psychotherapists also emphasize the value of getting in touch with feelings in order to free ourselves from the negative impact of past traumas. The combination of these two therapeutic approaches—delving into past experiences with all their emotional weight and developing a mindful-based emotion regulation—characterize the work I did with Anna as well as most of the other cases I have chosen.

And yet, in spite of increasing insight into human emotions, we still continue to deepen our understanding of their nature, function, and actual scope. Because emotions are such internal, private, and subjectively felt experiences, numerous hurdles hinder our attempts to study them. We also encounter many intriguing questions concerning emotions. How do we actually recognize emotions in ourselves and others? How do emotions feel experientially? Can emotions be unconscious to us, or do they feel real only when they can be verbally described (LeDoux, 2015)? Are emotions innate or, rather, learned concepts constructed through our experiences in the world (Barrett, 2017b)? Are emotions sufficiently different from each other that we can categorize them, and is it important to do so? What are the differences between emotions and feelings? Do raw emotions have additional dimensions that feelings don't have; and, if they do, what are they? Do emotions form a unique phenomenon that is separate from other mental functions such as cognitions and behaviors? Conversely, do thoughts and other types of cognition contribute to emotional states? And, above all, why is it important to understand our emotional lives with more depth, nuance, and scientific accuracy?

A central dilemma passionately discussed among researchers is whether emotions are innate (Barrett, 2017a), or, conversely, learned and constructed in response to general underlying states of arousal (Adolphs & Anderson, 2018; Panksepp & Biven, 2012). As you will see, neither of these approaches is completely satisfactory or sufficient to explain human behaviors.

The view that emotions are innate emphasizes the embodied nature of emotions—they are part of our brain circuits. Importantly, each innate emotion is unique and discernible. Anger, fear and panic, attachment needs, grief, lust, and love are some examples (Panksepp & Biven, 2012; Schore, 2012).

In contrast, the other view of emotions emphasizes the role of actual experiences in shaping how we feel. Through repeated experiences within our environment, we attach words and cognitive descriptions to inevitable positive or negative bodily sensations. Anna, for example, was able, with therapy, to identify her feelings and recurrent narratives; but it was also clear that her reactions in the workplace had deep roots in entrenched patterns of feeling and thinking, in old habits of framing the unpleasant sensations of anxiety in ways that doubted her competence. Although general hyperaroused states are innate, they do not contain specific emotions (Barrett, 2017a). Different, nuanced feelings become defined and increasingly recognized through experience and the words that describe them.

In some ways these two approaches to the nature of emotions also reflect previous attempts to decipher the nature of the mind. For centuries, and especially after the Cartesian split between body and mind, writers were certain that emotions were different from thoughts or cognitive processes. In recent decades, both neuroscience and psychoanalysis followed this line of thinking. For example, early neuropsychological research exploring how our brains process and encode a wide range of experiences mainly focused on the presumed cognitive characteristics of our brain/minds. Until recently, emotional experiences were largely ignored as a topic of study.

Similarly, but with a reverse emphasis, psychological theories tended to look at emotions as different and separate from cognitive processes. As a result, psychodynamic as well as therapeutic models looked to uncover and experience pure emotions or feelings. This was especially central to uncovering how one felt as a result of trauma and the painful emotions involved. Therapists pursued emotions, preferably unencumbered by thought, which was believed to make emotions less authentic and therefore lacking the power to start the healing process. However, as each of the cases discussed clearly shows, emotions are not just a state of physical agitation but also reflect other mental functions. In effect, healing often begins as we become more capable of using mindful reflection to recognize this inextricable interaction between our bodily states, perceptions, expectations, thoughts, and meaning. There is little doubt that with the growing knowledge of how emotions are essential to our overall functioning and how intertwined they are with other functions, we are increasingly better positioned to further understand our human nature (Adolphs & Anderson, 2018; Barrett, 2017ab, Panksepp & Biven, 2012; Pessoa, 2014, 2017; Schore, 2012).

THE INTEGRATED BRAIN

As we will increasingly see in the following pages, the story of emotions and how they are represented in our consciousness is much more complex and interesting. In actuality it reflects the many neural layers and interconnectedness that characterize brain processes as well as our conscious experience of them. In general, when we talk about our internal states, we use the term *feeling* more often than the term *emotion*. This is true for both clinical discussions and therapeutic practice, in literature and in the common jargon.

In essence, *feeling* is used to describe what we think of as an emotional experience, but in reality *feeling* describes the very complex and integrated conscious and unconscious processes among all our faculties. More specifically, feelings give a conscious expression to a host of enmeshed experiences; attention, perception, visceral sensations, emotions, past memories, and cognitive interpretations. All these brain/mind/body experiences happen at all at once (Pessoa, 2017).

When we say we are feeling sad, for example, we are describing a few interdependent processes. We experience unpleasant, painful, and heavy sensations in our body, usually in our chest and around our eyes when we cry. We can articulate the thoughts that accompany how we feel, thoughts that describe the pain of the loss we have suffered, the grief we experience, or the hopelessness we feel about the future. We display what we feel through body postures, tears, or the need to actively withdraw from others. These entwined brain/mind and body processes enable us to physically become aware of negative or positive changes in our body, interpret what they mean, and simultaneously put this meaning into words and actions, if necessary.

When particular brain/mind and body signals reach consciousness, they signify that some important changes have taken place in our internal state. As these physiological changes in response to changes in the environment become entwined with other mental functions, they become what we consciously recognize and identify as feelings. In effect, we can understand feelings as the culmination of and the conscious representation of all these unseen, unconscious neural processes (Adolphs & Anderson, 2018; Panksepp & Biven, 2012). Most of the time emotions do not really exist without the meaning they have as good, bad, or indifferent. Our feelings, then, contain all the expressions available to us: the integration of our bodies as a physical source of emotions, our understanding of what these reactive states mean, and our ability to put them into words. Acting on how we feel, like striking out or avoiding a task because of anxiety, is also part of our feeling states.

The following section explores emotions and feelings from recent research findings and insights. In particular, the cumulative body of neuropsychological data and the compelling conclusions gleaned from evolutionary science offer us a much more comprehensive picture of emotions and their function. What is significant about this new data is that it is no longer anchored in theory and speculation alone. Although there's still much to learn, these newer insights are largely based on close observations of the brain/mind and body in action. Discussing the origin and functions of emotions is a good place to start.

THE ORIGIN AND FUNCTION OF EMOTIONS

The origins of our complex emotional makeup are deeply rooted in our very distant past. Emotions like fear and disgust, social bonding, love, sexuality, and curiosity served functional roles in securing food and shelter, procreation, and regulating our social behavior (Panksepp & Biven, 2012; Sznycer et al., 2016; Tooby & Cosmides, 2008). In the service of survival and reproduction, evolution enabled us to instinctively react and adaptively respond to challenges and changes in the environment. More specifically, the ability to quickly perceive conditions of danger and threat and differentiate them from potential reward and satisfaction has been essential to survival.

Our encounters with the environment lead to either positive visceral sensations, indicating potential rewards, or unpleasant and discernible negative sensations that signal actual, or imagined, danger. Whereas initially these internal reactions are thought to have been entirely unconscious instinctual tendencies, with time they developed into more sophisticated, flexible response systems we now understand as affects or emotions (Adolphs & Anderson, 2018; Damasio, 2010). Those instinctual response patterns that successfully ensured the survival of our ancestors coalesced into basic and innate emotional dispositions (Panksepp & Biven, 2012). By allowing us to perceive, react, and adapt to internal and external environmental challenges, emotions have enabled humans to pursue the important goals involved in survival (Adolphs & Anderson, 2018).

As with our early human ancestors, these immediate evaluations of danger or reward automatically cause a cascade of physical, physiological, chemical, and hormonal events that are read by our brain/mind and body as physio-affective states; they are the physiological or mental signals that educate us as to what is going on and how to respond to it. Consider two different bodily states: the undesirable signals of hyperarousal signaling danger are dependent on stress hormones, while pleasant, at times euphoric, sensations suggesting potential reward are dependent on dopamine. Emotions, then, embody our innate ability to judge reality and respond to it.

In addition to the "is it good or bad for me" quality that every situation carries (i.e., valence), emotions also vary in their degree of arousal depending on how the organism perceives the level of danger or reward. Arousal refers to the level of emotional intensity subjectively experienced during an environmental challenge that calls for a response (Lindquist et al., 2016). This process starts in early infancy, when states of physiological arousal are inchoate signals that something unpleasant or upsetting is interfering with the infant's state of equilibrium. The positive or negative, pleasurable or dread-inducing valence as well as arousal itself constitute the characteristics that play a central role in most models of emotion (Lapate & Shackman, 2018).

Such automatic assessment processes respond to changing conditions in our internal environment as well. Hunger or remembered danger, for example, are rooted in internal changes in body and mind. Similarly, imagined rewards and punishment, anticipated threats, and many other aspects in our fertile imagination can conjure up a wide range of emotional responses. As in the case of our instinctual reactions to external stimuli, we fully experience internally projected threats or optimism about potential threats or rewards as if they are real. Imagination alone engages us in the same defensive, adaptive, or maladaptive behaviors. For Anna, the anticipated threats (e.g., judgment by her peers) and fear of looking inadequate (e.g., punishment) caused a range of emotions, reactions, and body manifestations.

While one view of emotions is that they play a physio-affective function that ensures our survival, that view does not account for the full nature and range of emotional experiences. As we develop, emotional states become entwined with thoughts, concepts, interpretations, meaning, and defensive behaviors (Clausi et al., 2017; Panksepp & Biven, 2012). Raw visceral emotional states, from dread to happiness, are crucial for forming memories. Similarly, they underpin much of our learning about ourselves and others. We know now that early learning that occurs in the context of strong emotions sticks and more often becomes part of our conscious knowledge and habits.

Finally, emotional states are often inseparable from the automatic behaviors we implement in order to respond to a situation. When we feel fear or sense danger, we run. When we feel enraged, we may punch an object close to us. Simply put, emotions express themselves as physiological states and interact with other mental and behavioral functions.

WE ARE OUR EMOTION STATES

Research into affective neuroscience (Panksepp & Biven, 2012) has identified seven core affective systems that, in essence, represent our innate emotions: (1) seeking/expectancy, (2) fear/anxiety, (3) rage/anger, (4) lust/sexual excitement, (5) care/nurturance, (6) panic/grief/sadness, and (7) play/social joy (Panksepp & Biven, 2012). Timely avoidance of danger, the effective pursuit of food and a mate, strong attachment bonds with family members, or getting along with others are examples of essential emotion states. Avoidance is an innate reaction to fear and anxiety, and similarly, pursuit of goals and getting along are rooted in the seeking and social joy emotions. These emotion states and the action tendencies embedded within them have helped us survive and thrive. However, in order to be more efficient, these emotional states needed to incorporate other functions as well. They had to develop a neural infrastructure that enabled optimal functioning. First, this entailed an effective attention system that quickly and accurately deciphered signals of threat and reward. Second, this necessitated an ability to remember environmental cues, their context, and the appropriate responses to them. And, finally, this required a generalized ability to learn from experience and predict future consequences.

The results of this evolutionary necessity resulted in extensive interconnectedness among brain regions and functions. In effect, the increasing discoveries regarding this interconnectedness among different brain regions underscores one of the most significant advances in recent neuroscience research. We can no longer view emotions as an isolated branch of human experience. Rather, brain evolution is increasingly viewed in terms of the intertwined nature of brain circuits and processes. During millennia of human evolution, the brain developed comparatively new regions, primarily the prefrontal cortex residing in the front of the brain. However, the neural activity these newer areas generate does not occur within a layered architecture; in other words, the newer additions do not lie on top of the lower ones, controlling them, as was previously thought. Instead, evolutionary development demonstrates that these new systems are embedded within old ones (Pessoa, 2008; Pessoa & Hof, 2015).

The neural activities arising from the interconnected brain-wide regions are the result of two types of neural links: structural connectivity, where there is physical proximity among regions, and functional connectivity, where neurons in faraway regions of the brain act simultaneously in response to particular stimuli. In this way, even remote regions are functionally connected through reciprocal neural signals that result in a far-reaching yet integrated neural network. This brain-wide integration is particularly relevant to how emotions influence all of our conscious and unconscious feelings, memories, beliefs, relationship to our bodies, attachment styles, goals, and behaviors.

As a result of the interweaving and interconnectedness of multiple brain/ mind systems, ancient and new, areas that mediate emotions became utterly entangled, physically and functionally, with skills essential for effective functioning (Okon-Singer, 2018; Pessoa & Hof, 2015). A good example of this type of mutual embedding is the amygdala, which has extensive connections with most other brain regions, both physical and functional. When the amygdala detects a stimulus and categorizes it as dangerous, we experience fear; this entails inferring the likely source in the environment, engaging past memories, and automatically enacting a response across parallel and numerous regions.

These responses include the sensory cortex that transmits visual or auditory stimuli, the fear circuit, which gives rise to the visceral sensations of fear, past memories, and learning pertaining to similar events encoded via the amygdala, the basal ganglia, and the hippocampus, motor systems that initiate action, and higher cognitive functions that further assess the situation (Pessoa & Adolphs,

2010). Furthermore, these various networks mutually affect one another and are, in turn, affected by previous expectations and predictions based on past experiences. More specifically, as we will discuss in the following chapters, this neural interconnectedness fuses emotions of fear and anxiety into explicit and implicit memories early on. This shapes our growing concepts of ourselves, unconscious expectations, behavioral tendencies, and relational styles.

Perhaps the best way to understand emotions is through their assimilated nature. When we say we are feeling upset and anxious or happy and content, by definition, the description of this state contains other human skills: perceptions, awareness of our mind and body, descriptive language, and a deep understanding of what a particular feeling means to our well-being, survival, and intactness.

In order to fully understand the emotional brain, it is necessary to understand the cognitive brain, and vice versa (Pessoa & Hof, 2015). Our very first emotions, in the form of pure instinctual reactions, develop into emotions and, together with cognition, express themselves as feelings. As we consider the functional differences between instincts and emotions, we should be thankful that consciously experienced feelings provide us with more flexible and complex assessments of and responses to situations (Smith et al., 2019).

Obviously, these processes are unconscious; we have no awareness of what or how the brain-wide assessments and conclusions transpire. (This topic is explored in depth in Chapter 3, looking at the fear system.) What we do become aware of is the culmination of this extensive integrated activity across numerous regions: the intermixing of information related to perception, memory, cognition, emotion, motivation, and action. From the beginning, as emotional states of arousal engage our chemistry and physiology, they are increasingly encoded and represented as concepts and personal meanings.

THE MEANING AND SIGNIFICANCE OF NEUROPSYCHOLOGICAL EMOTION RESEARCH

One of the mistakes we often make is assuming that neuroscientific research is too esoteric and reductionistic, therefore making it irrelevant to psychological inquiry. I would argue that this is a very erroneous conclusion, which effectively inhibits our knowledge of precisely what we want to know: how emotions, especially fear and anxiety, explain our human functioning. As challenging as it is, it is indispensable to integrate specific neuropsychological data on emotions and feelings when dealing with clinical observations and therapeutic approaches. It is important to create a better picture of how the brain/mind perceives, interprets, and experiences stressful situations, both consciously and unconsciously. Such enhanced knowledge further enables us to learn how individuals and societies perceive and react to inevitable crises and develop effective ways to deal with such challenges.

Such integrated knowledge can help us better understand, for example, what makes it difficult to tolerate and regulate difficult emotions. It can help us identify how we arrive at and why we maintain feelings of worthlessness. We can better understand why irrational fears that are no longer relevant persist and at times control our lives, and why we are so vulnerable to believing outlandish ideas when they play to our worst fears. We must understand how the neuropsychological mix of emotions, cognitions, and response tendencies shapes our beliefs about ourselves and others, our defenses and behaviors. This will allow us to become aware of how emotions such as fear and anxiety make us more vulnerable to a wide range of upsetting feelings and defensive behaviors. At the same time, accepting our vulnerable tendencies can also lead us to develop more effective ways to live with them and still thrive.

How can we understand the roots of Anna's suffering, her inability to release herself from distorted convictions about her abilities, and modify her avoidant behaviors? Although her internal experiences were not rooted in any external reality, she still responded to them as if her thoughts and projections were real threats. When we try to understand such upsetting internal states and the roadblocks to better emotion regulation, we are confronted by questions surrounding the roots of such lingering fears, anxieties, and narratives. Why are more reality-bound voices not strong enough to overcome the fears that influence her behavior? And why does she experience these powerful negative narratives regarding her competence as the only reality, disregarding and overriding her actual, demonstrable achievements?

The answers to these questions are rooted in the outsized influence that the fear system has on our other mental faculties. In this way, fear and anxiety can be considered as uniquely powerful emotions that, because of their evolutionary function, are front and center within our human experience. In order to optimize survival, the functional purpose of the fear system took a central role. When we try to understand the fear system within the larger frame of emotions, we further understand how the particular states of fear and anxiety can become so prominent.

It is this essential survival function that gives fear and anxiety, elements of the fear system, such outsized effects on how we develop and on who we become. Chapter 3 illustrates how the functional aspects of the fear system have resulted in its pervasive presence in our psyches. We will explore how the fear system came to organize what we know, how we remember and learn about the world, and why fear and anxiety have acquired such staying power in our brain/minds.

CHAPTER THREE

The Fear System and the Amygdala

As part of my efforts to translate neuropsychological findings into psychological insights, I am excited to further explore the emotions of fear, anxiety, and other negative feelings and thoughts shaped by them. From unpleasant visceral feelings to anxious expectations, fearful predictions, negative ruminations about the past and the future, self-doubt and other negative self-narratives, and deep-seated fears about being shamed and found out—the effects of the fear and anxiety in our lives are undeniable. To truly understand this oversized role of the fear system in our lives, we must integrate neuropsychological data with our considerable clinical knowledge. We need to better understand the origins of the fear system, its vast influence on our earliest learning and memories, and its tendency to take over our conscious experiences. Finally, in order to develop more efficient ways to deal with the ill effects of fear and anxiety, we need to get a better neuropsychological picture of its brain-wide influences. This chapter focuses on some of the complex characteristics of the fear system.

THE PRICE OF SUCCESS

As discussed in the last chapter, the evolutionary purpose of emotion states has been to ensure adaptive responses to a wide range of environmental threats and internal needs. All innate emotions have enabled us to survive, seek close bonds, reproduce, manipulate environmental challenges, play, create beauty, and become productive (Adolphs & Anderson, 2018).

Of the seven primary affective systems (Panksepp & Biven, 2012) examined in Chapter 2, the fear system has evolved into the key signifier of danger and potential threats. From the dawn of life, all organisms have automatically assessed environmental conditions as advantageous or disadvantageous for survival. As evolutionary pressures favored and reinforced survival mechanisms, the fear system became an important, if not the most crucial, emotion state. Its two major states, fear and anxiety, became the initiators of very obnoxious physiological and emotional states. Simultaneously, these particularly unpleasant sensations became very efficient signals warning us of potential threats, real danger, and the need to initiate coping and defense mechanisms.

As this alarm system was frequently activated across many situations, its responses became fast, automatic, and often unconscious. This led to a more generalized perception of threat, erring on the side of fear, caution, and overreaction. The result was that ambiguous or even neutral situations were often perceived as threats to survival. The fear system's automatic tendency to anticipate fear, even when no threat was present, kept our ancestors safe. But in order to efficiently maximize responses, the fear circuit in the brain/mind/body could not work alone. It had to recruit other mental functions such as attention, memory, and learning; these brain circuits retained important information necessary for future encounters with similar dangerous situations.

Memories of fearful situations, for example, did not disappear even when the immediate cause was no longer present. It was essential to remember dangerous situations and unconsciously learn all there was to know about them. Similarly, consciously mulling over past and future danger situations, frequently reliving them alone, or telling and retelling one's experiences in groups was important preparation for future threat situations. But living with memories of danger, and frequently thinking about future dangers, real and imagined, created a fertile ground for states of sustained fear—which in essence describes anxiety.

What we are left with today are easily aroused emotions that respond to a wide range of real, remembered, or even imagined threats. We learn what to avoid quickly and efficiently, but at the same time we tend to generalize fears; consequently, we avoid situations that present no real threat physically or emotionally. We are encumbered by bouts of worries and anxious ruminations on what can go wrong. And, most importantly, because states of fear and ongoing anxiety are embodied parts within our brain/mind/body circuitry, we have also inherited a difficulty in disengaging from the visceral manifestations of panic and from worries, negative predictions, and fearful expectations. For some people, this difficulty has become a complete inability to disengage, leaving them in a state of perpetual fear and anxiety. Often, just the thought of potential threat triggers a cascade of upsetting feelings, thoughts, and expectations.

The adverse sensations that fear and anxiety created in our distant past ensured fast and automatic reactions in the face of danger. We all know, of course, about the fight, flight, or freezing defenses. But what is so interesting about psychological insights into our personality traits is that with the evolutionary development of more cognitive areas like the prefrontal cortex, and with the resulting interconnections among neural networks, most brain regions and functions also became part of the survival enterprise. Neural circuits that alert, process, remember, learn about, and defend against perceived threats developed and became interconnected. This whole brain/mind/body dedication to survival and to the maintenance of well-being explains the perpetual presence of fear, stress, and anxiety in our lives. In short, survival as the most important goal ensured that the fear system with all its tentacles became prominent as well.

These circuits became part of our genetic makeup, staying with us in spite of the environmental changes we have gone through. For many people in today's world (although sadly not all), we no longer have to face the dangers of hunting and confronting daily threats. But an efficient fear system innately primed to react to and obsess about danger will inevitably find external and internal targets identified as threat. Generalized fear, panic with no apparent cause, and chronic inchoate anxiety are frequent manifestations today.

Indeed, anxiety disorders are among the most prevalent psychiatric disorders worldwide, estimated at between 15% and 20% of the population; these disorders often result in debilitating subjective suffering, somatic symptomatology, and comorbidity with other mental and behavioral difficulties such as depression and a wide range of addictions. Within the class of anxiety disorders, phobias, social anxiety disorder, agoraphobia, panic disorders, generalized anxiety disorder, separation anxiety, obsessive–compulsive disorder, and post-traumatic stress are among the most common. Anxiety disorders, characterized by a high degree of chronic anxiety conditions, tend to start early in life and, therefore, cause years of disability. Such disorders impose an enormous burden on the individual, society, and the economy; enormous resources are devoted to health care costs and lost productivity (Kessler et al., 2005; Shackman et al., 2018).

A vast body of research has focused on anxiety disorders and their neurobiological underpinnings. But beyond these difficulties, contemporary neuropsychological research and clinical experiences suggest that fear and anxiety are not only present in clearly diagnosed symptoms. Rather, these innate emotions have a wide range of characteristics and manifestations. From the very beginning of life, they infiltrate other emotional, cognitive, and behavioral traits. Whether we are aware of their ongoing effects or not, fearful and anxious states underpin our entrenched negative patterns. This early co-opting of many developing emotional and mental functions has wide-ranging implications, ensuring that inevitable fear and anxiety throughout our development shape other feelings, thoughts, and behaviors.

There are no other emotions as easily triggered and no other emotional states so reactive to both external and internal threats, real and perceived, as fear and anxiety. There are no other feelings so tightly bound together with the power of our imagination to expect, predict, and worry about what was wrong in the past, what is wrong in the present, or what can go wrong in the near and far future. Similarly, there is no greater emotional distress as when our conscious experience is aroused by fear, panic, stress, anxiety, and the elaborate feelings and thoughts they generate. In the midst of extreme anxiety, even without external reason, we are actually convinced that the worst is about to happen. One might say that these consequences are the price that we pay for a successful neural system that allowed our ancestors to survive, evolve, and thrive.

NEUROPSYCHOLOGICAL ASPECTS OF FEAR

Fear and anxiety are not just mental states. The deeply unpleasant physiobiological symptoms generated by the fear system are familiar to most of us. The fear system releases chemicals such as epinephrine, norepinephrine, and glutamate that mobilize signals of danger and activate the arousing and dysregulating sympathetic nervous system. This branch of the autonomic nervous system mediates states of hyperarousal, which are physical and emotional states of great intensity and unpleasant qualities, or valence. Physiological expressions of a hyperaroused state include increased heartbeat, higher blood

pressure, shortness of breath, lightheadedness, and extreme, very frightening sensations of unreality and dread. In general, a hyperaroused state signals danger and the sense that something is terribly wrong. These processes
generate the fight, flight, or freezing defenses, coping mechanisms inherited
from our ancestors.

Intermingled with and inseparable from such physical sensations are irrational fears, catastrophizing thoughts, excessive ruminations, negative predictions,
and self-doubts. Significantly, other disturbing feelings such as shame, guilt, loss
of trust in one's judgments and competence, and other aspects of our sense of
self also become linked to fear and anxiety. In a bidirectional process, worries,
fearful ruminations, and imagined negative predictions can intensify the physiological manifestations of the fear system (Forbes et al., 2019). The resulting
state—the inextricable combination of physiological, emotional, and mental
functions—is hard to tolerate, and is what we try to avoid and defend against.
As Panksepp and Biven (2012) stated, "the FEAR system generates a negative
affective state from which all people and animals wish to escape" (p. 36).

All emotions, including fear and generalized anxiety, start early, arouse automatically, and are embedded in our genome (Damasio, 2010; LeDoux, 2014;
Panksepp & Biven, 2012). The role of epigenetic processes is important because
the interactions between genes and environment largely account for the individual differences in how we perceive potentially dangerous situations; these
interactions determine how well we experience, tolerate, and regulate negative
feelings. This continuous interaction between the individual's innate tendency to
perceive danger and the actual degree of external threat is still with us. In addition, throughout evolution, with the essential need to avoid calamity, our ancestors needed to at times react to imaginary threats as if they were real, slowly
enhancing the centrality of the fear system.

These interactions between the over-sized influence of the fear system and
the challenges presented by the environment are especially important during the
early years when the brain/mind/body is most plastic and, therefore, very sensitive to environmental stressors. Indeed, numerous studies have shown that temperamentally shy and anxious infants, children, and adolescents are more reactive
to fearful cues and show more fear responses as adults. In particular, the interaction between increased sensory sensitivity to the environment and the quality
of childhood parenting resulted in an elevated reactivity in the amygdala and the
prefrontal cortex among adults (Acevedo et al., 2016; Acevedo et al., 2017).

THE INNATENESS AND PREVALENCE OF FEAR

The manifestations of fear and anxiety are quick to arise, feel bad, and are utterly convincing while they are happening. From the combined neurobiological and evolutionary perspective, stress and anxiety are generated by the older parts of the brain, those literally under the cortex—primarily the amygdala and its related regions (Broschot et al., 2016). According to researchers (Broschot et al., 2016), a major function of the fear system is to assess and respond to conditions of uncertainty and lack of safety. Significantly, such responses are not simply generated anew each time but preexist in a state of default; they are always there, waiting to quickly inform us of danger.

Only when safety is detected is there an inhibition of the fear circuits mediated by the vagal nerve system (Porges, 2001). Continuous threats to safety and prolonged uncertainty trigger this default stress response, promoting chronic anxiety, insecurity, and sadness. Furthermore, the price of erring, of not paying enough attention to threat and lack of safety, and not reacting immediately and appropriately, is potentially severe (Brosschot et al., 2016). This has clearly led the fear system to develop quick and automatic reactions even to nonexistent threats as if they were real and imminent. This tendency to generalize and exaggerate threat is very much with us, and as we'll see in the following chapters, can be intensified by many factors during early development. As habitual overreactions to perceived threats become part of an unconscious pattern, we tend to react to current situations through the old, fear-biased lenses developed in childhood. This invariably results in a chronic state of vigilance and anxiety.

The innate tendency to react with heightened fear and anxiety to lack of clarity and threatened safety is exacerbated in times of personal, physiological, and societal insecurity. Not surprisingly, at the time of writing this book, feelings of stress, anxiety, and even panic have greatly intensified as a result of the COVID-19 pandemic. Beyond fears of being sick, what has been most difficult to tolerate has been the lack of certainty and fear surrounding an unknown future. The uncertainty about controlling the virus and the disruptions to our everyday lives have added to real worries about financial insecurities and the sense that the economy and life as we knew it could never fully recover.

On all levels, our perceptions of clarity and safety have been seriously compromised with the complete uncertainty about how and when the pandemic would end and how we would all get back to normal. These feelings have plunged many of us into unrelenting states of stress, anxiety, dread, and depression. Such reactions are entirely expected and normal. Due to the survival value of paying greater attention to threats and uncertainty, the tendency to err on the side of fear and anxiety passes into our genes; therefore, we are hypervigilant to any threat, real or perceived. In effect, our collective anxious reactions to the calamity of COVID-19 are the embodiment of the fear system's success; we have been paying extra attention to what could kill us and how to avoid becoming sick. Collectively, we have been more anxious, stressed, frustrated, and sad. Now, as we continually mourn the many dead, we still fear the worst for ourselves, our loved ones, and many others we don't personally know.

Indeed, the continuous anxiety has even found its way into our dreams. A common theme in some of my clients' dreams has repeatedly focused on them finding themselves without a mask on in the middle of a big crowd of unmasked people. Upon realizing how vulnerable they are to the virus, they wake up experiencing intense fears about their survival.

FEAR AND ANXIETY: DIFFERENT AND YET THE SAME?

So far in this discussion, I have used the terms *fear system* and *fear and anxiety.* Are there clearly discernible differences between these states, either subjectively or neuropsychologically? Based on studies analyzing presenting anxiety disorder symptoms, some researchers concluded that there is in fact a distinction between states of fear and of anxiety (Kotov et al., 2015; Lang et al., 2016). They describe fear as intense and short-lived, whereas anxiety is considered to be a state of fear that is continuous and sustained over time (Shackman & Fox, 2016; LeDoux, 2015).

On the other hand, an examination of the vast literature on the fear system clearly reveals that the terms *fear* and *anxiety* are often used interchangeably, including in the American Psychiatric Association's (2013) *Diagnostic and Statistical Manual of Mental Disorders* (*DSM-5*). Similarly, various therapeutic approaches and theories treating conditions such as PTSD and anxiety disorders use *fear* and *anxiety* interchangeably or inconsistently. The difficulty of drawing sharp operational boundaries between these two terms is rooted in the neurological brain structures that generate these emotions—specifically, the amygdala, its connected structures, and related networks (Perusini & Fanselow, 2015).

THE AMYGDALA: THE BRAIN/MIND'S ALERTING SYSTEM

Many studies have consistently established the amygdala as a central mediator of fear, stress, anxiety, panic, sadness, and anger. It is also involved in processing positive emotions, although these reactions are not as well studied (Fox et al., 2015; Gaffrey et al., 2016; LeDoux, 2002; LeDoux & Doyere, 2011; Ohman, 2009; Pattwell et al., 2017; Phelps, 2006, 2009). As part of the limbic system, the amygdala belongs to the older regions of the brain; although we think of the amygdala in the singular, there is one in each hemisphere. Together, the two parts of the amygdala receive input from all sensory areas—visual, tactile, auditory, and olfactory. (As most other publications, I will refer to these bihemispheric brain regions as the amygdala.) The amygdala is always at the ready to react to incoming information and, based on the received neural signals, proceeds to generate emotional reactions, behavioral responses, and cognitive assessments (Davis & Whalen, 2001; Freese & Amaral, 2009).

The amygdala comprises a collection of nuclei. The basolateral part of the amygdala relays sensory signals of potential threats to its central nucleus. Unsurprisingly, amygdala activation has been seen in practically all the imaging studies that have investigated the effects of fear and anxiety on attention, learning, performance, short- and long-term memory, decision making, and perception. The amygdala has been found to visibly respond to sad, fearful, angry, and neutral faces; as discussed in later chapters, these findings have particular significance to early childhood development. Just anticipating a shock, for example, or watching negative stimuli such as sad or angry scenes increases amygdala activation (Callaghan et al., 2019; Lebow & Chen, 2016; Fox & Shackman, 2019; Shackman & Fox, 2016). In addition, old memories, imagined threats, and intrusive disturbing images, as well as scary stimuli presented subliminally or out of awareness, can all trigger an overreaction in the amygdala. At the same time, due to bidirectional links between the fear system and the body's physiological reactions, raised levels of anxiety will trigger all these unpleasant internal experiences (LeDoux, 2015; Lewis & Todd, 2007). Often, a chronic high level of anxiety is the reason for a host of addictive cravings and behaviors. This is especially so when an individual has a difficult time identifying, understanding, and therefore regulating their anxiety.

Significantly, this inseparable connection between states of hyperarousal and unpleasant sensations only emphasizes the power of the amygdala to create dysregulating states within us. Whether activated by real threats, by internally generated perceived and imagined threats, or by habitual hypervigilance, the amygdala releases neuromodulators. These chemicals mediate communication between synaptic connections throughout the brain (LeDoux, 2002; LeDoux & Schiller, 2009). In effect, the amount of neuropsychological information regarding the amygdala is vast and growing; the number of studies is literally too numerous to cite. Consequently, I will highlight only a few.

As the sentry in charge of danger detection, the amygdala is connected to two pathways of emotional perception and processing (LeDoux, 2002). The so-called low and dirty pathway—operating outside awareness—sends threat signals directly to the amygdala, where a state of fearful arousal is generated, bypassing the cortex and conscious awareness. The second pathway, the high road, generates similar physiochemical processes; but it goes through the cortex where these signals are immediately translated into conscious experiences of fear, anxiety, and other feeling states. Both modes influence each other and work in a coordinated way (LeDoux & Schiller, 2009). Indeed, both imaging studies and self-reported information from patients with amygdala lesions indicate that the amygdala plays a critical role in selecting and prioritizing cues and stimuli that signal threat.

The amygdala's level of vigilance and response to threat is highly individual and reflects complex interactions between genetic and environmental aspects; these interactions regulate what genes become activated. For example, children born with an extremely anxious, shy, or inhibited predisposition show an increased risk for anxiety, depression, and substance abuse in adulthood (Fox et al., 2018). Conversely, negative feelings can increase and become worse when they are exposed to high degrees of stress or trauma during childhood and adolescence. For example, negative life events such as the death of a caretaker, close relative, or friend, academic difficulties, or constant family strife are associated with increased anxious feelings later in life. Similarly, failures of parental attunement and conflicts and emotional ruptures within the family and with peers heighten feelings of insecurity about the safety of relationships and one's self-worth.

The neural circuits that are involved in learning about, remembering, and encoding threat-relevant cues are all interconnected with the amygdala: the hippocampus, the anterior insula, the bed nucleus of the stria terminalis (BNST), the midcingulate cortex, the orbitofrontal cortex, and the periaqueductal gray.

The amygdala and the hippocampus, for example, are part of the circuit that processes fear, anxiety, and memories. This system is particularly sensitive to the effects of early stress and hyperarousal brought on by fear and anxiety states. Early stress increases the amygdala's susceptibility to all types of aversive stimuli and conditions. The resulting tendency to experience fear and anxiety in a wide range of situations also increases one's vulnerability to experiencing post-traumatic stress responses later in life (McCoy et al., 2019; Vonderwalde, 2019). Importantly, when relying on early learning and sensitization to fear, the fast-acting automaticity of the amygdala will amplify and distort the meaning of current situations. Unless it is extinct, or part of our conscious awareness, past learning about potential threat will determine our reactions in the here and now. As a result, a more sensitive and reactive fear system can predispose an individual to an exaggerated stress response when a threat is encountered but also when it is internally generated in one's memory, expectation, or imagination (Shackman & Wagner, 2019; Uddin & Karlsgodt, 2018).

Researchers studied PTSD reactions among new army recruits exposed to combat conditions (Hendler & Admon, 2016). The soldiers' degree of amygdala reactivity was evaluated before and after they took part in combat. Those who were shown in the fMRI to have an overactive amygdala at rest (i.e., when not participating in a task) were more likely to display pronounced PTSD symptoms after a traumatic event during battle. Similarly, other researchers have demonstrated amygdala hyperresponsiveness to fearful faces among PTSD patients (Whalen et al., 2001). Conversely, people with amygdala damage exhibit a profound lack of fear and anxiety in response to both diffusely presented vague threats and also to more acute threats such as spiders or snakes (Bechara et al., 1995; Fox et al., 2018; Todd and Phelps, 2016; Korn et al., 2017; Mobbs et al., 2015). As we see, the amygdala's role in the generation of fear responses and automatic defenses is established. Similarly, its connections to other brain circuits and the resulting influence on the brain/mind are also proven. The following section discusses in more detail this unique structure and its close connection to another region involved in fear detection and processing.

The Extended Amygdala and the BNST

Recent studies have focused on another structure adjacent to and interconnected with the amygdala—the bed nucleus of the stria terminalis. Together with the central amygdala, these areas form a central hub that underpins the fear circuitry: the extended amygdala (Fox & Shackman, 2019; Lebow & Chen, 2016). The extended amygdala integrates and evaluates all threat-relevant information, generating internal states of fear and anxiety as well as appropriate coping defenses.

Some studies have explored whether these distinct structures may be related to the potential differences between fear and anxiety and have shown that the amygdala reacts rapidly to clear and immediate threats (e.g., cues associated with an imminent delivery of shock). The BNST, on the other hand, engages more slowly and is responsible for sustained or anxious responses to threats that are assessed as diffuse, uncertain, or remote. These differences are assumed to underlie two different states: intense fear and sustained anxiety; the latter involves negative expectations, predictions, worries, and ruminations.

Like the amygdala, the BNST is interconnected with essential emotional processing regions, including the prefrontal cortex, hippocampus, and the amygdala itself (Fox & Shackman, 2019; Miles & Maren, 2019). Some studies support separate functions of the two regions of the extended amygdala: the BNST and the central amygdala. Some researchers conclude that both areas possess distinct roles in the development of clinical anxiety. The paths engaged by the BNST might be related more closely to networks involved in cognitive regulation of anxiety, whereas those engaged by the central amygdala might underpin automatic value coding and regulation. These findings are important for better understanding the role of the extended amygdala in pathological anxiety (Torrisi et al., 2019). More specifically, this division of labor corresponds to the two main emotion regulation strategies, one controlled by cognitive efforts and the other guided by more automatic regulation.

Other imaging studies, however, show that the central amygdala and BNST exhibit similar functions. Both are sensitive to a range of aversive situations, including immediate danger, uncertainty, remote threats, and anticipated social vulnerabilities. Both structures become activated among patients who subjectively reported symptoms of both fear and anxiety. In addition, although subjects' extended amygdala (most publications refer to the amygdala) have displayed short-lived reactions to passing acute threats, they also show heightened neural activity during sustained exposure to less clearly threatening stimuli (Fox & Shackman, 2019; Lebow & Chen, 2016).

Similarly, the extended amygdala becomes activated when subjects quickly perceive a variety of interpersonal cues such as facial expressions, body postures, and vocal expressions. These structures seem to unconsciously assess and interpret these facial expressions and postures for potential threat and meaning (Fox & Shackman, 2019; Sladky et al., 2018). It is interesting to note that with elevated defensive responses, both the amygdala and the BNST showed heightened activity. In sum, these two structures composing the extended amygdala have similar response tendencies (Fox & Shackman, 2019).

On the whole, the brain imaging literature suggests that the central amygdala and BNST, while not interchangeable, are more alike than different. In humans, both show transient responses to clear and immediate threat and sustained activation in contexts associated with uncertain, longer-lasting threats. Both regions show heightened activation in patients with anxiety disorders and individuals at risk for developing them (Yassa et al., 2012).

Such neural characterizations of the fear system validate the centrality of the amygdala and its circuits to our sensitivity to stressful emotions. In some contexts, fear describes an acute and potentially short-term reaction to a specific threat or imminent danger. Most often, however, initial fears, especially those that started early in our lives, slide into more sustained anxious and apprehensive states intermingled with physiological markers of fear. Cognitive aspects of anxiety—worries, negative projections, and ruminations—are also intertwined with the more acutely felt hyperaroused fear responses. This suggests that, in most cases, we can use the words *fear* and *anxiety* interchangeably, while the term *fear system* refers to both.

THE FEAR SYSTEM AND ITS PRACTICAL IMPLICATIONS

This section illustrates how the extended amygdala and its related regions influence and inform other circuits to pay special attention to threat cues. By focusing on threat cues and making sure they reach many other brain circuits, the amygdala becomes an efficient teacher (Beebe et al., 2010; Pessoa, 2014, 2018; Pessoa & Hof, 2015; Satterthwaite et al., 2018; Tottenham, 2019; Tottenham & Gabbard-Durnham, 2017; Tronick, 2007) to the rest of the brain/mind. Attention biases, implicit and explicit memories, habits, learning processes, and other feelings become entwined with the emotions of fear and anxiety. Severe early life stress has a particularly noxious effect on ongoing dysregulated anxiety and, in turn, its effects on other mental functions. Enduring and negative reactions are augmented in the context of an innate anxious temperament. But another, equally significant question is whether what was previously termed normative disruptions—the inevitable slings and arrows of infancy and childhood—also lead to injured and vulnerable self-states.

One of the highlights gleaned from our growing understanding of the fear system and its emissary, the amygdala, is the realization that this innate circuit is extremely reactive and easily aroused in a wide range of contexts. This may result in lived experiences that highlight perceived emotional assaults felt by the child even in seemingly benign interactions. The child's need for love, attention, and full recognition of their autonomy and internal experiences is often painfully negated by careless, dismissive, or unwittingly critical behaviors from caregivers. With an immature prefrontal cortex, children lack the ability to understand the actual meaning of an adult's behaviors and, more so, the very personal motivation behind a hurtful exchange. Children, and even adolescents, often cannot see that injurious parental behaviors have nothing to do with the child's actual being or behaviors. An emotionally hurtful exchange with a parent induces not only anxiety about displeasing them and losing their love but also other injured, dysregulating feelings such as shame, humiliation, and guilt. The following chapters further explore the numerous effects of such common interactions on a child's unconscious self-concept. With each exploration, the outsized place and influence of fear and anxiety on our experiences, entrenched negative patterns, and personality traits will become clearer and more convincing.

CHAPTER FOUR

The Brain-Wide Influence of the Fear System

The realization that brain-wide networks are inextricably interconnected is particularly significant for a better understanding of the human mind in all its complexity (Lewis & Todd, 2007; Okon-Singer et al., 2015; Pessoa, 2017; Todd et al., 2020). In effect, long-held ideas are no longer supported with regard to the assumed conflictual relationships between emotion and cognition, passion and reason, and the authenticity of affect versus the defensiveness of thought. Rather, each internal self-state state contains emotional, perceptual, cognitive, and behavioral traits that are inextricably intertwined (Pessoa, 2008). Already at the very beginning of life, as the infant automatically assesses what feels good or not, other innate capacities are recruited. Innate skills such as perception, memory, and learning facilitate the process of adaptation to a range of situations, both threatening and rewarding. The recruitment of such skills also helps generate the essential responses of approach and avoidance (Todd et al., 2020).

Even prior to the most recent neuropsychological findings, working with patients has reinforced for me the integrated nature of our internal states. People describe their emotions with words, most often calling them feelings; they enact old patterns of defensive behaviors meant to protect them from hurt, and they experience the hyperarousal intensity of some emotions in both body/mind and behavior. For example, we can often witness how anxious and insecure states are conveyed through all aspects of one's experience: visceral discomfort, perceptual biases, self-denigrating thoughts, anxious ruminations, habitual negative expectations, and rigid defenses that are no longer adaptive. Similarly, in the case of intrusive anxious thoughts and images, a burst of physically unpleasant sensations of anxiety is usually the culprit. Interconnected with all other brain/mind networks, fear and anxiety will invariably trigger other memories, thoughts, and images that became associated with these particular emotions in a particular encoded and implicitly remembered context (Pessoa, 2014). Intrusive images are oftentimes part of a PTSD response pattern but are also triggered by anxious ruminations and worries. As in Mimi's case from the previous chapter, ongoing anxiety that started early in childhood occasionally triggered fearful and dysregulating images: memories of her abusive brother, pictures of her silently suffering mother, and "disgusting" images of illness for which she had no explanation.

From a clinical point of view, a negative pattern informed by the fear system and its influence on other feelings, mental functions, and behaviors seems to be the most significant and consequential aspect of our development. Furthermore, the outsized and pervasive role of fear and anxiety and their effects on all the other mental and behavioral patterns seems to explicate most of the ills and suffering we encounter at therapists' offices as well as in our lives in general.

This chapter further explores the interactions between the fear system and other disturbing feelings, thoughts, and images, and the interconnected nature of the brain/mind and body. In particular, this chapter focuses on the influence that the fear circuits have on our developing brain and, consequently, on our conscious and unconscious patterns. What consistently stands out in neuropsychological research is the disproportionate impact of the fear system and its executing arm, the amygdala, on the vast knowledge that the brain/ mind encounters, encodes, learns, and retains. I would like again to reiterate that throughout I do refer to perceptions, feelings, thoughts, and behaviors as separate entities. But I only do it out of the wish to convey the totality of our internal experience.

FEAR AND CHILD DEVELOPMENT

From early on, the amygdala significantly determines the relevance and personal meaning of incoming stimuli, making it crucial for learning about threat (Opendak et al., 2019). As the amygdala communicates the presence of threat to other regions of the brain, it leads the infant to experience what feels good or bad, calm or stressful. As the amygdala instigates negative moods, terror, fear, and defensiveness, it shapes other growing functions: attention, memory, unconscious learning, interpersonal representations, and the child's growing sense of self (Brosch et al., 2013; Desmedt et al., 2015; Okon-Singer et al., 2015; Todd et al., 2020; Tottenham & Gabard-Durnam, 2017).

Significantly and with implications for the unique nature of our development, the amygdala and its early circuits are detected prenatally, reaching maturation in utero by 8 months of gestation (Gabard-Durnam et al., 2018). Postpartum, the interconnected networks of the fear system go through rapid growth before 3 months of age. Studies using sophisticated fMRI reveal existing functional connections between the amygdala and other brain regions in children 3 months to 5 years of age (Gabard-Durnam et al., 2018). These regions include the motor, visual, and auditory regions of the cortex, some prefrontal areas, and subcortical networks such as the hippocampus, periaqueductal gray matter (an emotional hub), the basal ganglia, and the cerebellum (both learning and habit-forming centers). These subcortical areas play important roles in shaping emotional states, creating memories, forming habits, influencing learning processes, and establishing unconscious expectations and predictions.

With time, these networks grow in volume and connectivity, continuing to influence many emotional, social, cognitive, and behavioral functions (Lewis & Todd, 2007; Pessoa, 2018; Shackman & Shackman, 2007; Shackman et al., 2018; Todd et al., 2020). From ages 4 to 10 years, the amygdala's structural connections with these regions resemble the brain connectivity seen in adults (Posner et al., 2016). From infancy through childhood and adolescence and into early adulthood, these functionally interconnected networks are sensitive to and respond to a wide range of threatening emotional stimuli. Among the more devastating ones are physical and sexual abuse, failing attunement from caregivers, lack of safety, shaming interactions that cause intolerable humiliation, and terror-inducing events such as frequent fighting between parents and being bullied by peers. Among infants and children, dysregulating negative emotions may be activated by unpredictable and loud noises, negative facial expressions, and tense, chaotic, or inconsistent parenting.

Such experiential lessons, both negative and positive, gradually shape the ongoing pruning processes of the young brain. Synaptic connections that are used and reinforced get stronger, while networks that are not engaged by outside stimulation weaken and fade (Hebb, 1949, 2005). Networks that fire together become part of a vast neural network that forms the basis for future additional synaptic links (see Chapter 1). Paralleling the discussion of the evolutionary importance of the fear system for survival, the effects of the amygdala carry particular clout. With the amygdala's relentless sensitivity to emotional cues and especially potential threat, its quick activation spreads to most other brain regions. Through bidirectional networks, it communicates crucial information about what's good or bad to other regions of the brain.

ATTENTION BIAS FOR FEAR

To some degree or another, we all are vulnerable to and carry within us unconscious negative biases directing how we perceive ourselves and experience the world. Whereas some biases are innate, developed through evolution to serve the fear system, others are reinforced by environmental events. The constant onslaught of environmental stimuli creates strong competition for our limited attentional capabilities. The amygdala, in its role as the primary threat detector, designed an attention system that is especially attuned to potential danger (Aue & Okon-Singer, 2015; Aue et al., 2013; Okon-Singer, 2018). Together, the amygdala and the attention system act as the initial appraisers of incoming stimuli. Based on evolutionary demands, this appraisal system automatically allocates excess attention to aversive stimuli and the emotional arousal they create (Pattwell et al., 2017; Posner et al., 2016). For example, infants and adults alike prioritize objects and events that provide information about fear and danger. Outside their awareness, humans of all ages respond quicker to angry and fearful faces than to positive or neutral expressions (Morales et al., 2017; Okon-Singer et al., 2015).

This is supported by studies examining skin conductance responses, a good measure for hyperarousal levels (Nava et al., 2016). The autonomic nervous systems of infants 3 to 4 months old respond to both happy and angry faces at the subliminal and supraliminal levels. Higher levels of arousal in response to angry faces occurred compared to happy faces, regardless of whether the faces were presented consciously (i.e., at the supraliminal level) or not (stimuli that cannot be detected consciously). Similar to other findings, this study showed that infants can differentiate between happy and fearful expressions. Furthermore, this occurs in both the conscious and unconscious modes of perception.

The fact that infants pay more attention to fearful and angry faces clearly hints at some consequences; biases toward negative stimuli come online early and efficiently (Callaghan et al., 2019; Tottenham, 2019). Infants also show attentional bias toward threatening stimuli such as fear-inducing toys, even when they have little experience with the stimuli. Not surprisingly, 5-year-old children are quicker to detect angry faces, and 8- to 12-year-old children are quick to detect social threats in stories (Camras, 2019; Morales & Fox, 2019). In another study, 7- to 9-year-old children showed greater attentional bias toward unfamiliar animals; significantly, the negative bias toward unfamiliar animals became stronger after the children received negative verbal information about them (Diano et al., 2017; Morales et al., 2017).

Negative attention bias toward social threat is more pronounced in temperamentally fearful children. Compared to a nonanxious group, fearful children show greater sensitivity toward social threat cues, as depicted on illustrated story cards (Diano et al., 2017; Grossman & Jessen, 2017; Jessen & Grossman, 2017; Morales et al., 2017; Todd & Anderson, 2013). This shows how the interaction between innate fearful tendencies and environmental threats work together to influence the nature of our attention to threatening stimuli in the environment. Some biases are innate in us all and constitute remnants of the fear survival tool kit.

But our environment can also reinforce and strengthen this tendency. With repeated threats and fear-inducing experiences within our environment, emerging patterns of attention bias toward negative stimuli become practiced and entrenched. Eventually, in many obvious and nuanced ways, negative affective biases unconsciously focus greater attention on both real and imagined threats (Todd & Anderson, 2013). Such an exaggerated automatic attention to threats leads to the emergence of maladaptive patterns of perception, which readily and unconsciously misinterpret situations as more dangerous or negative than they really are.

The results of the early interaction between an innate attention bias and environmental pressures that enhance bias may very well be behind perceptions of the proverbial glass as being half empty. This happens when unconscious perceptual styles become entangled with developing attentional biases and the verbal meaning they may signify. The result is a propensity to perceive a wide range of situations and emotional cues as threats. Such misperceptions and exaggerations of automatic tendencies to perceive and interpret events in the environment as immediate threats to one's sense of well-being eventually generalize to the most mundane situations (Tottenham & Gabard-Durnam, 2017).

EMOTIONAL REGULATION AND FEAR

Some researchers (Todd et al., 2012) argue that fear-biased attention and perceptual styles are in effect an important component of emotion regulation. This regulation is executed by two opposing perceptual modes that start in infancy. In the first, we tune our filters of automatic attention to perceived threat, thus being more predisposed to experiencing dysregulating threat. In the second, we consistently utilize the very effective defense of avoidance against engaging with or even noticing threats. In both modes, the negative perception of what the threat means to the individual drives the reactive responses. A study exploring the relationship between stress and executive functions (Shields et al., 2017) found that stress impairs working memory, cognitive flexibility, and cognitive inhibition. This finding suggests that stress contributes to weaker regulation of automatic habitual reactions, in effect, compromising emotion regulation.

Unsurprisingly, clinical experience has taught me that among the plethora of defenses people unconsciously recruit (see Chapter 9), avoidance seems to be the strongest and most insidious tactic with the greatest consequences for everyday life. The power of avoidance to paralyze, promote procrastination, and completely work against what needs to be done comes from fear's innate existence and the very early attempts to regulate fears as infants (Todd & Anderson, 2013). This very early defense pattern becomes completely entangled with other cognitive and behavioral functions. As we grow, we genuinely don't know why certain tasks seem overwhelming, why we avoid them, why we don't take risks, or why we tend to postpone what we need to accomplish. Furthermore, often we are not even aware that we are avoiding a challenging task; we just don't take it on and then come up with justifications. As we often witness, this early, anxiety-driven defense tactic of avoidance is very difficult to change. In a sense, we may look at avoidance as among the most efficient strategies to deal with early fear and anxiety, a strategy that becomes an inseparable and unrecognized part of our functioning.

LEARNING AND EMOTION

Learning is the encoding and retaining of emotional, cognitive, and behavioral information. When we think about learning, we tend to focus on a process that is volitional and informed by awareness and choice. Early learning processes,

however, occur automatically and outside our awareness. From a neuropsychological point of view, learning starts in utero. Furthermore, no type of learning
depends on one particular brain region or function; learning involves different
interconnected circuits that are distributed throughout the brain but still work
together to encode and retain habits and information. It is this interconnectedness of networks that determines what we learn, remember, and internalize
during our development.

From the very beginning, infants enter the world fully equipped to acquire
knowledge about the environment. Guided by our genome, the brain's neural
activity in response to internal and external stimuli is uniquely fast and dynamic.
The process of pruning, described in Chapter 1, is very much at play. Neurons
that fire together in response to stimuli form hubs and networks that continue to
react in the same patterns to similar stimuli (Bar-Haim & Pine, 2013; Bar-Haim
et al., 2007; Hebb, 1949, 2005). Neurons that are not stimulated and engaged die
off. Sadly, extreme deprivation of stimulation in the first few years can be devastating to a child's brain/mind. For example, orphans raised in deficient institu-
tional settings may have great difficulties in forming attachments with adoptive
parents (Bowlby, 1973, 1982).

We know now that any learning necessarily changes synapses and neural
pathways. Early networks that learn to react to particular stimuli in the environment, for example, to a caregiver's caring and attuned vocalizations, become
well established. With repeated experiences, those initial networks, both positive and negative, perceive subsequent experiences as good or bad as well. As
they become more robust, these networks co-opt new stimuli into the already
existing learning schemas. A strong negatively based network will continue to
color new learning with anxiety and negativity. Throughout life, early emotional
and cognitive habits suffused with anxiety and fear may erroneously inform us
about impending but nonexistent threats, especially to one's self-esteem.

Indeed, one of the biggest threats to our sense of well-being is association
of anxiety with feelings of deep insecurity and self-doubt. When we feel loved,
valued, and fulfilled, our sense of agency confers on us courage and approach-
oriented behaviors. Conversely, when feelings of insecurity and a sense of fragility dominate, many develop an intense fear of being injured and hurt by words
or behaviors that are perceived to undermine them. The pain of feeling undermined, unaccepted, or unseen is so real, intense, and dysregulating that any
threat of igniting it triggers anxiety and automatic defenses against it. Ian, for

example, was exquisitely sensitive to perceived threats to his internal sense of competence. His immediate and unconscious response was competitive push-back. In order to protect himself, Jerry tended to disarm people, to charm them to come around to his point of view. In both these cases, the ultimate goal was to avoid feeling the enmeshed feelings of injury and fear about their self-worth. The following segment further shows how such unconscious associations happen and are maintained.

Conditioned Fear Learning: Not Just in Mice

Pavlov's classic model of conditioning has been used for many years now to demonstrate fear learning by association (LeDoux, 2000; Pavlov, 1927; Sigurds-son et al., 2007). Most studies on conditioned learning have been conducted on generations of mice; but more recently, studies have focused on humans. In conditioned learning, an aversive stimulus (e.g., an unconditioned stimulus that causes a hyperaroused fear response resulting from administered shocks) is paired with a neutral stimulus (e.g., a conditioned stimulus of a ringing bell, a flashing light, a specific shape or color). With one trial or several of them, the formerly neutral stimulus acquires the same ability to arouse autonomic fear responses. After such conditioning, the mere presentation of the previously neu-tral stimulus is sufficient to elicit physiological markers of fear. Now a bell, a light, or a particular shape or color have become fear-inducing. This is consis-tently demonstrated in both animals and human subjects (Alberini, 2005; Alber-ini & Chen, 2013; Schiller et al., 2008).

Although a great deal of knowledge about this fear learning model comes from lab studies, the implications for associative fear learning in humans of all ages are significant. It can help us better understand the underlying brain/mind mechanisms that promote negative patterns of perception and behavior. Fear conditioning is particularly impactful during development when the brain/mind is most malleable.

In the lab, studies showed that presenting the neutral stimulus without the shock disables the previously formed association between fear and the neutral stimulus. However, once the association between fear and the neutral object is reintroduced, the pattern of the generalized fear returns. In effect, the BNST is involved in the reinstatement (or relapse) of a conditioned freezing response to neutral stimuli (those paired with unconditioned stimuli like shocks). This return of fear-guided reactions occurs even after the association between the shock and the neutral stimulus was previously extinguished or broken (Goode & Maren, 2017; Torrisi et al., 2019).

Again, such findings teach us about the ease with which fear patterns are established and how they can come back when neutral situations are once again associated with fear. It is noteworthy how fast and automatic in nature such associative learning and conditioning are. Moreover, this Pavlovian fear conditioning tends to stick unless a prolonged process of extinction occurs. The evidence shows that an established learned association between fear and neutral stimuli does not actually die. It may lie dormant until it is triggered again by the return of the old association. This may explain why phobias and other anxiety-induced learned behaviors are difficult to extinguish.

Clinically, such information enhances our knowledge about how unconscious associations between a wide range of situations and anxiety persists from infancy. It is quite possible that from early on, an infant's and then a child's level of innate stress and hyperarousal serve as the unconditioned stimuli—very unpleasant experiences which they want to avoid. As other interactions and behaviors become associated with this scary internal state, they too acquire a very unpleasant tone. Becoming conditioned fear reactions, they also lead to unconscious avoidant behaviors (Goode & Maren, 2017). Such complex but entirely out of awareness connections may indeed shed light on the stubbornness of avoidant tendencies. Without any awareness, they are continually enacted as part of one's unquestionable way of functioning. Often people do not even know they are avoiding risks, a greater engagement with the world, or important tasks.

UNCONSCIOUS LEARNING

One important aspect characterizing this model of associative learning is its unconscious nature. Studies exploring unconscious learning have been conducted with both animal and human subjects; they have consistently shown that fear learning and conditioning can occur entirely outside awareness, with subjects completely unaware of what they learned (LeDoux, 2002, 2016). It is not surprising that fMRI scanning studies have demonstrated that the amygdala becomes activated during unconscious perceptions of fearful stimuli, such as facial expressions or words with fear connotations. Finally, even a conscious experience of fear cannot be separated from the unconscious physiological processes that underpin it (LeDoux, 2016; Taschereau-Dumouchel et al., 2018).

Similarly, we may not be aware of the internal or external stimuli that trigger anxious worries or ruminations. For example, at times in relationships we do not know why we become angry at a partner or anxious about the security of the relationship.

Several studies have shown that words presented outside our awareness (e.g., masked stimuli too fast for the human eye to perceive) are cognitively processed outside our conscious awareness. After a presentation when masked stimuli were used, the words were rapidly and accurately remembered and categorized. In another series of experiments, subjects were presented with two lists of masked words that, again, were presented outside awareness. Through repeated presentations, the subjects were taught to find a relationship between the two lists. The results showed that unconsciously they did just that (Greenwald & De Houwer, 2017).

The important conclusion of these studies is that it is possible for people to attend to events, objects, and stimuli in the environment without conscious awareness (Prasad & Mishra, 2019). This ability to process information outside awareness has many implications for our early development, and later on for our unconscious reactions to triggering situations. During development, selective unconscious attention will inevitably focus on interactions deemed important to the child and, most of all, on situations that arouse anxiety. We can safely say that this brain/mind ability to attend to events that grab our attention without awareness underpins a great deal of how learning occurs. Of the many stimuli surrounding the child, those that arouse his attention will be learned. The intense, aggressive emotions between frequently fighting parents will get extra attention from a child; this sets up an unconscious learning process that associates the child's aroused anxiety about his parents' relationship with an awareness of fearful ideas about interacting adults.

I have intentionally chosen to reintroduce this well-known learning model into the more practiced and accepted psychodynamic models we have become more comfortable with in the field of psychology. I do this not as a way of reducing the foundations of our psychic being to stimulus-response connections, like some psychologists did in the past (Watson & Greenberg, 2011). I do this because, within our expanded understanding of how we build our sense of self and come by our subjective experiences, we need to fully recognize how central learning from the environment is to our internal world. When trying to understand negative patterns, we need to acknowledge that some of those fear- and anxiety-suffused feelings and behaviors were formed very early and entirely unconsciously. Without any ability to select, reject, or remove themselves from painful situations, infants and children are at the mercy of ongoing learning processes that create lasting associations between the fear system and a range of feelings, thoughts, and behaviors (Farisco et al., 2017).

When we remember the amount of learning that takes place in the context of anxiety commanding our attention, we can appreciate how a child encodes, remembers, and internalizes negative experiences that later become part of their habitual functioning. Outside the awareness of parents, infants, and children, injurious words, feelings, and behaviors may be unconsciously paired in the child's brain/mind with fast-occurring states of arousal. This can happen even when the state of fear is short lived. Interacting with the child's temperament, such repeated experiences bind together the unconditioned stimulus (e.g., fear and anxiety aroused by parental behavior) and the conditioned stimuli; in this case, relational patterns, words, thoughts, feelings, and defensive behaviors may become associated with fearful emotions. Based on the Pavlovian fear conditioning model discussed earlier, these established fearful associations contribute to anxiety even in neutral situations.

The effects of fear learning are especially devastating under conditions of early childhood emotional and physical stress. Conditions of sexual and physical abuse, neglect, poverty, racial inequality, and others like the COVID-19 pandemic, for example, create environments deeply suffused with fear, anxiety, and stress. These situations inevitably result in a vast neural map that contains within it an uncountable number of learned associations with upsetting or unpleasant experiences and interactions (Pattwell & Bath, 2017).

At the same time, even benign conditions in which normative fears, anxieties, and parental failures are experienced can result in innumerable negative associations, again driven by the amygdala's influence on early memory and learning. For example, a pattern of painful interactions with a loving but frequently tired or distracted parent will create states of fear associated with being hurt or rejected within any close, intimate relationship.

THE INSIDIOUS POWER OF EMOTIONS

An important factor contributing to the effects of emotions on learning is the fact that emotional experiences linger from minutes to hours. Such lingering experiences, especially those with a hyperaroused negative valence, can taint or bias experiences that follow. After a dysregulating event passes, the lingering state of upset can change the valence of subsequent experiences. This happens even if the following experiences are more neutral or even positive in nature (Diano et al., 2017; Shalev et al., 2018; Tambini et al., 2017). Similarly, changes in the amygdala-hippocampal functional connectivity persist for more than two hours following exposure to an intense social stress (Vaisvasser et al., 2013). In this case, as negative emotion states linger, they can cause us to remember subsequent positive social situations in a negative light. Such negatively biased neuropsychological processes strengthen our tendency to perceive and expect negative events, often at the expense of positive ones.

It seems that especially within the intersubjective realm—where interactions can be a source of anxiety, shame, and vulnerability—lingering dysregulation will continue to color subsequent memories and associative learning processes. Emotional states of vulnerability and dysregulation can influence subsequent interactions; we will still perceive them as hurtful even when they hold a different emotional tone. For example, consider a child being scolded and shamed over a minor age-appropriate behavior; even when the parent has forgotten the event and completely changed their mood, the child may still feel rejected or diminished. The child experiences subsequent interactions through the lens of these hurt feelings. This can lead to an accumulation of distorted conclusions about the self that can continue through adolescence and into adulthood.

And finally, another contributing factor at play in this tendency to negatively color the meaning of interpersonal experiences is the slower development of the prefrontal cortex. Lacking the ability to properly regulate feelings and regain perspective in a momentary conflict, children learn and internalize their parents' perceptions of them as a factual reality. They don't possess yet the ability to differentiate between their subjectivity and that of a parent (see Richardson & Saxe, 2020a, 2020b). In a child's as yet immature brain, the meaning of an unpleasant interaction carries with it negative knowledge that teaches the child how to see himself.

Emotion and Memory

As we know from both personal experiences and research, memories of emotionally significant events have a vividness that stays with us. In particular, negatively charged events are better remembered. In addition, random events and other stimuli that were present in the environment during a negative event can also acquire negative meaning in one's memory (Admon et al., 2018; Phelps & Sharot, 2008). The proximity and the bidirectional links between the hippocampus and the amygdala underlie the strong connections between emotion and memories. The hippocampus, which mediates the creation of short- as well as long-term memories, is situated in the medial temporal lobe, near the amygdala. Patients with lesions of the hippocampus suffer from amnesia and have difficulties retrieving old memories or forming new ones (Dudai, 2011; Fernyhough, 2013).

The emotional signals from the amygdala reach the hippocampus and affect the emotional valence of newly formed memories. In turn, through other interconnected processes, such as with the prefrontal cortex, these memories become part of a wider network of memory traces, their contextual meanings, and their associations to other similar memories (Clewett et al., 2019). In this way, the amygdala is central to the processing of explicit and implicit emotional memories by way of its interactions with hippocampal memory formation and all other brain regions (Fernyhough, 2013; LeDoux, 2002).

Memory processing can be divided into three stages: (1) encoding, or the processing of information at the moment of perception; (2) consolidation, or the storage of information throughout the brain; and (3) retrieval, or the moment of remembering (Baddeley, 2012; Fernyhough, 2013). Each one of these phases can be influenced by emotions. Just as in the case of biased attention, the amygdala's sensitivity to threat promotes the encoding and retaining of negatively tinged memories. Events and interactions signifying threat to one's physical or psychological well-being, or memories encoded at a time of severe emotional upheaval (e.g., September 11, 2001 or the COVID-19 pandemic), are more often remembered and easily retrieved.

This is also the case for implicit memories encoded in the first few years of life; although most of these emotional memories, or more accurately memory traces, cannot be accessed by verbal expression, they are still favored to be encoded (Okon-Singer et al., 2015). As I have mentioned a few times, research often refers to memory traces because we now know that memories are not stable and accurate, like pictures snapped in the brain. Rather, we can see them as snippets that represent all aspects of an experience. Furthermore, not being stored in one place but distributed throughout the brain, the traces forming memories have a dynamic and changing quality.

The power of threats in determining the strength of encoded memories influences how we remember and how memories feel to us. As studies have noted, emotion colors the encoded nature of memories but also their retrieval into explicit memory. Emotion may also interfere with memories by emphasizing certain emotional qualities, thus distorting them (Kensinger & Ford, 2020). However, because of the acute vividness that emotional memories engender, they still tend to subjectively feel more real, and we may accept them as the only genuine and valid representation of what happened. This confidence in the realness and accuracy of negative memories at times defies the more objectively correct facts of what happened (Loftus, 1996). In effect, because we are not conscious of this tendency to focus on, remember, and retrieve negative memories in real time, especially during negative moods, we are not aware of these hidden machinations (Tarder-Stoll et al., 2020). We can literally rewrite our personal life narratives based on feelings and not the facts of what actually happened. This can cause us to exaggerate both positive and negative experiences, distorting our sense of self and influencing our relationships with others.

This sense of greater accuracy and trust in emotional memories, especially negative ones, corresponds to evolutionary forces ensuring that threats of all kinds were encoded and retained as part of our primitive human survival mechanisms (Fernyhough, 2013). When confronted with real danger, our ancestors had to rely on past memories, especially those that identified particular dangers and the behaviors that led to successful results.

Even if the automatically retrieved memories were not entirely accurate, they nonetheless provided invaluable information on how to navigate a dangerous world. In situations that required quick response to an immediate threat, any hesitation to use past learning and embedded memories could lead to injury or death. Unsurprisingly, this tendency was accompanied by increases in amygdala activation. This reminds us again of the assertion that throughout evolution we had to err on the side of seeing and imagining danger even if it wasn't there (Brosschot et al., 2016). This tendency, of course, explains how we so readily encode, maintain, and retrieve negative memories when a wounded, anxious, or vulnerable feeling state becomes activated.

Some researchers explored whether negative memories had more staying power among subjects tasked with remembering a range of stimuli. A series of findings suggests that the negative valence of negative memories causes them to tend to be remembered more often and more intensely. This particular enhancement, mediated by the extended amygdala, seems to occur in addition to the expected processes of encoding and retrieval. This process possibly contributes to the early consolidation and enhancement processes of negatively toned memories (Bowen et al., 2018). This also provides evidence that particular dedicated connections guided by the amygdala give rise to remembering more of the bad than the good (Kark & Kensinger, 2015, 2019a, 2019b).

This line of research raises critical questions and caution as we work with our own emotions and memories and those of our clients. What if this very innate tendency to encode and remember threats ends up convincing us that the negative is much greater than the positive in our history; that our parents were more malevolent than they actually were or meant to be; that our self-value deserves to be in doubt; and that the power of our agency was compromised? This is, in fact, often the experience when a negative self-state reaches consciousness and takes over; positive experiences, more reality-bound facts, and positive memories of strengths, love, goodness, and resilience recede and remain inaccessible. The potential prevalence of negative memories forms a critical aspect of the negative self-narratives we develop about ourselves, our families, and others, a process discussed in Chapter 11 (Ginot, 2012, 2015).

These complex neuropsychological processes almost guarantee that we all carry with us a host of implicit and explicit memories that highlight negativity. As we often see in psychotherapy, in the midst of a dysregulated state, memories of pain, insult, and anxiety dominate; they push aside other more positive memories, regardless of how frequently they occurred. At such times, we are more in touch with the unregulated negative story of our history and who we are.

Even the best of caregivers cannot eliminate all stressful situations and moments in a child's life, especially outside the home. Nor can a child always modulate their own inner fluctuations of stressful feelings generated by an anxious temperament. Similarly, a parent's ability to shield a child from the consequences of a hostile marriage or a challenging peer group may be limited. In other words, as our brain/minds acquire unique rules of engagement with the exterior world, we are vulnerable to inevitable fearful, painful, or shameful memories that underlie our anxious and vulnerable selves. As these processes often result in a web of negative narratives about one's parents and their intention to injure the child, these beliefs should be explored in psychotherapy. Obviously, as I frequently reiterate, I am not talking about cases of outright abuse. And as we see in Chapter 7, the definitions of trauma are not entirely clear-cut. Clinically, however, there is a great deal of benefit in helping a patient develop a diverse, mixed, and balanced picture of their childhood. Achieving this will reinforce in clients a deep understanding and acceptance of human frailty and inevitable human imperfections. In addition, this new perspective will also help clients reconnect with their more positive and resilient narratives—narratives that can reflect the more positive aspects of their internal and interpersonal existence.

REGULATION AND SELF-REFERENTIAL RUMINATIONS

The relationship of the amygdala to the prefrontal cortex (PFC) is especially important. We saw the evolutionary benefit of recruiting cognitive functions such as memory, learning, and fast memory retrieval with respect to confronting danger. The PFC, the seat of our executive functioning, is evolutionarily, ontologically, and individually the most recent brain region to develop. It is largely responsible, among many other functions, for conscious learning, planning, reasoning, and regulating emotions. Its connections with the amygdala have long been thought to mitigate the effects of an overreactive amygdala, thereby reducing the harmful effects inherent in the amygdala.

The medial PFC is part of the default mode network (DMN), which focuses on interior or internal processes. These areas are involved in self-referential cognitive processes that are carried out in a state of rest (i.e., when we are not actively engaged with tasks in the external world). While away from busy activities, we enter a state of rumination or an internal dialogue; this includes, for example, things like mulling over past experiences, envisioning the future, shaping opinions about oneself and others, and forming autobiographical memories. These complex processes also occur when children construct their nascent sense of self and form their understanding or interpretations of past memories.

Because of the amygdala's connections with the DMN, the amygdala has the ability to influence many of these processes with dark, hurtful, or threatening affect. The result is a growing neural map of negative self-referential feelings, thoughts, fantasies, and relational patterns. For example, in fMRI studies, patients who abused drugs or reported severe negative ideas about themselves were shown to have strong connections between the amygdala and the DMN (Ramirez-Barrantes et al., 2019). This finding suggests that patients with clinical anxiety maintain a strong communication between the amygdala and the BNST with circuits involved in attention, self-referential thinking, and visual-spatial processing (Torrisi et al., 2019). A strong association between the central amygdala and the medial prefrontal cortex correlates with more severe social anxiety symptoms. This may reflect the greater reactivity of this pathway in people prone to anxiety. This pathway may support the maintenance of the active and automatic negative responses to emotional events and also color one's interpersonal and social difficulties (Torrisi et al., 2019).

With an overreactive amygdala, we experience fear more frequently, thus becoming more vulnerable to the influence of the amygdala on our own internal monologues. With the development of language and many more nuanced behaviors, the conceptual meanings gleaned by toddlers and children about their experiences carry even greater opportunities for them to develop a deeply vulnerable sense of self, a self that is organized around multiple distorted and negative interpretations about who we are (Ginot, 2012, 2015; Ramirez-Barrantes et al., 2019).

AN EPILOGUE TO INFLUENCE

As this chapter shows, the fear system's effects on a range of brain/mind functions and eventually on our personality traits is one of the hallmarks of its outsized influence. But as we also see in other chapters in this book, despite such neuropsychological and evolutionary odds that favor the presence of anxiety-driven feelings, thoughts, and behaviors, most of us still develop self-states organized around resilience, positive feelings, optimism, and security. Furthermore, the chapter on therapeutic approaches (Chapter 15), as well as the discussed cases, clearly demonstrate that we can attend to and change the impact of negative or destructive patterns. To do so, however, we need to acknowledge the far-reaching influences of the fear system; recognizing and accepting its inevitable presence and at the same time striving to soften its more harmful effects.

DANA'S CASE: THE BRAIN-WIDE INFLUENCE OF THE FEAR SYSTEM

Dana was one of the more anxious and insecure young women I have encountered. When she started therapy, at the age of 27, Dana was taking antianxiety medication that significantly reduced the number and intensity of her panic attacks and what she described as "constant agitation; everything makes me jump in fear." She started taking medication three years previously after a particularly intolerable anxiety attack that "came out of nowhere but paralyzed me for days." She was afraid to leave her apartment, took leave from work, and became even more dependent on her boyfriend with whom she was living at the time.

Dana finished a 2-year college program and specialized in fashion design. She loved the job she had when we met, although it paid very little and had few benefits. Dana described a mixed work history. Before her anxiety became more manageable with medication, she had too many absences to hold a job. Each time she had to leave a position, she was devastated, convinced that her ability to function would never improve. Now she still felt anxious about her performance and dreaded any evaluation or criticism of her work, but at the same time felt great relief at being able to get up every morning and function well. She was very thankful to her physician for recommending that she take medication, "something that totally changed my life."

Dana's stated reason to start therapy again was a tumultuous relationship she struggled to leave but couldn't. Dana cried when she described the many ups and downs of a difficult relationship that had changed over the years and became increasingly painful and unsettling. She hinted at some serious problems that she could not raise in the first few sessions.

Dana, a very good-looking woman, met Judd when she was 23 and immediately fell in love with him. He was 34 at the time. She loved the attention he showered on her and the exciting lifestyle and parties he introduced her to. She especially enjoyed their sexual relationship and frequently thought she could never be with anybody else. She felt, she said, loved and supported. Judd encouraged her to be more ambitious, to try to get better jobs and ask for higher pay. He knew all about her "crazy anxiety" but totally accepted it. "He really calmed me down," she said. In effect, Judd was the only one who could do it. As they moved in together, she became dependent on him to feel "anchored and even normal." She said that Judd seemed to like her emotional dependency on him and could spend hours listening to her problems and offering advice.

Judd, however, had a cocaine habit that got more serious over the years. Only few of his friends knew about it and, as he kept saying, it didn't harm his work performance. At the beginning Dana did not consider Judd's addiction "a big deal." She was just happy to be with someone who was so kind and understanding. With time, however, Judd's behavior became more erratic and unpredictable. He would come back to the apartment very late or not at all, without contacting her. She would lie awake imagining the worst, praying that he would be okay. In those years she was still utterly convinced she could not live without him, that she would be lost and so vulnerable that she would "fall apart and literally disintegrate."

Dana did not like the latest version of Judd. During the previous year, the frequency of their lovemaking had dropped precipitously. She suspected that Judd was having sex with other women and indeed found evidence for it when she surreptitiously looked at his phone. When she confronted him, Judd admitted to having hookups with other women. But he loved her, he insisted, and wanted them to be together forever. What he needed in order to feel more alive and fulfilled, he said, were varied sexual experiences. He craved these adventures before settling down and having a family. Sheepishly, he asked her if she was open to an open relationship, to experience her sexuality with others.

Dana's reactions surprised and frightened her. Her initial anger, hurt, and intense feelings of rejection were mixed with what seemed to her like "a sick curiosity." She had heard about such relationships and even knew a couple who were engaged in polyamory and seemed happy. After some more cajoling on Judd's part, she agreed to go along with his suggestions. Judd promised her that he would not push her to be with someone else as long as he had his freedom. He also suggested they go to special parties where people could freely flirt and hook up with each other with the full understanding that it was all just about sexual encounters. The most Dana could manage at one of those parties was to "lightly flirt with some guy." She realized that she could not tolerate seeing Judd flirting with other women and stopped going out with him.

Dana became increasingly unhappy and distraught, reexperiencing panic attacks and increased general anxiety with the same old intensity. Her close friends begged her to leave Judd. And although rationally she knew that she needed to do so, her entire being resisted the idea. She still could not envision living without Judd, flawed as he was. Despite the changes in his behavior and his increased use of drugs during the previous year, she trusted his love and saw him as her only savior, a caring person who also happened to have different sexual needs. This was the time when she decided to try therapy. During the first sessions, she repeated to me what she repeatedly said to her friends, that she did not see his behavior as "cheating or unfaithful" because there were no emotions attached to any of these short adventures. She even said she could live with such an arrangement for a while because she was confident that once they had children, he would change and revert to the old Judd she loved.

But as we both witnessed, Dana's desperate determination to play along became harder and more heart wrenching with time. Feelings of jealousy tormented her, and she increasingly became insecure about Judd's feelings for her. Whereas once the certainty that he loved her anchored and gave her the comfort she craved, this new situation became emotionally unbearable. The more she tried to convince Judd that his ideas and behaviors were ruining their bond, the more he reiterated that this was "a contemporary way of life and many people live with such choices." Dana oscillated between desperately wanting to believe him and a growing agitation. But even when she realized that this forced arrangement was destructive and unnerving, she still could not leave.

As we started therapy, her feelings of anxiety, grief, and loss intensified. She repeatedly said, while crying, that those feelings were not new, that they reminded her of something deep within her, something that was even deeper than her anxiety. She felt that if she let these indescribable emotions surface, they would take over everything, and both of us would drown in sadness. I remarked that it sounded like she didn't trust me to contain such strong feelings, to help her deal with them. She agreed and, thinking a bit, said, "Nobody." After a prolonged hesitation she very quietly added, "except for Judd."

Dana was born to very young parents, neither of whom was ready to take care of an infant. They both had insecure, part-time jobs that generated very little income and stability. When she was 6 months old, it was decided that Dana's paternal grandmother would take care of her for the first couple of years, until her parents achieved stability. Her grandmother, although a well-intentioned woman, believed in a rigid set of rules that did not consider the possibility that children can be vulnerable to outside pressures or disappointments. She did not think that infants and toddlers have subjective and unique needs and preferences. Feeding and sleeping schedules were strictly enforced, and Dana was left to cry things out for long periods of time. While Dana's grandmother was very efficient in providing for all of Dana's physical needs, she was not an affectionate woman and minimized the time she held Dana in her arms for fears of overindulging her. Later, Dana found out from her parents that when they visited, she told them that she was very careful not to spoil Dana. It was important to toughen her up, she told them, and prepare her for dealing with life's difficulties.

From what she gleaned from her parents, Dana cried a lot as a child and was difficult to console. Her grandmother, however, did not see anything unusual about the crying. When she was asked about it by Dana's parents, she said that "children are supposed to cry but they always grow out of it." The most important thing, she kept saying, was not to "fuss over them too much." As Dana became a toddler and increasingly displayed fearful and avoidant behaviors, her grandmother's rigid rules did not change. As a matter of fact, with a growing number of challenging anxiety-induced situations, she became even more harsh and impatient, trying to control Dana's behaviors. There was little empathy for Dana's distress and anxiety.

At the age of 4, Dana finally went to live with her parents, who by then had a stable income. She was initially confused about the move. She also missed her grandmother and the friends she made at day care. Her crying and agitated states were again inconsolable. Her parents later told her that she had sounded bereft and very sad. With time, however, as Dana's parents consistently showed attuned caring, she cried less and became less agitated. From then on, Dana characterized her childhood as a happy one. She liked school and made friends. All along, however, Dana felt that something was always bothering her, something that could erupt and shatter her. She didn't know how to describe it even to herself.

When she was 14, however, Dana's anxiety grew and, not feeling like she could burden her parents who struggled with two younger siblings, tried to cope with her fears on her own. She tried to maintain her grades, but there were quite a few days she stayed home, not feeling well enough to go to school. She couldn't explain it. All she knew was that during those days she had to stay home within her safe environment. After finishing high school, to her surprise, better than she had anticipated, she went on to the local community college. Her love for fashion and for creating things made her time at college easy and fun. Upon graduating, she worked for a couple of years while still living at home but then decided to leave her state and move to New York in order to pursue her career. At the beginning Dana was miserable. Despite sharing an apartment with roommates, she felt lonely and invisible. During that time her panic attacks intensified, seriously interfering with her work life. It was also during that time that she met Judd.

Dana's therapy has lasted a few years. At the heart of it is Dana's intense vulnerability; her deep-seated anxiety about "falling apart" and disintegrating without the comfort of an attuned other. She realized that in Judd she had found the caring she always yearned for, the other person who truly saw her as she was and accepted her, including her fears. This acceptance became so essential to her continued psychological functioning that for a long time she was convinced that she could not give it up.

We explored how it was that her own parents, who were mostly understanding and caring, did not make up for those first three and a half years with her grandmother. Dana could articulate that somehow their love was not enough to heal the "dark hole at the bottom of her soul," as she came to call the early wounds. It was all there, their support, encouragement, and frequently expressed guilt over abandoning her, and yet it was not enough to fully heal her. As the exploration of her childhood continued and acquired increased specificity and texture, new disappointments surfaced as well. As loving as her father was, for example, he occasionally reminded her of her strict and unaffectionate grandmother. When under stress or in a bad mood, Dana said, "he would withdraw from the family and behaved as if they all were an imposition on him." He would then become irritated, impatient, and distant. Dana described being fearful that he would never revert to being the father she loved and needed.

On the other hand, her mother frequently expressed her guilt and shame at not being able to care for Dana herself during those early years. Dana was very ambivalent about her mother's feelings: on one hand she felt sympathy for her, but on the other she could not tolerate the intense vulnerability and pain that these conversations induced in her. In addition, she also felt that she had to comfort her mother, relieve her of her guilt and make her feel less remorseful. Eventually, she felt suffocated by these conversations and asked her mother not to talk about that painful past.

It seemed that Dana's first years without an attuned caregiver initiated and sustained an ongoing trauma that shaped many of her other
feelings and behaviors. The deprivation and emotional neglect of these
first years activated a predisposition for anxiety she inherited from her
mother's side of the family. But regardless of this inevitable interaction,
Dana's anxiety clearly worsened as a result of severe lack of an attuned
early attachment. When Judd came along and swept her off her feet, his
very presence consciously and unconsciously promised to provide the
deep attunement she craved.

Even after he withdrew from her and abandoned her for other "insig-
nificant" affairs, she could not give up on the idealized fantasy she developed about him. By staying with him, she simultaneously reenacted her
yearning for an idealized love, but at the same time also the deprivation
and heartbreak that came from being abandoned and frequently hurt. The
more Dana understood the underlying dynamics of her anxious clinginess
to Judd, the easier it became to imagine leaving him.

In addition, our therapeutic relationship provided Dana with some emotional resonance and the sense of visibility and importance. We spent a
great deal of time focusing on her intensely felt sense of loss, and that
empty, dark hole she felt but could not clearly articulate. The more she
allowed herself to feel these states with me, the greater her personal
strength became. After about a year and a half in therapy, she left the
apartment she shared with Judd. The separation was not easy. She still met
with Judd, and each time some of the old feelings came back. With time,
however, as the frequency and intensity of their dates decreased, Dana's
need for Judd's attention decreased as well. In hindsight she realized that
as long as she was unconscious about her motivation to cling to Judd, she
"would have done anything to keep him happy and make sure he stayed"
with her.

These days, as Dana mulls over the years she spent with Judd, she still
can't fully grasp what she "was doing with a cocaine and sex addict who
was out of control." But of course, what drew her to him were not conscious
and thoughtful processes. Rather, as is so often the case, she was guided
by unconscious emotional patterns that were organized around and continued to express painful and cumulative childhood traumas. Her grandmother's emotional limitations and her inability to provide the infant and

then the toddler with the empathy and understanding she needed to emotionally thrive left Dana in a state of constant hyperarousal. She became exquisitely attuned to anxiety-inducing situations, especially those that reminded her that she was all alone and without others' caring attention.

Being alone became intolerable, entwined with thoughts and ruminations about a certainty that without somebody there to pay attention, she would crumble and disintegrate. This was the sense of falling apart, in essence a state of utter dysregulation, that she experienced more than once in her frequent crying and agitation episodes when she was an infant and toddler (Winnicott, 1969). Indeed, repeated experiences of emotional disintegration, of intense panic, grief, and loss became the cornerstones of an unconscious state that, outside her awareness, sought both the remedy and the repetition. Early anxieties informed her attachment needs, while unconscious expectations of abandonment made it almost impossible to leave Judd.

Like many of us, whether in therapy or not, Dana eventually found the courage to confront the most painful and anxious parts of herself, learn from them and grow. She knows she cannot undo those painful and difficult first years. But she is also fully confident that the more she experiences, understands, and accepts her past and how it has informed her feelings and behaviors, the more it can become an integral, life-affirming part of who she is becoming.

CHAPTER FIVE

Other Emotions and the Fear System

··

So far, we have focused primarily on the emotions of fear and anxiety, and their wide-ranging effects. But, of course, our inner world includes many forms and nuances of other feelings. As most of us can attest, the subjective, conscious experience of feeling reflects the inextricable mix of visceral sensations, thoughts, beliefs, memories, and expectations, to name a few experiences. As a result, feelings can be complex, especially when they contain a mix of good and bad sensations and thoughts. Remembering the brain-wide interconnected neural circuits, we can easily understand how the input from different neural networks accounts for the complexity of our feelings.

By now we have seen how interconnected the extended amygdala is with most other brain/mind functions. As a result, the fear system very often influences other feelings and emotional patterns. For example, a sense of nervousness, doubts about the authenticity of good feelings, and false beliefs that something bad will happen are common when we allow ourselves to feel pride in our accomplishments. In this way, old ideas about what it means to feel good can dampen the intensity of positive feelings. In effect, the presence of nagging anxiety, even in the midst of feeling good or happy, is quite common among many of us, especially when we don't quite believe in the durability of a good state. Recalling the outsized effects that the fear system has on our thinking, it is not surprising that anxious mindsets developed during childhood find their way into positive states as well. This was the case with Mimi.

MIMI'S CASE: A PERFECT STORM OF ADVERSE CIRCUMSTANCES

Mimi, a grade-school teacher, sought therapy in her early 40s when her marriage to her wife Beth was on the brink of a painful breakup. In our first session, she appeared to be timid and unsure of herself, often asking me if I understood what she was saying and what she meant. Mimi had been in what she described as a committed relationship for five years in her 20s; she was extremely disappointed when the relationship ended and did not understand why it had.

Mimi's second relationship started with "great romantic promise." Two years into the relationship, Mimi expressed her desire to have and raise a child. Reluctant at first, her wife, Beth, believed a child would disrupt their carefree life and put a great deal of pressure on them both. Mimi agreed, but her yearning for a baby did not lessen and eventually Beth agreed to have a child. They both agreed that Mimi would become pregnant through an anonymous sperm donner, and when she was 5 months pregnant, the two got married.

Mimi started therapy when their son, Noah, was about 7 years old. Mimi initially had trouble describing what was bothering her about Beth and their marriage. She reported that they were having too many conflicts, many of which focused on the daily decisions that needed to be made in the course of balancing home, raising Noah, and work. Mimi felt that Beth was impatient with her, especially when Mimi found it hard to make a quick decision or second-guessed herself. Mimi shared that Beth also accused her of being too anxious and afraid of making mistakes. Beth believed these behaviors were not good for Mimi or their son, whom Beth feared "would grow up to be like" Mimi. Mimi desperately wanted to be a good mother and a good wife; however, she felt that the harder she tried, the more upset Beth got with her.

Although Beth encouraged Mimi to start therapy to tackle her anxiety, Mimi did not focus on her anxiety and self-doubts; rather, she described her difficulties in her relationship with Beth and, to a lesser extent, with Noah. Mimi did not think her anxiety was "such a big deal as Beth makes it to be." She admitted, however, that throughout her life, she had been aware of what sounded like chronic anxiety.

Mimi's anxiety seemed to be exacerbated by and more debilitating when she was under stress; this caused her to be more hesitant in making decisions and to feel more vulnerable and insecure. She was often terrified of making mistakes, and she tended to second-guess herself even about inconsequential issues. This was especially true in regard to Noah's upbringing and well-being. According to Mimi, because of her cautious deliberation, "Beth lost her empathy for my struggles." After a few weeks Mimi slowly began to examine her lifelong anxiety-induced behaviors, unpleasant feelings, worries about what could go wrong, ruminations about her perceived flaws, and persistent doubts.

Mimi's childhood provided clues to her anxiety. Mimi grew up with parents who moved frequently from state to state as her father, an engineer, sought better positions. The frequent moves forced her mother, also a teacher, to forgo a full-time, stable position. As a result, she became a substitute teacher who was often out of the classroom. Mimi, the second of three children, described her parents as "totally normal and predictable." She had a close relationship with her younger sister but did not speak to her brother, who was two years older.

As therapy continued, Mimi's slowly opened up to reveal a childhood "where everything was not what it seemed to be." Mimi's relationship with her brother was particularly destructive and abusive. Even as a young child, she remembered frequently being bullied by him verbally and physically. As they reached elementary school, he would often laugh at her, making fun of her intelligence, her looks, and her difficulty making new friends each time they moved. He took any opportunity to boast about his achievements and his friends and compare them to Mimi's. The older they grew, the more cruel his teasing and physical harassment became.

Each time the family moved, on average every three years, Mimi suffered. With each move, her ability to adjust diminished and she made fewer and fewer new friends. The frequent moves to different schools diminished Mimi's ability to excel in her studies, and she constantly felt like she was behind. Each time she was closing the gap and starting to do better in school, the family moved again. Mimi could not wait to leave home and become independent. She couldn't wait to come out as gay in college, something she was reluctant do while at home. She was particularly worried about mocking reactions from her father and brother.

"So much was going on that shouldn't have," Mimi said at the start of a session one day. This was a breakthrough and a gateway for Mimi to understand her anxiety. Although not outwardly abusive, Mimi's quiet and well-mannered father was often directly and indirectly dismissive and belittling toward her mother. He also requested her full-time attention and "needed to be coddled like a baby." He often and only half-jokingly reminded her mother that he was the "breadwinner." In addition to her occasional school jobs, Mimi's mother did all the shopping, cooking, and the cleaning; she often complained about being exhausted, with no energy left for anything fun.

Since childhood Mimi realized that her mother tried hard to avoid confrontation with her husband and keep the peace. But as we continued to explore her childhood, Mimi also understood that the older she got, the more defeated her mother felt. Outwardly, she seemed to cope with her husband's belittling, disrespectful, and verbally demanding behaviors. But Mimi knew her mother was in pain. Wishing not to add to her worries, Mimi did not complain to her about her brother's abusive behaviors. She often hoped that these behaviors would be noticed, but both her parents saw them as natural sibling rivalry. Mimi now realizes that even when her mother noticed her son's aggressive behavior, she still saw it as expected and quite normal. There were frequent attempts to restore peace, but the extent of her brother's bullying was well hidden by him. She could only complain to her younger sister, who was helpless and struggled herself.

The more she talked about her past, the more Mimi focused on her mother's state of mind. She remembered her mother becoming increasingly quiet and apologetic, negating her own thoughts and feelings. Aside from the household chores, she did not participate in or influence the bigger decisions that made a significant difference in the family's life, like moving. When Mimi's mother tried to verbalize her opinions, Mimi's father dismissed them outright, emphasizing that as the main earner only he had the responsibility to make all such decisions. Mimi also remembered her father's insistence that her mother was not smart enough, competent enough, or worthy enough. At those moments, Mimi felt rage at her father, "wishing he would disappear" and felt deeply sad and sorry for her mother.

With time, more memories surfaced about her mother's timidity and acquiescence in front of her father. On the other hand, to her surprise, Mimi also got in touch with a pervasive discomfort at home, anxious feelings unrelated to their frequent moves. Her father's dismissive and insulting control of his family, her mother's defeated behaviors and her abusive brother all contributed to a constant anxious state of brain/mind/body. She also realized that at times, her mother as well "lost it with the kids," and as Mimi sees it now, took out her frustrations about her husband and ruined career by yelling at them. Mimi is convinced that her mother "was totally unaware of her short-tempered behaviors or she wouldn't have yelled." These conversations induced severe anxiety states during the sessions, emotions that she took home with her. For a while, her anxious self-doubts, insecurity, and long internal debate increased, testing Beth's patience even more. Old feelings of sadness for her mother along with great personal distress also came rushing back. Mimi's anxiety and how it influenced her thoughts and behaviors took center stage in her therapy.

Mimi's anxious insecurity seems to have developed and maintained as a result of a perfect storm, as we came to call it. The inevitable dysregulation caused by each move and the need to adapt to entirely new interpersonal situations made her anxious and insecure; in her words, she "freaked out" each time she had to leave old friends and make new ones. Colored by constant anxiety, her belief in her ability to catch up all but disappeared. Upset and crying during many sessions, Mimi relived that anxious state and the self-doubting feelings, thoughts, and behaviors that were formed as a result. She was never free of anxiety, she said, always being in between a painful separation from the old school and friends and having to anxiously adjust to the new. The anxious, emotionally-loaded atmosphere at home did further damage. By the time she reached high school, Mimi described herself as "an anxious wreck."

Mimi's sense of being a secure, confident young girl was seriously undermined by her brother's abusive bullying. Although she tried to internally negate the effect of his words and behaviors, part of her still believed her older, "way more outwardly successful, cool brother." Inevitably believing her brother and interpreting his behaviors as a true statement and evaluation of who she was affected her feelings and thoughts about herself. In addition, unconsciously and unavoidably, Mimi's identification with her mother's anxiety and pain added to her already anxious and frequently destabilized sense of self. Like all children, she unconsciously learned and internalized her mother's hesitant sense of self. Questioning why she has not learned more from her father's controlling behaviors, she now thinks that her emotional alliance was completely with her mother, while at the same time recoiling from the pain he inflicted on them all. Only recently did Mimi's anger at her father for his "selfish and totally inconsiderate decisions and behaviors" surface. Jokingly she says that she doesn't "want to be like her meek mother anymore, but much, much less to resemble her father or brother in any way."

And finally, but importantly, adolescence proved particularly hazardous and even dangerous to Mimi. Her fears and anxiety about coming out as a young gay woman consumed her waking hours and her dreams at night. She was particularly mortified when imagining her father's and brother's reaction, their critical, mocking, and teasing attitudes. She knew she had her mother's support but still delayed coming out until she left for college. Only there did she finally get her yearned-for support of a stable community of friends.

Although she still worries about the anxiety she might have transmitted to Noah, she has begun to understand that becoming mindful about her feelings and behaviors would curtail this unconscious generational transmission of anxiety-suffused mental, emotional, and behavioral patterns. Mimi also came to understand the dynamics of other important relationships. Understanding that her first girlfriend "totally became fed up with [her] hesitating and self-effacing behaviors," Mimi was able to forgive her. She became more committed to saving her current marriage to Beth. She hoped that their love and respect for each other would survive their interpersonal difficulties. As Mimi increasingly became engrossed with her internal world, increasingly understanding her childhood and its effects on her, she also expressed a wish for more active tools to tackle her anxiety in real time.

As Mimi's ability to regulate her emotions and behaviors has grown, her inner experiences became less haunted by old anxieties and self-doubts.

She became more secure in her opinions and decisions; and relied much less on old, distorted emotional/cognitive patterns. Mimi's increasing capacity to stay calm in the face of routine pressures surprised her; she had been unable to imagine she could become a calmer and more self-confident woman. This has been especially important and helpful during the COVID-19 pandemic, as Mimi, Noah, and her wife were quarantined together, got along well, and even managed to enjoy themselves.

SHAME: THE FRAGILITY OF OUR SENSE OF SELF

Not surprisingly, often our most uncomfortable and painful feelings are experienced within interactions with others. Indeed, the intersubjective realm seems to be the most significant space for feelings of shame, insecurity, anger, and envy. For example, at its core, shame expresses our most intense worries about how others judge us. Real or perceived negative opinions can seriously rattle our own sense of self and reaffirm the worst opinions that we already carry about ourselves. Feelings of shame can be triggered just by thinking about real or imagined negative judgments. Such disturbing thoughts about disapproval from others are inevitably intertwined with anxious ruminations about the very personal meaning that negative evaluations have for us and our sense of self. Others' negative reactions to our performance, behaviors, characteristics, and traits can be devastating in the moment. And, as we saw with Mimi, these devastating experiences can impact us for years. Mimi's suffering at the hands of her brother caused her to doubt herself in both of her marriages and as a mother to Noah.

What is so difficult to tolerate when feeling shame is the injury to our conscious sense of who we are and how we want others to see us. In extreme cases, the disapproval of others, real or imagined, can lead to intense anxieties about the intactness of our sense of self. As part of negative ruminations about our value, we may incessantly compare ourselves to others; this process often also highlights our perceived flaws, aggravating feelings of shame in a vicious cycle. Anxious thoughts of being inferior and ongoing, irrational fears of being found out are a common aspect of the cycles of shame. Mimi's constant anxiety and fretting had its roots in her brother's constant comparison of their abilities.

Shame is not learned but innate (Muris et al., 2018). Accordingly, it can be considered part of the alerting system, warning us that something negative and upsetting has happened or is about to happen. One wonders whether the evolutionary function of shame is that it motivates humans to fit in, to adhere to expected rules, and to feel as competent and successful as others in the group. Indeed, in early human history, the survival of an individual was entirely dependent on membership in and protection by the group; shame ensured survival. In any case, shame is a response pattern that is rooted in a set of complex narratives and beliefs about the self. Like other feeling states, shame primarily occurs in an interpersonal context, often when we react to others' perceptions and opinions of us. For Mimi, these patterns were established as a result of her primary interactions with her brother and her second-hand empathic encoding of negative messages inflicted on her mother, with whom she closely identified.

In particular, our awareness of disappointing others or being judged by them and found to be flawed leads to acute dysregulated feelings. When experiencing shame, we may wish to die, hide, or disappear. At times, acute feelings of shame result in confusion, an inability to speak, or a sense of a true catastrophe where the body shrinks away in self-disgust with little hope for redemption (Lewis, 2019). Shame can be experienced internally or in the presence of others, whereas embarrassment is usually felt in the presence of others. Shame is often felt as we step away from the perceived exposure of our mistake or flaw. Similar to the feelings of anxiety, and no doubt as a result of the strong interaction between these two states, feelings of shame cause many of us to avoid situations that may trigger shame (Cibich et al., 2016). Often, we shy away from taking risks and from fully using our talents. For Mimi, this manifested in a reluctance to make decisions and a pattern of second-guessing the decisions she did make.

THE DEVELOPMENTAL PROCESSES OF SELF-CONSCIOUS FEELINGS

Self-conscious feelings, especially the emerging consciousness of shame, begin between 18 and 24 months of age. Mimi reported her earliest memories of shame and incompetence as beginning in toddlerhood. These feelings are linked to a toddler's nascent sense of competence and the demands from attachment figures (Lewis, 2019; Schore, 2012). Feelings of shame and embarrassment require a more sophisticated set of cognitive abilities, especially the ability to evaluate oneself in relation to others. Additionally, self-evaluative processes depend on an internalized sense of right and wrong as well as a basic understanding of what *good* and *bad* mean to those caring for the young child (Lewis, 2019). Similarly, an internalized understanding of adults' expectations, and the spoken and unspoken rules that determine good behavior and acceptance by others, are part of this growing process of self-evaluation. The self-conscious awareness of disappointing others begins to arouse fears about losing a caregiver's love, support, and validation (Muris et al., 2018).

Immediately, we can see how anxiety about how we compare to others is an inextricable part of feelings of shame. Indeed, as adolescents and adults, one of the significant features that accompanies shame is our internal comparisons with others as we gauge our looks, social standing and prestige, level of recognition by others, competence, success, and much more. In addition, fears of shaming oneself through words or deeds in the future, and thus losing respect and acceptance, are part of this state of rumination as well. The results of these comparisons are usually informed by our entrenched denigrating self-narratives, adding a sense of inevitability to feelings of inferiority, shame, and increasing anxiety.

Most of all, I think, we dread the actual feeling state of being shamed and the physical, extremely unpleasant and painful sensations that are part of it. The thoughts that make up this state are just as unpleasant; once again, in our fertile imagination, failures or awkward interactions with others provide further proof that, indeed, we are fundamentally flawed. The ongoing anxiety of making mistakes and exposing those parts of ourselves we perceive as flawed in front of others haunts us. This anxiety and painful feelings of shame are often enacted in private, away from others. We may mull over how we presented ourselves to others, things we said, actions we took, and repeatedly beat ourselves up for being inadequate. Although such emotion states are often intense only temporarily, they still exact their toll in heightened negative feelings that make us feel hopeless about ourselves.

It is not surprising, then, that several studies found connections between the feelings of shame and symptoms of social anxiety. This association was found among patients diagnosed as suffering from social anxiety as well as among adolescents who were not formally diagnosed with this form of anxiety (Muris et al., 2018). Shame was also present among adults who were diagnosed with generalized anxiety disorder, excess worry, and rumination (Fergus et al., 2010;

Levinson et al., 2016). Similarly, shame was associated with the sense of inadequacy, excess vulnerability, and avoiding participation in the world (Cibich et al., 2016; Gouva et al., 2015; Rüsch et al., 2007). In a sense, Mimi's inability to make decisions was a way of shielding herself from feeling vulnerable and participating in the world. But it set up a vicious cycle; the more she avoided making decisions, the more Beth felt frustrated with her, heightening Mimi's sense of inadequacy.

An important aspect that these studies highlight is the fact that, like all other feelings and traits, shame is strongly influenced by temperamental factors. Young adults with a predisposition for anxiety and shyness experience shame more intensely and in more areas of their lives (Levinson et al., 2016). This may explain why Mimi suffered so intensely, while other children who are raised in dysregulated homes or who move frequently do not grow into anxious, fearful adults. It may help us to understand why, even after leaving home with all its dysfunctions (i.e., entering a new environment), Mimi still struggled with shame and anxiety.

At the same time, shame seems to be present among individuals without a formal diagnosis of anxiety. These individuals show clear patterns of interpersonal anxiety: vulnerability, a sense of inadequacy, and fear of fully participating in the world. Even without formally suffering from an anxiety disorder, children, adolescents, and adults may experience shame and other self-referential feelings (Oexle et al., 2017).

The question that arises from such findings is a proverbial chicken-and-egg question. Does anxiety heighten shame, or does shame increase anxiety? Again, considering how interconnected our brain circuits are, the answer is most likely found in the interaction between fear and anxiety with other feelings. Feelings of shame, like other feeling states, are complex and often run deep. They do not just reflect a legitimate, reality-bound reaction to injurious external events that cause us to adaptively rethink our mistake. Most often, a feeling state of shame integrating visceral sensations, emotions, thoughts, and behaviors resides within us in a self-perpetuating way. Furthermore, such a state leads to distorted perceptions of ourselves and greatly exaggerate the significance of others' opinions as the arbiters of who we are. In effect, our innate state of shame can be seen as a default mode of seeing ourselves, a part of ourselves that, through predisposition and early learning, can convince us that without the validation of others we cannot trust our own value.

OTHER VULNERABLE FEELINGS:
MORE ALIKE THAN DISSIMILAR

There are many other emotions that leave us feeling vulnerable and self-conscious; they act in ways similar to shame. For example, a strong sense of guilt involves attributing to ourselves the source of failure and the act of disappointing others (Lewis, 2019). At times, feelings of regret and remorse are also present. Often, however, these feelings of self-blame are based on an imagined failure, a perceived act of opposition, or a projection of the injured party's hurt. This is particularly acute when it comes to our families.

In some cases, a young adult's feelings are intense enough to prevent them from fully claiming their independence. Doing so means disappointing a parent who is perceived as needing the growing child to remain within the parental orbit. In some cases, the parent encourages the child's dependency; in others, the child's own guilt and ambivalence prevents full separation. Underlying this complex process is the anxiety of losing a parent's love and approval, but also the enormous fear of hurting them. Frequently, adults and young adults seek psychotherapy because they feel that their life is stuck; they are unable to move forward with their stated goals in their career or love life. Upon untangling these complicated ties, both adaptive and maladaptive, with their parents, they internally free themselves to claim their own identity and pursue their own desires.

Another example of self-conscious, vulnerable feelings is anger. Anger is closely connected to states of heightened distress, frustration, or is a reaction to blocked goals and desires. Anger is experienced when individuals feel disappointed that expectations have not been fulfilled (Dollar & Calkins, 2019). The functional aspect of anger is to overcome these blocking elements. In cases of extreme anger or rage, especially when these feelings are enacted and directed toward others, there is also the failure of adaptive emotional regulation (Kiel & Kalomiris, 2019).

Similar to shame, fear and anxiety play a role. For example, a child's emotional and behavioral reactivity may be a response to excessive limitations, or direct or subtle messages undermining the child's self-confidence or individual identity. The child's developing patterns of dealing with states of frustration can persist into adulthood. A reactive pattern that lacks emotion regulation is physiologically linked to the role of the parasympathetic system in regulating emotions, attention, and cognition. The vagus nerve provides input to the heart, affecting cardiac activity that guides the body's responses to the environment (Porges, 2007). Vagal regulation to the heart in the midst of emotional upheaval has been studied as a visceral activity that promotes emotional regulation.

Outbursts of unregulated anger, on the other hand, are the result of compromised emotional regulation resulting from a skewed balance between regulating and dysregulating systems. Angry or rageful responses may be adaptive in the short run, when we are faced with interpersonal pressures or control, a potential fear of the loss of autonomy and independence, or severe injury to our sense of self. But as unconscious fears of authority persist and become generalized, reactive rage and anger become increasingly maladaptive.

Temperamental tendencies interact with the child's family life and shape the developmental trajectory of anger (Calkins, 2011; Dollar & Calkins, 2019). Numerous studies have found that anxiety disorders in children are typically characterized by heightened emotional reactivity (Kiel & Kalomiris, 2019). Easily hyperaroused children often experience a range of negative feelings more frequently and intensely; additionally, their level of subjective distress tends to be greater. Among these children, the ability to regulate emotions automatically and efficiently is compromised. As we learned in previous chapters, many studies have found that the amygdala lies at the root of an overreactive and fearful temperament. Again, it is important to remember that this interaction between temperament and environment determines oversensitive or overreactive personalities in both children and adults.

One of the interesting points that can be raised as we try to understand the role of the fear system in other feelings is the common thread among all distressing and negative feelings we have mentioned. Reconsidering the seven primary emotions (Panksepp & Biven, 2012), we realize that negative feeling states are more similar than different; these seven primary emotions are seeking/expectancy, fear/anxiety, rage /anger, lust/sexual excitement, care/nurturance, panic/grief/sadness, and play/social joy. Different feelings often bleed into one another, overlapping in physical sensations and thoughts, and leading to similar defenses. Some researchers (Barrett, 2017b) have even argued that all feelings are physically rooted in a common arousal state; what differentiates among these states and gives them their unique identities are the different cognitive interpretations we assign to those aroused states. Clinical experience supports this observation that feelings are often messy and cause similar physiological disruptions, negative thoughts, and convincing narratives. We see this in clients and in ourselves:

sadness in the midst of anger, fear in the midst of joy, and vulnerability in the midst of confidence (Pérez-Edgar, 2019).

What seems to unite these negative feelings and states is the anxiety that drives them. For example, a sense of vulnerability is often based in a fear of being exposed, hurt, or humiliated. It may include feelings of defenselessness, especially in the face of real or imagined power that others have over us. Often, such feelings are entwined with convictions that we have no agency or actual control over our own decisions or even our own well-being. Underneath most of these feelings is ongoing dread in the form of anxious predictions and expectations that something very hurtful is always around the corner, ready to injure us. The role of the amygdala with its specialized nuclei, reacting to a wide range of threats, is one of the unifying elements of all negative feeling states (Lebow & Chen, 2016).

The amygdala, as a rule, reacts to more attention-grabbing or salient stimuli that are unpredictable and that signal threat or reward (Adolphs & Anderson, 2018). It is also involved in reacting to other emotion states such as disgust, happiness, anger, and sadness. From infancy to adulthood, the connectivity between the amygdala and other circuits is mostly stable, blending different emotional and feeling states (Panksepp & Biven, 2012). With the development of the frontal regions of the brain, the connections between the amygdala and the medial prefrontal cortex grow as well. These changes in connection help children and adolescents develop a richer and more nuanced understanding of feeling states. Just being able to label this wide range of feelings has been found to increase effective emotion regulation (Gabard-Durnam et al., 2018; Lane et al., 2014).

CHAPTER SIX

Setting the Stage for Emotional Difficulties: The Significance of Early Intersubjective Resonance

The exploration of the fear system in our early years is not unlike an archaeological excavation, attempting to get a picture of past cultures and a glimpse into their early characteristics. Unearthed and often fragmented artifacts speak to us, and from them we try to conjure the old world. Similarly, none of us has direct access to early memories of events or how such events made us feel. But by translating neuropsychological findings into a brain/mind-centered paradigm, we can significantly expand our understanding of our emotional vulnerabilities.

Neuropsychological research enables us to literally see the neural manifestations of normative as well as problematic development. It allows us to pinpoint with accuracy the foundational circuits of emotions, cognition, and behaviors; we can see how they are entirely interconnected. We can better understand what encourages healthy neural development or, conversely, reinforces a maladaptive one.

An important result of the increasingly sophisticated and informative neuropsychological findings is the following realization: We all need to accept the presence of fear and anxiety in our lives. From birth, the course of development presents us with inevitable moments in which frustration, physical pain, and hyperarousal take over the emotional and physical states of infants and children. Indeed, it's important for us to accept that early fears and the physical distress they cause are an essential part of growing up human.

As we continue to connect neuropsychological findings to a wider clinical understanding, we must start by examining the relationship between an infant's innate needs for attuned attachment and the ever-present dysregulating fear system. During a period when the infant is entirely dependent on caregivers for attachment needs, physical proximity, warmth, nutrition, and attuned responses, the caregiver's ability to regulate the infant's physiology, emotionality, and behavior is particularly crucial (Callaghan et al., 2019; Schore, 2012; Tottenham, 2017).

Our mammalian brains developed through a process of biobehavioral synchrony with a parent, especially through face-to-face communication, eye gaze, and vocalization (Feldman, 2007; Jaffe et al., 2001; Tronick & Cohn, 1989). A large body of research shows that mother and infant dyads together generate complex, multilayered communication channels. Starting at 3 to 4 months of age, face-to-face interactions engage the infant's most advanced communication capacities. The mother–infant dyadic partners can hold their gaze, look away, engage in different intensities of smiling, or remain unresponsive. During such intersubjective exchanges, infants may also express distress through facial expressions, vocalization, or attempts to steer their faces away from the interaction (Beebe et al., 2010; Feldman, 2016).

Such mutual communication leads to a synchronized exchange of hormonal, emotional, and physiological signals between parent and child. Coordinated hormone levels, heart rhythms, and breathing are an inextricable part of intersubjective interactions (Abraham et al., 2020; Bos, 2017; Feldman, 2012, 2020). When such early caregiving relationships are profoundly disturbed, such as in cases of neglect, abuse, and trauma, their effects on emotional and social development can be devastating. On a endocrine–neurological level, the quality of parental care which may depend on their ow neurobiology, is tightly linked to the child's neurobiological development and the trajectory of their neuropsychological development. This close intersubjective interchange and mutual resonances of parent and child mediate the oft-seen intergenerational transmission of trauma. It seems that the verbal and nonverbal communication between parents and children carry the imprint of the parents' emotional states, and their roots in the endocrine and neurobiology. For example, the role of variations in neuropeptides, steroid receptors, testosterone, and oxytocin systems have been recently studied as mediators of parental behaviors and therefore intergenerational intersubjective transmission (Bos, 2017).

Research has repeatedly emphasized the importance of mutual attunement between caregiver and baby. An infant's capacity for physiological regulation, emotion regulation, expressions of empathy in childhood and adolescence, and infant attachment and cognition are all associated with those early interactions. Significantly, an infant's ability for sustained eye gaze has been associated with secure attachment and less sustained gaze with avoidant attachment. Finally, the irreplaceable importance of sustained, comforting touch as a means of attunement and regulation during infancy cannot be overstated. Direct skin contact is capable of shifting an infant's mood from hyperaroused and agitated to calm and relatively anxiety free (Beebe et al., 2010; Margolis et al., 2019; Schore, 2012; Tronick, 2007). Through facial expressions, tone of voice, and body language, the caregiver provides nonverbal signals of safety and resonance. What allows for healthy, empathic, and growth-promoting attunement is the nonverbal communication between the right brain hemispheres of both baby and mother. In an intersubjective process, both baby and caregiver communicate and resonate with each other's emotional states. This work describes the neuropsychological processes of the right brain that underpin this intersubjective communication (Schore, 2012).

As we have learned, the importance of intersubjective communication in the first years of life cannot be overemphasized. Empathic and attuned communications can establish and reestablish the infant's state of homeostasis—the sense of safety, well-being, and physical and emotional comfort. This communication can offset the dysregulating consequences of amygdala-driven hyperarousal, pain, and discomfort. On the other hand, negative, impatient, or simply unattuned communications from the parent provide limited comfort and can exacerbate the child's distress (Beebe et al., 2010; Tronick & Cohn, 1989).

The story of infant-parent intersubjectivity and the potential dysregulating interference of the fear system begins prenatally, with the nature of the mother's attachment to her unborn baby. As the amygdala activates during the last two months of pregnancy, it can already render the developing brain susceptible to aversive or disruptive states. For example, the mother's physical health, her emotional well-being, her emotional support during pregnancy, financial pressures, and family stresses have all been shown to affect the unborn child

(Gabard-Durnam & McLaughlin, 2019; McLaughlin, 2016; McLaughlin et al., 2019). Such internal and environmental stressors seem to reduce mothers' ability to form a loving attachment to their unborn babies.

Maternal levels of anxiety and distress, for example, influenced the duration and quality of a mother's attachment to her unborn baby (Bos, 2017; Hopkins et al., 2018). More anxious mothers were less positively preoccupied with their unborn babies. Other studies indicate that ongoing maternal stress during pregnancy becomes part of the child's genetic inheritance (Yehuda et al., 2005). The assumption is that an active amygdala will react to the mother's stressful states through signals sent by stress hormones. Attachment processes starting in utero are the embodiment of the earliest mutual communication, which continues into infancy. An important aspect of such early attachment is the mother's ability to nonverbally regulate her unborn baby's states of distress. Postnatally, the parents' ability to modify the infant's emotional, biological, and neural responses to internal and external stressors is an essential factor for healthy development (Abraham et al., 2020; Bouvette-Turcot et al., 2017; Callaghan et al., 2019; Callaghan & Richardson, 2012; DiPietro, 2012; Papousek & Papousek, 1990; Schore, 2012).

Following birth, parents can either buffer (i.e., downregulate) or amplify (i.e., upregulate) an infant's fear responses; this is true into childhood and to a lesser extent adolescence. This depends on the parents' own emotional internal states and how they enact them, and as was already mentioned, on parent' own internal neurobiology (Bos, 2017; Gunnar et al., 2015). Given the important role of parents in affecting emotional maturation, it is not surprising that emotional variations in caregiving are important predictors of children's mental and physical health (Callaghan & Tottenham, 2016; Callaghan et al., 2019).

THE INTERSUBJECTIVE REALM: MUTUALLY RESONANT EXPERIENCES

The most noticeable structural changes to the amygdala occur during the years prior to adolescence and continue into early adulthood (Fareri & Tottenham, 2016). The first year of life, especially, shows rapid growth and changes. This parallels the plasticity of the amygdala and, consequently, its tendencies to react to many felt and perceived threats. This is particularly true for the psychosocial environment (Callaghan et al., 2019; Fox et al., 2015). With the growing number of studies establishing the enormous plasticity of the amygdala, the focus on the buffering benefits of attunement has grown as well. Bowlby's (1969) work on the importance of early attachment has taken center stage in our understanding of human development (Schore, 2012; Tronick, 2007; Winnicott, 1969). Today, in light of the increasing number of neuropsychological studies that examine the actual brain/mind processes during the early years, we can arrive at a clearer and more tangible meaning of attunement and parental buffering.

Child development studies have demonstrated the important role of caregivers in regulating infant physiology and behavior. This is a key feature of early life attachment. In effect, there's an interesting and significant balance between the infant's amygdala-driven threat learning and parental buffering, which suppresses this learning. These learned fears are suppressed if the mother or father is present to block the amygdala from encoding learned fears and fear memories. The neurobiology of parental regulation of infant fear is made possible by their presence, which suppresses fear learning (Opendak et al., 2017, 2019).

Information about parental presence to the amygdala is transmitted through dopamine signals from the ventral tegmental area. This circuit is part of the extensive connections that the amygdala maintains with circuits involved in encoding reward and emotion. However, across a wide range of events, parental presence can reduce an infant's level of stress but may not block it entirely. This may result in very early forms of aversive learning—encoding and retaining anxiety states connected to frustrating situations (Callaghan et al., 2019). In such situations, aversive experiences compete with the rewarding and comforting experiences of attachment. This points to the role of temperament that is at play. The nuances of the two states—the rewarding and the aversive—and how they are subjectively experienced by the infant may depend on an innate tendency toward negative bias. In this case, more aversive experiences than rewarding ones will be encoded. These processes underlie the very delicate balance between fear learning and the internalization of a sense of safety and comfort.

Indeed, infants' innate styles of communicating and relating have been explored, focusing on an infant's social capacity for communication behaviors (Margolis et al., 2019). Researchers evaluated this based on second-by-second videos of mother-infant face-to-face communication when infants were 4 months old. Four infant behaviors were assessed: gaze, facial affect, vocal affect, and head orientation. Unique behavioral profiles representing natural types of infant communicative behavior emerged. For example, one group of infants displayed various forms of affective dysregulation. In this profile, sustained negative vocal emotionality was linked to disorganization; random vocalized emotion was associated with attachment resistance; and random facial affect and vocal affect, either positive or negative, were associated with difficult temperament.

Such specific and controlled studies further indicate the intricate interactions between infants and caregivers from early infancy and the mutual effects they inevitably have on each other. Even without fully understanding the effects of such innate relational tendencies on future personal difficulties, we can clearly imagine that an infant's communication struggles can interfere with a caregiver's ability to sustain a buffering and fully attuned interaction. The mutuality embedded within the infant–caregiver dyad may also result in anxious and disorganized reactions on the parent's part. In response to the infant's sustained negative affect or resistance to full emotional participation, a parent may withdraw and give up, acting on their own feelings of disappointment and sense of failure. Such behaviors, in turn, will further increase the already existing states of discomfort within the child.

Furthermore, in light of the discussion recognizing the importance of a mother's relationship to her unborn baby and the plasticity of the amygdala in the first few months of gestation, we can also speculate that at least some of the infants' behaviors in this study may have been influenced by those early processes. Although we can't actually decipher all the possible and varied influences on an infant's temperament, we can nevertheless identify and address some of the difficulties as they become more obvious. As this study suggests, clinicians can be trained to look for emotional and behavioral signals in infants that may indicate communicative and attachment difficulties. For example, clinicians can be trained to look for rapidly shifting gaze patterns or to identify an infant's tendency to become overly aroused. Clinicians can help parents shift to a lower level of arousal by maintaining a slow pace, accepting infant visual disengagement, and providing moderate-level (rather than high-level) greeting behaviors when the infant responds (Margolis et al., 2019).

THE INTERSUBJECTIVE EFFECTS OF ABUSE AND NEGLECT

Research across species has shown that initial abusive and neglectful caregiving impair the caregiver's ability to regulate the infant later on; this is associated with adverse mental health outcomes across the life span (Callaghan et al., 2019; Schore, 2012). What is so significant about such emerging information is that although parental presence suppresses regions involved in threat circuits during and after the sensitive period, parents may have a difficult time providing calming attunement if there's a history of severe misattunement. In this case, fear learning becomes dominant (Callaghan et al., 2019; Fareri & Tottenham, 2016; Opendak et al., 2017). Depressed mothers, for example, are less capable of blocking amygdala-dependent signals. This is because cold or impassive facial expressions cannot provide the necessary positive emotional buffering against hyperarousal.

Importantly, this decreased ability of parental emotional regulation was observed in parent-infant pairs. Following a history of neglect and misattunement in such intersubjective pairs, parents were less able to lessen their infants' anxieties. In effect, these initial and enduring results of early negative attachment relationships attest to the robustness of the earliest encoded circuits (see Chapter 1). Due to the great plasticity of the developing brain during those sensitive periods, and because of the power of the fear system, early fear learning demonstrates a particular staying power. This sets the stage for an increased bias attention to threats, both real and imagined.

The Dance Between Threat and Safety

Throughout development and into adulthood, social and affective signals gleaned from facial expressions, vocal tones, and body language provide a primary source of information about the state of mind and emotional intensions of others. But at no other time in our lives are these physiological and social cues as important as during infancy when parental facial expressions hold the key to providing infants with emotional and physiological regulation (Schore, 2012). Infants are innately hungry for, ready for, and open to receiving the soothing messages reflected in their caregivers' facial expressions and the important mutual eye gaze. But, paradoxically, again driven by the strong presence of the fear system in the brain/mind and body, infants are also innately drawn to faces that convey fear and threat. In this context, the parents' ability to communicate positively attuned affect is particularly important.

From early on, infants show an innate tendency to pay more attention to fearful faces and to threat-related expressions that engage the fear system—the amygdala and its circuits. In fact, many studies exploring human amygdala development use fearful facial expressions as threatening stimuli. Most studies exploring how infants react to fearful faces track the length of time they stare at different images. In general, infants display attention bias to faces, especially to fearful ones. At 5 to 12 months old, there is a clear attention preference to fearful faces. Likewise, at 12 and 36 months, babies pay greater attention to fearful over happy facial expressions. Such results indicate that the attention bias to fear starts early and is specific to this emotion. A more generalized bias to other negative expressions such as anger follows later on, around 36 months in toddlers (Leppänen et al., 2018). In a staring task that tracked the direction of a baby's gaze, babies 10 to 18 months old could perceptually categorize facial expressions of anger and disgust (Ruba et al., 2017). At 18 months old, they also showed heightened sensitivity to angry faces, suggesting that during the second year of life infants develop a growing ability for emotion categorization (Ruba et al., 2017).

Research (Leppänen et al., 2018) suggests that even normative or ordinary parental variations in relating to the infant may influence their attention bias to faces. For example, changes in a parent's expressions due to anxiety, depression, or shifting moods can heighten an infant's sensitivity to threat. Insensitive mothering, for example, may accelerate the development of the amygdala–medial prefrontal cortex circuit (Thijssen et al., 2017). Similarly, a reduction in the parent's ability to be attentive to the infant's emotional communication regarding their needs affected the infant's biases to threat. For example, a change in the quality of a parent's vocal communication with the infant may be disruptive and threatening, causing more anxious attentiveness to faces. If the caregiver's facial expressions do not mirror the infant's anxious state of mind, very little attunement takes place (Schore, 2012; Tronick, 2007).

It is not surprising, then, that a study showed a positive relationship between an infant's (4 to 24 months old) attention bias toward threat-related stimuli and their mother's level of anxiety (Morales et al., 2017). In this study, infants' attention bias was measured through eye-tracking behaviors accompanied by psychophysiological arousal measures. Infants of mothers who reported high levels of stress and depression showed higher levels of hyperarousal and stronger tendencies toward biased attention to threat (Forssman et al., 2014). Interestingly, neutral and ambiguous expressions may also be more threatening early in life. Not being able to receive sufficiently strong stimuli about threat potential, the amygdala's automatic evaluation tends to read neutral expressions as potential threats.

Another study found increased attention to threat-related faces compared to neutral ones among young children (Opendak et al., 2019). The attention bias toward fearful and angry faces was related to maternal anxiety. These results support a growing literature suggesting that attention bias toward threat is present in early development. Even though attention bias toward threat did not change with age, it was positively related to maternal anxiety, a known risk factor for the development of anxiety. This study, like others, implies that attention bias toward threat during infancy and childhood is affected by the mother's levels of anxiety (Morales et al., 2017).

THE NEUROBIOLOGY OF SYNCHRONIZED COMMUNICATION

As we saw, maternal presence has a strong buffering effect on infants' fearful and stressful states in all primates (Feldman, 2016, 2020; Howell et al., 2017). But what in such early attachment experiences provides the protective level of buffering?

Human attachment bonds do not merely reflect facial, verbal, and close bodily exchanges, but also the actual coupling and synchronicity of neural activity. Affective and biobehavioral sharing is particularly important to the development of bonding attachment early in life. For instance, a study found that a mother's and child's social brains were neurally coupled—showing similar patterns of activation—only during episodes of behavioral synchrony compared with non-synchrony (Levy et al., 2017).

Scanning studies also showed the importance of mutual gaze to neural mirroring in areas of the temporal lobes. Again, such coupling was seen only during eye gaze interaction. This biopsychological mutuality was also related to the degree of dyadic reciprocity and cooperation (Mu et al., 2016; Tang et al., 2016). At these moments, both participants of the dyad were experiencing attachment as deep and emotionally rewarding experiences, laying a solid basis for further mutual attunement.

INTERGENERATIONAL TRANSMISSION OF EMOTIONAL DIFFICULTIES

A remarkable study (Abraham et al., 2020) that began in 1982 explored how qualities of attuned care by depressed and nondepressed parents shaped their children's social brain circuits. The study examined 44 dyadic pairs of fathers and mothers through the first 16 years of their children's development. The study examined the brain's neural synchronicity between parents and their children. In particular, the researchers wanted to find out whether the social circuits in children of depressed and nondepressed parents resembled those of their parents.

The results provide the first neurobiological evidence for parent-child synchronicity in specific brain white matter connections, such as between the basal ganglia and temporal cortical areas. The basal ganglia–temporal cortex connections, including the temporoparietal junction, are implicated in our ability to relate to others and to see them as separate entities from us. In general, this area mediates what we call theory of mind, the knowledge that others have minds and desires of their own (Richardson & Saxe, 2020ab).

The neural connections between the basal ganglia and the temporal lobe networks are involved in human attachment and the formation and maintenance of parent-child bonding. They also mediate learning and habit forming. Both these circuits are extensively and bidirectionally connected with the amygdala, illustrating the delicate balance between parental buffering, the nature of attunement, and anxious states. When triggered but not buffered by an attuned parent, the fear system will take over the infant's internal experience. With repeated misattuned and nonprotective parental behaviors, more negative attachment experiences will be encoded as learned experiences. Remembering the role of the basal ganglia in forming habits, we can see how implicitly remembered and encoded negative experiences coalesce into enduring interpersonal patterns of anxious negative expectations.

This is especially important to our understanding of how early parental attachment styles literally shape their infant's growing brain (Abraham et al., 2020). Better parental care by nondepressed or moderately depressed parents resulted in stronger neural connections in the particular circuit responsible for social attachment. Parents with strong neural connections in this circuit were better able to provide buffering attunement against emotionally stressful situations.

On the other hand, dyads where parents suffered from depression showed diminished neural connections in this circuit. Significantly, their children were also found to have weaker neural connections in this circuit. In other words, more attuned parental care, underpinned by stronger connections in this social circuit, predicted greater neural concordance with their children. Indeed, parents suffering from depression tend to speak less, make less eye contact, are generally slower in their responses to their children, express less positive emotion, and show limited empathic understanding (Granat et al., 2017; Hummel et al., 2016).

The implications of this study are clear. It provides neurological evidence of synchronicity in parent–child dyads. Indeed, such relationships appear to set the stage for typical brain development (Fareri & Tottenham, 2016; Tottenham, 2012a, 2012b). The effects of early care were mediated by the severity of parental depressive symptoms. These parents tended to be less attuned, less responsive, and less empathic. This disruption in attuned caregiving constitutes a considerable risk factor for intergenerational transmission of psychopathology (Abraham et al., 2020). Parental basal ganglia–cortex connectivity predicted fewer aggressive symptoms for their 6-year-old children. This effect was mediated by attuned and collaborative coparenting in the preschool years (Abraham et al., 2020; Opendak et al., 2019).

Research also showed that the interactions between a parent's levels of depression and the quality of early care behaviors they administered resulted in a wide range of behavioral difficulties in their children (Abraham et al., 2020). This is not a surprising finding; rather, it reflects the wide range of emotional and social difficulties and other personality traits that may characterize parents. A moderately depressed parent, a parent who is primarily self-involved, an over-controlling parent, or a critical and nonempathic parent will all interact differently with their children's temperament, providing different and unique building blocks for the child's developing personality.

This transmission of emotional difficulties from one generation to the next goes beyond symptoms of depression. Dynamic intergenerational transmission encompasses a wide range of adaptive and maladaptive emotions and behaviors. When excessive anxiety, lack of empathy with the child's internal experiences, criticism, and shaming behaviors are part of the parent's psychology, they often become part of the child's internal dynamics as well.

Epigenetic Considerations

We also have to consider the fact that a temperamentally overreactive amygdala will naturally find more reasons to become activated and sound the alarm bell of danger. Inborn characteristics may also make children more sensitive to fear information (Aktar et al., 2013). However, even in these cases, the buffering effects of sensitive and empathic parenting provide an opportunity for less anxious feelings and behaviors (Abraham et al., 2020; Callaghan et al., 2019; Opendak et al., 2019). Thus, there is compelling evidence that, depending on particular parental traits, experiential learning within daily intersubjective interactions can result in excess anxiety and attention bias to negativity (Field & Lester, 2010; Tottenham, 2020). For example, in the face of novel stimuli, the parent's facial expressions provide essential cues and emotional feedback that teach infants and children how to respond to new stimuli and to nonstop daily challenges more generally. If parents directly or indirectly provide fear-related information to older children (e.g., talking about or implying that some events are dangerous), it may lead to increased anxiety and attention bias as well (Morales et al., 2017).

Finally, genetic and environmental factors do not operate independently. Innate characteristics that predispose children to experience fear, anxiety, sadness, shame, or excessive agitation may evoke specific emotional and behavioral responses from their caregivers. In turn, the ensuing intersubjective entanglements generate additional fears, anxiety, shame, and aggression; this necessarily interferes with attachment and closeness. For instance, negative overreactive emotions among adopted babies 9 months old predicted more anxiety symptoms in the adoptive parents (both mothers and fathers) 18 months later (Brooker et al., 2020). The authors suggest that these infants' constitutional tendencies contributed to their adoptive parents' anxieties. In a negative feedback loop, these anxieties further contributed to the children's difficult behaviors.

Obviously, we cannot overlook the interplay of genetic and environmental factors in affecting the quality of attuned bonding between parents and children. For example, genetic factors, such as variations in the 5-HTTLPR allele, are related to anxiety, negativity, and attention bias (Morales et al., 2017). Similarly, genetically informed studies (e.g., twin studies) find that attention bias toward physical and emotional symptoms of anxiety such as a racing heart has considerable genetic connections (30–40% heritability) (Zavos et al., 2010). But this still leaves environmental factors to explain a significant proportion of the intergenerationally transmitted difficulties. Did some of the children in Abraham et al.'s (2020) longitudinal study inherit the propensity for greater emotional and social difficulties? The findings of this particular study, showing a neural correspondence between a parent's and a child's brain/mind networks, suggest the presence of interactional forces. This leaves significant room for intergenerational transmission through the parent's own internal dynamics and behaviors.

This chapter sets the stage for a deeper exploration of how emotions, in particular the fear system, become an inseparable part of early intersubjective processes. Furthermore, as the following chapters show, our innate vulnerability to states of fear and anxiety, especially within the intersubjective dyad, lies at the heart of our dysregulated and distressed states as adults.

Emotional states, including normative and unavoidable distress and frustration, are triggered and engage the amygdala (Fareri & Tottenham, 2016; Pattwell & Bath, 2017). If we put parental behaviors on a continuum, the more destructive parental misattunement is, the more serious are the negative learned responses. Let's begin, then, by exploring the nature of our emotional lives.

IAN'S CASE: THE FATHER'S FEARS AND THE SON'S ANXIETY

When I first met Ian, a young African American man, he appeared to be content with his teaching career. He was about to get married and seemed to have a wide circle of friends. His reason for seeking therapy, however, was what he described as "frequently obsessing about any decision," past and present. He described frequently second-guessing himself, wondering if he was making the right decision. With great hesitation, he admitted that he was even questioning his love for his fiancée and his decision to get married. He was so used to thinking, rethinking, and ruminating on both the small and big decisions he needed to make that he described "wasting hours contemplating alternatives and what-ifs." He just wanted, he said, "to be 100% sure that I am doing the right thing." He wanted to know, he continued, that whatever he decided was the one perfect decision.

Ian remembered similar periods in his adolescence and young adulthood. During that time, he was heavily involved with playing soccer, a sport he was very good at. But still, each game was followed by a meticulous step-by-step play-out, asking himself whether he made the right call or the right move. Mostly, he would conclude, that he could and should have done better. Similarly, his college and initial teaching assignments brought frequent second-guessing bouts as well. Although Ian accepted his ruminations as inevitable and something he "just had to live with," he felt that "something was not quite okay" with him.

During the first few weeks of therapy, as we tried to explore the nature of Ian's ruminations and their possible beginning, Ian continually "hit a wall" and repeatedly went back to his annoying thought processes as the obvious problem. His main interest, he kept saying, was to be perfectly sure about the big decisions in front of him; whether to look for a new teaching position and, of course, his approaching wedding. What was quite puzzling in Ian's case was the fact that while these heavy self-doubts took so much mental space, he was not aware of any other disturbing feelings. He was only aware of "doubts and of the need to be sure" of himself.

However, as treatment continued, Ian became more open and ready to explore other aspects of his internal experiences. This became possible when we both realized that just talking each time about his incessant, obsessive second-guessing was not going to be helpful to him. He was doing it repeatedly on his own. Ian needed to get in touch with other parts of himself, mostly, I thought, the live emotions of anxiety and the experiences they affected. I also wanted to explore any feelings he carried around his experience as a part of discriminated minority group.

As we settled into our sessions, I asked Ian to pay deeper attention to other aspects of his experience, for example, becoming more aware of his interactions with others and his reactions to them. As Ian became more mindful of his internal states and behaviors, he could describe what he called "all kinds of funny sensations and unusual reactions." For example, he watched himself frequently "pushing back and dismissing other people's ideas or suggestions." In staff meetings, especially, he caught himself "tensing up" when colleagues were "too invested in their own opinions and ideas." He could even identify "an edge" in his responses to others, especially when he thought they pushed their views at the expense of his.

At that point, Ian was not aware of the unacknowledged fears and insecurities that were behind his behaviors; behind his difficulties to make decisions and trust his own mind. But as Ian continued to pay attention to his internal states and behaviors, he also started to notice unpleasant sensations in his chest and belly, sensations that until now he had been only partially aware of, and when he was, they were quickly dismissed.

When Ian became aware of how often he compared his life, his talents, and his achievements to those of other people he knew, he became more anxious, and experienced a great deal of agitation during our sessions. At the same time he also became curious about "what was going on" in his mind. He wanted to find out what was behind his self-doubting thoughts and his "defensive behaviors." In sessions, he said, "The more I am getting to know myself, the less I recognize myself and the less I like myself." He readily acknowledged the role that race played in his self-doubts, the continuous comparisons to his mostly white classmates at a NYC school. However, he also began to mull over and occasionally say that something else was also going on, some influence that he needed to understand, but at that point was still unknowable.

At the same time, however, the greater awareness of his visceral feelings opened the door to a greater exploration of his self-doubting thoughts, self-judgmental ruminations, and mistrust in his ability "to make right decisions." In an important way, the understanding that a host of anxious feelings underpinned his ongoing difficulties was an immense relief for Ian. He could finally "put a name to what was going on with" him. He was now "fully ready to deal with what led him to feel so anxious and insecure." He was "tired of what it did" to his life.

Ian's understanding of what it meant to feel anxious increased when he started to explore his childhood. He quickly realized that his father was an anxious and insecure man, often expressing worries of not being able to overcome his difficulties or achieve what he wanted. Ian remembered his father's frequent complaints about the way his life turned out and his conclusions that his disappointments were far greater than the rewards he experienced. He frequently suggested that "in another world, another time, another race, he would have done much better." Ian's father tried a few times to own his own business, but financial difficulties were always there. What Ian remembers most were the disagreements between his father and his partner. He remembers how unappreciated and victimized his father felt. Overhearing his parents talking, Ian felt sorry for his father's difficulties and wished he could stand up for himself and "put his partner in his place." In other painful moments during sessions, Ian remembered his father's repeated anxiety about "losing everything and becoming poor and homeless." Ian deeply felt for his father's "wounded pride" and the sense of defeat and disappointment.

In following sessions, Ian further remembered his father's fretting insecurities, his frequent doubts. As a young child, Ian realized now, he could not really put words to what he was feeling. He remembered, however, that he often had butterflies in his stomach. Just listening to his father's fears about losing the business filled him with dread. From the time he was 7 or 8 years old, Ian's fears and preoccupation with what might go wrong also included many ideas of what his father should or could do to succeed. He kept his ideas to himself, but watching his father and listening to him very carefully, he was always looking for signals that his father "finally did the right thing." Looking for some reassurance from his mother, Ian attempted to talk about his fears with her. Although she acknowledged that his father was an anxious man, she also told Ian that his father's anxiety "made everything look much worse." Things were not so dire, she said; after all, "they still paid the rent, and they had enough to eat."

Ian really wanted to believe her, he says. But his vigilance did not let up. He remained exquisitely attuned to his father's moods and verbalizations, always looking for clues that would reveal where things were heading. When he reached adolescence, Ian's preoccupation with potential doom lessened somewhat, and, as he said, "I put all my energy into soccer, my team, and my friends." But although he was no longer thinking about his father's business and his father's impending "failure," his focus became his own decisions and his perceived quality of his performance. This is when he started second-guessing himself, pulling everything apart in his head, not trusting himself to have taken the "right step literally and figuratively," as he said.

Being so fully attuned to his father's states of mind and self-defeating behaviors not only intensified Ian's sense of anxiety but also created serious doubts about his own competency. The idea that every decision was literally a matter of survival took root and informed all the decisions in his life. But because so much was seemingly at stake with each decision, Ian could never be fully certain that he took the right path. Many what-ifs always followed, tormenting him. This happened at school, with his diverse group of friends, and after each soccer game.

In a complete fusion of predisposition, learning, and identification processes, Ian's developing brain/mind internalized his father's internal states and behaviors. His father's anxiety became his, and his father's nonverbal worries, expressed self-doubts, self-denigrating narratives, and fears of going broke were experienced by Ian as originating from within his own mind. His father's internal states were experienced as Ian's own, setting the stage for self-doubts, incessant comparisons to others, and a wide range of convictions that questioned his own ability to function as well as others. To feel more in control, he needed to be totally sure.

As therapy continued, it became clear to Ian that a large part of his personality lived out his father's internal and external experiences both as a Black person in NYC and as someone with a great deal of drive and ambition, but also insecurities that undermined his abilities to stand up for himself. The process of internal separation from his father's inner experiences was not easy, however. The insights he got were not enough to change the automatic feeling, thinking, and acting patterns that were built and reinforced throughout his childhood and adolescence. The defenses against his unconscious narratives of incompetence and the dread of imagined mistakes occurred entirely out of his awareness. When a smart suggestion from a colleague unconsciously triggered his insecurity and thus threatened him, he actively pushed back or passively ignored it. When his anxiety about not performing well enough felt out of control, he tried to reign it in through a detailed examination and reexamination of each step he took. But of course, these coping strategies did not offer any sustained help; the self-doubts they created only added to his anxiety.

What helped Ian, however, was his growing ability to identify these patterns as they were occurring in real time. He became increasingly aware not only of his disturbing thoughts, but also of the physical sensations that seemed to be totally intertwined with them. And as his ability increased to tolerate his anxiety and understand its roots as he was experiencing it, he was also able to create distance between himself and the disturbing negative state. With increased self-confidence in his own separate subjectivity, Ian began to let go of the narrative that only perfect decisions were a guarantee for a safe life. It was not only the realization that perfect decisions do not exist, but the deep understanding that he no longer needed to derive his peace of mind from the illusory promise of perfection.

As an adult he needed to find his own ways of coping with both failures, racial discrimination, as well as successes, and thus let go of what he learned and unconsciously adopted as his own. Increasingly he looked for ways to note the differences between himself and his father and, unlike him, he was consciously determined to be much more at peace with his decisions. As expected, Ian's anxiety did not disappear—after all, it has been an integral part of his neurobiology. But it no longer controlled him. He recognized how it felt and was not terrified when he periodically felt its physical and mental manifestations. Moreover, as he developed the ability to reframe his anxious sensations and remember that his recurrent self-doubts were in effect the result of the automatic firing of old brain circuits, these aspects of his anxiety lost their bite.

CHAPTER SEVEN

Childhood Trauma and Its Aftermath

Research as well as numerous clinical encounters has consistently documented strong links between exposure to childhood trauma and lifelong emotional, physiological, and interpersonal difficulties (D'Andrea et al., 2012; Spinazzola et al., 2018; van der Kolk et al., 2019). Many studies and clinical experiences have established that childhood trauma, both episodic and cumulative, is a devastating condition that can result in a wide range of emotional, interpersonal, and behavioral difficulties. As will soon become clear, a history of abuse and neglect can lead to a range of debilitating emotional and cognitive difficulties, including increased fear and anxiety, flashbacks, derealization, depersonalization, and recurrent symptoms of depression (Choi et al., 2017; van Huijstee & Vermetten, 2018). In addition, as the *DSM-5* specifies, "following prolonged, repeated, and severe traumatic events (e.g., childhood abuse, torture), the individual may additionally experience difficulties in regulating emotions or maintaining stable interpersonal relationships, or dissociative symptoms" (American Psychiatric Association, 2013). Dissociation manifests clinically as avoidance, detachment, and intrusive thoughts (Şar, 2017).

What happens in the brain/mind/body in the wake of a trauma that makes it so enduring? We already know that memories encoded at the time of an emotional state are intense and more readily remembered. But what allows these particular memories to have such a hold on the majority of those who suffered trauma, especially during their early years? Why is it so difficult to avoid the injurious emotional learning that took place and to integrate it into our emotion regulation system?

SCOTT'S CASE: THE PAST IS NEVER FULLY GONE

Scott sought therapy when he was in his early 60s—when his wife, after many years of expressed unhappiness, had finally left their suburban house and moved to another state. She was not asking for divorce, but as Scott himself said, she needed to be away from him. Scott had two grown children who also lived outside New York state. He was an attorney in a small law firm based in the city, but expressed great dissatisfaction about the nature of his work. Although he was a partner in the firm, he often ruminated about choosing the wrong career. He also expressed bitterness and disappointment with his standing in the larger law community, his perceived lack of recognized professional achievements, and low status. Scott did not seem to have close friends, and often denigrated the people in his orbit. The most important goal he wanted to achieve was resolving the long-standing conflicts with his wife and developing closer relationships with his two daughters, their spouses, and his grandchildren.

From the beginning, Scott seemed very opinionated and rigid, with a limited ability to examine his own role in his difficulties. He often sounding controlling and dismissive of the feelings and points of view of others, including me. When I wanted to explore what appeared to be a strong tendency to blame others, he quickly dismissed any interventions encouraging him to further explore the possible causes for his interpersonal difficulties. Indeed, Scott stated that the reasons for his recurrent struggles with his wife, children, and colleagues at the law firm were their shortcomings and disappointing behaviors. He, on the other hand, was the smart one and therefore always in the right, he said. He described himself as quick to anger but emphasized that in all cases his anger was fully justified. According to Scott, throughout adulthood he had struggled with an addiction to alcohol. Over time he noticed that his alcohol consumption increased when he was under stress and when he felt all alone. In effect, feelings of loneliness, not being respected and appreciated for his talent, and feeling unloved by his family were at the core of his emotional but unacknowledged suffering.

Scott's childhood and its aftermath was a picture of verbal abuse, neglect, chaos, and violence. Scott and his sister were children of immigrants who came to this country as adolescents with their own poor families. Both his parents worked long hours, but his childhood was nevertheless financially stressful. Occasionally his father drank excessively, and when he did, he tended to be short-tempered and physically violent. On occasions he slapped the children with considerable force. Scott was afraid of his father, and when his father was drunk, he tried to stay out of his way by leaving the small apartment they shared with his mother's parents. He remembered some affection from his father and even some "fun or quality time" when his father was in a good mood, but feelings of unpredictability and fear persisted throughout his childhood. In his memories, the presence of his mother's parents, who were very strict and critical themselves, only made things worse. When Scott was 9 years old, they moved out. From around age 8, Scott stayed out in the streets on his own as much as he could. He tried to avoid his parents as much as possible, he said. Scott's 's most devastating memories revolved around his interactions with his verbally and physically abusive mother. In sessions, Scott frequently stated with full confidence that he had always known that his mother did not love him and that he was unwanted. In effect, she frequently told him that she did not want to have a baby when she got pregnant with him and that she wished he had been stillborn. She also often said to him that he was a "terrible, very bad little boy who only caused her trouble and endless work." Her attitude toward his sister, 4 years younger, was much different; "supportive and even loving," he said, chuckling. It was surprising to me that Scott often justified his mother's abusive and hateful behavior. He defended her by saying that she herself grew up with a violent, abusive father whose treatment of his wife, Scott's 's grandmother, was horrendous. Scott himself witnessed his grandfather's violent tendencies when they all shared the apartment. One of the highlights of his life, he said, was when his grandparents left for their own apartment.

Talking about these childhood memories, Scott did not show much, if any, emotion. It seemed like his memories and narratives about his childhood occupied a prominent place in the way he thought about himself, but there were no indications that he consciously felt wounded by these experiences. On the contrary, although he grew up feeling unloved, neglected, and frequently physically abused, he still could not see the effects such abuse unavoidably had on his emotional health, personality, and adult relationships.

Scott found refuge in school and in a small group of friends he made on the streets. As he says today, he "hung out with them, they served some purpose." He did not bring any homework home and, in his telling, his parents never knew whether he attended school or not. He was convinced that they did not care. They did not attend meetings with teachers and were not interested in how he was doing. With some amusement, Scott related a few incidents where concerned teachers tried to reach his parents through messages and through the mail but got no response. If he got sick while at school, there was nobody to call to pick him up, he said. Even as a very young kid, his parents expected him to get home on his own. They certainly did not prevent him from "practically living in the streets. They were both trying to survive," he said, "and the grandparents were useless." Again, Scott showed very little emotion and even smiled at these difficult memories of neglect, carelessness, and outright abuse. On the contrary, in his telling, he felt free to do what he wanted and as a result grew up fast to become an independent person. "His childhood," he often confidently asserted, "made him a stronger person."

In spite of all this, Scott was a very good student, who received a great deal of recognition from teachers. In effect, the positive attention from teachers and mentors became the center for any good feelings he developed about himself. His intelligence became his source of comfort, but it was also frequently a tool he directed to decimate and humiliate others. He needed to win all the arguments.

Scott started college at age 16 on a full scholarship. At that time, his parents divorced, and he never stayed with either one of them again. School dorms and then cheap rentals became his base. At 21, looking for a warm, consistent home, Scott married his girlfriend, and they soon had their first child, a daughter. During his years in law school and increasingly over the years, Scott was involved in a great number of affairs. Each time, however, although unhappy with his own marriage, he came back to his wife.

Inexplicably to him—although he really did not want to know why—his wife tolerated his affairs, and their younger daughter was born 4 years later. His wife's sense of betrayal and her anger and resentment toward him, however, grew and intensified with the years. The more successful she became in her job as a corporate administrator, the less tolerant she became of him. She often said that it was not only the affairs that alienated her from him, but the way he needed to control everybody. Witnessing the many tribulations and conflicts between their parents, the children took their mother's side and increasingly sought to distance themselves from him.

As therapy continued, some of Scott's greatest sources of pain began to take center stage. His perceived failures tormented him. How could he "only be a small-time attorney" when he had such an early promising academic life? How could he be such a mediocre lawyer when, against all odds, he overcame an abysmal background that few of his colleagues could even imagine? Why had he not achieved more professionally and financially? How was it that some less talented people had higher status and recognition and earned more? How was it that, at this late age, he found himself so alone and lacking friends? He was most upset that even his daughters kept their distance from him.

With time, Scott could no longer avoid the scarring reality of his childhood trauma. Although he still automatically raised objections to the possibility that his childhood had, in fact, been devastating to his emotional well-being and affected many of his choices and decisions, recurring dreams where he was chased, threatened, and mocked repeatedly surfaced. In a couple of his anxiety-suffused dreams he watched helplessly as he was killed or injured and left for dead. Paralleling his childhood experiences, his dreams placed him in situations where he was rejected, lost, frightened, doomed to fail, and even annihilated.

As we connected the very visible dots between past and present, Scott's internal struggles and interpersonal impasses also became clear. His chronic denigration of women, for example, or his tendency to cut people off when feeling slighted or dismissed, were examined in the context of his past. His perceived professional "underachievement" came to be understood as a repetition of an internal, very wounded self-state filled with the dread of rejection and overshadowed by persistent but unconscious threats. The automatic expectation of abuse and rejection were often projected onto other people, even when in reality they expressed no such intentions. But as Scott realized, "In order to save myself I needed to constantly be on guard and fight to the death." There was no in-between, he now says: "Either I win by being stronger than others or I become the abused, neglected, and helpless kid who is totally controlled by them. I can never let others be stronger and I can never allow myself be weaker."

The more we talked about his past, the more Scott came to realize that underneath his anger and dissatisfaction were his unusually painful childhood experiences. Deep fears for his very survival unconsciously permeated his developing ideas about himself and others. If he was not wanted by his mother, he would totally reject her as well. Inevitably "believing" his mother that he should not have been born, that he was a burden, had devastating effects. From early on, these repeated messages unconsciously informed his perceptions, feelings, thoughts, defenses, and behaviors. The ensuing profound sense of insecurity and self-loathing as well as early defenses that proved maladaptive in the long run shaped the actual trajectory of his life. In Scott's case, despite the prevalence of memories, he was utterly unaware of their many emotional effects. For many years, confronting and becoming aware of the pain that his childhood experiences embodied was literally too much to contemplate, let alone try.

But as we've seen, unconscious patterns based on traumatic childhood experiences still exert continual influence on all aspects of our personality. These unconscious self-states or patterns actively guide our feelings, thoughts, interpersonal relationships, dreams, and behaviors, allowing us to gain some sense of their pervasive power. Indeed, in spite of a promising path, this unacknowledged painful and anxious self-state unconsciously led to Scott's timid professional choices, troubled relationships with colleagues, and, most significantly, his unhappy marriage and rocky relationships with his daughters. Scott's abused and defensively rejecting relational pattern could not appreciate his wife's love and acceptance of him; repeating what he knew best, he could only relate to her and to his children by being entirely preoccupied with his own needs and unconscious drive for emotional survival. Doing what he wanted without considering others and the constant automatic tendency to control and always be right gave him a sense of being on top, of not being vulnerable under perceived threat. But of course, none of these unconscious ideations worked in his life.

As the strong links between childhood traumas and his adult behaviors became painfully clear, Scott expressed remorse and regret for the many "insults" he had directed toward his wife and the neglectful and dismissive behaviors toward his kids. He still felt like he tried to be a good father, different than his own was, but now saw that by unconsciously repeating his own childhood experiences he had little ability to maintain good, consistent relationships with them. It was important to me to fully show Scott how his traumatic childhood inevitably became part of what he learned and internalized about close relationships. Being rejected and neglected by people who were supposed to take of him was what he knew as a child. Without sufficient awareness of what havoc these early experiences produced within him, he often related to his wife and children in the only manner he knew.

As in many cases of childhood trauma, despite Scott's initial love and need for his wife and his welcoming response to her ability to take care of him, he was not able to regulate the negative state within himself. As in so many intimate relationships, Scott's traumatized self-state was frequently triggered by the countless disappointments, disagreements, and perceived rejection. The unconscious need to protect himself from any potential attack, real or imagined, caused quick and angry defensive reactions. Entirely out of his awareness, the aftermath of his early trauma became so consuming that he could not develop empathy for others. Although he saw himself as a "considerate and fair person," the learned state of being a victim of painful betrayal and cruelty led him to reject the love he had, look for new superficial connections, and entirely forget himself with excessive drinking.

Becoming more accepting of the emotional costs of his past freed Scott from being controlled by the destructive aspects of his childhood trauma. Scott embraced self-reflection and mindfulness when he realized how much they helped him modulate and eventually overcome his alcohol addiction. This was especially helpful in real time when he was feeling angry and anxious about his loneliness. The progress he made allowed him to be more open and truthful with his wife and grown-up children, and he successfully pursued a relationship with his grandchildren.

However, Scott's many complex feelings grounded in being a victim of abuse naturally did not leave him, and they proved themselves to be quite persistent and resistant to change. These feelings were frequently directed at me as well. At times, especially when angry and upset, Scott treated me the way he was treated as a child, expressing a self-state or pattern that was unconsciously convinced that the only way to survive was to protect himself, to fight back and win. When feeling attacked by a question, he belittled and dismissed me, reverting to the stereotype of a psychologist who only pretends to care about her patients, doing it only for the money. At those moments, I could feel the unarticulated depth of his anguish and his fears at being annihilated by an automatic perception of dismissal or indifference toward him. But as difficult as such interchanges were, they also provided great opportunities for increased awareness and change. In effect, in all therapeutic encounters, the ability to verbally process, to discuss and understand the meaning of such emotional exchanges, is one of the most valuable therapeutic processes we have. Emotional entanglements between therapists and patients (or enactments as they are called in the therapeutic literature) can illuminate unconscious patterns and tendencies in both patients and therapists (Ginot, 2009, 2015; Meroda, 2021).

Because of my genuine empathy for Scott's painful difficulties and my total acceptance of the devastating effects of his childhood traumas, I have been able to accept and relate to these interpersonal difficulties in a therapeutic way. I can point out to him how, at times, he does not see me as a person on his side but as an adversary. In effect, such behaviors are the unconscious manifestation of the wounds he himself suffered. The intersubjective process of transference–countertransference, as difficult as it has been at times, has allowed us to explore many more layers of Scott's emotional and behavioral patterns with others.

But the path to awareness and change was not smooth. Sometimes, a thoughtful Scott accepted all these realizations; other times, a rigid and overly defensive Scott rejected them, fighting with my observations. When I felt I could, I would deflect his resistance by joking with him. Mostly, though, I tried to engage him in discussing and exploring the two very different emotional and behavioral patterns within him: the considerate and even on occasion empathic Scott, and the easily angered, insulted, inconsiderate, and even ruthless Scott. The struggle toward greater integration and improved awareness and emotion regulation continues, but now we are both much more optimistic that with time and hard work, Scott's thoughtful and regulated states can increase in frequency and length.

....

WHAT TRAUMA TEACHES THE BRAIN/MIND/BODY

One of the most important functions of the human brain is to efficiently learn all it can from the environment (Tottenham, 2014, 2020). The brain's ability to learn and retain internal and external experiences is especially remarkable during early development. This neural plasticity, in essence neural reactions and changes in the brain in response to outside events, is particularly present in the fear system. Under the amygdala's influence, memory and learning networks encode severe fears and disruptions that trauma situations generate. In general, learning is associated with significant changes in the child's and adolescent's neurobiology—in the quickly forming neural circuits and the connections among them. But the most significant influences on early neural circuits are negative environmental events and ongoing stresses, often called early life adversity (Jovanovic & Ressler, 2010; McLaughlin et al., 2019; Milad & Quirk, 2012). Scott's story demonstrates the tragic and lifelong damage of negative environments and serious stress on children.

Post-traumatic stress disorder, in particular, is the consequence of a conditioned response to a traumatic event. An exposure to a traumatic event serves as the unconditioned stimulus, the basic event that triggers the innate system of fear and dread. But the trauma itself is not the only fear-arousing stimulus; in fact, many of the neutral aspects present at the time of the trauma (i.e., the conditioned stimuli) also acquire the neural ability to elicit fears and negative expectations. These learned fear associations are part of post-traumatic stress responses. Consequently, a wider range of learned associations to traumatic events becomes generalized to more benign situations, giving rise to frequent and recurrent PTSD.

In Scott's case, a whole swath of relational aspects became infected by his abusive relationships and became generalized to other relationships in his life. Convictions that those who are supposed to love will turn out to be cruel and indifferent; the inability to trust the other's good intentions, the ever-present fear and the need to defend against it, and much more. These learned, internalized unconscious beliefs made it difficult for Scott to trust feelings that people had for him, and defensively he did not even allow himself to surrender to them, especially with his wife and kids. Similarly, treating himself the way he was treated by his parents, and unconsciously harboring the same negative feelings toward himself, he could not make and execute the best decisions on his own behalf.

One does not need to encounter a precise reminder of a traumatic situation itself in order to be triggered; rather, a variety of associated stimuli invoke neuropsychological responses similar to the original trauma responses. For Scott, he saw threats where no threats existed. He acted in ways that protected his fragile and vulnerable sense of self from people who intended him no harm. Sadly, his triggers and self-protective mechanisms often produced the very relationship dynamics he feared, creating a lifetime of self-fulfilling prophecies about the "danger" posed by people who got close to him.

As a result of early emotional and physical abuse (e.g., neglect, deprivation, physical and sexual abuse, severe disruptions of attachment needs), what takes center stage in the child's brain/mind/body are those internalized destabilizing experiences and the many associations they generate. As these fear-related learned experiences, including PTSD, become dominant, they take over many of the processes involved in paying attention to, classifying, and encoding internal states and inbound stimuli. Consequently, much greater attention is focused on negative stimuli and trauma-related cues than on positive or rewarding signals in the environment. The skewing of these mechanisms leads to many emotional and interpersonal difficulties, including anxiety disorders, phobias, depression, tendencies to act out, impulsivity, and substance abuse (McLaughlin et al., 2019). As in Scott's case, a split can also occur between the trauma-related experiences and the unconscious defenses utilized against them (see Chapter 9).

A great deal of research has shown that childhood adversity can have long-term, harmful effects on mental health in adults. Not surprisingly, patients with a history of child abuse have significantly higher levels of hyperarousal, greater frequencies of comorbid disorders such as depression, and higher suicide risk. These adults have a greater prevalence of panic disorders, social anxieties, phobias such as agoraphobia, and psychotic symptoms. Finally, they also show a higher propensity for serious sleep disorders, nightmares, and substance abuse as a way to ameliorate states of distress. Many of these factors played out in Scott's life, repeatedly causing him anxiety, stress, and unhappiness as well as driving away the people he most desperately wanted to build relationships with.

TRAUMA HAS MANY FACES

But in spite of exposure to emotional and physical forms of victimization, and despite behavioral and interpersonal problems, many children do not meet the set criteria for a formal PTSD diagnosis. In response, notable figures in the field have expanded the definition of early relational trauma. Reviewing the research on the consequences of severe and chronic exposure to interpersonal violence and impaired primary relationships, these experts formulated the concept of developmental trauma disorder (D'Andrea et al., 2012; van der Kolk, 2005). This concept integrates the diverse forms of affective, behavioral, cognitive, relational, somatic, and self/identity dysregulation associated with early interpersonal trauma.

The concept of cumulative developmental trauma expands our picture of disrupted and impaired early attachment relationships. Such ongoing disruptions are particularly detrimental to the developing infant and child (Farina et al., 2019). These researchers emphasize the close, interpersonal nature of chronic impaired attachment experiences (Isobel et al., 2019). For example, hurtful, belittling, humiliating, shaming, and ultimately fear-producing interpersonal experiences refer to stressful and traumatic events that occur repeatedly and cumulatively over a period of time (Sar, 2011). Many forms of psychological trauma are known to develop interpersonally within important relationships, particularly familial ones (Farina et al., 2019; Liotti & Farina, 2016). In many cases, emotionally and physically traumatizing events are perpetrated by those who are expected to care for a child and protect them from pain, discomfort, and hurt (USDHHS, 2017). For this reason, cumulative developmental trauma is also seen as attachment trauma (Farina et al., 2019; Isobel et al., 2019). This is, in part, why Scott's early experiences were so devastating. The very people he depended on the most, his parents, failed to provide Scott with a safe, secure environment. On the contrary, throughout his young life, ongoing rejection and violence were constant ways of relating.

Trauma is not limited to overtly dysfunctional families like Scott's. People who work in this field estimate that potential attachment problems and their detrimental effects on children are more widespread than is currently being documented.

Despite the high prevalence of attachment problems, abuse and neglect may be masked in many apparently well-functioning families. Parallel to my clinical experience, researchers have found that the results of such interfamilial difficulties and conflicts can remain unexpressed until the onset of a disorder in adulthood. For this reason, childhood relational cumulative trauma may be called a "hidden epidemic" (Lanius et al., 2005). Among the more prevalent problems are traumatic attachments, which can take many forms and intensities, eventually interfering in one's ability to pursue meaningful and fulfilling relationships in adulthood.

Children have great vulnerability to misattunement; thus, unhealthy environments can result from a wide range of negative emotional, physically hurtful, and rejecting parental attitudes. When parents are exceedingly harsh, critical, dismissive, or belittling, or when they use physical force as a disciplinary tool, even in the absence of severe neglect and outright abuse, a child may feel utterly unprotected and unseen. Their growing personality patterns will be shaped and burdened by implicit and explicit memories of pressure to submit to authority, by critical, anxiety-inducing expectations, or by chaotic households that have no boundaries. In response, children will form learning pathways that emphasize negative expectations, rebellious and oppositional tendencies, and unsatisfactory attachments (Farina et al., 2019; Isobel et al., 2019). It is significant that recent findings in the field of child development demonstrate that chronic relational traumas are as damaging to mental health and relationship outcomes as sudden and acute traumatic events that are not related to the child's relational ties (Anders et al., 2012; Şar, 2017).

As Scott's therapy continued, he became able to directly experience the pain connected to the profound rejection and fearful existence of his past. The neutralized, distanced memories were still there, but along with them came more alive feelings connected to these experiences. Later still, he was able to reflect on his negative feeling states while they were happening.

Interestingly, other adults who grow up in seemingly good or normal families may find the roots of their anxieties, fears, and dysregulated behaviors more difficult to access. But as we keep being reminded, other much more benign ways of relating and being with one's child can be injurious as well.

Finally, it is important to note that, as a result of such observations, cumulative relational traumatization in the early years of life has been differentiated from acute stressful and traumatic events such as extreme domestic violence; war, refugee, and immigrant experiences; acute illness; divorce; or single calamitous events such as the death of a parent (Courtois, 2004; Herman, 1992; van der Kolk & McFarlane, 1996). Similarly, findings underscore the importance of differentiating between childhood maltreatment and relational conflicts and difficulties due to family dysfunction. Some researchers have emphasized the role of intergenerational transmission of trauma within families. In effect, throughout this book we see how such intersubjective processes provide a continuous source for children's internalized fears and vulnerabilities. Such findings stress the importance of understanding the discrete forms and pathways of transmission of psychological trauma between individuals, including transgenerationally within families (Atzl et al., 2019).

ADULT-ONSET PTSD

Adult-onset PTSD patients with a history of childhood abuse and trauma often have more severe clinical symptoms, higher rates of treatment resistance, and poorer outcomes following psychotherapy. Other reactions may be entirely internal, resulting in emotional and social withdrawal (Böthe et al., 2020; Gekker et al., 2018). In a recent study, the sense of alienation in adults who experienced abuse mediated the relationships between childhood trauma and later life difficulties (Mitchell et al., 2020). These feelings of alienation, disconnection, and loneliness are some of the anxiety-suffused feeling states common to the aftermath of early trauma. For Scott, persistent alienation and loneliness were themes in our therapy sessions. He felt like he did not belong in almost any group he was part of. Defensively, he looked down on "joiners," people who liked to spend a great deal of time with others.

Epidemiologic research has focused on early trauma as one of the risk factors for adult-onset PTSD. The earlier a trauma takes place, the greater the risk for PTSD. Thus, PTSD in adults may represent an ongoing symptomatic reaction to childhood abuse and adversities; more importantly, post-traumatic symptoms can appear a long time after the original events. Such delayed responses can sometimes be triggered by a subsequent trauma later in life (Gekker et al., 2018; McLaughlin et al., 2019).

Some Neuropsychological Considerations
Some of the neuropsychological hallmarks of PTSD are the amygdala's hyperresponsiveness to fearful cues, its exaggerated fear responses, and the emotional

arousal they generate. As we saw before, the fears detected and generated by the amygdala extend to other important brain regions and functions. The memory circuit is among them. Research with animals and humans has shown that exposure to early stress causes abnormalities in the neural structures and functions of the hippocampus. Such neural changes are associated with problems accentuating the pain of trauma in one's autobiographical memories. The resulting stronger interconnectivity between the amygdala and hippocampus affects what memories we encode, consolidate, and eventually retrieve. As the intense fearful aspects linked to trauma may lead to greater memory intensity, this increased connectivity between the amygdala and hippocampus may store and maintain negative autobiographical memory at the expense of positive experiences. This is evident among quite a few individuals who were exposed to the many variations of trauma. Clients, as well as others, seem to display a higher proportion of negative memories with very few positive ones. It may be that this reflects the reality of their childhood; but often, even when they know things were not all bad, they cannot come up with nice or comforting memories.

An MRI study conducted with adolescent girls diagnosed with PTSD due to sexual abuse showed a bilateral decrease in volumes of the amygdala, anterior cingulate, and hippocampus, and diminished thickness of the prefrontal cortex compared to healthy controls. Even among a nonclinical population of people with early attachment trauma, there was a deceased neural volume in the prefrontal-limbic regions, such as the hippocampus, the anterior cingulate cortex, and the medial prefrontal cortex. Long-term effects of acute stress on the prefrontal-limbic system were seen in healthy adults as well. These studies indicate how vulnerable to stress these interconnected circuits are. As the volume of amygdala and prefrontal cortex areas decreases and their interconnectedness increases, both structural and functional changes result from trauma and prolonged stress (María-Ríos & Morrow, 2020; Li et al., 2017). We may remember less, but what we do remember is suffused with fear and other emotional injuries.

Indeed, as we see in clinical practice, people's reactions to early traumatic experiences vary in their nature and strength. Some people with a history of early trauma may display real difficulties in retrieving memories from their childhood. They feel as if much of what they experienced has been literally wiped out and is entirely inaccessible. Typically, the memories that do come up as therapy advances reflect and embody the most painful and fearful aspects of their childhood.

Conversely, another group of patients may tend to defend against the emotional impact of such memories. They remember traumatic events and past experiences and yet, as they recall them, these memories are not seen as part of an emotionally or physically abusive childhood. In these cases, parents may be idealized or held blameless. Most often unconsciously, the painful lessons from traumatic relationships are explained away or turned against the self in hate, blaming oneself for the pain and interpreting it as a personal failure.

While Scott did not idealize his parents or hold them blameless, he also did not see his childhood as abusive. Rather than fully acknowledging the horrendous level of neglect, verbal abuse, and physical violence, he contextualized various events as part of the story of his traumatized, victimized childhood. While Scott could retell stories from his past, it was only through therapy that he began to access the pain and fear associated with these stories.

Many researchers believe that one of the reasons for the severity and complexity of post-traumatic responses is linked to the brain/mind dissociative processes. In response to traumatic attachment relationships with caregivers during the early years of life, children unconsciously develop coping mechanisms that keep them psychologically removed from the dreaded pain of past or still ongoing traumas (Farina & Imperatori, 2017). For Scott, his own abusive behaviors made it hard for others to connect with him, unconsciously keeping him safe from being hurt by others and from the disappointment of unmet expectations in his adult relationships. However, at a conscious level, Scott was painfully aware of his loneliness and isolation from others and actually worked hard to change this entrenched pattern.

We have now set the appropriate context for the next chapter, which deals with children's vulnerabilities to a wide range of unsettling, hurtful, and anxiety-inducing interactions with their caregivers. Consistent with the general theme of this book, even in the absence of clear situations of abuse and neglect or severe family dysfunction, many situations may be interpreted by children as anxiety inducing and emotionally taxing.

As we remember, the qualities of the relationships between children and their parents are determined by the interacting forces between innate dispositions, the nature of the intersubjective interactions and unconscious tendencies, or traits that get enacted out of awareness. Even when we consider the effects of temperament on a child's vulnerability to how parents relate to them, children are still influenced by the caretakers they love, depend on, adore, and idealize. Exploring how these interfamilial forces shape children continues in the following chapters.

CHAPTER EIGHT

Inevitable Fear and Anxiety: Normative Early Life Stress

At first glance, the effects of daily normative stresses on growing children may pale in comparison to the severe damage that arises from any form of abuse. Severe early-life stressors play an important role in elevating the risks in adolescence and adulthood for anxiety, depression, compromised emotional regulation, addiction disorders, and PTSD (Lebow & Chen, 2016). Indeed, the enduring and often debilitating consequences of sexual, physical, and emotional abuse are fully recognized and documented in the research literature. However, we increasingly understand the ease and speed with which the fear system perceives, reacts to, and processes threats; this makes it equally important to explore the effects of normative stresses.

Therefore, this chapter examines the many facets and nuances of early stress on infants, children, and adolescents. The increasing number of fMRI studies showing actual changes in the fear circuitry in response to a wide range of stimuli is expanding our definition of what may represent trauma; innate reactions to being exposed to stressful but still normative situations exist on a continuum of adversity. In effect, daily, stress-inducing events, especially with caregivers and later with peers, give rise to and shape patterns of anxious self-doubt and vulnerability. Understanding how influential these early processes are is important for a few reasons. First, realizing the many psychological forces that affect us as children can help us accept our vulnerabilities without self-recrimination, self-blame, or shame. Second, a clearer picture of how negative patterns are created and persist, especially in the context of the interactions between temperament and caregivers' behaviors, will increase our acceptance of human complexity and even flaws. This new lens can greatly improve therapeutic approaches. In particular, a new understanding of the role of everyday fear and anxiety in our psychic lives strengthens the importance of developing mindful awareness.

A third point may seem paradoxical, but such understanding should increase our empathy toward parenting in general and our own parents in particular. As we better recognize how sensitive our fear system is and how we tend to hold on to negative memories and perceived threats where they do not exist, we can appreciate the inevitable frustrations between parents and children. My intent here is not to take parents off the hook but rather to focus on the inevitable mishaps embedded in every family dynamic: misplaced impatience; frequent parental fighting; hostile divorces; emotional and interpersonal insensitivities; lack of awareness among parents of their own unconscious patterns; and parents who tend to be anxious, depressed, controlling, critical, or self-absorbed, to name a few. Significantly, depression or excessive anxiety compromise the attuned synchronicity between parents and their infants and often cause a host of internal problems among children and teenagers. Often kids exposed to such parental difficulties develop acute anxiety about abandoning the suffering parent whom they feel responsible for (Abraham et al., 2020; and others). Special situations and stressors, such as the COVID-19 pandemic, are important as well; this is discussed in Chapter 12.

Fourth, parents' heightened stress due to difficult circumstances such as poverty, unstable living situations, racial discrimination, and incidents of household violence affect children very negatively. Keeping in mind that the brain's primary purpose is to learn about the environment, and that this learning is greatly influenced by the amygdala, we can state that each one of these parental behaviors and situational difficulties can result in the development of vulnerable, anxious, and self-blaming patterns in children. In effect, we have seen in Jerry's and Scott's cases, for example, how immigration enhances parents' anxiety and creates relational instability. As these factors interact with the parents' own psychological histories, they may exacerbate existing interpersonal and internal difficulties. Such destabilizing factors as immigration and financial worries may have contributed to their parents' inability to provide both Scott and Jerry more attuned caretaking.

Fifth, and finally, understanding the great vulnerability of a child's growing brain may actually help parents become more mindful about the power of their words and actions. Recognizing their emotional stamp on the child's actual implicit memories, and the unknown meaning that the child gives to upsetting interactions, can motivate parents to employ both more effective emotional regulation and more mindful ways of interacting. Obviously, in our very human world, all parents make mistakes; parents, like all human beings, have no choice but to express their personalities. Parents carry their past with them and, like all humans, succumb to personal and environmental pressures. Nevertheless, we cannot underestimate the power of mindfulness and its relationship to greater empathy toward a child. This empathy for what children may experience and accepting their need to develop their own tendencies can place both parents and children in a less painful and negative dynamic.

EARLY LIFE ADVERSITIES AND THEIR EFFECTS

The terms *childhood adversity* or *early life stress* refer to negative environmental experiences that represent a deviation from the expected environment. In infancy and childhood, innate expectations for safety, empathic attunement, and emotional and physical comfort may occasionally be thwarted or even negated (McLaughlin, 2016). Remember here that even very young infants can differentiate between emotions conveyed in facial expressions; from early on they show an innate sensitivity to fearful and angry faces. When presented with negative expressions, infants tend to focus on them longer than on neutral expressions (see Chapter 3). A lack of mutual gaze, an absence of an empathic vocal and physical attunement, can create states of a generalized hyperarousal and discomfort, and consequently teach the brain/mind to expect negative experiences.

Childhood Adversity and Its Impacts

When innate expectations for safety and attunement are negated, such situations may elicit emotionally and physiologically based experiences of threat to the child's comfort or psychological needs. Although such perceptions may span a wide range of sensations, they still represent a disturbance of the physical and emotional homeostasis or well-being (McLaughlin et al., 2019).

There are many forms of childhood adversity; population-based studies in the United States show that approximately half of all children experience at least one form of adversity by the time they reach adulthood (McLaughlin et al., 2019). Some researchers conceptualize adversity as events that involve multiple underlying dimensions of experience; others see adversity as specifically organized around two experiences: forms or expressions of threat toward the child and the many possible layers of emotional deprivation or neglect (Callaghan et al., 2019; McGrath et al., 2017; McLaughlin & Sheridan, 2016). What this chapter seeks to highlight, however, are the anxiety-inducing and injurious aspects of inevitable everyday emotional hardships within one's family and outside it. Chapter 9, for example, expands the discussion to examine the effects of exposure to violent social media and the internet.

Emotion Regulation

The body of research that shows how early repeated frustrations and hurt damage our ability to emotionally self-regulate is robust. However, like most aspects of our personality, there is a continuum for both early adversity and the degree and type of emotion regulation it generates. At this point, it is impossible to pinpoint the exact degree and nature of adversity necessary to create difficulties in emotion regulation. This is especially true in light of the numerous studies that have focused on resilience and the presence of well-functioning adults among people who experienced early adversity.

However, our internal unconscious and conscious states alike do not follow any easy categories or diagnostic labels. Most often and within most of us, different emotional and behavioral patterns coexist and when enacted express different levels of contentment and joy but also anxiety, worry, and despair. Anecdotally, we can identify, in patients and ourselves, those moments and phases during which we seem to sink into and drown in anxious, self-doubting, or worried internal states. The greatest challenges come when confronting anxiety-inducing triggers that remind us of old hurts and lack of understanding from those we depended on. While in the midst of a dysregulating state, without modulation or a calming internal monologue, we are utterly convinced of the veracity of what our negative feelings imply about who we are and how much to trust others around us.

With varying degrees of success, effective emotional regulation results in reactions that are more measured and automatically slowed down. It is important to remember that, for most of us, these experiences are transitory. This is often the case even among people who suffer from pronounced difficulties in emotional regulation. What is behind a wide range of negative experiences during our adulthood in essence reflects the susceptibility of our brain/mind/bodies during development. From infancy to young adulthood, brain circuits exquisitely sensitive to fear and anxiety spread out and educate all other mental and behavioral systems (Tottenham, 2020; Tottenham & Gabard-Durnham, 2017).

Neuropsychological Factors

As the body of developmental neuroscience continues to grow, we are learning more about the reactivity of the fear system, which is compelling in its specificity and consistency. Numerous findings have demonstrated how susceptible some brain regions are to adverse stimuli during our early years. Increasingly precise fMRI has helped to identify neural networks that link early adversity with the activation of the hyperarousing hypothalamic–pituitary–adrenal (HPA) axis as a precursor to compromised regulation and the hyperactivation of the amygdala circuity (Tottenham, 2014, 2020; Tottenham et al., 2011).

The brain's plasticity during the first years of life renders it vulnerable to more commonplace and moderate-level stressors as well. The first year of life, especially the beginning of the second half of the first year, is a unique period for the development of fear. This period is typically characterized by a developmentally appropriate rise in fear, as infants increasingly engage and interact with their caretakers and their environment (Leppänen & Nelson, 2012). For example, in one study, 5-month-old infants who had witnessed verbal anger directed against their mothers displayed changes in their parasympathetic system, the part of the autonomic nervous system that mediates physiological calm. Following a witnessed angry scene involving their mother, infants reacted with visible frustration and stressful interactions with their mothers. Following these difficult interactions, the infant took longer to calm down (Moore, 2009). These results clearly indicate that infants as young as 5 months experience physiological stress and a reduction in the calming protection that the vagal nerve provides in reaction to fear-inducing situations (Moore, 2009).

Sources of Vulnerability

We need to acknowledge, first, that there are no perfect emotional and social conditions into which a child is born. We all are raised by humans, who may feel deep love and caring but who also inevitably enact their more problematic personality traits within any relationship. In addition, there is no human group more complex and nuanced than the human family in all its forms. It is important to note here that *family* has many expressions: the traditional nuclear family, extended families, single-parent families, blended families, nonparental relatives raising children, adoptive families, foster families, and multifamily living, to name a few.

The complexity of the human family is far from surprising. Even in the context of intimate relationships, where strong attachment ties are typically present, parents unavoidably express and project unconscious patterns that reveal conflicting feelings, anxious emotional states, vulnerabilities, rigid or controlling behaviors, and dysfunctional belief systems. Going back to Chapter 1 of this book, you may remember the tendency of such mostly unconscious patterns to be triggered and enacted in our relationships to ourselves and others.

A parent's unconscious patterns—resulting from their own childhood experiences, perceptions, expectations, memories, and beliefs—are not exempt from influencing their interactions with their children and with their partners. From infancy on, the many relational and attachment styles that parents possess are enacted within the family system. For example, we previously saw the harmful effects of parental depression on the emotional and physiological synchronicity between parents and children (Abraham et al., 2020). But depressed and anxious moods come in many nuanced forms and expressions. The following sections of this chapter examine some of these patterns and their influence on infants and children.

For example, in utero, a mother's stress during pregnancy affects the intrauterine environment in ways that can have lasting consequences on the developing fetus. Disharmonious family dynamics often elevate a mother's stress levels. This is a particular risk when there is excessive fighting, hostile disagreements, and unacknowledged anxieties surrounding the birth of the baby and reorganization of the family. Elevated stress levels are associated with an increase in cortisol production, changes in placental enzymes, and a less effective maternal immune system. All these physiological changes may affect the HPA function of the fetus, thus determining the trajectory of their emotional well-being even before they are born (Leerkes & Bailes, 2019). More specifically, elevated maternal cortisol levels predict poorer emotional regulation for infants at 6 months (Bolten et al., 2013). Prenatal maternal depression has also been linked to later emotional dysregulation and increased disorganized attachment (Hayes et al., 2013).

With the baby's birth and the child's early development, new stresses can interfere with parental emotional and relational functioning. Compromised parental emotion regulation, such as shifting moods, unpredictable behaviors, and emotional outbursts are linked to less sensitive attunement and to increased instability and anxiety among children. More prevalent during infancy, perhaps, are hurried or distracted caregivers who do not provide the needed sustained, comforting, and therefore regulating touch when it's most needed (see Chapter 6). Obviously, all these regulating behaviors vary tremendously within any adult–infant dyad and are greatly affected by life circumstances such as working parents, siblings that still need their parent, and the many tasks and worries involved in keeping the family going. It's very important to accept that instances of misattunement are inevitable and likely more prevalent than we realize. However, knowing the power of touch, mutual gaze, and vocalization, caregivers can attempt to pay attention and find ways to help babies regulate their fussy, agitated, and hyperaroused states (Schore, 2012). Parental anger especially is associated with harsh discipline and overly controlling attitudes. Children exposed to angry outbursts tend to develop a couple of internal unconscious patterns. On the one hand, they become fearful and learn to expect anger and disapproval from others. But they also unconsciously encode, learn, and internalize dysregulated anger as a mode of interpersonal behavior. At times, unless they become aware of this pattern, they may unconsciously repeat it in their adult relationships and with their own children. Some researchers have found that erratic parental behaviors are associated with unhealthy attachment patterns, such as disorganized attachment (Leerkes & Bailes, 2019; Lyons-Ruth & Jacobvits, 2016). And interestingly, often parents' attempts to control their children's behaviors in order to instill emotion regulation and self-discipline were actually linked to a decreased ability among their children to regulate their behavior and feel autonomous and independent (Thijssen et al., 2017).

WHAT WE MAY MEAN WHEN WE CONSIDER PSYCHOPATHOLOGY

While the question of what might constitute psychopathology is extremely relevant, it is not often answered in the detail it deserves. In many studies, parents, primarily mothers, are diagnosed as suffering from depression or anxiety. While these are important categories to consider, they are often insufficient to describe the myriad and ongoing characteristics of interactions

between a parent's personality patterns and their child's needs and temperament. Furthermore, as individuals, we experience these common states of
depression and anxiety in uniquely subjective ways. Some of us experience
chronic but "light" difficult feelings, while others only have periodic "dips."
Some of us are not even aware that, as parents, we carry and enact our own
parents' anxious or depressed attitudes; we don't understand the consequences
of our own parents' relational and attachment styles. As we saw, children's
ability to unconsciously connect to their parents' internal emotional states,
identify with them, and imitate them only emphasizes the many opportunities
for the transmission of a wide range of both injurious behaviors and anxiety-
riddled states. This is especially so when the children themselves have anxious
temperaments (Kagan, 1998).

Such detailed, rich, and nuanced pictures of our early environment often
emerge during psychotherapy; this is a place where we can reconstruct our
experiences and consider how they may have affected us. Both the negative and
the positive aspects of our relationships with our parents, and later with peers,
create a fuller picture of what helped shape our unconscious and conscious patterns. What seems to be part of almost all our childhood stories are anxious
feelings and worries that result from a wide range of intersubjective experiences
with parents who were resentful, controlling, or needy; overprotective or not
involved enough; or who sent nonverbal messages to us as young children that we
should not internally separate and define our own individuality.

A parent's personality traits, especially those that raise the infant's and
child's fear and anxiety, find many ways of expression. Parental personality
traits can be expressed directly through verbal communication, behaviors,
and many types of emotionally loaded actions. They can also be expressed
insidiously and nonverbally, through implicit communication. For example,
when anxious parents verbally express their fear, even if they do not direct
such expressions at their children, they will still raise the child's anxiety level,
just as in Ian's case growing up. Furthermore, such messages will be unconsciously remembered and learned as a way of seeing life's challenges. Even
without explicit expressions of fear, a parent's behaviors and attitudes toward
potentially fearful or challenging situations are unconsciously internalized by
the child. The mirror neuron system, neurons that resonate with other people's emotions, underpin such emotional contagion. This has the potential of
teaching the child's amygdala to pay more attention to and perceive vague or

neutral situations as threat-inducing (Todd et al., 2011, 2020). Finding such anxiety-inducing threats even in neutral situations starts a vicious cycle that may greatly affect one's self-confidence.

As we have seen before, parental facial expressions constitute an incredibly important guide as to how to feel or react (Hatfield et al., 1994). Even a parent's physiological dysregulation during upsetting situations may contribute to infants' and children's physiological dysregulation (Feldman, 2007; Leerkes & Bailes, 2019). With repeated experiences, such automatic and largely unconscious reactions on the part of parents will undermine their children's ability to develop effective emotional regulation. Similarly, parents' facial expressions in response to stressful situations may raise their infants' and children's cortisol levels (Laurent et al., 2013).

SIBLING RELATIONSHIPS

In addition to interactions between parents and children, with the many opportunities for raised anxiety, sibling relationships also play a role in a child's emotional development. How parents prepare an older child for a younger sibling's arrival and how much empathy they express for their older child is essential for the older sibling's well-being. Especially important, of course, is attending to the older child's potential anxiety regarding changes in the family structure. A sensitive and attentive approach in this situation may modulate the older child's excessive worries about the loss of parental love once the new baby is born. Although this is one external circumstance where some anxiety on the part of the older child is inevitable, the parents' attitude can influence which narratives the child may develop about their apparently diminished importance in the family, thus affecting their attitude toward the younger sibling.

Another important yet underappreciated source of potential anxiety at home is the nature of sibling relationships themselves. Again, based on quite a few patients' life histories, it seems to me that the contributions of these important relationships during childhood and beyond are not considered enough in our psychodynamic models. At times, these early relationships are so suffused with jealousy, hostility, and physical violence that one sibling or more experience daily stress. As I have often witnessed, when sibling relationships are hostile, one of the siblings (typically the older one) wields power over a more timid, obedient, and therefore vulnerable sibling.

Such older siblings may become controlling, extremely demeaning, and aggressive; sometimes solving conflicts with physical violence. In my psychotherapy practice, adult clients who were victims of hostile siblings still carry the emotional scars of this relationship. Often, under a demeaning and critical older sibling, they develop an unshakable belief in their own inferiority and flaws. As young children, they had no choice but to believe an older sibling whom they idolized. As a result, they often carry into other relationships the fears instilled by their sibling and the negative narratives about their own shortcomings, victimhood, and helplessness.

The internalized and distorted narratives that injured siblings develop is made worse when accompanied by a perception that a parent or parents were not there to protect them. In my experience, it is not unusual for parents to remove themselves from sibling conflicts, even severe ones. In some ways, the failure to intervene and ultimately the failure to protect the vulnerable sibling reflects some failure to recognize each child's unique personality. Parents may not take seriously enough the victimized child's complaints and dismiss the victimizer's repeated offenses; in general, they may not be sensitive enough to what is going on. A parent's motivation may be rooted in looking at their kids through the same lens, and not appreciating enough the enormous power that one sibling may have over another. In Chapter 10, we clearly see the results of such family dynamics on the development of Roger's narcissistic personality traits.

The overall quality of sibling relationships greatly depends on the ongoing family dynamics, especially the parents' empathic understanding of each child's individuality, including their innate temperament. Furthermore, the quality of attachment between mothers and older siblings can determine how the older child welcomes a new sibling. For example, from ages 1 to 5 years, children who had an insecure attachment to their mothers displayed greater difficulties in relating to a new sibling; a jealous pattern of relating may become entrenched. Similar difficulties were seen in children whose parents frequently fought (Volling et al., 2017). Siblings whose relationships were characterized by hostile aggression showed greater behavioral difficulties in childhood (Tucker et al., 2013). Finally, increased overt sibling hostility and aggression were linked to elevated levels of depression and poor emotional regulation among the offending siblings (Whiteman et al., 2015). In general, positive sibling relationships were associated with positive developmental trajectories into adulthood, including greater capacity for emotional regulation, attachment, and compromise (Leerkes & Bailes, 2019).

Obviously, parents cannot monitor and regulate every sibling interaction. They can, however, be more aware of their children's relationships and vigilant for unhealthy patterns. They may have to take more proactive supervision and action when necessary. In this way, parents set the foundation for healthy sibling and family dynamics that benefit all members of the household. Furthermore, this provides children with healthy models for adult behaviors that they can carry into their own adult relationships.

INTERPARENTAL CONFLICTS

The quality of the parents' relationship as partners seems to be a central factor that may raise a child's anxiety levels and heighten reactions to stress later in life. Between 6 and 14 months of age, babies become highly disturbed by interparental conflicts, paying more attention to negative emotions and displaying less play-like behavior (DuRocher Schudlich et al., 2011). Interparental conflicts undermine an infant's capacity to develop adaptive and effective emotion regulation. More severe interparental conflicts can result in greater emotional reactivity. As we see in Jerry's case, temperamentally anxious and reactive infants and children seem to be especially vulnerable to conflicts and hostile verbal exchanges in their environment (Mammen et al., 2017).

Such distressing and anxiety-inducing events result in actual physiological changes in infants and children. Higher cortisol levels and greater reactivity were found in infants, toddlers, and children exposed to loud and aggressive conflicts; as predicted, less anxious children displayed less cortisol reactivity and greater vagal nerve recovery. Conversely, toddlers who were exposed to positive interparental interactions showed calmer and more adaptive behaviors (Leerkes & Bailes, 2019). What happens, then, when young children are frequently exposed to hostile interparental conflicts? Again, we have to look to the amygdala as the mediator between a distressing environment and fearful reactions.

In a series of interesting longitudinal studies, the effects of what may be considered a common stressor within families—interparental conflicts and arguments during an infant's first year of life—were examined (Graham et al., 2013, 2015). Researchers measured the fear reactions and cognitive development of 48 six-month-old infants. Both the level of interparental fighting and the infant's general level of emotional reactivity were reported by the mothers. In general, fighting between caregivers was associated with changes in the level of stress hormones among young children, resulting in heightened emotional reactivity and behavioral and social difficulties as reported by their mothers (Graham et al., 2013).

The infants' connections between the amygdala and other circuits were also measured while the infants were at rest, and then compared to the circuits' activity following interparental arguments at home. Those neural changes in interconnectivity were recorded while the babies were asleep. Sophisticated fMRI data revealed increased functional amygdala connections with several regions of the brain including the insula, ventral striatum, and prefrontal regions. The observed connections were associated with higher fear responses. Additionally, higher levels of interparental conflicts were associated with greater neural reactivity in response to the angry voices. This reaction was seen in neural circuits that are involved in threat detection, learning, and emotional regulation.

These results provide empirical evidence for an association between early life stressors and their enduring effects on emotional overreactivity. Specifically, a common and understandable form of familial stress—nonphysical interparental conflict—is relevant for the infant's functional brain organization during the first year of life. Early exposure to common and moderate forms of familial stress contributed to observed changes in brain circuits related to fear and emotional regulation. These changes were seen by six months of age and persisted throughout the first year of life. We may wish to believe that infants and children are not capable of retaining the neuropsychological effects of upsetting events around them. But such findings suggest that disturbing emotional conflicts can elicit states of lasting hyperarousal and fear. Furthermore, when we consider the effects of such fearful hyperarousal on other brain circuits, we can appreciate the subtle but enduring effects on our developing personalities.

In this context, of course, the effects of divorce or separation may be lasting as well. Even when divorce seems the only way to reduce the levels of hostile and vocal fights, how parents separate and what they tell their children may provide an important buffer against the trauma of the breakup of the family unit. As in all cases, the adults' narratives about the reasons for a separation and how it will affect the child's life in the future are important aspects of communication. Empathy for the children's helplessness and lack of say is important as well. Parents often try to emphasize that the divorce has nothing to do with the children themselves, which is actually the truth of the matter. However, as we know now, as anxieties increase, so do distorted and child-centered interpretations of the difficult situation. In spite of the adults' proclamations, children may still blame themselves. Attentiveness to what a child may perceive or think needs to continue for a long time after children first learn about the divorce. In particular, a parent's repeated reassurance and reality-bound perspective about what a divorce really means or does not mean to the child is essential.

Within this context, I would like to discuss another somewhat common familial experience that may increase children's experience of anxiety and foster negative expectations of others and distorted narratives about relationships. At times, within complex family dynamics, one parent or both are excessively angry at one child, singling them out for more reproach and criticism. But the directly criticized or frequently yelled-at child is not the only one that is negatively affected. The other siblings who witness their brother's or sister's emotional states often are influenced as well. Through their mirror neuron system and their ability to internally identify with and sense their sibling's internal upheaval, other children may react as if they are criticized or belittled as well.

In addition, although it is not directed at all children, watching a parent's punitive behavior toward one designated child raises a child's anxiety about their own possible punishment. Indeed, patients who were exposed to such parental behaviors develop a wide range of potentially harmful narratives about what such behaviors mean to them. Some unconsciously decide that they have to put all their energies into avoiding incurring their caregivers' anger. The organizing emotion of avoiding a parent's anger continues to shape their timidity and consciousness toward others. As adults, such an unconscious motivation can seriously curtail a young adult's search for their own individuality and sense of agency. Other children may internalize such behaviors as a condoned and acceptable model of behaviors toward another who may be more vulnerable or who may struggle a bit more with daily tasks or school. At the same time, witnessing a parent belittle a child they are supposed to love and accept increases the other siblings' mistrust in what love actually means on emotional and behavioral levels. As young children cannot fully understand their caregivers' traits as a reflection of their own limitations and as separate from the kids' internal states (see Chapter 2), such behaviors hurt all children in the family.

WHAT THE BRAIN/MIND LEARNS

As we've seen, early life stress often accelerates the amygdala's development. Additionally, such stresses inhibit the development of more adaptive functional interactions through the ventral striatum—part of the basal ganglia significantly involved in habit forming and learning. Under the amygdala's influence, negative experiences quickly gain prominence; although the amygdala's ability to assess and react to positive values and valence of incoming stimuli may remain intact, the communication of these signals to the ventral striatum can become disrupted. In this case, what the ventral striatum encodes is greater negative learning and expectations (Fareri & Tottenham, 2016).

Such biases that facilitate threat identification over positive reward can interfere with other aspects of information processing. For example, children who have experienced violence exhibit difficulties remembering more neutral information in the presence of threat cues (Lambert et al., 2017). This may contribute to later difficulties by making it harder to discriminate between safe and dangerous environments. Significantly, this leads to the experience of fear even in safe contexts as the result of internally triggered signals of negative predictions and expectations. In addition, such biases in threat-related information processing are associated with a higher risk for anxiety and PTSD later in life (Briggs-Gowan et al., 2016; Shackman et al., 2007).

This observed decrease in reward response in individuals with a history of early life stress often emerges in adolescence in the form of blunted perceptions of cues that predict rewards (Callaghan et al., 2019). The implication that early life stresses reduce the recognition of reward cues but increase expectations for negative ones speaks to the crucial emotional context within which learning about the world occurs. Even occasional misattuned experiences that upset an infant's or child's homeostasis, or sense of consistent well-being, may train the amygdala and the basal ganglia about the primacy of negative expectations.

Such studies and clinical explorations of the roots of vulnerabilities and defenses further confirmed the amygdala's role as the neural bridge between environmental stressors and emotional development. In particular, the changed connectivity between the amygdala and the default mode network were associated with heightened sensitivity to perceived environmental threats. Remembering that the areas constituting the DMN are part of the prefrontal cortex, we can again see that early fear-inducing stressors inevitably influence cognitive thought processes. Specifically, as we grow, the DMN system progressively engages in a variety of thoughts, internal monologues, and the active rehearsal of autobiographical memories. Ultimately, these intertwined emotions and thoughts become a part of our narratives and sense of self. In effect, when listening to how people express their internal and often exaggerated anxieties, one can hear the voice of a small child who developed a web of distorted fearful perceptions, expectations, and interpretations.

We cannot overestimate the effects of genetic predispositions and an environment that can cause the activation of fear- and anxiety-related genes. As we have seen in previous chapters, negative experiences can give expression to genes that give rise to an overactive amygdala, more defensive behaviors guided by the amygdala, and compromised emotion regulation. As parents, we need to remember that an infant's reactions to frightening emotional stimuli may be influenced by their temperament. Children with a fearful tendency who already possess an overreactive amygdala will tend to react with more intense levels of fear and display higher levels of neural changes. This important understanding does not change the potential harm that a negative emotional environment can create for a child's growing brain/mind. However, if parents are particularly mindful of their inevitable influence, they may become aware of their child's vulnerable tendencies and difficulties in calming down.

In addition, as we'll see in Chapter 9, a great deal of children's development is determined by unconscious learning and identification with parental figures. In effect, through the mirror neuron system and the messages it sends to the amygdala, a child's internal state inevitably reverberates with the overly emotional states of parents. This lays the groundwork for a learning process that teaches the brain to acquire patterns of hyperaroused neural responses.

EARLY LIFE ADVERSITY IN THE CONTEXT OF LOVE AND CARING

We have learned that parents' personalities, unconscious patterns and quirks, human flaws, and the lessons that they learned in their own childhoods affect the children they raise. Throughout the previous chapters and in discussing my various client cases, we have explored many forms of parental misattunement, carelessness, and behavior that lacks empathy. However, what I have learned from working with many patients over the years is that a person's past and their ensuing psychodynamics combine to create an extremely complex human picture. I have come to believe that, most often, negative parental behaviors do not represent the overall love and caring feelings parents have for their child. Rather, I have come to believe that in many cases parents try to do their best; but they unconsciously act on what they learn and know. In these cases, parents' love and caring can easily be overshadowed by weak emotion regulation, impulsive behavior, or unconscious demanding, controlling, and narcissistic traits. And, knowing the complexity of human nature, we can safely assume that even the best parents lose it at times, become irritated at the wrong time, and express harsh feelings. Obviously, we cannot ascertain how injurious such behaviors are. We again need to remember that we are not speaking of the expression of isolated behaviors but rather of accumulating expressed messages that when repeated often enough become embedded in the child's unconscious as dismissive or rejecting.

Therefore, as an ending to this chapter on early stress and its varying severity, I would like to place the negative effects of early stresses within the wider context of normative family life. The power of the parents' personality traits often sets the trajectory of the intersubjective dynamics within the family. On the other hand, every child brings their own temperament and inclinations into those developing dynamics, influencing some of the parents' emotional and behavioral reactions as well. Nevertheless, being at the center of the child's emotional and interpersonal world, the parent carries the bulk of the responsibility for forming the intersubjective dynamics with the child. This is especially so during the early years. The parents' own emotional difficulties, level of stress tolerance, ability to regulate emotions, ability to see and respect their child's individuality, and, most importantly, their capacity for self-awareness, may greatly ease the occasional inevitable stresses, anxieties, and hurts.

BEN'S CASE: THE IMPACT OF MATERNAL DEPRESSION

Ben, a 30-year-old man, is tall and heavy-set. He walked into the office hunched over, as if he wanted to minimize his height and weight. The intricate tattoos covering both his arms were the only attention-getting aspects of his generally self-effacing demeanor. Ben started by saying that he had been chronically depressed for most of his life. He was on antidepression medications that seemed to help him a great deal, keeping him from sliding back into what he described as "a total mess with the inability to get out of bed and leave home." He wanted therapy to help him deal with what he called his "timidity and shyness." As a gay man, he tried to meet new people and go on dates but, as he said, his shyness and fear of rejection were in the way. Although he used a few dating applications, he often did not pursue others in a serious manner.

Ben was particularly worried about his weight and was utterly convinced that no man would find him attractive and desirable. Therefore, he said, "There isn't much point exposing myself to rejection." Ben had a group of good friends whom he frequently saw. Looking embarrassed and pained, Ben revealed that he was "in love" with one of his closest friends, a man in a long-term and committed relationship with another man. As Ben later realized, he had been involved in similar crushes before, often on straight men. Although he knew these relationships were not possible, he was gratified just to "think about them," yearning for these men to recognize their own love for him.

Ben worked as a cook in a big restaurant and spontaneously emphasized that he got along with everybody at work. He quickly added that he was good at making people feel at ease. He was particularly careful not to contradict others and thus anger any of them. He couldn't stand people being angry at him. In his words, the idea of making somebody uncomfortable made him anxious and pained. In order not to "make too many waves," he did not insist on reasonable work hours, pay raises, and his share of the tips.

We soon realized that Ben could not tolerate most situations where he was a target of somebody's disappointment, disapproval, or anger. Even imagining somebody angry with him led to anxious sensations and fears about being rejected by those he wished to engage with. At those rare times when others expressed negative feelings toward him, he promptly experienced shame and guilt, wishing "the earth would open up and swallow him alive."

Ben's mother suffered from depression throughout her adult life. His early memories, in effect, were of his mother frequently staying closed off in his parents' bedroom, "lying in bed, sometimes reading." He remembered that she would not leave the room for days at a time. For many years, Ben's mother refused any suggestions about seeking psychiatric help and trying medication. While his father was working as much as he could, his mother's parents came by daily to take care of him and his older sister, tending to their needs after school. His father tried to help as well but often expressed his own despair at the situation. Ben's mother's condition fluctuated. When she felt better, she could even work a little, helping an old boss run his office. "When feeling better, she could be fun," he said. She was affectionate and loving, helping them with schoolwork and projects. But even during these happier times, Ben has distinct memories of unexpected angry outbursts from her. These usually occurred when "things became too much." In effect, the more memories surfaced, Ben increasingly realized that he and his sister "could not win." When their mother was depressed, she was irritable, and during her better periods, she still often "lost it."

Throughout his childhood and adolescence, Ben could not shake off his worries about her. He also sensed, he said, "her underlying sadness" and, in order to maintain her good moods, made special efforts to "be as good as he could." Even as a young adolescent, Ben realized that his behavior toward his mother echoed the way his mother related to her own parents. Ben became convinced that his mother was making a big effort to protect them from knowing how depressed she really was. Because of their struggles as immigrants, and because of their hard life in their country of origin, he said, she was especially careful not to upset them in any way. He remembered her often making light of her depression in front of them. Her refusal to take medication was also meant to communicate to them that she was okay.

Ben seldom entered her bedroom when she was not feeling well, being afraid that he would burden and upset her. During her depressed periods, he was especially careful not to ask her for anything, regardless of how essential it was for his functioning at home or in school. In therapy, Ben realized that his decision as a child to avoid further burdening her was based on his unconscious need to save them both. He needed to save her from his own needs, but by avoiding demanding things of her he also protected himself from being disappointed at her inability to take care of him.

Ben occasionally relied on his sister and at times on his father and grandparents for what he needed, but for the most part he felt alone. He clearly remembered that throughout grade school he went to physical checkups and dentist appointments by himself.

After years of denying the need for treatment, Ben's mother finally saw a psychiatrist, and her depression considerably improved. At that time Ben was a junior in high school. Although she was more present in their lives,

Ben was still very careful about asking her for things he needed. In particular, Ben never talked to her about his struggles with his weight and how despondent he was about it. Becoming aware of his attraction to other boys increased his feelings of insecurity and confusion, but he kept all his feelings and thoughts to himself.

He had a group of male friends, but throughout high school he hid his sexual orientation from them as well. After high school, while he was trying to decide about a career in the food industry, his skills made him feel a bit more secure, but he was still unable to imagine himself approaching other guys. As his weight kept fluctuating, he gave up on ever staying at the weight he liked, and eventually abandoned dieting altogether. Starting therapy was an opportunity for him, he said, to give it another try.

Ben's mother's postpartum depression following the birth of both of her children and her subsequent periods of deep depression were clearly the base for much of Ben's psychological makeup. According to his father, after his birth and during her low periods later she really was "out of it." She needed to withdraw and be alone. It is not clear how much engagement she had with her children's emotional needs. Although her parents stepped in and provided some care, we clearly have to wonder about the nature of the emotional attunement that Ben received from the very beginning of his life. Based on his lingering reticence to express himself freely and his intense worries about hurting others, we can safely assume that from infancy on Ben unconsciously adapted his response patterns to his mother's internal states. In effect, he became really good at resonating with her states, hiding his own needs. Later this pattern of accommodation became generalized to everybody he came across.

In effect, Ben unconsciously welcomed not being seen by others. He was very comfortable in his role as a good listener. He "accepted not being attractive to other guys" and was quite sure that he would not find love. Some part of him was dimly aware that these beliefs defended him from self-exposure and potential rejection. And all along he had his crushes on a series of unavailable men, mostly married friends with whom he spent a great deal of time.

As treatment continued, Ben realized that loving unavailable guys from afar and in secret was preferable to encountering the threat of rejection. He could not imagine someone would want to take care of him, but he could imagine it with his secret passions. The idea that he deserved to be loved, that he could be important to somebody, was not a big part of his unconscious expectations. What he learned and became convinced of was an acute interpersonal insecurity where love might exist but had no chance of enduring. Unconsciously, he avoided any intimate relationship as a defense against becoming bereft when that love was snatched away. Realizing that this was how he felt each time his mother retreated again, and feeling emotionally distraught, he also began to feel compassion for the boy who needed to protect himself from further pain by hiding his needs and making do with what he could get. At the same time, as a result of the medication he took and his increasing ability to experience and tolerate many new emotional nuances, Ben's depression continued to improve.

It's hard, of course, to pinpoint the exact origin of Ben's own depression, which started during his adolescent years and intensified in his early 20s. At the same time, however, we can safely assume that a confluence of factors contributed to Ben's struggles. A most probable innate predisposition to depression and anxiety he inherited from his mother and an emotionally unstable and depriving environment culminated in depressive tendencies within him as well.

More specifically, the genetic predisposition he inherited from his mother was only the first steps in a complex developmental journey. From the very beginning of life, Ben was subjected to his mother's periodic withdrawal and minimally responsive expressions and behaviors. As we have seen in the many studies cited in these chapters, infants and children are especially sensitive to the caregiver's facial expressions, vocal mirroring, mutual eye gaze, and attuned engagement. As depressed parents have a difficult time mustering the emotional, mental, and physical strength to fully engage with their infants, children, and adolescents, what is lost is the all-important mutual resonance and recognition. To make matters worse for Ben, the good, loving periods did not last. He could not relax into them because he was anxiously waiting for them to end. And each time as the negative expectation of loss became reality, his young mind unconsciously decided to become more and more cautious in his expectations.

We also know that the process of identification with a parent's internal state is always ongoing. Part of the child is always attuned to his parents' feelings and behaviors. As an infant and a young boy, Ben already sensed that his mother was, in his words, "too fragile." The empathy and love he felt toward her only strengthened his resolve to keep his needs, opinions, vulnerability, and anger to himself. Inevitably, through identification and learning processes, his mother's anxious and sad emotional states became his feeling states as well.

During our sessions, the more Ben became aware of his unconscious emotional and behavioral patterns, and the more he connected them to his childhood experiences, the looser some of his entrenched internal self-imposed restrictions became. Becoming acutely aware of the fear involved in expressing needs and making himself vulnerable, he consciously and effortfully tried to change his old behavior patterns of hiding himself. The more he could express himself while still feeling anxious, the more he felt free to be himself, and the less preoccupied he became with potential disapproval and rejection.

CHAPTER NINE

Injury and Defense

· ·

Any discussion of the fear system also needs to focus on the many defense mechanisms that are automatically and unconsciously marshalled to reduce distress and restore a sense of well-being. Beginning in early childhood, fear, anxiety, and the defenses utilized against them are inextricably connected in the brain/mind/body. The evolutionary benefits of our fear system for survival became entangled with other innate mechanisms and skills that reacted to danger with fight, flight, and freeze responses. When a dangerous situation resolved, the aroused fear system calmed down and homeostasis returned. In safer conditions, our ancestors could regroup and think about the danger they had encountered; they would remember it and prepare themselves for the next inevitable stressful situations.

While vigilance was an essential aspect of survival, so was the need to regain a sense of well-being. Remaining in a state of constant vigilance and apprehension is too taxing physiologically and mentally. We might ask how it became possible for our ancestors to forget their fear reactions and engage in other activities. How successful were they in doing so? Of course, we cannot directly answer these questions; but we can certainly look for convincing neuropsychological clues. Essentially, how we deal with fear, stress, and ongoing anxiety is the story of our innate human defensive system as well; they work simultaneously and in tandem, both guided by the amygdala.

THE FUNCTION AND NATURE OF DEFENSES

Defense mechanisms are, in effect, unconscious brain/mind processes that provide self-protective effects by reducing or masking anxiety arising from stimuli that are difficult to tolerate or potentially harmful (Hayden et al., 2021). In this way, our defense mechanisms maintain physiological and psychological homeostasis (Miranda & Louzã, 2015). Freud (1926) described "defense mechanisms" as unconscious processes people use to manage stress and anxiety. Without our defense mechanisms, we would be continuously assaulted with negative emotions, such as fear, anger, sadness, and anxiety (Bowins, 2004). Thus, defense mechanisms are vital for a healthy relationship with the self, others, and the environment. This suggests a more appropriate description for defenses as "coping mechanisms" or our involuntary reactions to the inevitable slings and arrows of life (Freud, 1926).

Adaptive coping mechanisms enable us to function with a level of relative comfort in the face of a wide range of emotional states. These adaptive reactions help us react to both positive and negative situations without being seriously disturbed by them. More important, our adaptive defenses allow us to tolerate the presence of negative brain/mind/body experiences. This ability is central to emotional regulation and, therefore, our well-being because these defenses also allow us to enjoy positive internal and external states. Maladaptive defenses, as we will see in the following sections, make our lives harder and less enjoyable.

This observation is doubly important as there is growing evidence that utilizing our adaptive defense mechanisms and task-oriented coping strategies is significantly associated with a greater sense of well-being and more adaptive functioning. Research shows that those relying on maladaptive defense mechanisms and coping strategies were less able to regulate their emotions and act on their own behalf (Panfil et al., 2020). Although some psychologists differentiate between coping mechanisms and defenses, I use the term *defenses* to include both adaptive and maladaptive coping mechanisms (Frederickson et al., 2018).

Researchers have long viewed our earlier relational experiences through the lens of our defenses, including how we learned to avoid or cover up certain emotions (e.g., anger toward a parent; submission to a parent's authority as a way to avoid conflict) (Sullivan, 1953). In psychodynamic theory, defenses are understood as unconscious psychological mechanisms that reduce anxiety resulting from unacceptable or potentially harmful thoughts, conflicts, emotions, or impulses (Freud, 1959a, 1959b). However, more recent views maintain that the primary goal of defenses is to rid us—as fast and efficiently as possible—of subjective dysregulating experiences such as anxiety, emotional pain, shame, guilt, and uncomfortable negative thoughts about the self. By protecting our self-esteem or self-integrity, these defenses allow us to adapt to our environment (Cramer, 1998a, 1998b; Hartmann, 1964); they save important relationships from ruptures and ensure smooth existence with others and in groups (Bowlby, 1982; Sullivan, 1953).

Defenses, then, are mechanisms that are part of our innate regulatory self-management. These processes, mostly operating outside our awareness, primarily involve modulating activities against internal distress (Nevarez et al., 2018). Not surprisingly, neuroscience also recognizes defensive processes as inherent, built-in functions of the brain/mind. Using a psychodynamic point of view, researchers explored brain waves in response to conflict phrases. The phrases, based on individual interviews with the participants, were presented to them outside their awareness (Bazan, 2017). Three studies showed that participants presented with subliminal and subject-specific conflict phrases showed synchronization of a specific brain wave, the alpha wave, known for its inhibitory function. Researchers concluded that alpha synchronization could serve as a brain mechanism of unconscious defense.

Even more compelling is the work of LeDoux (2002) on the amygdala and anxiety. From birth and throughout our life cycle, the amygdala, in its role as a threat detector, gets information about emotional or physiological discomfort and recruits whatever visceral, mental, and behavioral processes and circuits are available in times of stress. Like all of our traits, defenses are a neuropsychological amalgam of our innate functions. As we know, the amygdala is a small almond-shaped brain structure in the center of the brain that receives information about fearful stimuli and transmits it to other brain regions to generate fear responses. Studies have shown that certain groups of neurons in the amygdala are crucial for the regulation of fear responses. They cause the body to release stress hormones and change heart rate or trigger fight, flight, or freezing responses (Whittle et al., 2021).

Starting in infancy, cues for threats affect all brain/mind/body functions: visceral discomfort, frightening emotional states, and interpersonal anxiety due to compromised attunement and empathy. Various forms of defensive styles evolve from infancy to adolescence and into adulthood. As development continues, defenses gain complexity and intellectual sophistication.

THE INEVITABILITY OF DEFENSES

I would argue that to further understand both defenses or coping mechanisms, we need to first acknowledge their innate inevitability and inextricability from who we eventually become as adults. These mechanisms should no longer have the negative connotations, and even the pejorative implications, we assign them as indicating a supposedly dysfunctional personality trait. Indeed, some theories frame defenses as a mechanism for hiding one's authentic feelings from those close to us and from ourselves, raising questions of denial. But defenses are much more complex processes; they are automatic self-protection mechanisms that were adaptive in childhood but often stop being adaptive as we reach adulthood.

When defenses are triggered but no longer serve us (e.g., they are not needed, no real threat exists, or they are distorted projections of another person's intent), they can cause real obstacles to emotional regulation and smooth, effective functioning with others. Often, denial is at the core of our lack of awareness of our defenses, and how frequently and consistently we utilize them. This minimizes or erases the existence of some crucial aspects of our experience. Similarly, we can often spot denial when individuals are not aware of their repeated patterns of feeling and behaving and how these behavioral patterns affect those around them. To some extent, defensive behaviors around others, especially those closest to us, are at the basis of many relational difficulties.

Defenses can also acquire a rigidity that can be quite resistant to self-awareness (Hayden et al., 2021). As adults, a variety of reminders of emotional injuries, scary events, and unpleasant feelings may unconsciously trigger old habitual defenses, whether they are appropriate or not. When these defenses, which were adaptive during early times of stress, become entrenched learned patterns, we often generalize them and respond to similar triggers. In these instances, we automatically respond to a wide range of perceived threats, creating dysregulated states and secondary interpersonal difficulties.

As we have seen in previous chapters, our parents' defenses and their typical ways of dealing with stress also shape our emotional development. For example, researchers found that healthier maternal defense mechanisms during pregnancy predicted better attachment security, greater social–emotional competence, and less problematic behavior in their toddlers (Nevarez et al., 2018; Porcerelli et al., 2016). Not surprisingly, more nurturing childhood environments are linked with more adaptive (i.e., mature) defense mechanisms used in adulthood and better relationships with one's children (Martin-Joy et al., 2017). Furthermore, many studies have shown that more adaptive defense mechanisms are associated with better functioning in adulthood (Malone et al., 2013), a stronger sense of well-being (Cramer, 2006), greater work satisfaction (Reid et al., 2010), and a more satisfying attachment to partners (Waldinger, 2017).

Similarly, researchers explored the effects of early life nurturance on satisfying and adaptive functioning at work as measured by earned income (Cristóbal-Narváez et al., 2016). The study found that adaptive defenses promoted engagement and led to healthier relationships. Interestingly, positively remembered childhood experiences were linked to stronger marital relationships and greater career satisfaction and achievement. The researchers attributed such positive levels of functioning to more adaptive defenses that did not distort reality or other people's intentions. Significantly, participants employing more adaptive defenses were not overly invested in being right and in controlling others as a defense against feeling inferior. Another study found that negatively remembered childhood experiences were associated with high levels of avoidance and greater difficulties in adult romantic relationships (McCarthy & Taylor, 1999). In such an environment, the stronger and more frequently used adaptive defenses become the more dominant ones, rather than the maladaptive ones.

HOW DO WE UNDERSTAND ADAPTIVE OR MALADAPTIVE DEFENSES?

This question is especially relevant when we remember that our defensive systems develop in infancy in response to environmental pressures over which we have no control. In this context, any defense used by a child to reduce internal distress is adaptive. We can evaluate defenses as adaptive or maladaptive according to their influence on our daily functioning, especially with regard to how we engage with our environment and other people, both close and distant.

For example, Allyson became automatically and unconsciously threatened when she perceived Michael's need for some distance as a reflection of his love (see Chapter 12). Distorting the meaning of his behavior, she projected intentions he did not really have. Her demands for proof of love were distancing themselves and created distance between herself and Michael. Her anxiety and defenses did not allow her to see Michael's point of view and acknowledge it without feeling threatened or unheard. Indeed, as we see in the other cases here, when some individuals experience anxiety-inducing vulnerability, they tend to either avoid confrontation or quickly negate the other or become argumentative. That was clearly the case with Ian.

Obviously, open and nondefensive interactions with our partners, coworkers, and authority figures are the optimal ways to be with others. Such internalized patterns lead to less suspicion of others, reduced hostility and anger, and greater trust. Nondefensive patterns of dealing with disturbing inner states actually save us from frequent and damaging interpersonal entanglements. But as we already know, the adaptive level of our defenses is essentially a matter of degree and intensity. Some defenses are much more conducive to a smoother, happier, and less conflicted life. As infants, children, and adolescents, we all had to process painful internal states. Even nurturing and supportive environments can still arouse inevitable stress and anxiety in children. So do difficult and traumatic situations such as frequent moves, poverty, systemic racism, natural disasters, and war, to name a few.

There is an old adage that no defense is the best defense. But we cannot develop without using some defense mechanisms; they allow us to deal with life's difficulties in ways that also enable us to pursue our goals and get along with others. For example, after assessing the confidence levels of 6- and 9-year-old children, a longitudinal study showed that children's decrease in self-confidence resulted in the use of more immature defenses such as denial. In contrast, children whose self-confidence increased did not demonstrate excessive use of such defenses (Cramer, 2015).

Similarly, another study explored the relationship between girls' social adjustments and the defenses they used. The results showed that girls who felt rejected by their peers and then were put in a situation in the lab where they experienced rejection used more defensive mechanisms to deal with their hurt. The girls who were higher on the social approval scale used fewer defensive mechanisms (Sandstrom & Cramer, 2003). These studies are especially important in light of current negative messages in social media about popularity and body image.

IMMATURE AND MATURE DEFENSES

All defensive styles express complex interconnected interactions among cortical and subcortical brain circuits and functions. In general, defenses that are less likely to promote emotional regulation are considered primitive or immature. They are primarily mediated by emotional circuits that are not tempered enough by those regions of the brain capable of reducing the intensity of perceived threats and automatic reactions. The regulating regions mostly involve neural circuits like the prefrontal cortex and the insula. They help us tolerate disturbing affects and thoughts by reducing perception of threat, thus lessening anxious reactivity.

The following sections briefly discuss a few commonly used defenses. They are immature only to the extent that they do not work well for us. They may defend against anxiety but hurt us in other ways.

Denial, for example, is considered to be an immature defense. It involves the quick and automatic dismissal of one's feelings, motivations, and actions; it may be viewed as the defense that underlies a lack of awareness about who we are. Denial is a subtle form of avoidance; we can acknowledge the existence of the stressor, but the intensity of avoidance of any recognition of our reactions and behaviors results in a serious blind spot.

Starting early in infancy, avoidance can become part of practically all developing psychological and behavioral capabilities. This is important because we often see clients who automatically and unknowingly avoid situations that may arouse their fears. Avoidance includes behaviors such as procrastination or not engaging with the world; clients can only fantasize about doing or achieving things but not actually pursue them. Importantly, even when anxiety is no longer experienced, the old avoidant behaviors persist with the full force of avoidant habits.

Often, just imagining engaging in an activity that involves effort and potential failure results in avoidance; we may explain this away as risk management, but it is often a form of avoidance. As a result, avoidance can lead to self-blame and self-loathing. As we helplessly witness our passivity and what we sometimes call laziness and endless procrastination, we despair at who we have become.

Another immature defense is acting out, fast and automatic reactive behaviors that unconsciously channel disturbing emotions into actions. In this case, we do not create any space for more moderate, slowed-down responses to surface. To avoid anxiety, we can only act.

Excessive worries about our health channel fears and anxieties into more concrete and potentially treatable conditions. Sadly, many of us experienced this form of displaced anxiety during the COVID-19 pandemic, discussed in Chapter 12. Fearing for our health may be a more accessible way to manage our wider fears about losing jobs, homes, social lives, and, most importantly, our loved ones.

Passive aggression, a behavior we are all familiar with, is a defense against fully expressing one's anger or opposition directly. Activating this defensive behavior are old fears of being punished or rejected for direct expressions of one's feelings and needs. Such a pattern may be learned when subtle communications from caregivers send messages that it's important to play along. Unwittingly, a parent may link opposition to the withdrawal of love.

Projection, a widely used interpersonal defense, is the tendency to assign to others one's own negative emotions, behaviors, and intentions. Often, such projections express our own unconscious or denied internal feeling states, thoughts, and motivation. Projective identification also occurs entirely outside our awareness. We first project feelings and negative intentions onto others, then proceed to act as if our assumptions are correct. Not surprisingly, despite efforts to rid ourselves of negative feelings, this defensive behavior actually raises our experience of anxiety. Assuming the worst about someone else—and believing that they are utterly responsible for our own internal suffering or victimhood—leaves us in a state of greater agitation and anger. The problem-causing qualities of this defense are rooted in its deeply unconscious nature. During a disagreement, we can become convinced that the other person doesn't understand our suffering; we may come to believe that they are out to hurt, control, or humiliate us (Ginot, 2015). Obviously, such a defensive style can cause repeated problems in relationships, especially intimate ones.

Like the defense mechanism of projective identification, splitting is often, although not exclusively, found among borderline patients. Dissociation is similar in its function and activity. Splitting involves the blunt demarcation between feeling states. Out of the need for self-protection, we intensely experience only one emotional state at a time. When an entrenched anxious, depressed, or vulnerable state is triggered, our brain/minds are overtaken by all the aspects of the particular negative state, including overwhelming emotions such as sadness, anxiety, a great sense of fragility, ruminative negative thinking, narratives about potential danger, and feelings of despair and hopelessness. While consciously experiencing such a negative state, there is a total absence of any consciousness of other possibilities, a positive reality, or a satisfying shared history with the perceived victimizer. Often, such intense convictions lead a teenager or adult to entirely cut that person from their life.

Similar to other defensive mechanisms, splitting makes us suffer even more. Drowning in one state without perspective leads to emotional and physical dysregulation. When a negative state takes over, it pushes aside other more balanced neuropsychological networks. The opposite self-state, although suffused with positive emotions, creates its own difficulties. In the throes of total positivity, much of it projected, we can idealize ourselves and/or others, feeling completely secure and invincible; we forget the existence of a more balanced and reality-bound perspective. Many psychotherapies aim to bridge such an internal gap and thus enhance the integration between self-states (Bromberg, 1998, 2011; Ginot, 2015).

Defense mechanisms considered more mature incorporate higher levels of automatic and cognitive processes, which can downregulate disturbing emotions (Zanarini et al., 2009). For example, the defense of suppression involves ideas, activities, and specific therapeutic tools that can successfully distract us from anxious ruminations. Like all defenses, suppression can be used without thinking (i.e., unconsciously), expressing a well-developed regulation ability. But it can also involve mindful efforts to distract ourselves from disturbing states. There is a great deal of research on the efficacy of such mindful defenses. Some researchers found that just naming and describing a disturbing feeling reduces its aversive effects (Lane, 2008; Ochsner & Gross, 2005). Slowed-down anticipation and naming emotional states were found to be effective defenses against distress among borderline patients undergoing psychotherapy (Zanarini et al., 2009).

To a large extent, adaptive defenses depend on our ability to tolerate states of negative feeling and situations and simultaneously engage them in healthy ways. For the most part, they do not include the unconscious negation of our worst fears, externalizing our pain or projecting stressors on others. Such adaptive defenses include humor, self-deprecation, and sublimation. Sublimation is the complex process of being aware of our own inner world and, at the same time, channeling inner turmoil and self-doubts into creative and productive activities (Domash, 2020).

As we further understand the nature and function of defenses, we also need to emphasize that the way each one of us develops and employs defense mechanisms is uniquely individual to us. Based on clinical observations, it is quite clear that, to varying degrees, most of us possess aspects of both adaptive and maladaptive, mature and immature defenses, employing them habitually and automatically.

However, we are far from being doomed to endless automatic repetition of defensive patterns that no longer serve us well. Even defenses that are entrenched and automatic can become more conscious through the self-examination that most psychotherapies and other mindfulness approaches provide and encourage. As adults, we can work toward becoming self-aware of our defenses and of what feelings we are defending ourselves against. It is important to note, however, that becoming aware of how defenses shape our behaviors and become stable traits does not mean getting rid of our defenses; this is not a therapeutic goal. Rather, the key to more adaptive defenses and functioning may lie in our ability to acknowledge and embrace our vulnerability. This necessitates the understanding that our more anxious and deeply vulnerable feelings and fantasies about ourselves are an inevitable part of our human nature.

We cannot undo the conditions in which we grew up or how they shaped our unconscious defenses. Neither can we alter how our genetic predispositions influenced our anxiety levels and reactions to our environment. But we can strive to examine those defenses that we had to develop in the face of hurtful, shaming, and neglectful experiences, including situations where our caretakers did not intend to hurt us. Doing so can greatly reduce the effects of defenses that constantly and unconsciously activate as we bump into reminders of the vulnerability and helplessness we experienced as children.

DREW'S CASE: INJURY AND DEFENSE—
NO POINT DWELLING ON THE PAST

Drew was 29 when he started therapy. At the time he was just starting a new job as a social worker for the city of New York. He complained about feeling somewhat insecure and worried about his upcoming job. He was not exactly sure what his complaints were, except that he knew it was a big adjustment to build his life in a "crazy place like NYC." He expressed a vague wish to become less rigid and more trusting of others, attributing these traits to the trauma he suffered when his parents divorced.

Drew described that period as the "worst time in his life." After years of not getting along and frequently fighting, Drew's parents separated when he was 7 and his younger brother was 5 years old. He was close to his mother and described his father as a "workaholic and an on-and-off alcoholic who still functioned well no matter how much he had to drink." Drew also remembered that the family still managed to have fun together, especially during trips they took together. He felt loved, he said; his parents were both affectionate and invested time and energy in making the children feel important to them.

But he remembered nights when he heard his parents' loud fights. He did not, in effect, remember any time when his parents did not fight. As his parents' fighting got worse, his fears and worries increased as well. His mother increasingly distanced herself from her husband and eventually stopped engaging with him altogether. Drew did not understand why his mother acted like this; he wished for his father to stop drinking "so she wouldn't be so angry with him." He also remembered being very torn; he "loved hanging out" with his father when he was in a good mood, but he also felt worried about his mother, who seemed upset much of the time.

One of Drew's biggest fears was that the family would fall apart. When his parents told him and his brother that they would no longer be together, Drew was devastated; he could not accept this new reality and begged his parents to stay together. At the time of the divorce, Drew and his brother found out from their angry and hurt mother that their father was having a longtime affair with a coworker.

During an emotional outburst, she told them that their father badly betrayed and hurt her. She was particularly angry and pained, Drew remembered, that "after all she did for him, after all the efforts she made to deal with his drinking and absence from home, she found out that he was having an affair." She told the kids that he was running away from the family, from her and from them. She told them that for a while she had tried to convince him to leave his girlfriend, but he refused.

In a separate talk, their father told the children that the situation at home was too difficult for him; as he and their mother did not get along and fought so much that he had to leave. Without explaining much, he told the children that he had suffered during the last few years and that he experienced a very painful conflict about leaving. Finally, he told them that all these emotional problems made his drinking worse. Repeatedly, and separately, both parents promised the children that the divorce was about their relationship and had nothing to do with the kids. It seemed that they did their best to reassure the children as much as they could.

As Drew said in session, "It was all too much information for us as young children." Without fully understanding what was going on, he was filled with intolerable dread about the future. These feelings of dread kept "telling him that nothing was safe, that something terrible could happen at any moment and change everything." Soon after the separation, his father moved in with his girlfriend. In a shared custody agreement, the children spent time with both parents equally.

Drew's father remarried and soon began a new family. When Drew's father's new young family absorbed much of his time and attention, the joint custody agreement slowly became less reliable. Drew himself was very angry with his father for having the affair and, with many ambivalent feelings toward his father's new wife, declined to stay with them after their first baby was born. He said that he missed his father terribly but made up for his father's absence with a very active social life.

All this information came tumbling out of Drew. It seemed as if he was still back at home, reliving both the painful moments of his parents' divorce and the enjoyable parts of his school days and friendships. After telling his story with a great deal of urgency over a few sessions, Drew's demeanor totally changed. He flopped on the chair with a visible lack of energy and few words. He did not have much to talk about, and his complaints were the same: vague insecurity and fears over the new job, hoping that it wouldn't interfere that much with his social life.

Drew talked little about his dating life. When asked about it, he emphasized that he was not interested in anything serious; he was after passionate sex with different partners. "I don't feel insecure about how I look or how girls see me," he said, but "I'm not interested in getting into potentially complicated dynamics where I have to cater to other people's needs." He could not really elaborate any further on this vague statement.

As we continued to talk over weeks and months, we both noticed that his initial urgency to talk about his childhood entirely left him, and he remained feeling deflated and indifferent, not wanting to deal with anything serious, a feeling he knew well. When we tried to understand this shift, Drew realized that the familiar mix of deflation and indifference, in effect, reminded him of how he felt following his parents' divorce and his father's remarriage. He remembered feeling intensely upset for a long while, but as "he went back to his life," he also noticed that he tried to think as little as possible about how things were and how he felt. As his mother also increasingly felt better and started dating again, Drew focused on his schoolwork, on his friends and activities.

As therapy continued, Drew seemed to emotionally distance himself from his trauma. In effect, he expressed a sentiment that maybe things were not as bad as he remembered them. Fifty percent of marriages, he said, end in divorce, and his family was no different or immune to it. It may even have made him and his brother stronger and more resilient in the long run. As Drew described it, he even managed to totally forgive his father and with time developed good relationships with his half-siblings.

Alongside Drew's current seemingly accepting and easygoing attitude toward the breakup of his family, there was a deep-seated cynicism expressed as an avoidance of taking anything seriously. Everything was a subject for a joke or a cynical observation, at times sliding into outright rejection and opposition to what he thought was expected of him, for example, feeling badly for himself. He did not directly connect his ideas about dating and relationships to his parents' relationship, but he did say, "Between my parents' fights and the underwhelming relationship I had in college, I have had enough for a while."

Overall, Drew was not aware of how his avoidance of directly feeling anxiety and pain was totally intertwined with his cynicism. When prodded to relate some memories from his childhood, he repeatedly minimized his emotional reactions. When I reminded him how eager he was to relate his past to me during the first couple of sessions, he said, "Yes, I felt the need to get it out, but basically, I've said everything." In addition, Drew expressed the wish to focus on help with negotiating the new job, especially how to deal with both his superiors and the clients he dealt with. He showed little appetite to go back to his past.

This left me in a therapeutic dilemma: being new in his position, Drew indeed benefited from discussing the many, at times overwhelming, situations within the complex labyrinth of the NYC social services department. Recognizing it, I was open to spending as much time as he needed on his current personal growth in his profession. At the same time, I was still very much aware that something very important was missing from Drew's therapy. As helpful as our conversations were, they felt somewhat sterile and lifeless. Drew's inner life was missing, the essential core that contained his feelings, memories, and narratives. This was especially noticeable in light of his own initial description of the divorce as traumatic.

Part of the dilemma for me was how much to respect Drew's avoidance of revisiting his painful past. At that point, I was convinced that it was not just the divorce that was traumatic, but years of being exposed to angry fights (see Chapter 8 for the effects of parental fights on children). Was it better for him to just focus on the present, or would it be better to push him to get in touch with some other parts of himself? In some ways, the path was presented to us when Drew settled into the job and performed his many tasks with increasing competence and growing self-assurance. "What do we do now?" we both asked. The question came up when Drew admitted that despite doing well at work, he was still somewhat on edge and unhappy. He was also getting tired of the many dates he went on and had recently deleted some of the apps he was using.

Trying to explore some of his internal feelings and thought processes led us to the realization that there was no way around it; it would be enormously beneficial to Drew to tackle both his past experiences and the very rigid avoidance defenses he had built around them. Half-reluctantly, and with a great deal of cynicism regarding "gazing at one's navel," we started the second phase of Drew's therapy. With time, Drew was able to understand how the painful experiences of his entire childhood shaped his conscious and unconscious sense of himself, behavioral patterns, and defenses. The more he looked inside for clues to how he developed and who he became, the more open he became to remembering and experiencing his difficult feelings.

Drew's growing openness to embracing his past feelings was not an easy road. His habitual defenses of avoidance, rationalization, and cynicism, among others, often reasserted their strength and persistence. But the more we worked together, the more accepting Drew became of his anxious child self, the self that reacted with inevitable and overwhelming fears to the verbal violence that surrounded him and infused him with dread. With these changes, his relationships with both his parents improved as well.

With the pandemic, as Drew switched to working remotely, he became even less defensive and more open to others. Surprising himself, he lamented that now, as he was becoming more interested in exploring relationships in more serious ways, it was no longer as easy as it used to be. It was smoother, he said, when he had been "determined to keep all his dating encounters short and unencumbered." But as Drew keeps bringing a similar determination to become a "more balanced guy," he is well on his way to reconnect with the more vulnerable and needy part within him.

CHAPTER TEN

We Are All Narcissists

••

Of the personal and emotional difficulties we typically see in clinical practice, narcissistic personality disorders seem to embody much of what the previous chapters have described—the many of implications the fear system for who we become. In a clear way, we can look at clients we label as narcissistic as exemplifying the intricate behavioral patterns we all develop in our attempts to cope with psychic pain, vulnerability, and anxiety. When crushing and intolerable feelings of anxiety and shame overwhelm a toddler, a young child (Braten, 2007; Braten & Trevarthen, 2007; Schore, 2012), or an adolescent (Grawe, 2007), innate defensive processes automatically and unconsciously struggle to compensate and restore a sense of well-being. The emotional injury and the various defenses employed against it coalesce into an unconscious pattern that includes both experiences. This is the essence of narcissism. Ironically, narcissism develops from the exaggerated power and habitual activation of entirely natural and necessary defense mechanisms.

Most often, memory traces of the painful tangle of injuries are implicit, especially those reflecting experiences in the first three or four years of life. Only when enacted as emotional and behavioral patterns do they reveal some of their embedded intensity. What we communicate outside our awareness are the encoded representations of enduring anxiety about one's self-esteem and the defenses automatically employed to regulate them. Clinical experience reveals that narcissistic personality disorders are made up of two emotional struggles: the tendency to feel injured, victimized, and deflated, with considerable low self-esteem; and the tendency to display grandiose, hypomanic, and/or sadistic defensive patterns (Bach, 2006). By experiencing and articulating the depth of negative feelings and thoughts regarding their self-worth, the deflated narcissist often appears to be depressed and clingy. Conversely, other narcissistic individuals may repeatedly come across as self-aggrandizing, tirelessly seeking the approval of others, competing with others, and needing to see as themselves superior and always right.

In the midst of emotional dysregulation, the self-narrative of deflated narcissists focuses on their insignificance in relation to others and on their perceived inferiority. In therapy and in their relationships, they often look to the other to validate their narrative of an inferior, hurt, or victimized position, experiencing anger when these unconscious expectations are perceived to be true or when they are projected onto others. The overinflated narcissist often comes across as arrogant and all-knowing; they automatically emphasize their superiority, often at the expanse of the other (Kernberg, 2007). They consciously experience themselves as the center of attention and, therefore, important; they expect others, including their therapists, to mirror their subjectivity without any doubt or skepticism (Bach, 2006). Researchers have observed that the core issue of some narcissistic individuals is their inability to depend on others because any dependency is unconsciously experienced as humiliating (Kernberg, 2007). As a defense, these individuals try to control others, even those who love and support them.

Often, while engaged in the therapeutic process with narcissistic clients, I have witnessed their wide mood swings; they become embroiled in very negative or, conversely, grandiose self-states. Being indirectly asked to confirm either or both, I have come to realize that, directly or indirectly, all narcissistic self-states convey a great deal of misery (Kohut, 1971). At times, when being attacked for failing to see a client's point of view, or when being subtly and competitively put down, I can momentarily lose my own regulatory capacities and sink into a victimized mood or a sullen, somewhat hostile withdrawal. More typically, however, holding on to my reflective awareness, I maintain the fragile thread of connection to the injured part of my client. As the patient and I get to know and immerse ourselves in that vulnerable self-system, I find myself more empathetic to the client's desperate but unconscious attempts to save face.

MELODY'S CASE: A NONNEGOTIABLE NEED FOR PERFECTIONISM

Melody was a physician in training when she sought therapy because of severe and persistent anxiety. She could not explain what made her so stressed and anxious, except for the competitive atmosphere, frequent evaluations, and high stakes attached to her performance. Pretty soon it became clear that her professional and interpersonal life embodied a constant struggle with self-doubts and nagging thoughts of imminent failure. She was utterly convinced that she would be found out as a fraud (i.e., imposter syndrome). In one of the first dreams she brought to treatment, she could not diagnose a patient; both the head of the ward and her direct supervisor were becoming increasingly frustrated and angry with her. She woke up in total panic, with inchoate and inarticulate feelings of dreadful shame.

From the beginning of our sessions together, it was evident that Melody was actually living this nightmare in her daily internal life, expressed as her constant doubts and fears of being found out and identified as less smart than the others around her. She became aware of how afraid she was to be seen as incompetent. If she were judged as such, she felt she would be rejected and unloved; unless she was perfect, she would not be good enough. Her unshakable and unexamined conviction that unless she was perfect she was an utter failure personified the torture chamber that characterizes some of the internal structure of the deflated narcissist (Bach, 2006). It is a no-win situation where perfection is not possible: the sense of self, dependent on perfection as a lifeline, is not connected to the individual's real strengths, and they continually feel crushed.

How is it that an unconscious injured self-system and its accompanying conscious dysregulated self-state compels intelligent and often highly functional people like Melody to lose sight of the irrational aspects of their experience? As we often witness, dysregulated states display such intense negative emotions that they end up strengthening faulty thought processes, which are represented in narcissistic dysregulation or collapse (Bach, 2006). The following sections further examine how these unconscious narcissistic systems—based in old patterns and triggers encoded by the fear system— still exert an enormous power on perception, emotions, and cognition.

VULNERABILITY AND DEFENSIVE SELF-REGULATION

Melody's emotional and cognitive patterns demonstrated complex aspects of a deflated internal structure, accompanied by a great deal of anxiety and depressed affect. Her automatic attempts at securing a sense of well-being reflected an ineffective and unrealistic conviction that perfection was proof of her self-worth. She did not actually experience herself as perfect, but she held the desire to be seen as a perfect and flawless professional. It is important to note, without going into too much detail, that Melody grew up with a bitter, critical mother; she often witnessed her mother being belittled and put down by her maternal grandmother, who lived with them. As a child, Melody seemed to have encoded many memory traces that implicitly carried very critical communications from her grandmother to her mother. Her identification with her criticized mother and anguish about her mother's miserable reactions led to her internalization of these critical voices and sense of injury as her own. These experiences fueled her later extremely anxious and self-doubting narratives.

We need to remember that although the pervasiveness of dysregulation and self-regulatory defenses in narcissistic disorders may be more obvious than in other situations, we all embody the dual systems of hurt and protection—occupying spaces on the continuums of consciousness and flexibility. In effect, our sophisticated self-regulating mechanisms are surely among the most essential and intriguing aspects of the human brain/mind, with significant individual variations. We have yet to understand why two people can grow up in similar environments but encode fear and trauma very differently and with different results. As we have seen before, the predisposition to experience fear and anxiety usually runs in families. But beyond innate tendencies like shyness and felt anxiety, environmental factors may further cause a genetic expression of the fear system and its influence on other emotions, thoughts, and behaviors.

In addition to what she witnessed between her mother and grandmother, Melody was also directly subjected to her mother's criticism and sarcasm—behaviors clearly internalized and unconsciously enacted against her own daughter. Melody had no choice but to develop an unconscious self-system that oscillated between two self-states. The first self-state held very anxious, shame-filled, self-doubting, and critical beliefs and narratives. The protective state, on the other hand, constantly created unrealistic pacts and imposed childlike conditions to achieve a sense of well-being; mostly, only perfection would negate her sense of shame and low self-esteem. We can imagine the role of the default network—the brain's activity at rest—being preoccupied with the inward processing of feelings, memories, and ruminations about what it felt like to be criticized and what it took to overcome injured and anxious feelings (Gusnard et al., 2001; Raichle et al., 2001). In reality, Melody's conviction that only perfection would bring relief became just as tortuous as her internal suffering about her perceived shortcomings.

We can see how a pattern of deflated narcissism embodies such an emotional collapse and loss of self-esteem; we experience any flaws or mistakes as if they were catastrophic and capable of potentially annihilating our very essence as human beings. Such perceived vulnerabilities serve as the ultimate proof of our worthlessness and, thus, arouse inordinate levels of anxiety. Any realistic perspective or wider prism on life and reality does not exist when threats to our integrity come up. Melody's extreme doubts about her self-competency developed as a response to a critical mother, who was often humiliated by her own mother. As Melody came to understand her childhood, she realized that watching her mother being continually put down by an angry and rigid grandmother caused Melody a great deal of anxiety and pain. By unconsciously identifying with her mother's shame, it became her burden of shame as well. Being criticized by her own mother seemed natural and justified to Melody; the negative self-system with its hyperaroused states of anxiety and their self-diminishing narratives was never questioned until Melody entered therapy. As we have seen with Scott, Anna, and Jerry, the unconscious nature of triggers and narratives is universal to humans. Like Anna, Melody experienced imposter syndrome, feeling that she didn't belong and utterly convinced that she wasn't simply good enough. Unlike Anna, Melody's early encoded neuropsychological networks expressed themselves through narcissism in adulthood.

As we see in clinical practice, deflated patients are often preoccupied with comparing themselves to others, constantly trying to assess their perceived value, and often judging themselves as lacking or inferior. They feel diminished when others succeed, as if such successes are a reflection on their own competence. In extreme cases, patients are loath to read, learn new material, or seek help, unconsciously convinced that such acts in and of themselves are proof of failure.

Overinflated patients, on the other hand, are extremely sensitive to any intimation that they harbor within them human weaknesses or flaws. It is as if the very acknowledgment of a human need, vulnerability, or flaw has the power to throw them right back into the unconscious web of intense and intolerable shame wrapped in anxiety. Even dependency on others may be unconsciously perceived negatively given the narcissist's belief that having a human need renders them weak and vulnerable (Kernberg, 2007). For that reason, they often have a difficult time with interpersonal disagreements or conflict.

Within bonds, even close ones, narcissists unconsciously look to avoid the dreaded experience of the weak and vulnerable self. They have to be right and have the last word. As part of the constant and unconscious campaign to promote the self, some narcissists unconsciously seize on any opportunity to assert their superiority and remind others preemptively that they hold the power. Being unaware of themselves and their behaviors, they are often unaware of others existing as separate subjectivities, with needs, perceptions, and opinions different than their own. Their main internal preoccupation is their own fight for psychic survival, so others mainly exist as tools to achieve the narcissist's sense of well-being.

ROGER'S CASE: VICTIM AND VICTIMIZER

When Roger was about 3 years old, growing up in an upper-middle-class family, his older brother started abusing him verbally and physically. His parents were not aware of the severity of their son's aggressive bullying and refused to acknowledge it even when they were alerted to it. Throughout his childhood, Roger remembered complaining about being bullied by his brother, but his parents did not take him seriously. They told him to "be a man" and insisted that both brothers assume equal responsibility for the conflicts. Roger felt helpless and lacked any resources to fight back; even when he tried, his brother accused him of instigating the fights, and at times even convinced Roger that he was to blame. After many such fights, Roger felt that his parents also blamed him, so Roger concealed his sense of helplessness and rage. Underneath Roger's hidden feelings were unconscious triggers resulting from the encoding of fear and trauma from his childhood. Not only was he negatively impacted by his brother's bullying, but he was also further traumatized by his parents' failure to listen and protect him.

Roger started therapy in his 40s due to serious problems in his marriage, especially repeated fights and disagreements that caused a great deal of stress for the entire family. Paradoxically, he appeared at once brittle and arrogant. He was convinced that he was the victim in his marriage just as he had been the victim in his family of origin. He attributed the problems in the relationship to his wife's unfulfilling part-time career and her frustrations at having to sacrifice her professional life to take care of their two sons. His frequent expressions of righteous indignation, self-confidence in his own assessments, total lack of self-doubt, and a withering attitude toward his wife were delivered without any reflective awareness. The narcissism in these behaviors is obvious; what is less obvious is the defensive mechanisms at work, protecting Roger's fragile sense of self. The self-aggrandizing behavior was often triggered when he felt vulnerable and helpless, as he had in childhood. The greatest difficulty in our initial therapeutic encounter was Roger's sensitivity to any exploration that required some sort of self-examination or a more nuanced understanding of his marriage and other relationships. He would bristle when asked to reflect on the connection between his difficult past and his present relationships.

It's not that Roger did not recognize that his past affected his present problems, but that understanding was only couched in the context of being a victim. In essence, Roger had unconsciously interpreted his fear of his brother and his trauma at not being protected by his parents as a narrative of being a victim. He was still a victim of his brother's bullying, his parents' unempathetic neglect, and his wife's complaints and dissatisfaction. He rejected any possible links between painful emotions and the enacted need to be on top, to control others, and, at the same time, still see himself as the only victim. Similarly, his automatic expressions of self-aggrandizement and the importance of being vindicated at all costs remained unconscious. More than a year into therapy, Roger would get angry with me when he perceived the intrusion of my own subjectivity in our interactions, sometimes rightly but other times with a great deal of projected and not entirely reality-bound certainty. I could not freely express my own ideas about what I perceived was going on; this was often perceived as a disagreement and an insult. Roger wanted me to completely accept his version of who he was and the nature of our interactions.

The level of sensitivity to disagreement and perceived slights permeated his relationship with his wife. If she disagreed with him or insisted that he examine his behavior, he felt attacked and devalued. Over time, Roger viscerally realized that some of his intense and recurrent problems with his two boys might be related to his past experiences. He came to see that his frequent complaints about his wife were an expression of the deep wounds within him. Only then did he slowly begin to let our interactions sink in, with less defensive argumentation. "Fear for my marriage and my sons made me brave," Roger later said. Yet, as his therapy continued for several more years, we still encountered the automatic enactment of his entrenched defensive modes and the inevitable entanglements that our interactions created.

The lengthy therapy was an important aspect of Roger's progress toward an enhanced ability to look inward with less panic and defensiveness. During that time, again and again, his life experiences, his many interactional difficulties, and the many distortions embedded in the ways he saw himself and others were felt, identified, and analyzed. Whereas Melody's internal shifts occurred relatively rapidly—within a year both her internal states and her encounters with her external environment changed considerably—Roger's path was more difficult.

It is entirely possible that, from the onset, Melody possessed more flexible and, thus, more open connections between her cortical and subcortical systems, allowing for a quicker attunement to and integration of novel ways of feeling and thinking about herself and others. Roger's learning curve, on the other hand, was impeded by the enactment of a more entrenched narcissistic self-system. With time, his complicated and rigid web of hurts, resentments, and defenses softened as well. A growing reflective ability and an increased affect tolerance enabled him to eventually construct entirely new ways of understanding himself and others. Roger realized that he embodied and enacted both victim and victimizer, hurt and rage, helplessness and defenses against it. This enabled Roger to modify his internal reactions and interpersonal behaviors. He deepened his capacity to tolerate and sit with difficult feelings, feelings that in the past would have been quickly responded to with familiar patterns. With this growing awareness, the automaticity of Roger's emotional, cognitive, and behavioral reactions greatly diminished. Time may indeed be an important aspect of the therapeutic process, especially when it comes to changing entrenched neural pathways. This brings up an important consideration in relationships with clients: We need to set realistic expectations that healing the aftermath of fear and trauma takes time. In a society that values quick fixes, this is an important foundational piece of effective therapy.

LEARNING AND AUTOMATICITY OF DEFENSE

The process of developing unconscious and automatic defensive systems is closely intertwined with implicit and explicit learning processes. We saw this with both Melody and Roger, who implicitly learned their parents' definitions of who they were as children. Learning occurs when specific behaviors, emotional reactions, comforting thoughts, or soothing internal monologues lead to a favorable outcome of restored well-being. In this context, we can empathetically hold narcissistic behaviors as an attempt to restore a sense of well-being, no matter how dysfunctional and ultimately ineffective.

We can fully understand how internal or external responses, from simple avoidance to complex cognitive machinations such as the tendency toward grandiose self-soothing, take hold in the face of early painful blows to the self. Roger, a victim of bullying and the failure to be protected by his parents, escalated his self-soothing and self-affirming behaviors into full-blown narcissism. Melody, on the other hand, became stuck in a continual neuropsychological loop of negative narratives underpinned and reinforced by her growing anxiety about her self-worth.

Learning is crucial when a negative and faulty self-evaluation develops; a child has no choice but to internalize his parents' impatience, criticism, neglect, or lack of acceptance as his own. These communications become the dominant measure of a child's self-worth. We see this clearly for Melody, who internalized two generations of negative patterns, her grandmother's criticisms of her mother and her mother's criticism of her. Learning determines the strength of the defense response, whether it is automatically recruited to reestablish a more positive emotional state or whether a child succumbs to the parents' definition of them; the latter is a possible reaction against defying the parents in order to secure their love. We see this in Roger's story as he succumbed to victimhood in the face of his parents' refusal to defend him and a vain attempt to earn their love.

UNCONSCIOUS SYSTEMS AND EITHER-OR RESPONSES

Often narcissistic clients who have just entered therapy seem to enact unconscious self-systems with a remarkable degree of obliviousness as to the opposing
emotional and behavioral extremes that characterize these systems. This certainly
was true with Roger early in his therapy. An either-or way of relating to oneself,
others, and the world at large is common. For example, Melody frequently shifted
between a self-state where she felt like an utter failure and a self-state where she
was convinced that only perfection would confirm her self-worth. For Roger,
people were always mistaken or correct, inferior or superior, victims or victim-
izers. Both Melody and Roger exhibited polarized thinking, where gray areas of
perception or interpretation are nonexistent; one is either bad or good, guilty or
totally absolved of guilt, experiencing pain or pleasure, utterly alone or attached
to others (Bach, 2006). Some researchers see this polarization as a failure to
develop a "usable transitional area in which dichotomy, ambiguity, and paradox
can be acknowledged and contained" (Bach, 2006, p. 76).

The disconnect between self-patterns containing enactive representations of
injury and defense develops when parallel—but unconsciously interacting—
self-systems of pain and defense become exceedingly robust. Although the connections between these two emotionally significant maps is not conscious, these
relationships nonetheless foster separate pathways for self-experience. The more
pronounced and rigid the dissociation between the unconsciously held injury and
the defense, the more vacillation between them is experienced and enacted. As
a result, an either-or pattern of experience dominates one's personality. Good
and bad intersubjective encounters come to inhabit different self-systems and
self-states, resulting in a split between them with no linkages (Bromberg, 2006,
2011; Kernberg, 1975, 1997, 2007). This was the case for Melody, who saw herself as either an utter failure incapable of success or a person for whom success
necessitated perfection, which was in theory attainable.

For some individuals, the more devastating the emotional quality of the
injury, the more it may become split or disconnected from the defenses used
against it. However, while the linkages between the injury and the defenses are
unconscious, the actual memories of experiences of deep anxiety and trauma in
the wake of an injury can often be recalled by the individual. What facilitates the
persistence of the split between the two self-systems is the enormous emotional
significance that experiences of being shamed, criticized, or diminished carry

for the state of well-being and the survival of our own perceived integrity. Both Roger and Melody could clearly describe painful events from their childhoods but, prior to therapy, had been unaware of the linkages between childhood and adult challenges.

Some researchers suggest the existence of a bidimensional affective system that innately reacts to and emphasizes the positive or negative valence and perceived values embedded in every situation (Zachar & Ellis, 2012). This perceived—and often projected—good/bad value inherent in any internal or external context reflects how we interpret the meaning of most stimuli and states of arousal. In the context of human evolution, this innate dual approach helps explain the binary way of thinking often noticed among narcissistic patients, but a way not unique to them. From early on, driven by an actual or perceived blow to the sense of self, good or bad valence is automatically generated by what some researchers call core affects (Adolphs & Anderson, 2018; Damasio, 1999, 2000, 2010; Panksepp & Biven, 2012; Zachar & Ellis, 2012).

The core affect, whether positive or negative, is the basis for our emotional life, guiding cognitive and behavioral choices. Within its innate and automatic nature, the core affect will certainly influence all-or-nothing binary perceptions of ourselves and others, shaping the binary nature of narcissistic approaches to the self as all good or all bad. The developing defenses are shaped by a similar binary assessment—grandiosity or the unconscious fear of humiliation and narcissistic collapse.

Similarly, emphasizing homeostatic goals as the guiding principle of our innate response tendencies adds reward and punishment as the all-important incentives for exploration, action, or withdrawal (Damasio, 2010). Paradoxically, there is no single designated agency in the brain/mind acting as the "rewarder" or "punisher" (Damasio, 2010, p. 55). Yet, rewards and punishments are quickly assessed (Damasio, 2010, p. 55) by the emotional and personal value of an experience as rewarding or harmful. This ultimately determines how we react to it, internally and interpersonally.

THE COST OF NARCISSISTIC STRUCTURE: INTERPERSONAL RELATIONSHIPS

A narcissistic self-structure is characterized by an unconscious and unyielding conviction that the sense of self is fragile and extremely vulnerable, needing

to be defended at all costs. Often, narcissistic defensive systems enact a vora-
cious need—at times even an insistent demand—to be adored, recognized, and
appreciated. Other systems frequently seek validation and agreement, as in the
case of the garrulous, grandiose patients who do not understand the reasons for
their interpersonal difficulties. Again, seeing narcissism as a desperate attempt
to defend the self and the sense of well-being allows us to have empathy for narcissists; this creates the necessary foundation for healing.

At its core, a narcissistic structure of injury and coping may not be particularly
different from any other systems of conscious or unconscious self-organization.
As we have seen in previous chapters, we all embody variations in our vulnerability to hurt or trauma, and our innate need to psychologically survive. In the
midst of dysregulation, when our sense of self is threatened, an amalgam of conscious and unconscious emotions and cognitive convictions gets triggered (Bach,
2006, p. 21). The resultant swings between the unconscious sense of being oblit-
erated and old, rigid defenses seriously influence the qualities of relationships
that narcissists are capable of.

At first glance, this assessment may seem excessive; but, on closer examination, we can recognize that what characterizes a narcissistic coping mechanism
is indeed the tendency during dysregulation to be fully and solely attuned to
one's own feelings and thoughts. The narcissist's internal reality becomes the
only reality. In these cases, their internal experience does not align with or take
into account real-time conditions, nor can it pay any attention to others' needs
or separate subjectivity. This was particularly true for Roger, for example. These
modes of functioning affect all levels of the narcissist's relationships to themselves and others, especially within an intimate relationship. What we often witness among narcissists is the inability to consider others as whole individuals
with their own preferences, response patterns, and ideas. In some narcissist's
unconscious fantasies, others are there to psychologically support them alone.
For this reason, disagreements can cause serious interpersonal struggles. Narcissistic pathology, in particular, presents an extreme example of failure to take
reality into account, tolerate ambiguity, or accept multiple points of view (Bach,
2006; Kohut, 1971).

The unconscious and excessive preoccupation with protecting the sense of
self may lead to a lack of awareness about the consequences of our behavior for
others. Narcissistic individuals may come across as insensitive and selfish. As
some researchers suggest, narcissists are addicted to receiving and experiencing

positive self-esteem (Baumeister & Vohs, 2001). They may also be incredibly sensitive to what they perceive as critical or belittling remarks and often tend to misinterpret vague innuendos as negative evaluation.

Consequently, it seems that the biggest costs to a narcissistic personality structure are the many potential interpersonal entanglements created by their honed sensitivity and unconscious defenses. The tendency to disregard the other or, in more extreme cases, to disallow others from having subjectivities of their own make people with narcissistic tendencies difficult to live with. Conversely, some tend to begin every relationship by idealizing others, by imbuing them with a host of idealized qualities that in essence reflect the idealized opinions that narcissists may have of themselves. Predictably, following an inevitable disappointment, the newly flawed other is no longer tolerated as an object of love or affection.

Clinicians have observed that narcissists have difficulty establishing a sense of themselves as consequential agents in the context of other selves (Bach, 2006, p. 23). The anxiety about losing themselves as separate worthwhile entities drives them to unconsciously avoid any manifestations of vulnerability. As a result, they sometimes outwardly reject their dependency needs (Kernberg, 2007). This was my experience with Roger, especially at the start of our relationship. His noticeable drive to show his strength and superior knowledge and to have the last word was expressed through frequent attempts to challenge my observations and put his stamp on what was said and understood. The unconscious aim was to prove his resilience; he really didn't need me and my interventions.

The interpersonal limitations inherent to narcissistic personality disorder are also linked to the failure to develop a theory of mind in relation to significant others (Bateman & Fonagy, 2012; Fonagy et al., 2002). Linked by researchers to early intersubjective difficulties, the failure to develop a theory of mind dovetails with excessive feelings of panic regarding the survival and the integrity of the self. Therapy is especially challenging as a result of the frequent lack of self-awareness that characterizes narcissistic structure, the difficulties in taking another's subjectivity into account, and the general tendency toward unconsciousness about one's feelings and actions.

IMPLICATIONS FOR TREATMENT

Throughout the past few decades, major advances have been made in the treatment of narcissistic disorders. Kohut's (1971) seminal work focused on the therapist's role as a self-object to the patient. Such an attentive and support-ive relationship is designed to help clients heal their injuries and thus develop their stunted growth as whole, mature individuals. Some clinicians also empha-sized rupture and repair as inevitable and necessary interactional processes. A mutual repair of an interpersonal rupture strengthens the client's ability to tol-erate interpersonal disagreement and emotional struggles (Kohut, 1971). Clearly, like all interpersonal relationships, psychological treatments can never avoid such ruptures or enactments entirely. Therefore, the successful resolutions of inter-personal entanglements are a central element in psychotherapy, especially with narcissistic clients.

Obviously, much empathy is needed when offering any intervention address-ing emotional pain, defenses, and interpersonal difficulties. With the chang-ing view of intersubjectivity, however, the view of empathy has changed as well. Empathy is not seen simply as the feelings of sympathy or understanding, but as being part of an honest, freeing exchange between client and therapist (Aron, 1989; Bromberg, 2006; Chused, 1998; Ginot, 1997, 2001, 2007, 2009, 2015). This more interactive and authentic understanding of empathy implies a flow of communication, especially when attempting to resolve an enactment (Kernberg, 2007).

What points us toward more engaging and confronting interactions with the narcissistic patient, to my mind, is the knowledge that a client seeks therapy likely knowing that something in their way of being does not work. Often, these clients live their lives with emotional, professional, and interpersonal difficulties. As defended and sensitive as they are, a part of them still wants to get a handle on their lives, to feel more balanced, and to enact fewer destructive behaviors. A sensitive and unafraid therapist can create a place for honest communications and exchanges, even if they involve hard questions that have been long avoided. The defenses themselves should be held empathetically, analyzed, and under-stood in the context of the client's past.

This was the case with Roger's and Melody's therapeutic processes. In spite of Roger's need to always be right, to fight for and establish his autonomy at any cost, part of him was also engaged, surreptitiously, in taking me and our inter-actions in. This was especially noticeable when his defenses were lived and expe-rienced in the sessions. As treatment continued, he became increasingly curious about how his behavior affected his family, therapy, and me.

Melody's therapeutic process also addressed the emotional and the interpersonal costs of her unconscious self-systems and self-states. In her eagerness to reduce her intolerable distress and suffering, she was open to a different kind of dys-regulation: the one she experienced with me during sessions. But this time, she was simultaneously accessing her most painful experiences and memories while also reflecting on them in real time. Each time she could regulate her affect and negative thinking within a session, she took that ability with her to her work and her social life. The growing elucidation of her dual volatile systems of pain and defense greatly contributed to Melody's ability to become more aware and integrated. This very brief description of her treatment leads us to Chapter 11. Continuing with the theme of reflective awareness and mentalization, it discusses their centrality to the therapeutic process.

CHAPTER ELEVEN

Self-Narratives as Expressions of Unconscious Anxious Self-States

As we follow our inner experiences, we inevitably encounter stable and repeated self-narratives which, to a large extent, construct our conscious feelings of who we are. This chapter focuses on a particular form of narratives: familiar thoughts, beliefs, and ruminations that most often express deep anxiety about our own perceived flaws. When triggered, usually during a dysregulating state of anxiety, they enter our consciousness and center on important aspects of our self, especially in relation to others. We compare ourselves to others, feel inferior to them, and feel fear about being judged or found out as imposters. You may remember Anna's story from Chapter 4; she was plagued by these comparisons, which created in her a sense of being less competent than her peers and a fear of being discovered as an imposter.

These thoughts and narratives are often inseparable parts of challenging and anxiety-inducing situations. When triggered, old and familiar internal monologues and ruminations attack us with discouraging, demeaning, or anger-filled assessments of our abilities or lack thereof. To quote Panksepp and Biven (2012), "In humans these [affective states] are always accompanied by cognitive changes, such as emotionally entangled attributions, ruminations, all sort of plans and worries" (p. 451).

Anna's struggle to regain courage and confidence in meetings was often stymied in the face of her habitual tendency to drown in her own negative narratives about her competence. In the midst of these anxieties and extreme fear of being shamed, she would forget that she was at a meeting with her bosses for a reason, that they wanted her there and thought she had something important to contribute. These self-narratives or ruminations, in effect, give a more conscious articulation to unconscious patterns organized around a basic sense of inadequacy and fears of exposing this inadequacy to others.

Our repeated self-narratives essentially give shape to our conscious sense of identity. These narratives may be different, but they all are imbued with the core emotions that influence a particular brain/mind pattern (Bromberg, 2009). Most of us possess resilient, optimistic self-states that, through strong internal positive narratives, allow for smooth and productive functioning. Such narratives have allowed so many of us to push ourselves through difficulties, for example, with the COVID-19 pandemic. Other self-states, those influenced by fear and anxiety, produce more judgmental and harsh narratives about the self. Some states may be organized around unconscious or unresolved resentment and rage, expressing themselves through narratives of bitterness, victimhood, dissatisfaction, and anger. Other narratives unconsciously give rise to rebellious thoughts and actions dedicated to guarding against any perceived threats to our shaky autonomy.

What is so interesting about our human minds is that distinctly diverse narratives simultaneously coexist in our brain/minds, revealing our most essential patterns. Narratives may be triggered by different situational contexts such as recurrent memories, shifting moods, and unconscious expectations of rewarding or negative outcomes. These stimuli activate old patterns that react to our present circumstances in the same way they did in response to anxiety-inducing situations during our early development. When created under adverse conditions, such negative narratives acquire a particular neural strength. What is so illuminating about narratives is their unconscious repetition; in response to triggering situations, they surface with the same thoughts, convictions, and beliefs.

NARRATIVE PATTERNS AND THE INTEGRATED BRAIN/MIND/BODY

In a broad sense, self-narratives are an example of how brain/mind processes are integrated; visceral physiology, emotion, cognition, and action tendencies are intertwined within the brain/mind, even if we are not aware of this unity

(Damasio, 1999, 2010; LeDoux, 2002; Panksepp & Biven, 2012). In other words, narratives are the verbal expressions of all these entwined processes. We typically think of each of these as separate entities, holding on to the somewhat intuitive notion that in our felt experience, as well as within the brain, emotion, thoughts, and actions are different and distinct phenomena. But as we know now, subjectively felt experiences integrate and convey all mental functions; feelings actually give cognitive meaning to our emotions, and automatic behaviors are an unconscious expression of both feelings and cognition (Okon-Singer et al., 2015; Pessoa, 2016; Todd & Anderson, 2013; Todd et al., 2020). Cognition and emotions overlap in most areas of the brain and there are no regions in which either reside as a separate function. This is the result of the interconnectedness and the integrated processes of all brain areas and functions (Okon-Singer, 2018; Pessoa, 2016, 2018; Todd et al., 2011, 2012, 2020).

As we often see in clients and in ourselves, a recurrent narrative expresses a vulnerable self-state, giving it a familiar shape and feel. In the midst of an anxious state, visceral sensations, emotions, and thoughts are inextricably intertwined; feelings are embodied by words and words are fueled by feelings, both equally conveying the intensity of a negative state. Neurally, and therefore experientially, emotions and thoughts are one and the same.

Through direct connections to the basal ganglia, the hippocampus, and the prefrontal cortex, "the amygdala highlights particular interpretations, memories, and appraisals, which then become increasingly consolidated over time" (Lewis & Todd, 2007). Emotional learning and associations mediated by the amygdala not only regulate real-time cortical activity but also continue to shape the cognitive evaluations and thought processes of events and experiences. Remembering the influence of the amygdala on the brain during early development, we can appreciate the negative tones the amygdala confers on a wide range of experiences, including neutral ones. Through such negative influences, interpersonal situations, for example, may acquire meaning that signals fear, anxiety, negative expectations, shame, or low self-esteem. As they become part of unconscious patterns, these negative meanings give rise to self-narratives.

Although we don't have access to the vast brain-wide networks, we can become aware of the narratives they create. As a matter of fact, one of the most revealing manifestations of an integrated neural network suffused with anxiety and vulnerability is the recurrent negative feelings and thoughts that often surface unbidden during stress. Through familiar ruminations and internal monologues, narratives about who we are give voice to all facets of unconscious patterns. What is conveyed through narratives are some of the distorted conclusions children arrive at when they attempt to make sense of emotional experiences. It is during this process of meaning making that injured, fearful, vulnerable, angry, shameful feelings, or a mix of these feelings, establish a presence in our brain/minds.

THE INTERSUBJECTIVE ROOTS OF UNCONSCIOUS SELF-STATES

Although narratives are expressed through words, their first emotional foundations can be found in a child's early intersubjective environments. States of anxious dysregulation will shape much of the child's encoded memories, forming the earliest network representations of visceral and emotional states of well-being or frustration and stress. It's important to emphasize again that early-forming networks influence subsequent experiences. The neural strength of negative learning and expectations will influence how future experiences are perceived and understood.

Infancy

We have seen how sensitive infants, children, and adolescents are to fear-inducing stimuli; in addition, we know that the picture is more complicated. Innate temperament and inborn brain connectivity also affect the trajectory of our emotional growth. For example, specific proteins responsible for ways of coping with stress are transmitted from mother rats to their pups (Zaidan et al., 2013), and similar findings have been reported in humans (Vonderwalde, 2019). Still, developmental forces are most likely found in the interaction between genes and the environment and, more specifically, in the process of gene expression in the context of environmental influences (Callaghan et al., 2019; Schore, 2012; Todd et al., 2020).

In addition to the spoken words, a great deal of communication is actively transmitted by the caregiver through nonverbal processes. This is especially so within the all-important intersubjective field, the total sum of all aspects of mutual interactions and emotional resonance between parents and children. Intersubjectivity can be defined as these ongoing mutual experiences driven by conscious and unconscious, verbal and nonverbal communication. As a result, at all times, alongside the child's essential separateness and inherent temperament, there are self-states that are utterly attuned to the caregiver's physical presence, emotions, and vocal communications.

This lack of differentiation is not simply a result of the child's supposed nonexistent subjectivity. Rather, this deep attentiveness of the child to the parent's state of mind and behaviors is due to an active, evolutionarily determined psycho-biological need. This ongoing attentiveness is an aspect of the all-important attachment needs a young child has. Paying close attention to the caregiver ensures the child's sense of togetherness and, thus, security (Beebe & Lachmann, 2002; Braten, 2007; Braten & Trevarthen, 2007; Bromberg, 2006; Cozolino, 2006; Lyons-Ruth, 2003; Schore, 2012; Stern, 1985; Tronick, 2007).

Intersubjectivity describes an interactional model that changes over time but still has one enduring feature: the child's other-centered focus (Braten, 2007; Braten & Trevarthen, 2007). This model explains the power of learning and identification processes, showing them to be the essential building blocks of developing internalized patterns. The primary phase of intersubjectivity emphasizes verbal and nonverbal exchanges between parents and infants, and their mutual mirroring of each other's emotional states. These are the earliest intersubjective connections. We recall here that infants have shown particular sensitivity to their caregiver's expressions and vocal tones. As mentioned in Chapter 8, infants' brain circuits actually change in response to interparental fights. Infants also display a tendency to detect and pay more attention to threatening facial expressions. The strong attention paid to the adults around them and the identification and learning processes make infants especially vulnerable to fear- and anxiety-inducing intersubjective interactions.

Toddlerhood

In the secondary intersubjective phase, toddlers and their caregivers progress to a different mode of attunement. Here, toddlers seek and find shared intentions and interests with parents. The need for shared emotions, thoughts, and behaviors becomes the foundation for the child's sense of self in relation to the parent. During this phase, a shared agreement about the toddler's accomplishments is especially important. Toddlers often seek confirmations and emotional echoes to their exuberance and growing exploratory behaviors. During this period, toddlers are especially animated by feelings of pride and a quest for autonomy. Conversely, they are also sensitive to communications that arouse feelings of shame, disappointment, and a sense of deflation; these feelings are a primary focus for toddlers around 18 months of age (Braten & Trevarthen, 2007; Schore, 2003).

In addition, developing verbal skills enable toddlers to acquire new forms of intersubjectivity and additional modes of interaction. A toddler's ongoing attention to and involvement in the emotions, language, and behaviors of caretakers become more nuanced and sophisticated. At the same time, the automatic learning and identification processes that encode all these complex processes virtually guarantee an unavoidable internalization of the many facets of the parent's feeling states and behaviors. In effect, the child is exposed to two kinds of communications which they encode and make their own: the direct communications directed toward the child on the one hand, and the parents' verbal and nonverbal communication about their own internal feeling states and ways of coping with them, on the other. As we often see, we tend to enact both sides of these communications. We often oscillate between a self-state that acutely feels the hurt inflicted by others, and a self-state that can be the one inflicting pain on others.

The Preschool Years

Tertiary intersubjective participation occurs between 3 and 6 years of age; it is defined by an even greater understanding of, and absorption in, the thoughts and emotions of others. As a child's cognitive skills expand, they become increasingly entangled with their caregivers' emotional, cognitive, and behavioral personality traits. During this phase, there is a significant increase in children's ability to ruminate, think of themselves in autobiographical mode, utilize their imaginations, and give meaning to emotional events. These growing abilities lead to a web of interpretations that may distort the meaning of actual interactions and events (Gazzaniga, 2007; Gazzaniga et al., 2014).

This lag between a strong emotional circuit and slower-developing cognitive abilities causes two problematic outcomes for children. First, in the absence of emotion regulation, this gap intensifies, and at times exaggerates, children's emotional reactions to frustration and injury. Second, the lack of higher cognitive ability and perspective leads to distorted interpretations of the meaning of emotional experiences. Most often, such meaning making by the child focuses on the parent's verbalized disapproval, internalizing it as truth. Unconscious learning and imitative processes underpin what the child learns about themselves.

Studies that examined the degree to which children identify with adults' ideas, feelings, and actions have shown that during play, children often repeat whole conversations that they have been exposed to in interactions with their parents. In these observations, a caregiver's verbal comments and actions became part of the children's conversations and a way of acting with their playmates. Throughout these developmental intersubjective periods, then, there are increasing opportunities for children to learn from and imitate parental behaviors. Among the important internalized lessons are those that lead to children's erroneous interpretations of what injurious communications from parents actually mean.

As some researchers have found, children largely understand things in a literal way; a parent's statements, in the child's mind, describe things as they really are (Richardson & Saxe, 2020a, 2020b; Saxe, 2010; Saxe & Houlihan, 2017). Parental anger and disapproval of the child, for example, are perceived by the child as a true assessment of who they are. Children have no ability to see a parent's negative outbursts as an expression of their own personal turmoil, agitation, or limitations, not an accurate assessment of the child's character. The attentiveness to a parent's opinions and the power such opinions carry inevitably results in an immature and distorted interpretation about the source of emotional difficulties. The source of a child's injury is unconsciously seen by the child as coming from themselves—their own actions, feelings, and thoughts. When such experiences are put into words in a ruminative internal monologue, they become negative self-narratives (Braten, 2007; Ginot, 2015; Grawe, 2007; Lyons-Ruth, 2003; Olds, 2006).

When parents are not aware of their tendency to project and enact their own unconscious patterns, shaming and emotional bruising are inevitable. Such injurious interactions may be common within a child's peer group as well, leading to further hurt, feelings of rejection, and self-doubt. Beyond words as the basis for developing narratives, the parents' emotional states are crucial as well. Anxious parents, whether they talk about their feelings or not, transmit their fearful approach to the world, unconsciously teaching their children to be fearful. Although not fully grasping the source of the anxiety, through learning and identification the child's immersion in a parent's feeling state leads to the unconscious adoption of anxious ruminations as their own.

Furthermore, parental internal emotional states and behaviors that have nothing to do with the child will also be co-opted by the child as if they were their own. The child may come to believe they are the source of the feelings and behaviors emanating from the parents; examples include a parent's own tendencies to become irritated or impatient, episodes of depression or chronic low mood, frustration with a job or marriage, anxiety, self-denigration, and frequent parental fighting. As higher-order development continues, children increasingly see themselves as responsible coauthors of anything they feel or think, even though the experiences they are immersed in and ruminate about originate from a parent (Braten, 2007; Hermans, 2004; Lewis & Todd, 2004, 2007).

LANGUAGE AS A BRIDGE BETWEEN AFFECT AND COGNITION

Our self-narratives are constructed from words embedded in feelings; as such, they are primarily expressed through our personal language or internal monologues. Language itself develops within "(m)other-centered" continual interactions as well (Braten, 2007, p. 123). Being attuned to a parent's vocal communications, the child unconsciously but actively coarticulates the speaker's intentions and actual words as if he himself were a co-originator of what is being said. A parent's actions and communications become the child's own. Parents' language and expressions about themselves are integrated within the child's own growing language. Of course, this is not just about the words themselves but rather the emotional and behavioral messages they carry—messages of fear or resilience, hope or despair. This is especially so when words that convey a parent's own distress are suffused with affect.

Again, we need to remember the exquisite alertness of the emotional system, and especially the fear system, to any signals of stress or fear. The amygdala, as we saw earlier, will orient toward intense emotions, especially fearful and painful ones, reinforcing neural activations. This neural activity and its influence on many brain regions eventually coalesce into a solid pattern of narratives, fantasies, or thought patterns. What accompanies these thought patterns is an entrenched linguistic knowledge about various aspects of the self. Mundane parental criticism, disapproval, intrusiveness, and rejection present a threat to the child's emotional intactness, laying the foundation for such distorted knowledge and beliefs. It may take a few years of mature adulthood before the child realizes the extent of such influences on their implicit core self and behavioral patterns.

During the first few years, before a greater perspective becomes available, a parent's feeling states will catch the child's attention; a parent's anxious approaches and behaviors, sad moods, or personal frustrations will arouse the child's anxiety and sadness as well. Resonating with the parent's distress, the child may feel threatened, sad, and worried, both for the parent and for themselves. In addition, as we saw, memories that embody and carry an emotional punch will stick, further ensuring that a parent's emotional states as well as their verbal expressions become part of a child's unconscious patterns.

As language develops and becomes the symbolic carrier of emotions, narratives provide a link to a wide range of emotional experiences. In this process, associative memories mediated by the amygdala together with episodic memories mediated by the hippocampus lay down patterns of meaning that continue to be refined and shaped over a child's development and into adulthood. The distorted explanations given by the child are made even more destructive by the slower-developing left hemisphere (i.e., the explainer) and the prefrontal cortex as a whole (Gazzaniga, 2009; Gazzaniga et al., 2014; Lewis & Todd, 2007; McGilchrist, 2009). This immaturity adds to the self-centric meaning given to an emotional state. Consequently, while in the midst of traumatic, painful, or shameful experiences, children have no choice but to arrive at distorted conclusions about their self-worth, competency, and importance to the parent and later on to their peers. Young children tend to believe they are the sole reason for the distressing or destabilizing feelings they experience. As a result, the meaning of a shaming or injurious experience focuses on their perceived badness and inferiority.

In an inextricable interaction between innate temperament and environment, children, then, tend to develop a host of self-blaming narratives about who they are. As children, they are not aware of the child-centric distortions of their interpretations. They are not aware of how their limited understanding and perspective leave them at the mercy of intense emotional experiences that they then proceed to frame in a childlike limited and immature way.

Ideas about the effects of parents on their children's behaviors have been with us for a long time; after all, the apple doesn't fall far from the tree, as they say. However, the wide reach of intersubjective processes through which a child absorbs and internalizes a parent's internal states and behavioral patterns is much clearer today. Verbally, nonverbally, and mostly unconsciously, parents communicate a great deal about their internal emotional states and behavioral tendencies. Emotional states and moods, past traumas and parental ways of coping with past and current stresses and challenges, their verbal expressions about themselves, and how they relate to others are imitated and internalized. In the first few years, these characteristics become entwined with the child's own innate traits, in essence underlying some of the child's own growing unconscious and conscious narratives about their own traits.

Our expanded neuropsychological understandings and my own clinical experience both highlight how influential self-narratives are in our psychology and behaviors. They seep into all our modes of conscious and unconscious functioning. Our narratives, both positive and negative, are in essence who we are, or who we tell ourselves we are. When activated during stressful situations, they take over our consciousness, intensifying our insecurities and self-doubts. Even after lying dormant and in the face of positive, resilient self-patterns that enable smooth and adaptive functioning, anxious patterns and their narratives remain hovering in the background, informing our decisions and moods.

SELF-NARRATIVES AND NEUROPSYCHOLOGICAL PROCESSES

The infant, child, and adolescent bring their own innate tendencies and dispositions, their anxiety levels, and a predetermined pace of neural and intellectual development. A child's innate tendencies can also influence a parent's internal reactions and enacted behaviors. An anxious baby or child, for instance, may try a parent's patience, moving them to employ controlling and angry behaviors. In turn, this vulnerable and sensitive child may feel even more anxious, stressed, and upset with themselves for disappointing the parent.

Indeed, the term *intersubjectivity* implies that both parties consciously and unconsciously affect each other; they both operate from an other-centered point of view and engage in a process of mutual influence. However, within the parent–child dyad, the child is the most vulnerable participant in the exchange. Paradoxically, by being so essential for survival, the bonds of intersubjectivity can also carry with them the seeds of excessively anxious and injured self-patterns. Painful, traumatizing, and humiliating interactions emanating from the parent are given self-centric meaning that becomes an entrenched narrative for the child.

An important implication of these findings is the necessity to consider the developmental phases of middle and late childhood as well as adolescence, viewing them as equally powerful and influential as early infancy. In other words, the potential for painful and humiliating experiences that may cause dysregulation and shape negative meanings needs to be considered throughout development. This is especially true during preadolescence and adolescence, when acceptance by one's peer group is important for well-being, and the push for self-definition occupies a central focus. During childhood, for example, conflict between parents or a difficult divorce will contribute to the child's developing negative narratives (Graham et al., 2015). A child who is exposed to interparental conflicts may experience feelings of panic over a possible divorce and anxious ruminations about themselves and their family. In addition to heightened states of fear and anxiety, the child may also misinterpret the meaning of such fights, feeling shame and guilt about their own misperceived and projected role in them.

It seems, then, that guided by the amygdala and mediated by the default mode network (see Chapters 3 and 4), inner monologues and verbal narrative express the many shades of emotions, fantasies, and beliefs that were influenced by states of fear and anxiety during development (Lewis & Todd, 2004). This susceptibility to negative monologues, driven by the amygdala and the attentional system, seems to be an inevitable part of intersubjective bonds during development, especially when a child's temperament is taken into account (Kagan, 1998; Lewis & Todd, 2004, 2007).

The human need to give meaning to all events may also create biases and distortions. As we tend to rely on quick impressions about the personal value and significance of a situation and as we tend to favor negative and self-incriminating meaning, we are particularly susceptible to neurally encoding negative narratives. This tendency is especially strong in the case of an anxious temperament or when the very early neural circuits were already affected by enhanced amygdala activity (Cimpian & Steinberg, 2014). These innate brain/mind unconscious processes further reinforce and exaggerate a child's or adolescent's inclination to perceive even benign parental communications as more critical than they really are.

THE MIRROR NEURON SYSTEM AND ATTUNEMENT

As we have learned, dysregulated states can develop not only from what is directly done and said to the child but through an unconscious process of absorption and imitation of a parental emotional self-state. But how do such internalizing processes occur? Research on the mirror neuron system further demonstrates the child's susceptibility to negative states and the development of negative narratives. The mirror neuron system has been shown to establish a neuropsychological link between interacting subjectivities that observe or relate to each other. Specifically, this system, found in the premotor cortex, imitates and predicts the actions of others. When studied, the observer's brain activity resembles that of the observed. This phenomenon is mediated by a neuropsychological process of embodied simulation, creating in our own brains the actions, affects, and intentions of those we observe or interact with (Gallese, 2006, 2008, 2009). These processes constitute the roots of empathy and intersubjectivity (Iacoboni et al., 2005; Ramachandran, 2011).

The mirror neuron system, then, supports the intersubjective building blocks of interactions and attachment (Gallese, 2006, 2008, 2009; Iacoboni, 2008; Rizzolati et al., 2002). But the mirror neuron system is also underpins our capacity for empathy and understanding others in a direct, emotional and nonverbal way. In Iacoboni's (2008) words, "This simulation process is an effortless, automatic, and unconscious inner mirroring" (p. 120).

Recalling the child's vulnerability to a parent's emotional states, the mirror neuron system mediates not just a nonverbal understanding of action and intention. Through our ability to get absorbed in the other's emotional state, the mirror neuron system also enables the important functions of unconscious imitation and learning. This, of course, leads to the child's resonance with a parent's pain and anxiety or, conversely, with their positive feelings (Dapretto et al., 2006; Iacoboni, 2008).

Mothers' mirror neuron system reactions were studied by scanning their brains using an fMRI scanner (Lenzi et al., 2008). The scanning took place while mothers were looking at their babies' facial expressions as well as those of unfamiliar babies, all 6 to 12 months old. The four expressions shown to the mothers were joyous, ambiguous, distressed, and neutral. The mothers who were assessed as emotionally available were also given the Adult Attachment Interview to evaluate their maternal reflective functioning. Predictably, the researchers found that the mirror neuron system, the insula, and the amygdala were more active during a mother's engagement with the images of her own baby, and also when they viewed images of joyous expressions. These intersubjective processes affect both parents and children. But as young children are the vulnerable ones, their absorption in, imitation of, and learning from their parents clearly shape and determine their developing self-narratives.

THE MEMORIES AND NARRATIVES WE HOLD

The important field of memory research further illuminates how distortions in one's narratives may occur. Our memory reservoirs constitute who we are in our conscious narratives. But as we now know, memories, including emotional memories, are not an accurate replica of our experience. Rather, memories are always in a state of being constructed and reconstructed, especially when they are consciously recalled and then reconstituted. Memories are intertwined with a person's current mood and colored by already established emotional self-systems through which they are recalled (Churchland, 2013; Damasio, 2010; Fernyhough, 2013; Panksepp & Biven, 2012). Dysregulated self-states will tend to call up negative memories and the narratives they coalesced into.

Memories, of course, can be accurate and genuine; but they can also be prone to distortions and biases. To emphasize the fragile and distorted characteristics of memories is not intended to simply undermine their accuracy. Rather, the more we know about how complex memory processes are, the more we realize how fragile they are, the more we can understand many of the distorted negative narratives we carry and fully believe to be true. For example, memories, or more accurately memory traces, are stored throughout different brain regions according to their visual, auditory, olfactory, and visceral elements. Through neural association of the time and space in which events took place and these traces were encoded, they become linked together to form what we then view as our memories (Dudai, 2011; Fernyhough, 2013).

As children, we take on other people's emotional states and verbal behaviors; this is especially true for caretakers, where children can easily become immersed in the caregiver's emotional states. Thus, our memories can be both emotional and contextual. But, in spite of this knowledge, when we experience the familiar convincing feeling of remembering, especially within an emotional state, memories feel totally true (Fernyhough, 2013). This feeling of remembering seems to be important to our consistent sense of self. But we also know that each time we recall something, we do not retrieve a static picture, but in essence we only recall what we remembered the last time we thought about a particular event or memory. Memories, then, are constructed and reconstructed (Churchland, 2013; Kandel, 2001). And as we have repeatedly seen in these chapters, a negative bias to negative events will color our memories as well. As our narratives become entwined with our remembered past, they also become incredibly vulnerable to negative biases and distortions.

Consequently, when triggered within a dysregulated state, narratives are experienced as based on real and true memories and impressions. Unless we become aware of these processes, we do not realize that some of these narratives may be based on constructed and reconstructed distorted memories.

Indeed, some researchers argue that memory and narratives are completely intertwined. Neuroimaging studies as well as observations of brain-damaged individuals reveal that similar neuronal systems underpin memory and story-telling (Fernyhough, 2013; Rubin, 2006). Being a key organizer of experience, self-narratives incorporate autobiographical memories with all their biases and emotional qualities. If information does not fit into the developing system, it has less of a chance to become a conscious memory.

We now have a robust picture of how anxiety influences negative self-narratives. But I'd like to raise a caution that calls into question the very negative spin therapists and clients tend to have about past experiences and relationships. We often hear from clients, think to ourselves, or read in case descriptions that a parent "never paid attention" or was "always critical and controlling." The emphasis is, of course, on "always" or "never."

If we are learning new things from neuropsychology, it is the consistent data showing how complex and intertwined all brain processes are, both con-scious and unconscious. This complexity inevitably also determines how we perceive, react to, and internalize those all-too-human beings that raise us. And if we also consider the interaction between predisposition and environ-ment, this process becomes exponentially more complex and complicated. Par-ents who love and deeply care for their children can also unwittingly dismiss, hurt, and reject them at times. They can transmit their own inner conflicts, anxieties, and sense of failure. And they can enhance their children's fears and provide a compromised model for attachment if they engage in frequent fights and hostile relationships.

It is helpful to remember that oftentimes we actually can greatly help our children approach difficult situations with more positive meanings and inter-pretations. Relevant examples are an amicable divorce, peer relationships, and stressful events like the COVID-19 epidemic. At the same time, it is also true that under all circumstances and under all conditions, children will form their own idiosyncratic and singular impressions and interpretations, using their innately determined intensity of feelings and cognitive tendencies. Practically speaking, as much as we may want to pay attention and be mindful about our children's internal feeling states, we still cannot fully know how they feel, what memories have left outsized impressions, and how they interpret what happens around them. We can be mindful and do our best, but we also need to accept that children are their own separate subjectivities and hope that our good intentions can still positively guide their developing self-narratives.

SYLVIA'S CASE: INTERGENERATIONAL TRAUMA AND SELF-NARRATIVES

Sylvia was in her late 50s when she started therapy with me. This was the second therapy attempt for her. She described her two-year previous therapy some years before as helpful to the extent that she understood her problems better. However, she did not feel more secure and self-confident and still could not stand up to her "controlling" husband or her two teenage boys. Her therapist helped her see how timid she was, she said. She realized how like a child she felt, little Sylvia who would not be respected in any group of successful adults.

In reality, Sylvia was a popular high school teacher. It soon became clear that she embodied that common dichotomy between self-denigrating internal narratives and the many productive and satisfying actual contours of one's life. As she started therapy the second time, Sylvia often thought of herself as less talented than her colleagues, with fewer good ideas and less creativity. She often tried to prove to me that her negative assessments of herself, in faculty meetings for example, were entirely justified by her supposedly lackluster performance. Presenting "facts" meant to prove that the others were "so much more confident and eloquent" than she was, it felt like it was important for her that I collude with her negative feelings about herself. When this unconscious message was identified and analyzed, it started Sylvia's deeper encounter with the roots of her easily triggered negative narratives.

When asked about her actual position and achievements, she was quick to state that "a lot of it was due to luck." She was good with students, and she was also well-organized. "That helped a lot." Obviously, these observations did not in any way describe her abilities as a teacher. But it became clear that Sylvia's anxious feelings about her competence in comparison to others also prevented her from achieving more. Her entrenched narratives of not being competent enough prevented her from writing more and taking on extra projects that she was actually interested in. Believing these internal voices, she was too anxious to try.

Sylvia's "timidity," as she described it, was especially disturbing to her in her relationship to her husband, whom she felt "was too controlling and too demanding." Sylvia got married later in life because, as she says, she wanted and tried to "establish her independent self." In her husband she found a partner she thought would help her make her own decisions. With time, however, Sylvia found herself increasingly ceding control to him. Mostly, she said, she "gave in to him on all money matters, how to raise the boys, and where they lived." At the start, Sylvia was so identified with her ideas about herself that she could not see her own contribution to the dynamic with her husband and kids. She did not see how her internal anxieties and insecurities, her timidity and passivity at home, also determined the nature of her relationships within the family. In effect, she seldom tried to actively draw her own boundaries and resist what she perceived as "dominating behaviors" from her husband and the boys who she frequently felt were dismissing her wishes. She hated confrontations. They were "too upsetting and achieved nothing anyway." Most of the time, she said, she tried hard to avoid fights.

Sylvia and her older sister grew up with two Holocaust survivors. Whereas her father occasionally talked about his concentration camp experience and his first wife and two children who had been killed, her mother never talked about her childhood. Sylvia's mother was 20 years younger than her husband. At the beginning of the war, her mother's family ran away from Germany. To ensure her safety, Sylvia's mother was placed in a convent in a country whose language she did not speak. Her older brother was placed with a non-Jewish family. She was 8 years old at the time. A few years after the war, still in Europe, she met and married Sylvia's father, and they found their way to the United States. A few times Sylvia's father hinted that those war years were very difficult for their mother; she had no communication with her parents and brother and was severely taunted and discriminated against at the school that the convent ran. Upon reuniting with her mother and brother, Sylvia's mother was often scared, angry, and mistrustful of others. She deeply mourned her father's death, the circumstances of which were never discussed. Sylvia and her sister learned these sketchy details about their mother's past only when they reached early adulthood.

Sylvia's mother was still alive and lived in another state. At the peak of the COVID-19 pandemic, Sylvia was not able to visit her mother and constantly felt very guilty and worried about her, imagining her isolated and alone in an assisted living facility. Knowing that her sister lived close to her mother did not provide comfort as even her sister could not visit her. She has not seen her mother since then.

Sylvia's childhood and early home life seem to explain much of her anxious existence and negative narratives. She remembers her mother as a complicated and unpredictable woman, who relentlessly pursued perfection in her house, herself, and her daughters. Their physical flaws were often remarked upon with frequent suggestions for actual (nose) surgeries and trips to the hair salon to straighten their curly hair. In her quest for all things to be "perfect and according to her vision of how they should be," Sylvia's mother was often critical and disapproving. At times she became angry and belligerent. Most times both girls did not know what she was angry about and were too afraid to ask. Sylvia remembered herself thinking that her mother "was not quite okay." At times, the girls would rely on their father's support and calming words. He often told them that they all had to remember their mother's traumatic war years. In Sylvia's memory, whenever the girls did get into verbal conflicts with their mother, he took their mother's side. He would then ask the girls to apologize to her regardless of what took place. He often said that it was important not to upset her. With each such event, Sylvia became convinced that her mother needed protection.

The more Sylvia got to "know" her mother in therapy, the more she realized how insecure and anxious her mother had been. As she remembers, there was something very childlike and vulnerable about her mother. But her mother did not openly discuss her childhood or old memories, or verbally express vulnerable feelings. Based on her father's words, and on a great deal of reading about the Holocaust, Sylvia construed and intuited her mother's past and internal difficulties. As they grew older, when Sylvia and her sister confronted their mother about her unpredictable and angry behaviors, she denied her impulsive actions, shifting moods, and criticalness. Their mother could not acknowledge that she was ever wrong and could not see how much her behaviors affected her daughters.

As Sylvia remembers, she felt responsible for both her parents' well-being, a typical behavior for second-generation children of Holocaust survivors. When she was away with friends, Sylvia remembers worrying about her parents alone at the apartment with their painful memories. As a result, she did not like to spend too much time away from home. Throughout her childhood and adolescence, at parties or outings Sylvia felt compelled to call her parents to make sure that they did not need her. For that reason, she also avoided sleepovers, even with her closest friends. As she reached late adolescence, these behaviors became even more entrenched, and unlike her older sister, who became a vocal and independence-seeking teenager, Sylvia became increasingly determined not to upset either of them with her own needs for independence. She became, in her words, an "unrebellious teenager who most of all focused on the well-being of my parents."

Quite a few aspects in Sylvia's history highlight the sources of the self-denigrating assessment of who she was. Her mother's criticalness was a factor, of course, and it seems it was more influential than the frequent support, encouragement, and compliments her father offered. But it also appears that much of the fear and anxiety she internalized were nonverbally and indirectly transmitted to her by her mother. Her mother's unacknowledged horrific emotional memories found expression through her moods, anger, and the defensive need for control through the fantasy of perfection. In her inability to think about and integrate her painful past, Sylvia's mother nonetheless enacted these hidden traumatic events and emotions within her family. Unaware of her own shaky emotional foundation, she needed to be perfect and needed to see her daughters as perfect as well. What she could not tolerate in herself, her unacknowledged "vulnerability, rage, and self-loathing" as Sylvia described it, was unconsciously part of the home atmosphere and thus projected onto her daughters.

As Sylvia's feelings and memories about her mother became more nuanced, she also remembered her mother's utter devotion to her husband. She did not get angry with him; neither did she criticize him. In effect, he could do no wrong. She fully supported him and his work. Sylvia now thinks that he might have been a "replacement for the father she had lost in the war and the only island of security for her." In return, Sylvia's father was loving and devoted as well as accepting of his wife, even when she had angry outbursts.

Not surprisingly, Sylvia's negative self-narratives reflected all the differ-ent emotional and intersubjective forces she was exposed to. Her recurrent belief that she was a little girl with no real power to affect what happened to her in her marriage and the outside world was an inevitable echo of her parents' past—of her mother's unverbalized but real helplessness and utter lack of power as a child, and her father's known and detailed terrible time at the concentration camp. Sylvia's readily triggered, repetitious conclusion that she was not as smart or competent as others around her reflected her mother's frequent criticism of her daughters' looks, performance at school, and friendships. Her mother was the one who unconsciously "taught" Syl-via to automatically compare herself to their neighbors, friends, and dis-tant relatives, finding the girls lacking and on the losing end. As therapy continued, Sylvia also realized that their mother did not encourage the girls to be ambitious and succeed. It seemed to Sylvia now that, being unable to achieve what she wanted because of the war, their mother could not see achievement in her daughters as well. It seemed their mother uncon-sciously and perpetually lived the fears, fragility, insecurities, and helpless-ness she endured as a young girl. Without a coherent, conscious narrative about her past (Fonagy et al., 2002) she transmitted her hidden states to her daughters, and especially to Sylvia, who was more attentive to her internal world.

With time, as Sylvia became increasingly aware of the unconscious pat-terns behind her feelings, thoughts, and behaviors, she was also able to develop very different ways to approach anxiety-inducing situations in her life. The feelings that she was the incompetent little girl lost in the world of adults who controlled her life started to lose the power and conviction they previously had. By letting herself fully acknowledge the painful and anxious feelings she was carrying, by realizing that they were mostly her mother's emotion states, Sylvia was able to tolerate them and at the same time disconnect them from her negative narratives. At home, she increas-ingly tried to argue her points of view with her husband and increasingly stood up for her wishes. Slowly she became able to separate her current feelings from her past ones, and especially differentiate them from her mother's internal states; she was no longer at home with her mother, being fearful of her shifting moods and outbursts or unconsciously taking on her unprocessed traumatic memories. Significantly, she realized that standing up for her own needs was not going to break or hurt anyone around her. To her surprise, her husband and children cooperated with her. "Maybe it was mainly me all along," she said.

The largest shift in Sylvia's narratives was taking place at work. Looking back now, with the distance that her awareness created and with the inner separation from what she unconsciously internalized at home, Sylvia could not believe her past anxious and self-belittling convictions.

It may sound as if the changes Sylvia underwent in therapy came quickly and easily. In reality, however, her path to change involved a great deal of mindful effort and determination on her part. Her treatment also lasted a few years. During sessions, she fully allowed herself to explore her memories and the feelings they invoked, dealt with recurrent anxious dreams, and faced the very painful experiences of growing up with two Holocaust survivors. But Sylvia also practiced mindfulness in between sessions. She started to meditate regularly and began to carefully track her rising anxiety during meetings and classes. When becoming aware of her bodily anxiety and the old familiar narratives that went with it, she was able to tolerate the very unpleasant sensations of fear and anxiety. She no longer automatically employed her old narratives about who she was. The more she was able to practice this new way of living with her anxiety, and the easier it became to avoid drowning in disturbing feelings and narratives, the less in control they were.

•••

CHAPTER TWELVE

Parenting in the COVID-19 Pandemic: The Fear System and Its Intergenerational Effects

If I carefully think of many of the patients I have seen over the years, I can state without hesitation that what characterizes most is the presence of fear and anxiety in generations within a family. This tendency for anxiety and depression to run in families and the genetic vulnerability that may follow as a result should always be considered. Indeed, many times, when trying to understand the roots of a patient's anxious states, it is quite impossible to differentiate the effects of genetic predisposition and environmental factors such as learning from, imitating, and identifying with one's parent. Among the cases I have discussed here, most have reported that one or both parents suffered from various manifestations of anxiety and depression.

Going deeper into their cases, we can see that the interaction between temperament and environment almost guarantees the intergenerational transmission of myriad anxious and depressed states as well as ways to deal with them. As we previously saw, both internal states and coping strategies are easily picked up by children of all ages. One can see how any degree of genetic susceptibility will increase the effects of those parental communications guided and informed by anxious internal states. A wide range of carefully observed and imitated emotional, cognitive, and behavioral patterns can raise a child's own anxiety. A child's strong, innate need to identify with a parent as part of their attachment will cause them to take in the parent's internal states and automatically consider them as their own (Braten, 2007). For example, Jerry's, Anna's, Sylvia's and Ben's mothers all tended to experience anxiety and depressed moods and expressed these feeling states in various direct and indirect ways.

In Chapter 2, we explored the expanding neuropsychological picture of the processes underlying developmental stresses and the role of generational inter-subjective influences. In particular, the evidence concerning a child's vulnera-bility to parental messages is compelling in its timeless implications. Whether obvious or subtle, verbal or nonverbal, emotional and cognitive communications are implicitly remembered, learned, and encoded by a child. These subconscious messages will invariably become part of the child's anxious self-state, supported by self-narratives, concepts of self, and ideas about others.

What happens, then, when parents themselves are experiencing upheaval and stress? What are the possible effects of especially difficult circumstances within the family or the larger community? Can a parent's unsettled state consciously or unconsciously inject further negative complications into daily interactions? A question like this was acutely relevant to Jerry's parents when they immigrated to the United States; the fears, anxieties, and insecurities they felt were transmitted to him. As he became increasingly dependent on his mother for understanding his surroundings, her own anxiety in their new country became his. In addition, her verbalized and nonverbalized concerns for her son's difficulties and her anxious projections into the future interfered with her ability to provide Jerry with a more grounded adjustment to his new and unfamiliar environment.

We have seen the powerful effects of the amygdala on attention bias, memo-ries, learning, and thoughts. We have seen how sensitive children's brains are to real and perceived threats; we know how exquisitely reactive to facial expres-sions, anxieties in others, and worried or angry voices children are. This raises an extremely important question with serious implications for our children's future. What happens when both parents and children have unusual trauma, such as we experienced during the global COVID-19 pandemic? As we all know, unfortunately, this is far from being a hypothetical question, but rather an acute and important one.

Parents and children found themselves isolated and under quarantine, their daily routines and activities totally upended. For more than a year, these changes had no end in sight. You may remember from previous chapters that pervasive, chronic stress is typically more damaging than a single-event trauma. But the potential danger has not only been the result of the actual and very painful limitations regarding school and children's great need for social interactions with other children. Perhaps just as dire is the fact that during these many long months, the pandemic and its disruptive consequences allowed many new fears and anxieties to fester and grow. Parents and school-age children lived with recurring fear of disease, loss of jobs, and sudden financial insecurity. In many cases, having to help kids with their schoolwork while still having to work themselves added incredible burdens to parents, especially mothers. In March 2021, a year into the pandemic, more than 10 million mothers with school-age children were not working, a 12% increase compared to March 2020 (Heggennes et al., 2021).

Many researchers have already started to examine the psychological implications of the prolonged lockdown for families and communities of all socioeconomic levels, especially the social isolation forced on children and their inability to attend school. Many more are sure to follow. In this chapter, however, I want to focus on the potential effects the pandemic may have on some important developmental aspects among children growing up with its added pressures. Specifically, the following sections explore the important process of intergenerational transmission of fear and anxiety, and its potential impact on the growing brain/mind. As with all other threat-filled situations, the fear system and its sensitivity to danger has a great deal to say about how each one of us deals with chronic fears and anxieties. As we also know, the way that adults relate to, experience, and process difficult situations and the fears they arouse largely determines the child's response patterns and developing narratives as well.

It is essential here to repeat the obvious purpose of this expanded knowledge: to enable parents to pay more attention to their children's general vulnerability to negative experiences. A sensitivity to what children may hear, feel, and eventually internalize can go a very long way toward easing fears and developing effective regulation. There is little doubt that a heightened awareness of some of the insidious long-term effects of such ongoing stressful situations can eventually help parents, even those anxious by nature, better navigate themselves and their children.

THE FEAR SYSTEM AND THE COVID-19 PANDEMIC

One of the most relevant characteristics of the fear system is how easily it is triggered in reaction to uncertainty and insecure circumstances (Broschott et al., 2016). And, of course, the real and frightening threats posed by a disease that can turn deadly so quickly have resulted in intense fear in many people. Initially, with a nearly total lack of information about the virus, the uncertainty about its spread put us all into a generalized state of sustained anxiety. Most of us wondered how to minimize or avoid any potential danger to ourselves and those close to us. We became afraid of other people, even sometimes those closest to us. The fear that COVID-19 could spread out of control only added to the many layers of already triggered fears and sustained anxieties.

We can say with utter confidence that the COVID-19 pandemic has been a major trigger for the human fear system, whose evolutionary job is to alert us to danger and help us survive. The sense of heightened fear and anxiety that took hold once the presence of the virus became clear was compounded by the sudden and drastic changes we all had to implement as a result. We had to adjust suddenly to many new behaviors: being forced into isolation, avoiding proximity to others, working from home, essentially homeschooling our children and grandchildren, wearing masks, washing our hands, and disinfecting our groceries. In essence, each one of these behaviors as well as all the other adjustments became a constant reminder of what was at stake: that we could not get away from the very real presence of severe illness and death.

Any one of these forced behaviors would have been enough to activate the amygdala, the alerting system, thereby directing our full attention to the frightening aspects of the situation. A sense of inchoate anxiety was the inevitable result. Indeed, the unprecedented vigilance and the lack of certainty about the future engaged our fear system in the deepest ways possible. But even within the utterly justified pandemic atmosphere of uncertainty and fear, parents, like the rest of us, reacted according to their own unique emotional patterns. For example, the ability to tolerate a great deal of uncertainty and the lack of personal control it creates varies from person to person and parent to parent. In part, this ability to regulate intense fears depends on the habitual balance between the prefrontal networks that, outside our awareness, calm the amygdala's activity.

During the prolonged COVID-19 pandemic, any capacity for emotion regulation was severely tested by real and tangible obstacles. Usually, and especially in psychotherapy, therapists try to help people develop effective regulation of mostly imagined dangers. For example, fears and anxieties that characterize social anxiety may have their earliest roots in actual past events and experiences. But with time, people learn that the very same fears and the defenses that go with them are no longer relevant to their current reality. Similarly, many phobias center on irrational fears attached to insects, animals, or crowded places. With the pandemic, however, the dangers were not imaginary, and the fear was based on current events in real time. Each wave of spreading infections has resulted in serious disease and a mounting number of deaths. Sadly, this has continued even after the availability of very effective vaccines. And with the ever-present possibility of new virus variants and the unknown threat they may pose, it had been hard for many people to let their guard down. In addition, the growing cases of "long COVID" have also contributed to fear of becoming sick, especially as vaccinated children and adults could still fall sick. Conflicting facts and information, uncertainty, and the desire for normalcy in the face of the need to remain cautious have all made sure that the initial fears and anxieties remain with us. They have become an inseparable part of our lives, affecting our moods and feelings, and prolonging enforced isolation.

The various neuropsychological findings we have discussed so far consistently support our intuitive sense that the emotions and messages that surround infants, children, and adolescents impact their conscious and unconscious levels of fear and anxiety. And as evolving interpretations and meaning making become integrated with these stressful feelings, the effects of parental communication are substantial. In addition, the general environmental stress experienced by parents can increase their worries for what their children are going through, causing feelings of helplessness and frustration. In turn, the elevated level of worry is often felt by the children, further adding to the child's own anxious feelings and erroneous, childlike interpretations of the scope of the danger, future fears, and more positive perspectives. As with so many instances, but more so in the case of the pandemic, parents have found themselves having to walk the very fine line between not fully hiding reality while also providing their children with the age-appropriate tools for coping with it. Modeling coping behavior and balanced narratives can greatly help children of all ages.

In the face of such ongoing real difficulties, we need to consider, of course, the many layers of ongoing intersubjective mutual influences. The results are constant exchanges of moods, emotions, and verbal reactions between parents and their children. But as was emphasized before, when both parents and children are exposed to and experience emotional and behavioral difficulties, it is the child who is more vulnerable to the messages coming from the parent (Bowlby, 1969; Callaghan & Tottenham, 2016). It is the child's still-developing brain/mind that, without the benefits of a more reality-bound perspective, reacts to the expressed emotion. The absorbed fear, anxiety, and stress parents bring may lead the child to experience a sense of impending catastrophe and an utter lack of control.

PARENT–CHILD ATTUNEMENT DURING THE PANDEMIC

As we saw before, the mechanisms that facilitate intergenerational transmission of emotions, cognitions, behaviors, and general parental beliefs and mental states influence the child's own unconscious self-states and narratives. Understanding what gets transmitted, both positive and negative messages, is especially important when it comes to the struggles created by the COVID-19 pandemic.

When we realize the innate tendency of the fear system to be constantly vigilant and reactive to threat signals, we understand that an essential goal of early attachment is to provide a secure intersubjective space. Beginning in infancy, within a caring relationship, it seems that a parent's ability to counterbalance our powerful fear system and the hyperarousal it creates is vital. As an infant or young child primarily depends on external modes of emotional regulation, a caregiver's ability to attune and regulate their own emotional state can both buffer or intensify fearful responses in the child (Callaghan et al., 2019). This ability of a parent to regulate a child's physiological, hormonal, emotional, and behavioral reactions to stress is the most important aspect of the early parent-child relationship. This relationship creates an interesting and significant balance between an infant's amygdala-driven threat learning and parental buffering, which suppresses this learning. These learned fears are suppressed if the mother or father is present to block the amygdala from encoding learned fears and fear memories. The neurobiology of parental regulation of infant fear is made possible by the parent's presence, which suppresses fear learning (Opendak et al., 2019). It is possible that for many parents, the myriad challenges and pervasive anxiety presented by the pandemic interfered with their attunement to their young children. Parents who worked in health care were often forced to physically isolate from their children, some even moving out of the house in an effort to keep them safe.

Conversely, a gross and persistent failure to offer such regulation can inhibit a child's ability to develop their own ability to tolerate fear and anxiety. Some researchers even argue that these regulatory processes begin in utero and fully depend on the mother's ability to maintain a mostly calm communication with her unborn child (DiPietro, 2012; Opendak et al., 2019; Papousek & Papousek, 1990). The real risks of giving birth in a hospital during a pandemic, and the early prohibition against having a loved in the birthing room, made this type of calm communication virtually impossible for many pregnant mothers. Significantly, these early regulatory patterns determine the efficiency of those neural circuits in mediating emotion regulation (Tottenham, 2012a, 2012b, 2020).

We know from research that even natural variations in caregiving are important predictors of a child's mental and physical health (Callaghan et al., 2019; Champagne et al., 2003). At times, in spite of the caregiver's best intentions, the infant's constant needs for caretaking and attunement can be disrupted, and the child suffers. This can happen when a parent needs to attend to their own internal struggles, as when they are excessively preoccupied with a difficult situation or trauma. If maintained over time, a compromised caretaking relationship with an infant or young child can influence the child's affective development (Bos et al., 2014). Recent studies highlight the need to examine these pandemic-related parent–child difficulties.

A parent's (mostly) consistent presence can reduce adverse learning by sending dopamine signals to the child's amygdala. This can mitigate hyperarousal. But what happens when hyperarousal and adverse learning result from the parent's own fears and inability to modulate it? Given what we elaborated in previous chapters, children's sensitivity to their caregiver's emotional states is remarkable. Could infants, children, adolescents, and even unborn babies be affected by the real difficulties their parents endured, and continue to endure, because of the pandemic lockdown and the myriad problems it created?

COVID-19 AND INTERGENERATIONAL TRANSMISSION OF ANXIOUS STATES

The vast body of research describing the effect of early parental mental states and behavioral approaches is obviously relevant to our discussion of the potential effect of the pandemic on parenting. Although a great deal of research needs to be done, developmental neuroscience has already indicated that the lockdown experience presented parents with significant difficulties and even ongoing trauma, including but not limited to being confined together in small homes, working from home, job loss or financial worries, homeschooling while working, and the inability to visit older parents. These family difficulties all occurred in the midst of a panicked atmosphere fraught with insecurity and fear of a capricious disease. How parents deal with such enormous life challenges and the resulting anxieties presents particular challenges.

Revisiting Neuropsychological Mechanisms

For the sake of highlighting the increased vulnerability that the pandemic may cause in children, it is worthwhile to briefly revisit underlying neuropsychological mechanisms of fear and anxiety, beginning with intersubjective models (Braten & Trevarthen, 2007; Schore, 2012). An inextricable aspect of the mutual attachment between a parent and a child, from infancy to late adolescence, is the child's total attunement to the parent's shifting states of mind. This is especially so during infancy, when the infant is dependent on the caregiver's emotional states for comfort and well-being. From early on, verbal and nonverbal intersubjective interchanges carry significant information about how a parent feels. Needless to say, parents' states of mind were unusually unsettled and even volatile during the pandemic.

This emotional information is transmitted through the quality of the engagement between the infant and the parent, both communicating with facial expressions, tone of voice, and body movements. Through the engagement of mutual gaze, the infant can viscerally perceive excessive anxiety and worries. At such times, the infant's amygdala can correctly evaluate the threats embedded in an emotionally disconnected parental stance or in half-hearted, hurried, or perfunctory responses. Through an impassive and unresponsive expression, for example, a parent's depressed state can compromise the infant's sense of security and increase their anxiety (Abraham et al., 2020; Callaghan et al., 2019). We need to wonder about all the many shifting moods and subtle behavioral communications that inevitably have expressed caregivers' states of mind during the pandemic. Were parents more often emotionally distant due to the stresses of the pandemic, or did they become overprotective and even intrusive? And to what extent did their own preoccupation with health issues in general exacerbate their direct and indirect communications to their infants and children? Obviously, these questions and many others can only be answered in future studies, which I am confident will follow.

The sought-after information is crucial because a parent's heightened state of anxiety or depression can trigger and enhance an infant's amygdala's reactivity as it instantly evaluates the valence of the signals reaching the child from the parent. With a lack of attunement or compromised parental presence, the important balance between amygdala reactivity and a parent's attuned presence can easily become imbalanced. A parent's anxieties or incessant worried preoccupations make it difficult or impossible for the parent to provide the necessary buffering from negative states of hyperarousal for the child. It's as if, while struggling with their own internal upheaval and worries, the parent cannot save the child from their own internal states. In this case, parental presence does not suppress the child's activated threat circuit.

Even for nonclinical anxiety, the amygdala has great power to regulate development of corticolimbic processes. Through direct connections to the hippocampus, "the amygdala highlights particular interpretations, memories, and appraisals, which then become increasingly consolidated over time" (Lewis & Todd, 2007, p. 424). The emotional associations mediated by the amygdala not only regulate real-time cortical activity but also direct developmental trajectories by which events acquire lasting meaning. The amygdala also regulates other emotions such as anger and rage. Associative memories mediated by the amygdala, and episodic memories mediated by the hippocampus, lay down patterns of meaning that continue to be refined or directed throughout a child's and young adult's development. Because these limbic structures are plastic and sensitive to experience, they harness the cortex to frame the content and meaning of events as they change over development. Knowing this, we must make every effort to understand the outsized influence of the pandemic on children's amygdalas and explore ways to leverage brain plasticity to nurture healthy development.

Developmental Research

Developmental researchers suggest that even normative or ordinary parental variations in how they relate to their infant may further influence the infants' attention bias to faces; this is significant, in general, and more so during the pandemic. As we know, infants are innately oriented to look longer at faces and to linger on fearful and angry expressions. Numerous studies found a clear attentional preference for faces in 5- to 12-month-old infants and a preference for fearful over happy expressions in 7-, 12-, and 36-month-old children. Significantly, bias for fear in infants cannot be interpreted as a more generalized bias for expressions of other negative states among others (Opendak, Gould, & Sullivan, 2017).

Another large study found very similar results. Among children 4 to 24 months old, the presence of attention bias toward threatening facial expressions (as measured through eye tracking and physiological markers) did not depend on the child's age, gender, or tendency for negative affect. However, such a bias was positively related to maternal anxiety (Morales et al., 2017). These results support other research showing that children of anxious mothers display an attention bias toward threatening stimuli, compared to children of nonanxious mothers. This was found among older children as well (Montagner et al., 2016).

Furthermore, if parents are not sufficiently aware of their emotional state while they attend to the infant, changes in their facial expressions due to anxiety, depression, or shifting moods can heighten the infants' sensitivity to threat. The amygdala contributes to the attention-grabbing properties of emotional stimuli. It redirects a child's as well as an adult's gaze to the most emotionally noticeable feature of facial expression. Indeed, we reflexively focus on the eyes. A stronger biased attention to fearful expressions is associated with higher levels of anxiety later in life (Bouvette-Turcot et al., 2017; Gabard-Durnam et al., 2018; Okon-Singer, 2018). This may be due to a learned fear response that reinforces the innate tendency to pay more attention to fear. If, instead of finding a calming expression and an attuned gaze, the infant encounters anxious or depressed expressions, their fear system quickly learns to expect more of such unsettling experiences. In addition, changes in a caregiver's tone of voice (e.g., the lack of soothing quality) may be disruptive as well. It adds to the infant's perceptions of threat and causes more anxious attentiveness and predictions of perceived threats (Callahan et al., 2019; Leppanen et al., 2018; McLaughlin et al., 2019). This is another urgent research area as we move out of the pandemic.

Early disturbances in mother–child attachment can begin prenatally. In one study, prenatal attachment to the unborn infant was related to the mother's levels of anxiety and to the amount of social support that was available to her. Mothers with increased social support showed enhanced prenatal attachment to their unborn babies (Hopkins et al., 2018). Isolation and significantly reduced social support were hallmarks of the pandemic, especially for pregnant women; this research suggests that the earliest attachment between mother and baby may have been affected by the pandemic, possibly influencing later patterns of attachment.

In another study, 971 mother–infant dyads were studied; their interactions were microcoded for maternal and infant social behavior and synchrony. Mothers who reported postnatal symptoms of anxiety or depression were compared to a control group. They were tested again at 6 and 9 months after giving birth. The researchers evaluated the infants' negative and positive emotional demeanor and self-regulation in four interpersonal conditions: anger with mother, anger with stranger, joy with mother, and joy with stranger. The research showed that maternal depression in the first year of life disrupted the development of effective emotional regulation in their infants. Similar to other findings, the infants' difficulties resulted from the diminished social synchrony in the mother-infant dyad as well as a compromised attunement. The opposite was seen during positive moments that encouraged self-regulation (Abraham et al., 2020; Granat et al., 2017).

Similarly, a study of 6,894 women who were pregnant during the pandemic revealed that 31% showed signs of clinical anxiety or depression, 53% reported loneliness, and 43% showed signs of post-traumatic stress. Of the participants, only 7% had contact with someone with diagnosed COVID-19 and just 2% had been diagnosed with COVID-19 themselves (Basu et al., 2021). This highlights the implications from previous research as to the serious risks to infants and toddlers as a result of poor maternal mental health as a result of the pandemic.

Implications for Post-Covid Child Development

Not surprisingly, the impact of COVID-19 has been especially devastating among children, adolescents, and young adults whose social and academic lives have been severely interrupted, and in some cases, entirely ceased to exist in their previous form. There has been a considerable increase in pediatric mental health related struggles for both children 5 to 11 and adolescents 12 to 17. The reported incidents of general anxiety, depression, a sense of helplessness, and suicidal ideation are steadily increasing (see Leeb et al., 2020). Studies are already looking at the short- and long-term effects of the pandemic on children and adolescents. No doubt it will take time and effort to tease out the entwined social, financial, environmental, and emotional impacts that may result in enduring personal difficulties due to heightened anxiety. In some crucial ways, however, children and adolescents comprise the group most vulnerable to environmental pressures and to circumstances over which they have no control. We already saw the power of the amygdala to automatically react to threats, and consequently color memories, influence mood, increase negative bias, and often cause traumatic reactions to events. This is especially true during all phases of development. In the face of their disrupted lives, and with the continuous panic-suffused news, older children and adolescents may feel overwhelmed, helpless, and confused. These feelings will reduce their capacity for emotion regulation, which in turn may lead to impulsivity on the one hand and to depressed feelings of hopelessness on the other.

But in addition to the fears, anxiety, stress, and uncertainty generated within the youngster's own brains and minds, the verbal and nonverbal worried messages they absorb from their caregivers' emotional states only intensifies their own dysregulation. A parent's financial insecurity, reaction to a lost job, changes in their mode of functioning, and significantly, worries about the health and emotional state of their own isolated elderly parents, will inevitably worry the child or adolescent as well. Facing their parents' parents' vulnerability, children's empathic need to protect their parents, to see them as strong and invincible, will suffer and shake their inner strength and confidence as well. Finally, we have to deeply consider and pay special attention to the many children traumatized by a loss of a parent or another family member.

Unfortunately, even the ongoing vocal and passionate disagreements among parents regarding the importance of vaccination and masks may destabilize a youngster's sense of well-being. Large groups of parents, as well as teachers, are continuing to angrily express their oppositions to any safety measures against the pandemic, potentially contributing to greater confusion and inner angst. Finding themselves in the middle of angry and opinionated exchanges, children's unconscious conflicts as to whom to "believe" and identify with may further increase their anxiety. Embedded in this anxiety are worries, negative ruminations about the meaning of the situation to their parents and to themselves, which all affect the emotion regulation and the adaptive nature of their coping mechanisms. As a large body of already existing research shows, an increased sense of feeling overwhelmed coupled with impulsivity may lead to all forms of self-harm (Foulkes & Blakemore, 2016; Sebastian et al., 2011).

As the mirror neuron system facilitates nonverbal communication between interacting subjectivities, fearful feelings emanating from a parent will grab and inhabit the child's own experience. As a result, the child's attention to threat will grow. Additionally, learned attention bias to threat can become a fixed attitude toward the environment, highlighting the unintended damage that the pandemic may have on infants and young children during insecure and unsafe times

(Gabbard & McLaughlin, 2019; Okon-Singer, 2018). As attention bias to threat develops, it introduces habitual anxiety about the ways in which we experience the world. Again, one wonders whether the intensity of emotion, news, and real-life changes resulting from the pandemic have put infants and young children at increased risk for habitual anxiety and therefore influenced many of their ways of thinking and behaving.

We have seen that interpersonal transmission between parents and children can lead to the development of anxiety and attention bias. This is especially important when parents provide assessments about levels of danger regarding unfamiliar situations. It is the caregivers who provide cues and feedback that teach infants how to respond emotionally and behaviorally toward these situations and stimuli. When we remember the role of identification-based learning, it's not surprising that when parents provide fear-related information to older children (e.g., talking about or implying something is dangerous), it may lead to increased anxiety and attention bias (Field, 2006a, 2006b; Morales et al., 2017). This may increase the tendency of growing children to overemphasize threat in adolescence and adulthood.

We have so far emphasized the ease with which an infant's fear system reacts to fearful expressions and compromised attunement. However, a great deal of fear learning—which involves the amygdala—continues throughout toddlerhood, childhood, and adolescence. For example, a study of 18-month-old children revealed that toddlers could learn threat associations by observing an aversive social interaction between two adults in reference to a toy (Repacholi & Meltzoff, 2007). By measuring skin conductance reactions, 3-year-old children showed the ability to learn conditioned responses to aversive stimuli. This process of learning occurs outside conscious awareness. In this case, a regular tone elicited fear after it had been paired with an aversive loud noise. The results also showed that the degree of conditioned fear responses increased from age 3 to age 8. This suggests that even young children, observing tensions or fighting between adults in their household, possibly exacerbated by pressures due to a pandemic, may encode excessive threat associations.

Furthermore, this finding suggests that underlying or unconscious fear learning processes mature and strengthen throughout this period. From ages 6 to 16, children consistently demonstrate avoidance learning to threat cues. This behavioral tendency is associated with amygdala activation that occurs throughout childhood and adolescence. The increased pace and amount of learning is further supported by the maturation of the hippocampus (i.e., the memory system and the prefrontal cortex and higher cognitive functions) (Callaghan et al., 2019). Significantly, the connections between the hippocampus, the prefrontal cortex, and the amygdala continue to develop throughout childhood (Gabard-Durnam et al., 2014, 2016, 2018; Silvers et al., 2016, 2017; Swartz et al., 2014). Thus, during childhood, the fear circuitry is heavily dependent on and influenced by the fear system or amygdala reactivity. During this time, the amygdala increasingly interconnects with memory circuits and higher cognitive networks such as thinking and deliberate reflection (Callaghan et al., 2019). Consequently, much of the learning process increases the brain-wide interactions between affect, cognition, and behaviors. Under the influence of the amygdala, memories, thoughts, and beliefs can influence a developing negative self-narrative. Again, it is worthwhile to consider the potential effects of an unusually negative situation such as the pandemic on the developing identity and sense of self of young children and adolescents.

COVID-19 and Adolescent Development

Adolescence, the period roughly between 10 and 24 years of age, is an especially sensitive period. Adolescents are suspended between childhood and approaching adulthood, between puberty and full sexual maturation; they crave face-to-face interactions with friends and are often conflicted about their dependency on parents. The hormonal and biological changes cause profound psychological and interpersonal changes. For this group especially, the emotional difficulties created by the pandemic were possibly the worst: staying at home with parents and siblings, isolation from friends, and lack of a structured school environment and activities. Early data supports this assertion; in one study, 62.9% of young adults ages 18 to 24 reported anxiety, depression, or both; a full 25% had seriously considered suicide (Klass, 2020). The numbers were higher for adolescents living in poverty and young adults of color.

Adolescence is a unique period when the social environment is important for crucial brain development, construction of self-concept, and mental health (Orben et al., 2020). As it is, adolescents tend to experience emotional ups and downs and excess stress and worry regarding their self-image. Adolescents are indeed considerably more sensitive to peer acceptance, rejection, and approval than are children or adults (Foulkes & Blakemore, 2016; Sebastian et al., 2011). To most adolescents, peer groups, dating, and school provide the important environments in which they experiment with emotional and social skills, adult roles, and active engagements. Without these important resources, adolescents can become severely anxious and depressed. There is evidence that social exclusion and loneliness are risk factors for the development of affective conditions such as depression (Blakemore & Mills, 2014). Thus, the conditions imposed by the pandemic are of particular concern for adolescents and young adults.

Adolescence is also characterized by heightened vulnerability to mental health problems. Indeed, 75% of adults who have ever had a mental health condition report that they first experienced symptoms before the age of 24. Conversely, high-quality peer relationships appear to protect against mental health problems and strengthen adolescent resilience (Kessler et al., 2012; Orben et al., 2020). Consequently, widespread changes in the social environment, such as enforced physical distancing and reduced face-to-face social contact with peers, may have a negative effect on brain development. These effects, in turn, increase feelings of loneliness, craving for social contact, and decreased happiness (Orben et al., 2020). This positions the pandemic as the source of two negative impacts: the immediate stresses of the pandemic and the secondary stresses of isolation for peers.

One mitigating factor is the widespread use of digital technologies that lessen the pain of social disconnection. Among 13- to 17-year-olds, social media makes them feel more connected with friends, helping them interact with more diverse groups of people and allowing them to access social support during tough times (Anderson & Jiang, 2018). In addition, the development of high-level cognitive processes provides adolescents with the mental capacity to reflect on themselves and other people and to develop mutual relationships. As with most other regions within the human cortex, the structure of the social brain shows extensive development throughout adolescence.

During adolescence, there's a diminished ability to extinguish earlier emotional and behavioral patterns compared to younger children. Amygdala-driven learning about danger and safety become more entrenched during that time (Johnson & Casey, 2015). On the other hand, there is evidence that the prolonged and uneven development of the prefrontal cortex during adolescence leads to a lessened ability to regulate the amygdala's reactivity (Casey et al., 2005). As the prefrontal cortex continues to mature, an adolescent's ability to modulate the amygdala's activity grows as well (Gee et al., 2013). This indicates that with age there is increased prefrontal involvement in fear regulation (Callaghan et al.,

2019). We see again how significant is the developing neuropsychological balance between the emotional circuits and the ones involved in emotion regulation. A more effective regulation capacity can become an important factor in resilience during adolescence and later on.

The pitfalls for children and adolescents are vastly different, of course. Preadolescents still depend on their parents' approval and emotional states to guide their moods and behaviors. Through unconscious identification processes, children continually learn about potential danger and what constitutes safety. Their parents' internal fear states and how they express them will be unconsciously imitated and encoded, reinforcing an increasingly fearful self-state. In addition, at this age, children are particularly sensitive to feelings of shame. Overburdened parents may find it difficult to modulate their own impatience and frustration. They may demand too much of children in terms of good behavior and impulse control, expressing their disappointment and anger in ways that don't align with their child's developmental stage. Like children, adolescents need parental approval and support. They may externally deny the need for parental understanding, but sensitive parenting can help the isolated adolescent navigate loneliness.

ENVIRONMENT AND TEMPERAMENT

Genetic and environmental factors do not operate independently. The interaction between temperament and environment is crucial, of course. Highly fearful children may be especially sensitive and, therefore, susceptible to anxiety-related behaviors of anxious parents. It is possible that as both factors interact, they together contribute to the development of attention bias toward threat. With the certainty of the interaction between genes and environment, it is even more important to recognize and understand our children's potential vulnerabilities and sensitivities to fear. Knowing our children will enable us to be aware of and modulate our emotions as we directly relate to our children or when we are interacting with others and modeling behaviors.

This mindfulness is especially important during times of crisis. As we have seen, children's innate tendency to become immersed in a parent's feelings and thoughts makes them especially susceptible to influence from their parent's experience. Often, as a result of these intersubjective processes, the parent's experience can become the child's own. Unconsciously taking cues from the parent as to the seriousness and threat meaning of a situation, children will adopt the parent's feelings and cognitive points of view. As these internalized experiences take hold, they become central to the child's emotional memories, learning, and expectations. In effect, they can replace the child's own experiences and interpretations of these experiences.

Parents' mindful awareness of their children's state of mind is especially important because of the extra worry that began during the COVID-19 pandemic. As parents worry about their children, this worry will be encoded by the child as his own, making a difficult situation worse. We need only remember the enduring effects that Jerry's mother's anxiety had on him to understand the implications for this generation of children. The pressure to assimilate and fit in with other kids quickly and smoothly turned a difficult situation into a high-stakes one where failure was a possibility.

THE ROLE OF REFLECTIVE AWARENESS

As we already recognize, the influence of parental feelings and viewpoints can mitigate the results of a naturally reactive and even an overreactive fear system. In effect, the family unit has the greatest influence on the child's neuropsychological level of anxiety and the ways the child learns to manage it. A parent's own mindful behaviors can go a long way toward nurturing a child's healthy emotional life (Callaghan et al., 2019). This raises some interesting questions.

Can we help parents learn to provide buffering when they are under stress? While the amygdala and ventral striatum are active and functioning early in life, the evidence indicates that their functionality continues to develop throughout childhood and adolescence, making them highly susceptible to environmental influences throughout development. If parents understood these connections, could we encourage them to develop reflective awareness of their own behaviors with a goal of creating positive environments for healthy brain/mind development?

Fear of Death and Grief

We have discussed, so far, the many ways in which sudden and traumatic changes due to the COVID-19 pandemic inevitably have upended and deeply affected the lives of many families and communities. But unfortunately, for many families the pandemic has also meant the death of a loved one. In some cases, more than one family member has become ill and died. This magnitude of trauma, of course, demands a continual and special kind of attention and caretaking that needs to focus on all members of the family and on the children in particular. In light of what we have learned, all effort should be put into mental health services that can help families deal with grief and mourning, thus helping them provide their children with the emotional support they need for healing.

Children's developing understanding of death, their curiosity, and especially their innate fears should all be paid attention to and taken seriously by the adults in their lives. Adults, especially those who suffered loss, should continue to be especially mindful about their children's shifting moods, expressed and unexpressed worries, and the needs for safety and continuity. Grief, indeed, can be very overwhelming and consuming. Families, however, are also resilient, especially if people lean on available support systems and seek help. Keeping the future well-being of children in mind seems to be especially crucial during trying times when infants' and children's exposure to what is going on around them is inevitable and full of potential hazards.

ALLYSON'S CASE: THERAPY IN THE MIDST OF THE COVID-19 PANDEMIC

Allyson sought therapy two years ago when she was in her mid-30s, a few months prior to the COVID-19 pandemic lockdown. The reason she gave was a growing insecurity about ever being able to establish a close relationship. Allyson had gotten divorced six years before, and since then was not able to "find anybody [she] could connect with." She tried to use a few dating apps, but with little success. After meeting a couple of guys, she gave up and stopped using the apps altogether.

Following the total shutdown in New York City, Allyson was increasingly becoming aware of a sense of hopelessness and despair about her loneliness and her life in general. The pandemic naturally made things worse; Allyson could no longer engage in all the activities she and her friends did for fun, especially going out to bars. She could no longer find comfort in her daily encounters with other people at the office. Her job, which became remote, kept her busy, but she continually felt "as if something was not right." It was a mix of anxiety and sadness, accompanied by "crazy thoughts about how pointless everything is." She used to enjoy the daily challenges of her job but increasingly found it tedious and unsatisfying. She still bantered with coworkers on video calls, commiserating about the awful situation. She wished, however, that she "felt more alive." As the quarantine dragged on, she became convinced that only a close relationship would make her feel alive again. She even regretted her divorce, thinking now that she would have been better off with her ex-husband Michael. At least she would not feel so alone, anxious, and listless.

Allyson's marriage to Michael was filled with disagreements and fights. "We could not get along no matter how hard we tried." They went to therapy together to better understand why things were so difficult, but as she now says, each of them was too stubborn to listen to the other. They were both convinced that the other was to blame. Allyson was angered by what she saw as Michael's indifference to her feelings and wishes; she felt neglected and unattended to. Michael, for his part, said that he tried to do his best, and that Allyson was unrealistic in her expectations of him. Allyson mentioned that occasionally he had accused her of being too insecure and untrusting of him. In couple therapy he often said that what Allyson wanted was more a parent than a husband. Without much self-awareness at the beginning of our therapy, Allyson repeated to me that often in their joint therapy Michael said that he did not want to be a parent, he wanted a partner. She seemed entirely unable to understand what he could have meant at the time. But talking about these interactions, Allyson became both sad and angry. She could not forgive Michael's lack of acceptance, patience, and sensitivity.

As we started exploring her marriage dynamics, more details began to highlight Allyson's difficulties with Michael. Michael indeed needed his "space and time alone," two things that were difficult for her to accept. She often experienced his occasional aloofness as deeply rejecting and hurtful. She could not understand the reasons for his sporadic distance and interpreted it as a statement of his feelings for her. In response, her demands for attention grew, and her verbalized disappointments became more intense. She often told him how depressing the situation was for her. The more upset Allyson was, however, the more distant Michael's behavior became. When they stopped having sex altogether and when their fights intensified, they decided to give their marriage another chance, but therapy failed to bridge their crisscrossed needs and expectations.

Now, in the midst of the pandemic, experiencing her loneliness and chronic gnawing discomfort, Allyson said she was ready to understand what had happened and why. But examining her own needs and distancing behaviors was not easy for Allyson. Her inclination was still to blame Michael for not being loving and attentive enough; for ignoring what was important to her. All she was aware of was the disappointment and anger that this conviction caused.

Slowly, however, we started focusing on Allyson's internal world: how she saw herself, the nature of her recurrent narratives, her emotional needs and expectations, and how she dealt with painful emotions. In addition, Allyson's emotional and behavioral patterns clearly and repeatedly enacted in her past marriage provided a great deal of information about the unconscious forces behind her feelings and actions. Starting to delve into her childhood further provided important aspects of her unconscious motivation.

Allyson grew up in a small town, feeling awkward and misunderstood. As the youngest of three girls, she remembers feeling neglected and not important. She was ignored by her oldest sister, six years her senior, but felt closer to the middle sister, who was three years older. From a young age, Allyson felt that her hardworking parents "were already too tired to pay attention" to her and "just didn't care." They were not that interested in her school performances, her friends, or any of the sports and hobbies she took on. Like other parents around her, Allyson's parents lived from paycheck to paycheck and were often preoccupied by financial worries. In Allyson's memory, the little energy her mother had after a long work day went to attending to her husband, who tended to be controlling and demanding. Indeed, Allyson thought that most of her mother's energy went to placating and taking care of him. Allyson remembered thinking that she would never marry somebody like her entitled and ungrateful father. She saw herself with somebody very warm and attentive, but somebody her equal. As an adolescent, she was determined to attend college, leave her small town, and achieve more than her parents. She imagined herself as an independent woman who could take care of herself.

Allyson met Michael in college and fell in love with his reliable and at the same time carefree nature and fun-loving behaviors. After getting married, they left for New York. Whereas before her marriage to Michael, Allyson felt strong wishes to take care of herself, she increasingly relied on him for many of her needs. She enjoyed the fact that she did not have to take her own work seriously, as Michael's income was more than sufficient. She also became demanding of his time and was disappointed when she perceived him as neglectful or withholding affection when she "needed it most."

Without being aware, Allyson started to feel disappointment, frustration, and anger. The overriding mood became one of inexplicable sadness and loss, which Allyson felt in a visceral way, but could not yet put into words. Unconsciously she became convinced that all these feelings of sadness, disappointment, and anger meant that something was wrong with her marriage, and were actually the result of Michael's "distant and uncaring behaviors." Michael's attention no longer seemed to fill her up with good feelings of reassurance or make her feel less anxious, loved, or important. And although some part of her realized that her negative ruminations were somewhat irrational, doubts and blaming thoughts were stronger than her logic. In order to feel good, she had to be totally convinced of Michael's love, feel that it was there, but in her mind, it was absent.

As we continued to unravel Allyson's childhood experiences, it became clear that these sensations and feelings were not new but were enacted anew in her marriage. Throughout her early years, she often felt uncomfortable and anxious, wondering to herself why her parents and oldest sister showed so little interest in her. She concluded that "they did not care enough." Even on the occasions when her parents did ask about her schoolwork, her friends, and her sports and hobbies, she still did not feel that they really did it out of a genuine interest. Somehow Allyson still felt it was not enough to make her feel really seen and appreciated. She needed more engagement from them. "Yes, they made sure that I had food, a bedroom that I eventually inherited from my oldest sister, and I could go to the mall." She strongly felt that it was not enough. Even their support of her decision to attend college and their modest financial help fell short in her eyes.

What Allyson yearned for were frequent gestures of affection, recognition of her importance to the family. She wanted her parents to see her achievements, and more, to recognize her individual qualities. During dinnertime, she frequently tried to talk about her day and activities, but she was often drowned out by her sisters. Her parents made some effort to address and acknowledge them all, but the way Allyson remembers it, they lost steam when it was her turn. They often returned to the subject of how to deal with their expenses. She tried to raise her voice and assert herself, but the enthusiastic reactions she was looking for were not there. She would get hurt when she felt "they were just performing in order to move on and focus on their own stuff."

Allyson's sadness and anxiety in response to her parents' perceived indifference intensified with the years. In a case of intersubjective mismatch, her strong needs for affection did not match her parents' often preoccupied state of mind. Their focus on their own worries and their lack of overt affection left Allyson yearning for more. Outside her awareness, this achy yearning led to an unrealistic narrative of what love meant and to the defensive need to be presented with continual proof. Only total devotion and attentiveness could convince Allyson that she was important enough. Consciously, she really wished to become a self-sufficient woman, but a strong unconscious brain/mind circuit contained a yearning that overrode all else.

Allyson's choice of Michael as a lover and husband expressed these building blocks of her relational pattern. Michael was affectionate and attentive, and Allyson was intoxicated with his warmth and promise of devotion. His need for some distance was not yet part of their relationship. But once Michael's needs and behaviors became more nuanced, they triggered Allyson's worst anxieties about not being seen and cared for enough. She became deeply disappointed when the great deal of attention and affection she craved was limited by Michael's independence and occasional need to spend time on his own. It is common for our early patterns to be triggered within our important relationships. These early relational patterns forged during our early years inevitably become a part of any close relationship we form as adults. One could even speculate that by choosing Michael, intuitively and outside awareness, Allyson already expected some of his distancing behaviors. In this way, her unconscious patterns enacted both her deep wishes for constant affection, but also the entrenched learned belief and expectation that she would be disappointed. Unconsciously she was convinced that like her parents, Michael was not attentive enough.

After the divorce, which was in effect initiated by Michael, Allyson

felt "depressed for months." What she experienced as Michael's rejection of her felt like a total annihilation of her very existence. By ending
the marriage, he clearly said to her that she had no importance and value
for him. All Allyson could do was go to the office, work long hours, and
then go straight to bed. Her ability to take care of herself became even
more compromised. With time, however, Allyson resumed her social life
with her friends. She was still not ready to date and felt she could never
trust another man; old, deep insecurities about being loved returned and
intensified. This sadness, she began to realize, had always been there,
expressing how shaky and insecure she felt about her lovability. She could
also see how she coped with the perceived lack of recognition; she unconsciously upped the ante as she became increasingly needy, demanding,
and untrusting. These feelings, she realized, did not allow her to accept
Michael's individual needs.

The more Allyson remembered and emotionally relived some of her
childhood experiences and her interpretations of them, the more empathy and acceptance she developed toward her frustrated and anxious self-
state. At the same time, she also became increasingly empathetic toward
her parents; she saw their shortcomings but also the real difficulties that
preoccupied them. She could even express the totally new thought that
maybe she "was a sensitive child that wanted a lot from two people who
did their best, but being so limited by circumstances, by financial difficulties
and three kids to take care of, still hurt her." Understanding and accepting
the source of her feelings increased Allyson's ability to develop a different
sense of what it meant to be in a loving bond. Paradoxically, although the
pandemic period was particularly difficult for Allyson because it strengthened her feelings of not being loved and lovable, she also decided to use
her (remotely conducted) therapy well, to continue her self-understanding
and attempts to find recognition and strength within herself rather than in
another person.

CHAPTER THIRTEEN

Virtual Violence and Anxiety

Adding to the numerous conditions that easily arouse states of anxiety, life in the modern world has introduced another potential source of stress and anxiety: technology and the media. As we venture out of the family unit to widen our exploration of the roots of anxiety among children and adults, it is not possible, in my mind, to ignore our aggression-soaked popular culture. The ubiquitous presence of violence in practically all existing forms of media and entertainment is taken for granted and, therefore, not sufficiently questioned. Whether in cartoons, movies, television, or video games, the amount of aggression, misogyny, death, murder, mayhem, and gore that are habitually displayed is staggering. In any other context, much of what we are exposed to in our so-called entertainment would be considered traumatizing. So, how do we ascertain what, if any, effects such images have on a child or adolescent's growing brain/mind and behavior? And what unconscious entertainment-based vicarious trauma do we carry into adulthood?

The unconscious and automatic reactivity of the fear circuits when it comes to danger raises the question of whether we may be especially susceptible to lingering anxiety and depression as a result of exposure to the more injurious aspects of virtual violence. For example, do innate, complex negative feeling states take on additional weight as a result of repeated visual exposure to threat, injury, and death? Do video games where children take an active role as players whose purpose is to win by killing enemies affect them in any way? And what are the psychological, physiological, and social effects of the ubiquitous internet world and the anxiety and depression it can induce in teenagers?

In the context of what we have learned in the previous chapters, these questions are significant. We have seen that much of our early learning occurs automatically and outside our awareness. We have also learned that our innate sensitivity to threat and danger results in perceptual biases and increased fears. In addition, learning processes are particularly enduring when they are supported by identification with and imitation of others, or are accompanied by strong emotions. States of hyperarousal, whether conscious or not, seem to be inevitable when we are exposed to actual violence or when adopting an active role in violent games. I do not believe, however, that the effects of virtual violence are limited to the presence of fear or aggression alone. During development, through the interconnectedness of brain regions, such feeling states shape our worldview and influence our understanding of ourselves and others. Outside our awareness, emotion states underpin patterns of behavior that we carry out in our adult lives, with our children, spouses, other family members, friends, and coworkers. Knowing what we know about brain/mind development, this should be an area of further investigation.

VIRTUAL VIOLENCE IN ENTERTAINMENT MEDIA

Violence in entertainment media—including television, film, video games, music videos, and social media—is usually defined as depictions of characters (or players) trying to physically harm or kill other characters (or players). Aggression is defined as any action that is intended to cause harm to another character. Violence is an extreme form of aggression, potentially causing pain and physical harm or death. Not all aggressive behavior is violent, but all violent behavior is aggressive (Anderson et al., 2017).

For example, superhero films are soaked with violent acts. A group of researchers closely analyzed acts of violence depicted in superhero-based films released in 2015 and 2016 (Muller et al., 2020). In particular, they wanted to find out how many acts of violence were carried out by the hero (i.e., protagonist) in comparison to the villains and enemies (i.e., antagonists). The most common acts of violence for all major characters were characterized as "fighting"; "use of a lethal weapon"; "bullying, intimidation, or torture"; "destruction of property";

and "murder." Researchers found that protagonists carried out significantly more acts of violence compared to antagonists. The average number of acts of violence associated with the protagonist and the antagonists for all films over this two-year period was 22.7 and 17.5 mean events per hour, respectively; together, these characters carried out acts of violence every hour, or one act of violence every 90 seconds. This finding contradicts the common assumption that protagonists are the good guys, and therefore perform fewer acts of violence than their evil counterparts. In a narrative about good and evil, we may justify violence perpetrated by the hero, but our brain/mind/bodies make no such distinction; acts of violence are still perceived as such and are unconsciously encoded in our emotion, memory, and learning brain circuits. Furthermore, the study found that more acts of violence are performed by male characters compared with female characters. This discrepancy may be due to the predominance of male leading characters in superhero-based films. We need to consider that continuous exposure to this kind of violence may create different unconscious patterns for both males and females, leading to the perception that men are dominant and clearly more aggressive. This discrepancy may also subtly normalize violence against women at the hands of men.

The field of research exploring the effects of media violence on children is not new and has grown proportionate to the exponential growth of entertainment media (Hoge et al., 2017; Lissak, 2018). While there are many researchers who speak to the potential and actual harm attributable to virtual violence, there are also disagreements as to its effect on children and adolescents (Elson & Ferguson, 2014; Ferguson, 2015; Szycik et al., 2017). Some researchers argue for minimizing the effects of violent media in all its forms, emphasizing that people, including children, can differentiate between what is real and what is imagined. This ability, they argue, somehow confers a protective barrier between a child's psyche and potential damage from the visible and audible manifestations of what, in effect, are cruel acts of violence.

The central question is not whether we can consciously differentiate between real and vicarious violence, but whether the amygdala and its circuits know that they are being buffered from fictionalized violence. More specifically, to what extent do our automatic perceptions of threat, and the hyperarousal they induce, understand that it is only make-believe? Based on the fast reaction of the fear system, it is entirely possible and even likely that a young child exposed to violence on a screen may not be able to avoid ensuing lingering anxiety and unconscious associations with what they saw. Such violence, whether as a part of entertainment or the news, may also guide some of their conclusions and beliefs about their safety in a dangerous world. Clinically, we often encounter children who suffer from nightmares resulting from watching a scary movie or the news.

Virtual Violence and Children

Research on the long-term effects of media exposure on children's emotional development is still limited, especially its potential effects on their fears, anxieties, and emotional regulation skills. But the small body of existing studies reveals an association between entertainment and news-based programming and the creation of emotional states of upset. Predictably, these effects differ according to the child's age. Similarly, intense, trauma-like symptoms resulting from digital exposure are common in children and adolescents (Cantor & Riddle, 2014; Hoge et al., 2017; Lissak, 2018; Wilson, 2008).

The interaction between innate vulnerability to fear and the child's developmental phase may further enhance the effects of violence exposure. We need to remember that regardless of innate predisposition, our early years largely lack the regulating capacities mediated by the prefrontal cortex. This frontal brain region is the last to fully develop. Indeed, we can say that without the distancing effects of reality-bound perspective, which is mostly provided by the prefrontal cortex, all young children are particularly susceptible to images of violence. Therefore, the consequences of exposure to material that is frightening to a child of a specific developmental stage can be dramatic. It is often difficult to calm a child who has been intensely frightened by a video game, movie, or news item (Hoge et al., 2017). Other fear manifestations include loss of sleep, nightmares, heightened levels of reported stress and fears, loss of a sense of security, and excessive preoccupation with death. Consequently, researchers and clinicians strongly advocate for efforts to shield children from inappropriately disturbing content and, when needed, help them gain an age-appropriate understanding of news they have been exposed to (Cantor et al., 2010; Wilson, 2008).

Among fifth graders, for example, exposure to digital violence was associated with expressions of physical aggression. This association was significant and followed exposure to television, video games, and music videos. The authors concluded that the association between physical aggression and digital exposure to violence is robust and persistent. They argued that the effect of violent media on children's aggression may be at least as important as factors such as neighborhood violence, home violence, a child's mental health, and gender (Coker et al., 2015).

The differential effects of actively playing versus passively watching a violent video game on aggressive behavior were studied among 57 children aged 10 to 13. Three groups either played a violent video game (active violent condition), watched the same violent video game (passive violent condition), or played a nonviolent video game (active nonviolent condition). The children's manifestations of aggression were measured through peer reports of real-life aggressive incidents during free play sessions at school (i.e., time spent at recess or in the lunchroom). Following active participation in a violent video game, boys behaved more aggressively than did the boys in the passive game condition. For girls, neither game condition was related to aggression. These findings indicate that, especially for boys, actively playing a violent video game can lead to more aggressive behaviors (Polman et al., 2008).

Virtual Violence and Adolescents

Other researchers have examined the effects of virtual violence on anxiety among adolescents as measured by blood pressure and heart rate. Participants reported on their anxiety before and after watching violent movie clips as well as on their own previous exposure to violent content. Measures of blood pressure and heart rate were taken before and during movie viewing. Participants watching violent movie clips showed a greater increase in anxiety than those watching nonviolent clips. The findings demonstrate that a relatively brief exposure to violent movie clips increased anxiety among adolescents (Madan et al., 2014). What is particularly important here is that exposure to violence increased the participants' levels of anxiety. In turn, as we have seen, elevated anxiety will affect other brain/mind/body circuits. This heightened anxiety happened independent of whether or not the teens displayed more aggressive behavior later on. In other words, exposure to violence has been linked to independent but interconnected phenomena: the unconscious elevation of fear signals and the subsequent expression of aggressive behaviors.

The associations between playing violent video games and how adolescents relate to others was observed over a five-year period. Specifically, researchers investigated behaviors such as empathic concern, benevolence, and self-regulation. Participants included 488 adolescents and their parents who all completed self-reported measures as well as parental evaluations of their teens' behavior. Data collection occurred at three different time points, each one two years apart. The results revealed that early exposure to video game violence was associated with lower levels of prosocial behavior such as helpful cooperation (Greitemeyer & Mügge, 2014). More specifically, with exposure to violent video games the teenagers expressed lower levels of concern and empathy for others (Coyne et al., 2018; Hasan et al., 2013).

Another study investigated the relationship between violent video game exposure and accuracy in identifying negative emotional expressions in others. Studies with both adolescents ($N = 67$) and adults ($N = 151$) showed that violent video games were associated with less accurate recognition of negative emotional expressions, even when controlling for age, gender, and trait empathy (i.e., the general tendency for empathic resonance with others). The researchers argued that the ability to accurately recognize emotional expressions in others would have an impact on how we interact with people around us (Miedzobrodzka et al., 2021; Stankovi, 2015). This ability to identify distressing social cues and negative emotions is essential to our behavior in response to other people's emotional distress and needs. Even as we try to avoid a hyperbolic interpretation of these findings, they do raise the question whether the objectification of others and the indifference to their suffering may be unintended outcomes of the ever-growing violent entertainment.

Finally, the effects of screen time on symptoms of anxiety and depression in Canadian youth were studied; 2,482 students in 7th to 12th grade were assessed using the Children's Depression Inventory and the Multidimensional Anxiety Scale for Children-10. Screen time (e.g., hours per day of TV, video games, and computer time) were assessed using the Leisure-Time Sedentary Activities questionnaire. After controlling for age, sex, ethnicity, parental education, geographic area, physical activity, and weight, duration of screen time was significantly associated with severity of depression and anxiety. Video game playing and computer use were associated with more severe depressive symptoms and severity of anxiety. The authors concluded that screen time may represent a risk factor or marker of anxiety and depression in adolescents (Maras et al., 2015).

Perhaps not surprisingly, the specific consequences of exposure to virtual violence have focused on the effects of violent video games on growing levels of aggression among children and adolescents. Indeed, reviewing the existing research field, I found that the majority of studies in this field have explored the effects of media violence on children's and adolescents' aggression, desensitization to violence, and reactions to the feelings of others. Most studies indicate that exposure to virtual violence is correlated with an increase in aggressive thoughts and behaviors, angry feelings, physiological arousal, hostile evaluation of others, desensitization to violence, and decreased empathy (Anderson & Bushman, 2018; Anderson et al., 2010, 2017; Bushman & Huesmann, 2006).

These studies show that exposure to violent media can indeed increase the presence of fear, anxiety, and aggression in children and adolescents. What is missing so far is a more detailed understanding of what such findings mean. For example, understanding how elevated hyperaroused states guide a child's aggressive and angry narratives as well as their fears will help further assess the potential generalizing effects of violent content.

Virtual Violence and Young Adults

Another study explored the effects of violent movie scenes on the development of PTSD, more specifically, behaviors that resemble reactions to traumatic experiences among young adults. Specifically, the study investigated how exposure to traumatic scenes enhanced the participant's biased attention to other traumatic stimuli. The participants' responses to a variety of threats were measured prior to and one week after they had viewed either violent or nonviolent movie scenes. After both conditions, responses to traumatic images as well as threats unrelated to trauma were measured. The participants' responses to emotionally neutral images were also assessed. The findings show that traumatic exposure increased the participants' biased attention to traumatic cues. Those who had watched the traumatic scene became more sensitive to other traumatic stimuli than those who had not. The authors suggest that such increased attention bias to trauma-related stimuli may contribute to the development of anxiety and even PTSD (Schäfer et al., 2018).

By utilizing a violent movie scene as a traumatic stimulus, this study demonstrates the power of such exposure to enhance our sensitivity to other trauma-related threats. Furthermore, this enhanced sensitivity to trauma-related signals occurs and manifests itself entirely outside our awareness. Indeed, when we remember the fear system's influence on implicit and explicit memories, its tendency to linger as an emotional state, to become generalized, and to color all other mental and behavioral functions, the unconscious consequences of exposure to virtual violence acquire a particularly troubling slant. In this case, exposure to virtual acts of violence clearly increased participants' sensitivity to stimuli that reminded them of the upsetting clips they had watched a week earlier. The authors characterize these effects as post-traumatic intrusions into other mental processes. In addition, there was no enhanced attention to threatening stimuli that were unrelated to the traumatic movie scene. Rather, these intrusion effects were specific to biased attentional processing that developed in response to trauma-related stimuli. This indicates the activation of unconscious processes such as implicit memories, perceptions, and learning, among many others.

The effects of exposure to virtual violence on anxious dreams were also investigated. This study explored the effects of media coverage of the COVID-19 pandemic on the frequency of anxious nightmares in young adults. Results collected from 328 Chinese participants showed that exposure to media coverage was significantly associated with greater frequency of anxiety dreams. In addition, greater anxiety levels were associated with a lower ability to cope with states of hyperarousal provoked by exposure to news coverage (Guo & Shen, 2021). This, of course, created a vicious cycle of fear leading to greater frequency of nightmares, which in turn increased the perception of fear.

VIOLENCE, DESENSITIZATION, AND EMPATHY

One of the explanations for such wide-ranging effects is that virtual violence further primes and strengthens already existing aggressive patterns and cognitions. By increasing physiological arousal, these exposures trigger an automatic tendency to imitate observed behaviors and enact them in our own environment. The role of learning and identification may be substantial as well. Media violence may cause long-term learning through the emphasis on aggressive thoughts, motivation, and behavior. It may also strengthen aggression-colored beliefs about others and about the nature of social behavior. These aggression-tinted learned behaviors eventually overwhelm more accepting and empathic attitudes toward others (Anderson & Bushman, 2018; Anderson et al., 2003, 2010; Bushman & Anderson, 2002; Hoge et al., 2017).

An important mechanism that may underlie aggression following violent media exposure is desensitization, which some have defined as "a reduction in emotion-related physiological reactivity to violence" (Carnagey et al., 2007, p. 490). These researchers suggest that exposure to media violence may lead to changes in the processing of emotional information, including lowering our sensitivity to social cues (Carnagey et al., 2007). As we already saw, this reduced sensitivity shows up as difficulties recognizing emotional expressions in others (Miedzobrodzka et al., 2021). Impaired recognition of negative emotions was found to be a common problem in adolescent offenders (Bowen et al., 2014; Gonzalez-Gadea et al., 2014), people high in trait psychopathy (Hastings et al., 2008), and in young adults characterized by antisocial behaviors (Marsh & Blair, 2008).

The effect of violent video games on empathy is especially concerning. Empathy involves imagining others' perspectives and feeling care and concern for them. Empathy is especially important when it comes to promoting prosocial behaviors, such as helping, cooperating, and sharing (Batson, 2011). Although viewers of violent television, video games, and movies have a choice in taking on the perspective of the killer or the victim, players of violent video games are typically forced to take the perspective of the killer. Players have the same visual perspective as the killer in first-person shooter games. This may explain findings that individuals are more likely to behave aggressively themselves when they identify with a violent video game character (Konijn et al., 2007).

CONFLICTING CONCLUSIONS IN THE RESEARCH

In spite of what might seem to be overwhelming evidence with regard to the effects of virtual violence, the seemingly established association between violence on digital platforms and aggressive behaviors is still considered controversial. Other studies have found little or no effect of violent video game use on aggressive behavior (Ferguson, 2015; Ferguson et al., 2008). In one study, 15 pairs of excessive users of violent games and control subjects were matched for age and education. The two groups viewed pictures displaying either emotional or neutral situations, while fMRI brain activation scans were obtained. While the typical patterns of activation for empathy and theory of mind networks were detected, there were no significant differences in brain responses in these regions between the two groups. The authors interpreted these findings as evidence against the desensitization hypothesis and suggested that the impact of violent media on emotional processing may be short-lived (Szycik et al., 2017).

A general criticism of this field of research has been its emphasis on short-term effects. A study investigated the effects of long-term violent video game play among adults with a mean age of 28. The researchers used a large battery

of tests spanning questionnaires, behavioral measures of aggression, sexist attitudes, empathy and interpersonal competencies, impulsivity-related constructs
(i.e., sensation seeking, boredom proneness, risk-taking, delay discounting),
mental health (i.e., depression and anxiety), and emotional regulation functions.
All these measures were taken before and after three groups played either *Grand
Theft Auto V*, the nonviolent video game *The Sims 3*, or no game at all. The players used their games daily for two months. The results did not find significant
changes among measured traits. Again, there were no significant differences
between the three groups following the two months of game play. According
to the authors, these results provide strong evidence against negative effects of
playing violent video games (Kühn et al., 2018, 2019).

In a related study, the same group (Kühn et al., 2018, 2019) investigated
whether the type of video game influenced the participant's empathy responses
as recorded by fMRI scanners. The cues for empathy were scenes that depicted
individuals in situations of injury and pain. Here as well, no significant differences in brain patterns indicating empathy were found among the three groups.
In other words, there was no evidence for a decreased activation in the empathy
network for pain even in the violent video game group at any time point. These
results also question the frequently assumed negative effects of playing violent
video games.

The effects of four types of games on stress levels were measured through the
presence of stress hormones in participants' saliva. Salivary α-amylase concentration, a marker for stress, was measured in the following four groups: those
playing a fear-inducing game, a video running game, an excitement-stimulating
game, and a video puzzle game. Levels of the stress hormones decreased most
significantly after playing the puzzle game. Conversely, concentration of salivary
cortisol increased significantly after playing the running game, the excitement
game, and the fear-inducing game. Among these three groups, brain wave analysis also revealed that the level of stress was highest in the group playing the fear-
inducing game. According to these research findings, video games, especially
those involving fear, directly elevate the stress system (Aliyari et al., 2018). Such
out-of-awareness raised levels of cortisol may be one reason why so many studies
have found an association between violent games and aggression; increased stress
leads to fear, and in turn to defensive postures that involve aggressive behaviors.

As we see, the jury is still out on the effects of violent media on levels of
aggression and the blunting of empathy. However, the effects of violent media

on fear and anxiety among children seem less controversial. Moreover, states of hyperarousal while being exposed to violent content of all types may stimulate states of aggression. It is possible that the unconscious activation of the fear system becomes entwined with the unconscious development of automatic defensive aggression.

SOCIAL MEDIA USE AND EMOTION REGULATION

More recent research deals with the interactive nature of newer media, especially social media, and their impacts on anxiety and depression. The excessive use of screen time and social media carry additional hazards as well. For example, adolescents may seek digital distraction from emerging anxiety or distressed emotions, creating a reinforced behavioral avoidance of emotional experiences. Remember that emotional regulation is an essential skill that develops in childhood and adolescence. It allows us to learn to handle and cope with strong emotions by experiencing them and developing internal ways to regulate them without being deeply rattled by them. But individuals with internet overuse or addiction have reported using digital distractions in order to avoid negative emotions such as anxiety and depression (Greenfield, 1999; Spada et al., 2008).

Although no studies showing causal relationships yet exist, problematic internet use and overuse are associated with greater difficulties in emotional regulation (Vajda et al., 2014). In fact, the *DSM-5* (American Psychiatric Association, 2013) now has diagnosis categories for internet overuse and social media, including what is popularly known as "Facebook depression." Ironically, symptoms of depression predict an increase in the use of the internet for mood regulation, which "seems to act as a dysfunctional regulator of emotional distress" (Gámez-Guadix, 2014), creating a vicious cycle of internet overuse and depression.

Researchers have documented that the options of texting, instant messaging, and emailing have become preferred by some individuals over face-to-face interactions for some types of contact (Joinson, 2004; Leung, 2011). Such behaviors may actually increase adolescents' vulnerability to social anxiety. The defensive substitution of interpersonal communication with digital media is unconsciously chosen as a safeguard against potential hurt. But such behaviors may become cyclically reinforced over time, making the individual even more avoidant, thus increasing feelings of anxiety and lower self-esteem (Hoge et al., 2017).

Other sources of low self-esteem and self-doubts are the incessant comparisons to others on social media, cyberbullying, and ridicule from one's peers (Hoge et al., 2017). Exposure to social media can trigger among children and adolescents acute social anxiety that focuses on fears of embarrassment or humiliation. Such anxieties are, in essence, the embodiment of how unconsciously fragile and vulnerable young people may feel in the face of potential rejection and shame. The developing and internally reinforced negative self-narratives that accompany such anxieties only add to the lack of confidence. At a time when most children and adolescents desperately wish to be accepted and positively recognized, the rapidly shifting voices on social media and their potentially negative scope can become a serious and constant source of anxiety. In extreme cases, cyberbullying and fear of being shamed can lead to suicidal ideation, cutting, and eating disorders (Hoge et al., 2017; Lissak, 2018; Wilson, 2008).

WHAT DOES NEUROSCIENCE SAY?

Neuropsychological findings indicate that exposure to violent content may indeed alter some of our brain structures. For example, in a PET study performed on healthy young adult volunteers, visual evocation of unrestrained aggression was significantly correlated with reduction in blood flow to the ventromedial frontal lobe compared with an emotionally neutral scenario (Pietrini et al., 2000). Similarly, using fMRI scanning, violent visual images were shown to change the frontal lobe functioning of young viewers. In addition, among control subjects, brain activation patterns in youth with significant violent media exposure were different from those with a minimal amount of violent media exposure (Mathews et al., 2006).

Using fMRI data, a study examined the neural changes in young adults in response to violent and aggressive video games. Brain activity of 18 young men playing violent and nonviolent versions of the same video game were recorded in real time. The recorded brain patterns revealed a decrease in connectivity within six brain networks during the violent game but not in the nonviolent game, including the sensory-motor networks, the reward network, the default mode network, and the right-lateralized frontoparietal network. The authors speculated that these changes may underlie the short-term increase in aggressive emotions, cognitions, and behaviors that have been observed in people after playing violent video games (Zvyagintsev et al., 2016).

These last findings are perhaps the most interesting and useful in the context of understanding media violence and its effect on youth (Haslam et al., 2003). The implications for emotional regulation are clear. In addition to the inevitable activation of the amygdala circuits, the effects of virtual violence on areas in the prefrontal cortex may contribute to the lessening of a young person's ability to regulate emotions such anger and fear.

I started this chapter by wondering whether the very violent and aggressive elements so prevalent in our popular culture can trigger our fear system and the defenses it typically recruits. If we look at the general conclusions from the studies discussed here, two themes emerge. First, given their immature prefrontal cortex, a fast-acting amygdala, and an innate negative-biased attention, young children may be more vulnerable to the anxieties and worries brought on by exposure to virtual violence. Second, it seems that adolescents and adults may not be fully immune either.

Beyond the presence of conflicting data, what is important in the context of this book are the hidden physiological and neural markers of hyperaroused emotions resulting from exposure to vicarious trauma. The elevated stress that occurs while engaged in a combative game may result in a chronic physiological state that, in turn, can affect mood, biased attention, expectations, and narratives about oneself and the world. Such chronic stress can also compromise one's cardiovascular health (Porter & Goolkasian, 2019). Obviously, much more research is needed to clarify the effects of virtual violence in the digital world. We need to know whether young adults become more aggressive, numb to violence, and less empathic; or are they indeed buffered with the cognitive knowledge that this is only fiction and make-believe. We also need to better understand the addictive powers of video games and the pernicious effects of social media and the internet as they influence how children and adolescents feel about themselves.

Equally important is the clear antidote to the many pitfalls embedded within media: parental supervision. Central to any effort to neutralize the potentially destabilizing effects of exposure to virtual violence is limiting both screen time and the type of media consumed. With older children, the recommendation is to co-view movies as a family. Young children, particularly ages 8 to 12 years, are often eager to discuss what they watch with their parents. They welcome conversations about violence, its meaning, and impacts.

When parents do not exercise limits, the message to children may be that the parents approve of the content being viewed (Muller et al., 2020). In that case, children's and adolescents' identification with the violent hero, for example, may be even stronger given the perception of tacit parental approval. Some researchers have observed that without active involvement in the child's screen and media behavior, aggression among children and adolescents may intensify (Lissak, 2018; Muller et al., 2020; Wilson, 2008). In contrast, when parents take an active role in their children's media consumption via an active mediation of what it may mean, the negative effects of violent media are greatly lessened. Active mediation, explaining and discussing with children the content of a movie, for example, is particularly effective in reducing the potential hazards of aggressive content. When parental restrictions, active mediation, and coviewing were studied, findings showed their positive effects on children's anxiety and aggression (Collier et al., 2016).

CHAPTER FOURTEEN

Poverty, Racism, and the Fear System

So far, we have seen the many effects of the fear system on who we are and who we become. A great deal of this exploration focused on the presence of fear and anxiety in the context of our earliest relationships. We also highlighted the interaction of early developmental experiences with innate predispositions, and how environmental factors may unwittingly result in excessive anxiety. This chapter examines the neuropsychological costs of economic and social forces: poverty and racial discrimination. Admittedly, discussions of poverty, race, and racism can be challenging and confronting, especially for many white Americans. But beyond the calamitous effects of poverty and racial discrimination on affected groups and on our society as a whole, I think it is crucial to apply the accumulating neuropsychological research to further understand the impact of these social conditions on young children—on their developing brain/minds and bodies.

THE SCOPE OF POVERTY

Poverty cuts across all ethnic and racial groups in the United States. The Urban Institute projected that one in seven Americans, nearly 50 million people, will live at or below the poverty level by the end of 2021 (Giannarelli, Wheaton, & Shantz, 2021). But unfortunately, poverty disproportionately impacts people of color, with 18.1% of Black families and 21.9% of Hispanic families living at or below the federal poverty level, compared to 9.6% for white families; in 2021, the federal poverty level for a family of four was $26,500. The numbers are more alarming when we look at those living at or below twice the federal poverty level, or $53,000 for a family of four: 61.1% for Black families and 65.5% for Hispanic families compared to 34.9% for white families. The Children's Defense Fund (n.d.) reports that a shocking 71% of children living in poverty are children of color. While most of us have a basic understanding of poverty and its relationship to the overall economic health of our country, we must also contextualize poverty as another serious barrier to individual psychological health and overall public well-being.

All these factors and their many manifestations in our society are responsible for dangerously high levels of fear, stress, and anxiety in many families. When caregivers are under financial pressure or the ongoing stress of racial or ethnic discrimination, or both, children inevitably suffer. In fact, they are vulnerable in more than one way. First, they are directly affected by the dire situation into which they are born; second, they absorb and encode their parents' emotional states, which are exacerbated by poverty and racism. As we saw in different contexts, children become acutely aware of the anxieties and fears embedded in their families and communities.

Fear and anxiety are especially destructive, even lethal, to people who struggle with the ongoing insecurity that poverty brings. Similarly, the daily microaggressions, insults, and traumas related to systemic racism are a common cause of extreme anxiety and fear for people of color. The connections between poverty, racism, and physical illnesses are well established in the medical and psychological research literature. Additionally, we need to fully acknowledge that within certain populations, early anxieties and ongoing fears generate and support a constant state of hyperarousal and dysregulation.

We now know that the experience of early stress can actually change gene expression (Uchida et al., 2018). DNA methylation, a process that causes gene expression, results in genes being "turned on or off" (Vonderwalde, 2019). The major changes in methylation happen very early in life, and the exposure to ongoing external and interpersonal trauma has been showed to turn anxiety genes on in the amygdala. A more reactive amygdala influences how one processes fear, resulting in a heightened fear susceptibility to a wide range of events. Because it exerts a brain-wide influence on developing feelings, cognitions, memories, learning, and behaviors, early changes to the amygdala influence our conscious and unconscious patterns in childhood and throughout our adult lives (McCoy et al., 2019). In essence, the methylation and the amygdala shape our sense of ourselves, our internal narratives, and our level of self-esteem.

In fact, living with unrelenting and constant financial insecurity and the dangers of racism lead to some of the more damaging aspects of anxiety: actual threats to one's survival, fears for one's family, and substantial uncertainty and worries about the future. In a vicious cycle, these real-life pressures cause the amygdala to become ever more vigilant, resulting in increased fears and anxiety later in life. Remember that the implicit emotional and physiological memories colored by the visceral experience of fear go on to shape our traits. Those inaccessible implicit memories have been found to be more influential on subsequent perceptions, memories, feelings, expectations, and predictions, making them more difficult to modify (Pavlova et al., 2017). For example, adults with higher amygdala reactivity, who were shown both positive and negative emotional scenes, remembered more negative scenes compared to controls with no overreactive tendency (Kark & Kensinger, 2019a, 2019b).

As research shows, both poverty and racism cause substantial harm to children and adults alike. However, as I noted above, the harm to children is twofold: the immediate impact of poverty and racism; and secondary trauma due to the impact of poverty and racism on parenting. Thus, while this chapter references the impact of these factors on adults, the primary focus is on children.

CHILD POVERTY, ANXIETY, FEAR, AND TRAUMA

Children who live in poverty often suffer from food insecurity and hunger (Francis et al., 2018). In fact, households with incomes below the federal poverty level disproportionately experience food insecurity at some point in time (Coleman-Jensen et al., 2015). Nearly 16 million children in the United States live in poverty with food-insecure homes, defined as a household with any member who has limited access to adequate food (Francis et al., 2018). Real deprivation resulting from inadequate finances, cramped living conditions, a lack of shelter altogether, and the daily pressures experienced by parents under the strains of poverty can all lead to childhood trauma and harsh adverse experiences.

Psychological trauma is usually defined as an unbearable and inescapable threatening single or continuing experience in the face of which a person is powerless Herman, 1992; van der Kolk, 2015). Research on the effects of poverty on young children and adults consistently shows its devastating harms and lingering traumas. Neuropsychology, in particular, is starting to shed light on the mechanisms by which such aversive conditions actually affect the brains, minds, and bodies of a developing child.

The ongoing traumatization attributable to poverty increases fear and anxiety among children and leads to a significantly higher risk for difficulties in regulating emotions. Such early experiences also cause greater vulnerability to experiencing traumatic reactions in adult life (Schmid et al., 2013). Traumatization due to severe poverty heightens children's and adolescents' vulnerability to a host of developmental injuries to their growing sense of self. Difficulties such as impaired emotion regulation, interpersonal problems with peers, somatization, distorted perception of self and others, negative self-narratives, and self-destructive behaviors such as drug and alcohol abuse in adolescence are some results of chronic traumatization. For both caregivers and children, chronic stress results in a host of health problems as well (Schmid et al., 2013).

In addition, there is a clear relationship between early experiences of malnutrition and conditions or diseases such as high blood pressure, coronary heart disease, diabetes, comorbid mood disorders, and sleep disorders. Not surprisingly, children growing up in poverty often develop feelings of self-reproach, guilt, and shame (Brown et al., 2009). Their exposure to the humiliating and physical consequences of poverty, including hunger, and being fully attuned to their parents' struggles, inevitably creates a state of constant anxiety, hyperarousal, sadness, and insecurity (Rachel et al., 2017). Similar to children who are ethnic and racial minorities, children from poor neighborhoods are disproportionately enrolled in schools that are impacted by underfunding, overcrowded classrooms, bullying, and poorly trained teachers. These factors may compound the trauma these children are forced to endure within their families, schools, and neighborhood.

The power of the trauma that poverty creates, and its ability to metastasize and infect the child's developing feelings, thoughts, and behaviors, cannot be overstated. The various threats experienced by children living in poverty severely increase their sense of anxious vulnerability, resulting in an inability to tolerate and contain states of uncertainty as they grow older. Perpetually anxious feelings damage the child's self-esteem, reduce motivation, and dampen their hopes for the future. As a result, the development of a healthy self-image can be substantially impaired. Additionally, socially intense feelings of shame and low self-esteem caused by early traumatization are responsible for interpersonal problems in adulthood (Chicchetti, 2003).

Children who live in poverty are more likely to be exposed to multiple adversities and traumatic situations including but not limited to child abuse and neglect, household substance abuse, domestic violence, parental incarceration, community violence, homelessness, housing instability, and racial or economic discrimination (Halfon et al., 2017). These sources of chronic stress and adversity affect such children's parents, who are often unable to provide a safe, stable, responsive, and nurturing environment in spite of loving their children.

We know that a child's need for adequate nurturing and support is especially crucial during the first few years of life and into adolescence.

Several studies have shown that exposures to high levels of stress and poverty during infancy, childhood, and adolescence are linked to observable changes in brain development, particularly those areas associated with emotional regulation and cognitive development (Francis et al., 2018).

Poverty, Trauma, and Neuropsychological Development

Poverty is typically a chronic, multidimensional stressor. In addition to food and housing insecurity, poverty increases the likelihood of exposure to violence and maltreatment (Evans, 2004). Research has shown that the proportion of childhood spent in poverty is associated with decreased working memory performance in young adulthood (Evans & Schamberg, 2009). Research examining the neural effects of low socioeconomic status during infancy and childhood has found that some brain structures are actually smaller in volume compared to those of infants and children of high socioeconomic status. These regions include the frontal, medial, parietal, and temporal cortex as well as subcortical structures and total gray matter (Hair et al., 2015). Neurobiological evidence has shown that early life stress can have a particularly debilitating impact on prefrontal cortex structure and function as well as on the memory system (Taylor et al., 2020).

Significantly, one of the brain structures that was seen to increase in volume among children who grew up in severe poverty is the amygdala (Evans, 2016; Tottenham et al., 2011). These changes in the amygdala's size and reactivity have great implications for a child's developing ability to regulate emotions. A less efficient prefrontal cortex—the region of the brain involved in planning and emotional regulation—coupled with an overactive amygdala can create emotional reactivity and less effective suppression of amygdala responses to adverse stimuli. For example, individuals who were raised in poverty showed increased amygdala activation when they were presented with emotional scenes (Javanbakht et al., 2016; McLaughlin et al., 2016; Tottenham et al., 2011). Similarly, subjects who were raised in severe poverty are generally found to be more responsive to negative emotional stimuli, needing less perceptual information to identify angry and fearful facial expressions than other groups (Herzberg & Gunner, 2020). This makes sense from an adaptive point of view where the need to survive hardships necessitates developing enhanced attention to threat stimuli.

A study explored the association between disadvantaged socioeconomic status, amygdala volume, and symptoms of anxiety and depression. Both children and adolescents were examined, ranging in age from 3 to 21 years old. The group 7 to 21 years old also filled out self-reported measures of anxiety and depression. Lower family income was associated with a smaller amygdala among adolescents but not among younger children. Smaller amygdala volume in both children and adolescents was significantly associated with higher rates of depression (Merz et al., 2018).

In addition to having a negative impact on the development of the prefrontal cortex, adversity in early life is associated with lasting changes to the central nervous system (Kalia & Knauft, 2020). During infancy and childhood, while the HPA axis is still immature, children are particularly vulnerable to stress. Prolonged exposure to increased levels of stress hormones can interfere with normative development of the structure. For example, the reduced volume of the hippocampus and, therefore, compromised memory functioning, paired with ongoing activation of the HPA axis results in a constant state of anxious hyperarousal (Kalia & Knauft, 2020).

These processes derail the adaptive responses of the brain/mind/body to sustained stress. As a result, early life adversity can unbalance the normally adaptive physiological stress response and make it difficult to maintain stability in response to changing environmental demands. In addition, repeated stress responses to environmental pressures keep the interconnected arousal and fear systems in high gear, inflicting actual physiological damage. However, not all individuals exposed to early life adversity exhibit negative outcomes associated with early life stress. Individual differences in emotion regulation likely account for some of the observed variance in outcomes (Cameron et al., 2018; Troy & Mauss, 2011).

These neural and bodily changes are associated not only with heightened emotional reactivity and reduced emotion regulation but also with learned patterns of reduced sensitivity to reward processing. This is the result of unconscious learning processes that in effect already start in utero. Research has demonstrated that such consequences are associated with increased behavioral risks such as smoking cigarettes, drinking alcohol, drug addiction, and overconsumption of high-fat, high-sugar foods (Duffy et al., 2018).

Until recently, we have assumed that an infant is not responsive to environmental factors like poverty and race. However, as we saw in the previous sections, as early as the first year of life, disparities in socioeconomic conditions affect brain structures, their functions, and the stress system. Recent research has shown that among children in low socioeconomic status households, changes in brain function were found in circuits that support language, memory, executive functioning, emotions, and reward processing (Noble & Giebler, 2020).

Any discussion of brain development following early life adversities must be rooted in the underlying mechanisms by which stress "gets under the skin" (McEwen, 2012). This particular turn of phrase has been used to characterize the effects of stressful experiences across several systems associated with emotions and reward processing, particularly in the context of the neuroendocrine stress system (Danese & McEwen, 2012). Of all the systems involved in the developmental trajectories precipitated by poverty and food insecurity, the HPA axis may be the most influential and well-studied. The HPA axis acts to mobilize metabolic resources in response to external threats of sufficient intensity or specific nature; certainly, poverty and food and shelter insecurity are such chronic stresses. Cortisol is the primary hormone associated with this system. Basal levels of cortisol are important for maintaining healthy brain development and function (McEwen et al., 2015). However, repeated exposures to high levels of cortisol or its releasing hormone (corticotropin releasing hormone) can have negative effects throughout the brain and body. For example, elevated levels of cortisol exposure over periods of 48 to 72 hours can promote the formation of free radicals that are toxic to neurons themselves. Animal models of chronic stress in rats have correlated to dendritic shrinkage in the hippocampus; inhibited activity in the pituitary, hypothalamus, hippocampus, and amygdala; and reduced cell proliferation in subcortical structures (Eiland et al., 2012; McEwen et al., 2015; Treccani et al., 2014). Similar effects have been reported in humans with experiences of physical abuse, early neglect, and low socioeconomic status during childhood (Hanson et al., 2015; Sheridan et al., 2012). Understanding the effects of the neuroendocrine stress system on brain structure and function allows for the elucidation of one pathway by which experiences of poverty and all the adversities stemming from it shape the development of children.

The damage caused by cumulative trauma depends not only on experiences of deprivation and insecurity; it is also aggravated by the child's perception that the situation is hopeless or inescapable. For young children, the source of anxiety is manyfold: states of instability, actual food and shelter insecurity, parental fears and anxieties, and a chaotic existence over which they have no control. In one study, interviews were conducted with 94 socioeconomically diverse 4- to 9-year-old children. Additionally, their parents reported on their children's social-emotional functioning and on the levels of the family's socioeconomic disadvantage. As hypothesized, children from socioeconomically disadvantaged households who perceived their situation as disadvantaged showed more attention to problems and more anxious-depressive symptoms than socioeconomically disadvantaged children who perceived themselves as being less disadvantaged (Heberle & Carter, 2020).

Poverty and Emotion Regulation

Findings on emotion regulation in children exposed to adversity are almost universally consistent. Findings generally indicate that regardless of age, gender, or ethnicity, children growing up with significant adversity have poorer emotion regulation compared to nonexposed children. Moreover, in studies that have measured children's use of specific emotional regulation strategies, children exposed to adversity were more likely to use maladaptive regulation strategies, such as disengagement, blunted feelings, and negative rumination. Additionally, children growing up in poverty and adverse conditions use effective strategies such as cognitive reappraisal less often than children not raised in the same way (Boyes et al., 2016; Milojevich et al., 2018).

Emotional regulation depends on our ability to inhibit intense, dysregulated responses to emotionally charged stimuli. If a healthy automatic, unconscious regulation system is present, we still react with feelings but without a dysregulating emotional upheaval. Poverty, and the unrelenting daily stresses it brings, can interfere with such a foundation for effective emotion regulation. Behavioral and neuroimaging research has compared the emotion regulation ability of children from high-risk, disadvantaged environments and typically developing children. For example, a study of 4- to 7-year-olds looked at the ability to inhibit responses to irrelevant emotional information while busy with a task (Capistrano et al., 2016). The results indicated that experiences of poverty in middle childhood are related to a compromised capacity for regulated, more measured responses to challenges. Children coming from low-socioeconomic-status households became distracted and more emotionally reactive in the context of angry and sad emotional information, reactions that interfered with effective execution of the task. These deficits in emotion regulation were, in turn, associated with more frequent self-reports of feeling anxious and sad.

Other studies have focused on the association between childhood economic disadvantage and internalizing symptoms, such as numerous manifestations of anxiety and depression. Children from impoverished circumstances are more likely than their middle-income counterparts to develop states of anxiety and depression, such as fears, worries, lack of confidence, and negative expectations. These patterns of feeling and thinking often last into adulthood (Capistrano et al., 2016). Such results suggest that the observed deficits in children's ability to inhibit excessive behavioral responses to disturbing emotional stimuli are also associated with greater levels of childhood anxiety and depression (Kilford et al., 2015; Tottenham, 2019, 2020).

Another study looked at parental emotional well-being as a factor in a child's ways of coping. The parents in this study completed questionnaires regarding their own difficulties with emotional regulation. As predicted, greater exposure to parental difficulties with emotional regulation was associated with poorer regulation ability among their children. Significantly, parental difficulties with emotional regulation, but not the level of deprivation or actual threat, predicted their children's emotional regulation abilities. Unsurprisingly, among families living in poverty, the parents' level of effective ways of dealing with difficulties predicted the nature of their children's emotional regulation tendencies.

As we consider the influences of poverty on parents and their children, it is clear that poverty poses a significant risk to healthy childhood development. Thus, we must consider how to equip infant mental health experts, early childhood therapists, daycare centers, preschools, and elementary schools to provide effective support for the psychological needs of children growing up in poverty and their parents. This benefits not just children and families but society as a whole. The economic returns on early childhood interventions range from $4 to $10 for every $1 invested in the well-being of children (Reynolds & Temple,

2008), creating the foundation for psychological health that can begin to lift children and families out of generational cycles of poverty.

RACISM, ANXIETY, FEAR, AND TRAUMA

Racism comes in many forms and causes varying degrees of harm. Racism can manifest as bullying, verbal harassment, and subtle microaggressions. It includes discrimination in workplaces, classrooms, health care, voting, courts, and consumer environments. It manifests in hate crimes, from the vandalizing of property to physical violence to murder. And it shows up as exclusion, where people of color find themselves unrepresented, underrepresented, or negatively represented in many social outlets.

There is a growing literature on the damaging effects of racism on children's health. The study of the relationship between racial discrimination and anxiety confirms the insidious and direct ill effects on children's emotional well-being (Pachter et al., 2018). Previous studies have shown that over half of African American youth have experienced discrimination (Cronholm et al., 2015). A study of 277 children between the ages of 8 and 18 found that 88% had experienced situations that they perceived as racially discriminatory (Pachter et al., 2018).

Like poverty, and often intertwined with it, racism also is increasingly being considered as a childhood adversity, a psychosocial stressor that can potentially become a form of cumulative trauma. Indeed, experiences with racism are associated with significantly higher levels of anxiety and depression (Mouzon et al., 2017; Pachter et al., 2018). Among African Americans over the age of 18, 70% of symptoms indicative of trauma were significantly associated with racism. In general, findings reveal that race-based trauma seems to reflect a range of personal and collective experience. A study of 646 African American women who completed self-report measures of perceived racial discrimination revealed symptoms of anxiety and diagnosed chronic health problems; the study's findings highlight the potentially central role that anxiety plays in experiences of racism and subsequent chronic health problems (Carter et al., 2016).

Experiences with racism have been associated with many manifestations of anxiety states among nonclinical samples of African Americans: fear, negative narratives, rumination, chronic worrying, and somatic symptoms such as a racing heart and muscle tension. Heightened fear is linked to racism and, in some cases, to symptoms of post-traumatic stress (Jones et al., 2013; Polanco-Roman et al., 2016). Consistent with findings showing the ongoing effects of chronic anxiety, chronic stressors such as racism can also gradually increase anxiety and negatively change one's reactivity to stress (Young adult African Americans [N = 54]) were asked to report hourly on momentary racial discrimination (e.g., microaggressions), negative emotions, and the availability of psychosocial resources and coping strategies for two days. Racial discrimination was associated with a greater frequency of negative emotions such as anxiety, insecurity, and self-doubt. Interestingly, the relationship between the recorded racial discrimination events and negative emotions was stronger among individuals living in areas with fewer African Americans. Past experiences with racism contributed even more to reduced psychological health and coping strategies. Significantly but again not surprisingly, witnessing vicarious discrimination, the exposure to discrimination experienced by another person, was also associated with high negative emotions and reduced coping abilities (Joseph et al., 2021). We understand now the power of identification and the contribution of the mirror neuron system to processes of empathic connection.

Not surprisingly, everyday discrimination, particularly the frequency with which individuals were threatened, shamed, or treated as less intelligent or more dishonest, increased the odds of panic attacks in the following 12 months (Hearld et al., 2015). Such acts of racial aggression are also related to increased odds of social anxiety disorder among African Americans (Levine et al., 2014); they are also associated with both increased psychological distress and reduced measures of general well-being). Because of the amygdala's influence over other mental functions, individuals exposed to prolonged anxiety rooted in racism have also shown poorer self-concept, greater hopelessness, and anhedonia (i.e., the inability to experience pleasure) (Carter et al., 2016; Mouzon et al., 2017).

EMBODIED STRESS: THE EFFECTS ON THE BODY

Much like the pervasive effects of material hardships, such as poverty and food insecurity, the chronic nature of daily discrimination represents a persistent challenge to the emotional well-being of African Americans, indigenous people, and People of Color. The presence of ongoing, high levels of psychosocial stressors has severe consequences to one's physical health. As stress lingers, a cascade of biological processes takes place, most notably a dysregulation in production of cortisol. In a sample of 312 African American young adults (45.5% males, ages 21 to 23), the concentration of measured cortisol levels was significantly associated with symptoms of anxiety, but not with depression. Importantly, there were no gender differences in this pattern. The documented intersection between racism, anxiety, and health adds a significant factor to our efforts to better understand anxiety, fear, and trauma.

In this context, social structures and destructive hostility activate an already sensitive and vigilant fear system residing within us all. This is especially so when, in essence, People of Color still have no control over social structures or individual behaviors that actively discriminate against them, perpetrate aggressive words and actions, and threaten physical violence and even death. As a result, prolonged exposure to the stressors of active racism leads to the dysregulation of the HPA axis. As we already saw, periodic activation of the HPA axis is adaptive in the context of acute stress, when our body prepares itself for a fight-or-flight response; however, extended activation of the HPA axis exposes the body to the chronic presence of glucocorticoid cortisol, the primary byproduct of HPA axis activation. The repeated, accumulated pressure of such relentless biological activities takes a serious toll on important physiological functions; elevated blood pressure, diabetes, heart disease, and obesity have all been associated with excess cortisol and chronic anxiety (Adam et al., 2015; Lee et al., 2018).

Feeling States Linger

As the discussion on the nature of emotions showed, emotion states linger. As the amygdala automatically reacts to negative, threatening conditions, the state of hyperarousal and the feelings it embodies remain long after the interaction (see Chapter 3). In turn, this negative internal state colors subsequent, more neutral experiences. As research has shown, racism leads to inevitable and amplified physiological responses in the short term and, perhaps even more important, the neuropsychological reaction lingers long after the racist incident occurred (Hope et al., 2015).

For example, a study found that among African Americans, discriminatory experiences caused by whites had a prolonged effect on cardiovascular functioning as much as 24 hours after (Hoggard et al., 2015). Other studies suggest that the prolonged activation of the stress system also occurs when people emotionally or cognitively reexperience a racist event, or even when they simply anticipate future anxiety or fear related to race (Hope et al., 2015). As we recall from the discussion on unconscious processes (see Chapter 1), much of the encoding and categorization of our life experiences happen out of our awareness. The ongoing distress of racism—with the potential for psychological harm, physical violence, and even death—is obviously fully felt by the individual. But many more insidious and unseen injuries, both psychological and physiological, continue to leave their long-term marks.

Intergenerational Transmission of Racial Trauma

Direct and vicarious race-based heightened anxiety and psychological injuries are intensified by the ongoing traumatization of generations of African Americans and the process of intergenerational transmission of trauma (Kirkinis & Pieterse, 2021). As we saw in Chapter 6, children's emotions, cognitions, and behaviors are closely entwined with the internal and external experiences of the adults in their lives. During critical phases of development, children are especially vulnerable to stressors that cause their parents pain, fear, anger, intense insecurity, and ongoing anxieties, among many other feelings, thoughts, and behaviors.

Through unconscious learning, identification processes, and implicit memories, a parent's feeling states reverberate and echo within a child's subjectivity, thus becoming a part of their growing sense of self. Among children, he ever-vigilant amygdala is particularly sensitive to overt and nonverbal communications that transmit states of fear, distress, and a range of parental feelings that signal helplessness. Children's mirror neuron system will inevitably and unconsciously identify with and simulate within their brains those feeling states experienced by a parent.

A parent's sense of helplessness, insecurity, and indignation (e.g., the sense that they cannot protect their children from racism) raises the levels of fear and anxiety for both children and caregivers. A parent's emotions, attitudes, and behavioral responses become part of the child's own perceptions of themselves, others, and the world. Race-based negative stereotypes are particularly pernicious and unconsciously internalized by a child's developing understanding of themselves and the world around them.

As young children cannot understand and contextualize the reasons for a parent's shifting moods and distressing feelings, even when they are the result of external events over which they have no control, such darker moods may be attributed by children to their own failings. For older children, the situation is more nuanced. Given the realities of racism, hate crimes, and racial profiling, hypervigilance is both anxiety inducing but at the same time also an adaptive strategy. Many African American parents, for example, relate the story of "giving the talk" to their children, particularly their sons, about how to respond when interacting with police.

It is important to further understand how such talks, although utterly necessary, affect children's and adolescents' anxiety levels as well as their developing feelings and narratives about themselves and the world. As in all cases when dealing with trauma-inducing situations, parents' conscious and mindful attention to their children's responses and narratives is important. Similarly, the cognitive and behavioral modeling they provide may also mitigate some of the more damaging effects of dealing with such difficult and emotionally loaded situations. As has been observed, parents' ways of coping with the effects of racism can positively influence their children's resilience and motivation to succeed in spite of the external social constraints forced on them (Heard-Garris et al., 2018).

POLITICAL VIOLENCE AND CHILDREN'S ANXIETY

Another serious source of children's fears and anxiety is political violence, especially during times of war or political unrest. In one study, a majority of infants and children (81%) who were repeatedly exposed to war-related events showed post-traumatic symptoms and decreased coping abilities later in life. As we saw in previous chapters, infants, toddlers, children, and adolescents are prone to unconsciously experiencing the effects of traumatic events. The effects of direct traumas such as unnatural noise, situational chaos, and instability as well as vicarious trauma communicated by fearful parents are remembered and retained by the child's brain/mind. Such conscious and unconscious experiences are couched in levels of anxiety that can interfere with short- and long-term adaptive functioning (Halevi et al., 2016).

Children who actively look to their mothers for help display greater resilience than children who avoid asking for help and instead withdraw. A mother's own sense of calm and support is also a factor in children's resilience and in their ability to develop more adaptive coping and emotional regulation capacities. In middle childhood, children exposed to greater disruption displayed more post-traumatic stress symptoms, defiant behaviors, sensory processing and attention-deficit/hyperactivity disorders (Yochman & Pat-Horenczyk, 2020). The negative effects of childhood exposure to the many traumas of political violence and war appear to be widespread and are not limited to post-traumatic symptoms.

Again, with our overactive and stimulated fear system, such events may negatively affect the trajectory of a child's development. Because of the interconnectedness of the fear system with other brain circuits, a child exposed to traumatic events may display difficulties in emotional, social, cognitive, and interpersonal functioning in childhood and beyond. Their preoccupations, ruminations, worries, and continuous heightened anxieties can cause somatic symptoms, emotional dysregulation, and behavior problems (Conway et al., 2013; Pat-Horenczyk et al., 2015).

Using observational measures of a mother's emotional availability, researchers found that retrospective accounts of women's exposure to war-related experiences (mostly missile attacks in northern Israel) was related to elevated emotional distress. In turn, this emotional distress was related to higher levels of maternal separation anxiety, lower emotional availability during parent-child interactions, and lower levels of children's adaptive behaviors (Cohen & Shulman, 2019). In the context of children's vulnerability to parental emotional states, the intergenerational transmission of anxiety in times of war between mothers and children was also examined. Indeed, mothers' physiological stress levels influenced their children's developmental trajectories in regard to perceived stress or states of well-being (Halevi et al., 2017).

Studies suggest that, in comparison to an exposure to a single traumatic event, the effects of prolonged exposure to situations of political violence may be more pronounced in young children (Conway et al., 2013; Pat-Horenczyk et al., 2017). These events plunge both caregivers and their children into continual states of stress and anxiety with no clear end point. The need to continually adapt to unpredictable stressful events may result in increased biological dysregulation, a state in which serious pathophysiology can occur in the children's brain/minds and bodies (McEwen, 1998).

Unfortunately, what seems to connect the awful and stressful conditions of poverty, racism, and political violence is children's extreme vulnerability to these forces. A significant conclusion is that the best attempts of both children and caregivers to adjust to traumatizing situations may not always result in greater resilience; such situations still lead to increased fear and anxiety. The study concludes that the buildup of pervasive, unpredictable, and chaotic situations exacerbates emotional distress (Pat-Horenczyk et al., 2017).

Under threatening conditions, infants, toddlers, and young children cannot grasp the details of what is happening. However, their ability to absorb their external environment, and especially their parents' emotional states, all but guarantees the encoding and internalization of the many powerful and nuanced outcomes of extreme stress and fear. The results of poverty, racism, and social upheavals such as the COVID-19 pandemic, which are discussed next, all have the potential of greatly influencing the trajectories of children's development. Far from being an abstract understanding, all the chapters in this book point to the obvious fact that the underlying traumas embedded in these situations influence the nature of children's unconscious processes. And as has been established, these unconscious processes, continually and outside awareness, determine how we experience the world, how we interpret it, and how we react to inevitable challenges. Early emotional, cognitive, and behavioral patterns stored in these unconscious maps are then triggered and enacted, often in ways that are not appropriate to the current situations. This is why it is so important to keep in mind that the effects of poverty and racism go to the heart of who we are—our brain/minds and bodies.

At this point, however, our expanded knowledge regarding the effects of environmental cumulative traumas presents many opportunities for mitigating their worst effects. Understanding the importance of critical phases in children's development, the role of caregivers' emotional regulation, and the centrality of the intersubjective relationships within the family can guide us toward interventions aimed at derailing and improving the negative consequences of difficult situations. Parental attitudes have been found to lessen some of the most noxious effects. Evidence from the risk and resilience literature suggests that post-traumatic stress symptoms in caregivers increase parenting stress and may hinder their ability to provide adequate care at a time when their children most need it (Cohen & Shulman, 2019; Halevi et al., 2017).

Social support networks and early educational interventions can greatly reduce the stress felt by parents. In the case of poverty and racism, early educations programs for children such as Early Headstart and Headstart have proven to be significantly beneficial later in life. Above all, as caring humans we must not simply accept the existence of demeaning poverty, hurtful and debilitating racism, and the destructive violence of war. We must actively work against these powerful, and controllable, forces in our communities.

CHAPTER FIFTEEN

Fear, Anxiety, Therapy, and Mindfulness

As we have learned so far, as part of the human condition we necessarily coexist with fear and anxiety. From the acute emotional and physiological distress they cause to their numerous effects on our feelings, thoughts, imagination, internal narratives, and behaviors, these emotions seem to create the biggest impact on our internal states. Essential to our evolutionary survival and deeply etched into our neurobiology, the fear system cannot be eliminated from our brain/mind/ body. Nor should we try. After all, such emotion states are the ones that provide us with critical information regarding threats and impending dangers.

However, on the flip side, many of our personal difficulties have their roots in our anxious selves, the selves that developed early and entirely outside our conscious awareness. We only need to survey the vast number of self-help books, magazines, podcasts, and YouTube videos offering myriad strategies to tame symptoms of anxiety to recognize the hold that this emotion has on us. These attempts are a clear response to what we now know: Stress and anxiety seem to infiltrate every nook and cranny of our psychic life. The physiological sensations, worries, anxious ruminations, tortuous self-doubts, and questionable defenses combine to generate ongoing or occasional unhappiness in our lives.

But considering the neurobiology of the fear system and its widespread influence, what can we do to ameliorate their more upsetting and debilitating influences? We have learned that we cannot avoid experiencing fear and anxiety or escape their early developmental effects. In addition, unconscious patterns that were created under the influence of fearful and anxious experiences can easily be triggered, enacting negative feelings, thoughts, and beliefs even years later. We need to recognize, then, the need to pivot from thinking that we can entirely banish manifestations of anxiety to better understanding how to successfully and adaptively coexist within us.

For more than 100 years, since Freud began publishing his work, researchers, theoreticians, psychotherapists, and modern psychologist have tried to reduce the damaging effects of fear and anxiety. During the peak years of psychoanalysis as a therapeutic modality, the hope was that gaining enough insight into the origins of unconscious conflicts and repressed memories would be sufficient to get to the bottom of anxious or fearful symptoms. But unconscious processes, particularly entrenched patterns shaped by fear and anxiety, do not follow such premises. The fear system is biologically innate and omnipresent, and, as we have seen, guides many other mental and behavioral functions. Consequently, often, gaining insight into conflicts or old childhood experiences has not been sufficient to change the course of anxious self-states.

As we also learned, unconscious patterns are part of brain/mind processes that are automatically repeated and enacted. As a result, such unconscious patterns are also very resistant to change. This is because the mechanisms underpinning ancient, fast-acting, and unconscious reactions to the environment are still with us, often overriding slower, more reasoned and emotionally regulated reactions. And, finally, the recurrent fearful symptoms brought on by the lingering effects of trauma have also proven to be resistant to change. Encoded and learned within an intense emotional context, traumatic experiences tend to be vividly remembered and influential for our excessive sensitivity to fear; as a result, they create destabilizing, anxiety-suffused reactions to a wide range of cues in the environment.

The more we are influenced by patterns based on old fears, anxieties, distorted narratives, worries, and ruminations, the less we are able to pay attention to the actual cue and characteristics of our external environment. In effect, this is one of the costliest outcomes of negative states; distressing feelings, thoughts, and behaviors pull us away from experiencing the present moment and from what needs to be done in the here and now. In effect, when feeling anxious, our attention and perceptual biases unconsciously exaggerate the level of danger and see risks, often where none exist. As these automatic brain/mind processes create serious obstacles to more adaptive emotional regulation, we can see the obstacles in trying to treat anxiety-driven symptoms.

EMOTIONAL REACTIVITY AND EMOTIONAL REGULATION

In the last couple of decades, contemporary psychology research and psychotherapeutic practice have increasingly considered emotional regulation as essential to well-being and optimum functioning. In light of the interconnectedness of brain circuits, every state of dysregulation or emotional overreaction represents all aspects of our experience: intense and upsetting feelings, distorted cognitive expectations and predictions, repetitive negative thinking, rumination, worries, and defenses such as avoidance, rationalization, or narcissistic grandiosity.

In this context, emotional regulation can be described as all the conscious and unconscious strategies that we willfully or automatically use to influence which emotions arise and when, how long they persist, and how intensely these emotions are experienced and enacted (Frederickson et al., 2018; Gross, 2013; Guendelman et al., 2017; Gyurak et al., 2011). An increased understanding of the nature of dysregulation has led to new therapeutic approaches aimed at adaptively regulating the negative feelings, thoughts, and behaviors that are part of emotion dysregulation.

Paradoxically, we may be more familiar with how states of dysregulation feel. But what does a regulated state look like and how does it feel? The answer to this question may not be as simple as it sounds. Looking at the neurobiological data, we can state that, for most of us, eliminating anxiety and reaching a state of nirvana is not possible, unless, of course, it is assisted by illegal and extremely dangerous drugs. Consequently, we can rightly conclude that a state of regulated emotions does not have to do with the elimination of feelings altogether but rather with the ability to neutralize their painful and incapacitating effects. And, for many of us, this may create freedom from unrealistic expectations that we should never experience a negative emotional state; that feeling good means avoiding the various negative aspects of our bodily and emotional states.

Another way to understand a regulated state sees it as fully engaged with the present moment. This direct engagement allows us to approach internal and external pressures without drowning in them. It entails a conscious acceptance of life's difficulties and of the inevitability of struggles. And it involves a deep sense that many of our perceptions, expectations, and interpretations of our experiences are indeed heavily influenced by old unconscious patterns of feeling, thinking, and behaving, and that we can successfully live with them.

THERAPEUTIC APPROACHES

After decades of traditional therapeutic approaches, many clinicians and researchers have realized that words by themselves (i.e., talking about and repeatedly describing anxiety symptoms) may not be enough to diminish their debilitating effects. As a matter of fact, repetitive descriptions and complaints about our many manifestations of anxiety only tend to perpetuate negative thoughts and feelings, rather than improving them (Mischkowski et al., 2021). In a similar way, just complaining about states of anxiety and negative feelings without focusing on their meaning, origin, and function, and without implementing more active ways to neutralize their effects, changes little.

As a result, clinicians looked for more efficient ways to tackle these embodied emotions and ameliorate their many manifestations. Recognizing that the fear system is an innate and intractable part of us, these new approaches looked for ways to help people experience, tolerate, and eventually mitigate the many residual effects of anxious experiences. Research into the beneficial effects of meditation and mindfulness, for example, have shown a path to achieving regulation and relief from persistent anxiety through the very act of mindfully attending to and accepting it. Such developments have also opened doors to various mindfulness practices that can enhance regulation outside of the therapist's office.

Although this chapter focuses on the advantages of mindfulness as a therapeutic approach, we also need to remember the many irreplaceable benefits of more traditional talk therapy. In particular, although it may take time to develop, the safety and collaboration of the therapeutic relationship are essential for any progress. Similarly, deep and meaningful explorations of one's lifelong emotional and behavioral patterns are incredibly helpful and satisfying experiences. In effect, a supportive and collaborative therapeutic environment provides one of the few opportunities for many of us to find new and adaptive ways of becoming aware, and for new ways to experience ourselves and others. But keeping up with the book's focus on the fear system and its many manifestations, I have chosen to emphasize the benefits of mindfulness as a more active and actionable approach to the ongoing difficulties anxiety presents. Fortunately, the literature on psychodynamic psychotherapy is unusually rich and varied, and many books address all the emotional, theoretical, and practical aspects of what takes place (Bachant, 2019; Domash, 2020; Meroda, 2010; Nevis, 2020). My narrower focus in this chapter, then, aims to stay close to the wider context of fear and anxiety.

To state what is probably obvious by now, all the observable as well as unobservable changes in our emotions, feelings, and behaviors are actually modifications of existing neural circuits on the one hand, and/or the creation of new ones alongside the old. The more we practice new behaviors, the stronger their neural underpinnings become, while the older ones weaken. Eventually, new patterns can take over and operate more consistently than the dysregulated ones (Ginot, 2015).

Before discussing mindfulness, I would like to emphasize the occasional need for antianxiety medications. Far from being an easy and superficial solution, the right medication in the correct dose can offer many a reprieve from ongoing debilitating anxiety and depression. Medication is especially called for when the persistent presence of these emotions greatly interferes with one's personal and interpersonal functioning. Often, as physical and mental suffering subsides, individuals' engagement in the therapeutic process increases. With the edge taken off their distracting dysregulated emotions, thoughts, and behaviors, people are ready and more able to acquire and practice the necessary tools to deal with their internal states. In many cases, therefore, the use of medication is temporary.

FROM COGNITIVE–BEHAVIORAL THERAPY TO MINDFUL AWARENESS

An important contribution to treating the emotional, cognitive, and behavioral manifestations of anxiety was offered by Beck's therapeutic system of cognitive-behavioral therapy (CBT; Beck et al., 1987). CBT is a treatment modality that has shown success in treating the symptoms of anxiety and depression through cognitive and behavioral exercises. Clients track their upsetting behaviors and distorted thoughts, directly challenging their veracity, usefulness, and adaptability (Gomez et al., 2017). The encouragement to become aware of our negative narratives and other anxiety-induced misconceptions and behaviors in real time (i.e., as they are happening) has been an important addition to therapy. It has shown that the manifestations of fear-conditioned learning and irrational, anxiety-induced thinking can change when they become the focus of observation and reexamination.

Utilizing a similar framework, others created dialectical behavioral therapy (DBT), an invaluable therapeutic model that specifically addresses a range of emotional regulation difficulties, especially among individuals suffering from borderline personality disorder (Linehan, 2018). At its core is the idea that in order to function adaptively, opposing notions must be acknowledged and accepted. For example, in order to achieve a desired change in emotional regulation, one needs to embrace the balancing act between acceptance of internal states but also the work that needs to be done to change them.

In a nonjudgmental fashion, clients are taught how to become mindful of internal anxieties, of their tendency to entirely believe them, and finally, how to regulate repeated impulses and behaviors. This is usually done in a weekly group setting where clients learn to utilize reflective awareness and slowed-down reactions. This further helps clients identify and reshape emotional reactions and behaviors that do not work in the client's life. The results are newly learned skills such as enhanced emotional regulation, improved interpersonal relationships, and, importantly, a higher ability to tolerate upsetting internal states.

Another mindfulness-based intervention is acceptance and commitment therapy (ACT; Hayes & Wilson, 1994). The primary aim of ACT is not to eliminate anxiety symptoms but rather to improve our psychological flexibility (i.e., the ability to focus on the present moment) (Eifert & Forsyth, 2005; Hayes et al., 2013). This is accomplished by encouraging the mindful tracking and observing of internal experiences without judgment or efforts to change them. One of the goals, which in effect recurs in most mindfulness-based interventions, is to generate an internal distance from disturbing internal experiences. This is achieved when clients are taught not to fight off or mentally run away from upsetting feelings, thoughts, or bodily sensations. Instead, they are instructed to accept them and find more adaptive ways of dealing with them (Gomez et al., 2017; Hayes et al., 2013; Kelson et al., 2019). Even though reducing anxiety symptoms is not the primary focus of ACT, there is substantial evidence that by emphasizing mindfulness and acceptance individuals can significantly reduce anxiety symptoms (Swain et al., 2013). In addition, in order to change behavioral patterns, clients are encouraged to engage in exercises that explore their values and preferences. By committing to such personal values, clients can experiment with new ideas about what is important to them, thus developing new, more adaptive behaviors. Again, the goal is not to gain control over internal states and behaviors through logical analysis or cognitive attempts to push them away. Rather, the focus is on trying to accept one's internal states and commit to different coping mechanisms (Hayes et al., 2013).

Significantly, CBT, DBT, and ACT all assume that such mindful tracking, labeling, challenging, and reshaping of all aspects of dysregulation should not happen only within the therapeutic situation. Rather, a great amount of homework is given to clients and strongly encouraged. The importance of this shift to dealing with everyday behaviors as they are happening makes complete sense. If we remember the stubborn automaticity of unconscious brain processes, we realize that one hour of therapy a week is insufficient to extinguish old, learned emotional and behavioral habits. In addition, most of our life difficulties tend to occur outside of the therapeutic hour. When clients are given concrete tools to tackle anxious states in real time, they can practice them when they are most needed.

The existence of therapeutic techniques or practices that encourage states of emotional regulation away from the therapist's office is nothing short of amazing. In addition, such tools can prove to be essential during times of enhanced uncertainty and anxiety, such as the extended COVID-19 pandemic. Most of us can engage in mindful practices that, with persistent repetition, can help us regulate what might otherwise be intolerable states of anxiety. The following sections continue to examine some of the tools available to all of us inside as well outside a therapeutic environment.

Mentalization

Another approach based on mindful processes is mentalization. Mentalization is defined as the ability to think about and understand various mental states in ourselves and others. Mental states like feelings, desires, motivations, and behaviors become subjects of observation, reflective contemplation, and enhanced awareness. An important part of the mentalization process is the implicit understanding that people we interact with possess subjectivities different than our own. This mental ability to understand the content of our own mind as well as that of others develops within our early attachment relationships and is also dependent on the development of some areas in the prefrontal cortex (Choi-Kain & Gunderson, 2008; Guendelman et al., 2017; Saxe, 2018; Saxe & Houlihan, 2017). This trait, like all others, is the product of epigenetic interactions; it is central to how we understand our feelings and regulate them, as well as how we relate to others (Fonagy et al., 2002).

Compromised attachment experiences such as early interpersonal stress, neglect, and abuse results in difficulties realizing that others have minds and desires of their own. For example, in order to cope with uncertainty, shaming, or dismissal, children may become excessively preoccupied with their own self-protective ruminations. This will come at the expense of developing the ability to see those close to them as separate beings who mean well and are on their side. Secure interpersonal feelings allow children to relate to others with less apprehension, fewer negative expectations, and a reduced tendency to engage in victimized ruminations.

Psychotherapy can help children and adults to develop this mentalizing capacity. Pragmatically, this ability overlaps with mindful or reflective awareness, the ability to examine our internal states and those of others. This has been true especially for people diagnosed with borderline personality disorder or exhibiting various degrees of a narcissistic disorder. Oftentimes, both these groups have difficulty understanding their own internal mental states and those of others, leading to ineffective emotional regulation and impulsive automatic behaviors and defensiveness (Fonagy & Bateman, 2006). For these reasons, the goal of improved mentalization has been a part of psychodynamic therapeutic approaches as well as of more structured processes such as CBT and DBT (Björgvinsson & Hart, 2006; Lewis, 2005; Lewis & Todd, 2007).

Mentalization has been characterized as comprising four main processes: (1) observing mental phenomena, (2) describing or labeling those mental phenomena, (3) describing the meaning and motivation of one's own and others' behaviors as the product of mental states, and (4) understanding the intrinsic linkage and mutual influence of mental states in oneself and others (Goodman, 2014; Guendelman et al., 2017). The act of observing feelings and thoughts, and labeling them in real time, overlaps with the reflective processes that take place in other mindfulness practices (Goodman, 2014). Similar to the other approaches we have discussed so far, purposefully observing and labeling negative feelings, thoughts, and behaviors as they are happening can build more effective emotional regulation skills (Fonagy & Bateman, 2006). We will continue, then, to examine in greater detail notions of mindfulness and mindfulness-based therapeutic interventions.

THE BENEFITS OF MINDFULNESS

Although the previously discussed therapeutic approaches may differ in various aspects, they all share a direct focus on mindfulness. Of course, one of the goals of psychodynamically oriented psychotherapy has always been to "make the unconscious conscious" and help individuals become more aware of their unconscious motivations. However, mindfulness-based approaches directly engage reflective awareness as the chosen road to change. For example, CBT looks to change established maladaptive thoughts; DBT and ACT encourage acceptance of disturbing patterns rather than an active "cognitive restructuring" of them (Gomez et al., 2017). Still, even within a CBT approach, in order to identify, challenge, and modify our "faulty" thoughts and behaviors, one would first need to become aware of them. In different ways, all these therapeutic modalities enhance the development of a purposeful attention to and examination of feelings and cognitive processes.

"Mindfulness refers to a process that leads to a mental state characterized by non-judgmental awareness of the present moment experience, including our sensations, thoughts, bodily states, consciousness, and the environment while encouraging openness, curiosity, and acceptance" (Gomez et al., 2017). Unsurprisingly, with the growing appreciation of mindful approaches, some therapeutic approaches have incorporated Eastern-based mindfulness practices such as meditation.

An attitude of openness and curiosity about inner experiences such as visceral sensations, feelings, recurrent narratives, and anxiety-inducing inner monologues allows us to be less judgmental of them. As disturbing feelings and thoughts arise, we allow ourselves to experience them while we transform them into observable entities floating by, thus reducing their power to rattle us. During such instances, anxious feelings, thoughts, and expectations are seen from a more neutral point of view. We come to realize that what we experience is indeed a part of us but at the same time not the sum of us. We can remember in real time that negative states are neuropsychological representations of old patterns that were learned and reinforced entirely outside our awareness.

Numerous longitudinal studies have shown the efficacy of mindfulness-based interventions in a variety of populations, both clinical and nonclinical (Gomez et al., 2017; Guendelman et al., 2017). For example, Jon Kabat-Zinn, a seminal figure in the Western mindfulness movement, developed an eight-week treatment program designed to reduce stress through mindful meditation (Kabat-Zinn & Chapman-Waldrop, 1988). The program consists of weekly group meditation classes with a trained instructor, daily audio-guided home practice, and mindfulness retreats where instructions focus on developing skills to mindfully attend to the visceral sensations involved in breathing. These active reflective practices also incorporate various mind–body meditative practices such as body scans, stretching, and yoga. Similarly, others maintain that the most effective treatment for war trauma and related experiences, for example, comes from practices that engage the body, such as paying attention to our body through the practice of yoga and meditation (van der Kolk & McFarlane, 1996; van der Kolk et al., 2019).

Psychological Flexibility

During the COVID-19 pandemic, researchers explored the moderating effects of psychological flexibility on mental health outcomes in Italy (Pakenham et al., 2020). Unsurprisingly, they found that psychological flexibility mitigated the emotional effects of the COVID-19 lockdown on anxiety, depression, and COVID-19–related distress; psychological inflexibility exacerbated those effects. Individuals fared better when they could shift their attention away from the very grim, fearful, and uncertain aspects of the raging pandemic and internally rely on a wider, more hopeful perspective and use existing support systems.

This study provided valuable insights into the potential of psychological flexibility to buffer negative mental health outcomes during a time of severe communal and personal crisis. In addition, psychological flexibility was shown to lessen the negative effects of the enforced social isolation (Waldeck et al., 2017). A central mitigating factor in psychological flexibility was the individual's ability to accept a difficult situation with greater composure. Greater mental flexibility helped participants cope with the potentially harmful effects of increased social isolation amid the COVID-19 pandemic.

These findings show that the attribute of psychological *flexibility*—the *acceptance* of difficult psychological experiences—contributed to improved mental health functioning during the pandemic. By allowing individuals to adopt a stance of greater acceptance and wider perspective, mental flexibility served as a buffer against the detrimental impacts of the prolonged traumatizing crisis. What is significant about this study is its emphasis on psychological flexibility. When we recall that mindfulness-based interventions can increase our ability to avoid getting stuck in and swallowed up by negative states, we can see the healing potential of meditation. Meditation can increase flexibility by teaching us to shift our attention among different feeling states and pay attention to alternative experiential states. At the core of psychological flexibility and mindfulness is the idea that accepting an aversive experience, while at the same time recruiting other ways of dealing with it, diminishes the acute debilitating effects of anxiety.

Mindfulness-Based Interventions

Meditation has taken root in the West, and for many good reasons (Siegel, 2007). The rich body of research pointing to the efficacy of mindful practices emphasizes how mindfulness promotes emotional regulation. With the growing body of research indicating that meditation actually changes areas in the prefrontal cortex, it has become apparent that we need to counter the physiological, visceral markers of negative feelings, thoughts, and behaviors with practices that teach us how not to drown in our own feeling states (Davidson & Begley, 2012; Goldman, 2006). Indeed, meditation, for example, allows us to develop the right distance from our most dysregulating states. As a result, we can develop a more tolerant relationship toward our anxious and injured states, and those of others.

Individually or in groups, practices such as mindful meditation encourage us to increasingly become aware of body sensations such as skin temperature, shifting muscle pressure, and levels of pain and comfort—all visceral markers of emotions. These strategies contribute to the important goal of tolerating, accepting, and regulating difficult emotions (Guendelman et al., 2017; Kabat-Zinn, 2005; Ochsner et al., 2009; Siegel, 2007). In effect, we learn that as unpleasant as anxious feelings are, we can still tolerate a modified coexistence with them. It may be reassuring and calming just to realize that an anxious state is one of our innate reactions, and that in many instances its intensity changes or goes away all together.

MINDFULNESS AND THE PRESENT MOMENT

Mindfulness has been defined as "the intentional, accepting, and non-judgmental focus of our attention on the emotions, thoughts, and sensations occurring in the present moment" (Wehry et al., 2015). With rising popularity as well as fast-accumulating research data as to their effectiveness, mindfulness practices have been widely accepted as a way to promote health and well-being. Effectiveness has been shown among adults, adolescents, and children suffering from anxiety disorders. Two approaches have been widely used to increase emotional regulation and, thus, psychological health: (1) mindfulness-based stress reduction, and (2) mindfulness-based CBT (Burke, 2010). Both these approaches teach mindfulness skills, which are effective therapeutic interventions against many facets of anxiety.

Interestingly, mindfulness meditation can be seen as the antithesis to our prevalent states of mindlessness—our propensity to let our minds wander and shift attention away from the present moment. Indeed, if we monitor ourselves mindfully, we can easily notice how often we turn away from the present moment and from external situations, leaning into our well-rehearsed internal monologues. This appears to be the result of a default mode network that engages in mental self-referential processing when we are not busy with an externally focused task.

Studying the connections between mind-wandering and mental health has yielded some interesting findings. For starters, nearly 50% of our awake life is spent in states of mind-wandering; ironically, despite its prevalence, unfocused mind-wandering is associated with lower levels of happiness (Killingsworth & Gilbert, 2010; Marusak et al., 2018; Nolen-Hoeksema et al., 2008). In contrast, the capacity to keep our minds focused on the present moment is associated with greater psychological well-being (Brown & Ryan, 2004). One explanation is that a high level of self-referential thoughts often slides into negative ruminations about the past or anxious worries and negative expectations about the future.

These data have prompted interest in understanding the benefits of mental states that are *present*-centered and the ways in which such states can be cultivated. One neuroimaging study in adults, for example, identified four brain/mind/body states: (1) mind-wandering mediated by the default mode network, (2) attentional awareness of mind-wandering, (3) shift of attention back to the present moment, and (4) focus on the present moment (Hasenkamp et al., 2012). The suggestion is that each of these states corresponds to particular neural networks and the various connections among them. Mindfulness, according to these researchers, may increase more flexible shifts between these brain states, resulting in the ability to move more easily from mindlessness to a mindful connection with the here and now (Marusak et al., 2018).

Studies exploring mindfulness-based stress reduction have often used meditation practices that focus on breath awareness, body scans, walking meditation, and yoga. In each of these practices, participants are trained to focus their attention on present-moment experiences (Kabat-Zinn, 1990; Siegel, 2021). The results show that mindfulness-based stress reduction leads to reduced negative experiences and to quicker recovery from a negative challenge (Britton et al., 2012; Kral et al., 2018). Nonclinical participants who practiced meditation also showed improvement in emotional reactivity, distractibility by emotional inter-ference (Ortner et al., 2007), and, most importantly, decreased negative moods (Jha et al., 2010).

Mindfulness consistently seems to improve a stable state of mind and a calmer approach to general stress for adults (Kral et al., 2018). But exciting emerging data also support the use of mindfulness to improve the physical and mental health of children and adolescents. Mindfulness training has been shown to improve cog-nitive performance, emotional regulation, and stress resilience among children and adolescents diagnosed with anxiety as well as in children with low anxiety levels (Marusak et al., 2018). What some practitioners and researchers stress is that even subtle indications of anxiety among children and adolescents should be addressed before they lead to further entrenched negative feeling states. Thus, it is important to address early fear and anxiety with treatments and practices that enhance emotional regulation, particularly after traumatic experiences. For example, case studies have provided evidence for the efficacy of a CBT awareness protocol with preadolescents who displayed mild signals of anxiety, distress, and depression (Mariotti et al., 2021).

Mindfulness-based treatment modalities that have been found to help chil-dren in various levels of distress include relaxation training; deep breathing; cog-nitive restructuring by identifying and challenging anxiety-provoking thoughts; practicing problem solving and effective coping with anticipated challenges; sys-tematic exposure to feared situations or stimuli, including imagined scenarios; and a focus on neutralizing feared stimuli (Wehry et al., 2015).

The Ideal Versus the Practical

A frequent difficulty in clinical settings is a frank admission that many of us simply can't sit quietly with our thoughts and discomfort. Clients report that they have tried and failed to pay attention to their breathing without becoming distracted or even rattled by their familiar internal monologues and rumina-tions. In such cases, people note that, in contrast to the goal of neutral aware-ness, they become even more anxious and distracted. The struggles brought on by meditative practices are real and need to be taken into account in any treatment modality that incorporates them. Indeed, a review of studies with healthy adults found that most people choose to do mundane tasks, or even receive mild electric shocks, over being left alone with their own thoughts. Cli-ents often report taking on the practice of mindful meditation only to abandon it after a short while. This happens despite the wide availability of online meditation guides and numerous excellent mobile applications (Creswell, 2017; Kral et al., 2018).

On a pragmatic level, today's numerous apps and online meditation classes should facilitate engagement with mindfulness-based interventions. It is possible to overcome this obstacle, but it takes a lot of persuasion and confidence building. Convincing people to persist with the practice is the first step. As findings suggest, although mindfulness is a difficult state to achieve, the commitment to pursue it is well worth the great efforts it takes. Skills that develop as a result of mindfulness-based interventions, meditation in particular, can provide a lifelong ability to rely on an internal sense of well-being and resilience (Creswell, 2017; Kral et al., 2018).

My emphasis on the efficacy of meditation is guided by my conviction that current therapeutic approaches need to expand their efficacy in treating anxiety-suffused states. The incorporation of direct mindfulness-based practices is the most important step. Psychotherapy, of course, will always have a central role in providing a safe place to recognize, become aware of, explore, and change old, anxiety-driven patterns. Whether the therapist directly guides the patient or not, the acquisition of mindful ways to relate to oneself, others, and the world is one of many benefits of psychodynamic psychotherapy. The benefits are not limited to adults; a few well-designed studies examining psychodynamic psychotherapy with children and young adults showed improvement in their anxiety symptoms (Fonagy et al., 2006; Fonagy & Bateman, 2006; Levinson et al., 2014; Wehry et al., 2015).

EXERCISE AND PHYSICAL ACTIVITY

Finally, we need to acknowledge one more therapeutic tool that has long been found to reduce anxiety symptoms: physical activity. Numerous studies in the general population have found that individuals who engage in more physical activity have a reduced risk of being diagnosed with an anxiety disorder. When people who exercise do complain about anxiety, it is less frequent and with less severe symptoms (Baumeister, 2017). Conversely, physical inactivity has been shown to be a risk factor for developing anxiety and depression (Teychenne et al., 2015). This evidence suggests that physical activity appears to protect more active people from the debilitating effects of anxiety symptoms; this is true for the general population as well as among clinical populations (Kabat-Zinn, 2005; Kandola et al., 2019).

It is not a reach to see bodily movement as a practice that promotes mindful focus and attention. Exercise involves a wide range of physical sensations; paying attention to them strengthens our connection to the embodied physical and emotional aspects of our experiences. Physical activity also teaches us to tolerate painful sensations, at the same time showing a way of coexisting with them.

By combining evidence-based research, mindfulness-based psychotherapy techniques, and meditation, we have access to powerful and effective tools to mediate the influence of our fear system. We may not be able to eliminate fear and anxiety, but we can learn to mitigate its most damaging effects. And that is a source of hope in our increasingly complex, unpredictable, stress-filled world.

LAUREN'S CASE: THERAPY AND MINDFULNESS

Lauren is a 26-year-old woman who is currently in New York City for graduate school. She grew up in the Midwest in a family of second-generation immigrants of Asian origin. Lauren described her parents, siblings, and extended family as "successful overachievers who can also enjoy life." Lauren herself has struggled with a severe eating disorder since she was 12. Whereas her eating disorder started with symptoms of anorexia, for the last few years she has been binging and purging; until recently, almost daily. As we often see in such cases, her psychic and social life was consumed by her eating disorder.

Lauren described her parents as loving and affectionate. But alongside their obvious caring feelings and interest in their children's needs, Lauren's parents, and especially her mother, were very preoccupied with following social rules, fitting in, and how they looked to others. In particular, Lauren's mother was very attuned to people's appearances, how they carried themselves, and how successful they were.

Both parents, indeed, were quite successful, and growing up Lauren thought they were perfect and invincible. She remembers fantasizing how one day she'll be just like them, successful, witty, and good-looking. The atmosphere and the messages that surrounded Lauren and her older brother intimated that vulnerability and weakness were a real impediment to achieving one's goals. It was not exactly that failure was not accepted but that one "had always to strive, to achieve, and always set one's goals higher and higher." Looking back, Lauren has realized how anxious her father was, and how this anxiety did not let him relax and enjoy what he had and what he achieved. He continuously strived for greater business successes and did not take setbacks very well, verbally expressing his disappointment with a great deal of frustration.

Often, but especially at dinnertime, directly and through hints, both parents criticized Lauren's older brother for eating too much and already being "chubby." During these times, they expressed worries that he might gain weight, become a target of bullying, and face future personal and interpersonal difficulties. Lauren's mother frequently noted other people's weight, and verbalized what Lauren understood as a mix of disdain, disgust, and pity.

Throughout her childhood and until her young adulthood, Lauren desperately wished to get her parents' approval, to differentiate herself from her "big eater and chubby" brother. Dinner conversations often compared the children's achievements in school and according to Lauren were full of encouragements for both herself and her brother. At the same time, there was also an emphasis on how one should behave and appear to others. As the spotlight repeatedly landed on Lauren's brother's "weight problems," Lauren felt increasingly uncomfortable, and in her words, "very confused and cringy." She felt sorry for her brother but at the same time was glad and relieved that she was spared her parents' judgment. Listening to their witty, fun, casual, critical talk of friends and others in their extended family, Lauren secretly worried that one day her parents would criticize her looks as well. In hindsight, Lauren thinks that as a young girl the worrying thoughts and fearful ruminations about being criticized became enmeshed in her mind with the physical changes of her developing feminine body. Although Lauren did not remember her parents directly making any critical remarks about her looks, anxiety mixed with shame became a part of her ruminations about what was acceptable or unacceptable about her. In her young mind, she needed to make sure that she would stay "perfect and fit." In spite of her young age, when she was around 11 years old, Lauren started to restrict how much she ate.

Somewhat later, during adolescence, Lauren's states of anxiety became tangled with strong feelings of self-loathing that could only find relief when she binged and purged. In spite of her intense fears about gaining weight and worries that she was already overweight, she still managed to maintain good grades and a good social life. Doing well in school was very important to her, as it assured, in her mind, her parents' esteem. Only a couple of close friends knew about her troubled relationship to her body and food.

Lauren felt too humiliated, ashamed, and frightened to tell her parents about her inner turmoil and troubling behaviors. In effect, she was very good hiding it all from them, at times feeling proud about being able to pull it off. And although her eating disorder intensified over the years, she only told her parents about it when she was 20 and started seeing a college counselor.

In spite of her conscious efforts to stop her binges, Lauren could not avoid this cycle of overeating and throwing up. Each cycle began with troubling sensations of inchoate and painful distress. It was then followed by obsessive thoughts about food. She would experience an all-consuming craving for all kinds of food, especially sugar, then binge and purge. Most often she ended up feeling intense shame and guilt. Lauren came to think of her eating disorder as "a beast inside" of her, a monster that could take over and control her free will and determination.

The link between negative emotions and unbidden thoughts about food became evident in our sessions as well. Whenever she encountered discomfort during a session, thoughts about food surfaced. Sensations of anxiety in the form of physical pressure in her chest or wanting to jump out of her skin were accompanied by thoughts of worthlessness. Simultaneously, the defensive function of food also became clear.

The act of binging and purging was the only reliable way to gain some calm and relief from emotional upheaval. The moment she felt the pain in her chest, the familiar sense of agitation, she would turn to the rituals of overeating. Paradoxically, despite her attempts to get away from the physical manifestations of anxiety, binging and purging was the only way through which she could become connected to and feel her body. This cycle was enacted almost daily, often in the face of Lauren's daily determination not to give in to it.

Similarly to her adolescent years, when Lauren started therapy, she did well in graduate school. As she said at the beginning of therapy, sex also became important to her. It became another way to gain relief from anxious ruminations and feel her body in a positive way. However, as she lamented, she only got to meet "wrong, bad guys" and therefore had not yet been involved in a long-term relationship.

When trying to understand how Lauren's eating disorder took hold in such a forceful way, we may speculate that her genetic predisposition to anxiety/depression played an important part. Her father and his two siblings were either depressed or very anxious individuals. There is little doubt that, as in most cases, Lauren's difficulty represents a not yet fully understood interaction between genes and environment. Carrying the predispositions inherited from her father, the general expectation of appearing "just right," and the potential humiliation of being overweight gave this predisposition an embodied presence in Lauren's brain/mind/body and subsequent struggles.

We can also say that by unwittingly following their ideas of what makes a successful life, Lauren's parents greatly increased her levels of anxiety. In turn, as we saw in the previous chapters, this anxiety inevitably affected what she thought and did. In her young mind her food restriction began as a way to ensure control over how she looked and thus maintain approval from her parents. Within a family that also emphasized strong, loving bonds, Lauren came to believe that some of these essential loving attachments were somewhat conditional. Not yet able to ground herself in a nuanced understanding of how her parents' values were their own particular distortions, they inevitably affected how she felt about herself; their opinions and views reflected some unshakable true reality (see Saxe, 2018).

In addition, watching her brother being the focus of negative attention for being slightly overweight filled Lauren with and anxiety of her own. While watching her brother's discomfort at the dinner table, Lauren identified with his internal feeling state. She wished to come to his defense but was conflicted and confused. She could not reconcile, she says, her caring parents with their disregard for her brother's feelings, or with their tendency to put others down for not following their own vision. But as we repeatedly saw, a child's identification with her parents is always there (see Chapter 6). And indeed, a pervasive thought kept reminding Lauren that her parents knew best—that they were right, after all.

When Lauren turned to anorexia as a way to control her weight, her confusion lifted; she found a way to guarantee acceptance and praise. At the same time, she discovered that anorexia and bulimia were effective ways for her to cope with what became distorted self-denigrating and self-loathing thoughts that, when triggered, went on the attack.

Lauren's story illustrates the power of an unconscious internal pattern organized around ongoing anxious feelings and ruminations about what made her valuable and lovable on the one hand, and potentially rejected on the other. Out of awareness Lauren developed a convincing narrative that the only way to become like her parents and be accepted by them was to follow their most obvious verbal and nonverbal guidance: reach for full control over food and body.

We can see here how anxious feelings, the physical sensations that embody them, and the narratives that accompany both became inextricably intertwined. Anxiety about losing control, and the shame and humiliation that were sure to follow, would take over her consciousness with self-hating narratives. Finally, intertwined concrete behaviors around food consumption and elimination ensured the enaction of this pattern.

With time, as part of our work together, Lauren became able to focus on her body and her feelings, recognize them, and put them into words. With the help of mindful attention, she began to better tolerate what she was feeling, to engage in mindfulness and self-talk, and to develop a dialogue with the worried, confused, and anxious very young self-state. As many memories about her childhood surfaced, explaining her internalized ideas about body and self-worth, the automatic coping mechanisms came under mindful consideration. At the same time, while becoming more aware of her emotions and their automatic association with food, Lauren also became more understanding and compassionate toward her hurt part, the little girl who felt shame for no reason but was unable to differentiate her feelings from those of her parents. By allowing herself to fully experience the anxiety she felt as a child, tolerate it, and talk to it, she has begun to disconnect the automatic association between the bulimia and her visceral experiences. An increasing connection to her body and its sensations helped her to recognize and move away from the tyranny of the eating disorder pattern.

A Short but Essential Perspective: The Duality of Our Psychological Lives

The previous chapters illustrate the various and lasting effects that childhood fears and anxiety have on our personality and behaviors as adults. Using neuroscience as a guide, I emphasize the power of the fear system to educate and influence the rest of our mental functions. In effect, it is the brain's interconnectedness that enables such wide-reaching consequences. Understanding the nature of self-states organized around fear and anxiety, acknowledging negative behavioral patterns, and identifying anxious self-narratives are the first steps toward healing our past and changing our reactions and behaviors.

DUALITY: THE BAD NEWS

In some ways, acknowledging the extensive neuropsychological body of research confirming the evolutionary power of the amygdala may seem somewhat dispiriting. For example, states of hyperarousal triggered by frustration, a child's sense of being overly controlled, the hurt of injurious and critical messages, and the many restrictions resulting from overprotective behaviors by parents can all lead to uneasy, anxious states. These ongoing stressful states intermingle with our other feelings, narratives, and thoughts, affecting how we see ourselves and others and how we act.

Additionally, the brain/mind's susceptibility to distressing experiences contributes to the ubiquity of negative feeling states. Studies have consistently found that our memory system tends to recall more negative memories than positive ones (Bromberg, 1998, 2006; Kark & Kensinger, 2019). Furthermore, when distressing memories reach our consciousness, they are experienced as entirely real and therefore true; our brain/mind/body tells us that if we remember something so intensely, it must be so. This negative propensity is evolutionary and contributed to the survival of our species; but we pay a price today given how it leads us to construct our past, present, and future. For many among us, especially those of us who were more anxious as children, the amalgam of negative experiences crowd out the positive ones. Indeed, imaging studies have identified amygdala activity in unborn babies during their last two months of gestation, setting the stage for a tendency toward hyperaroused states.

The possibility that none of us can escape some form of early emotional injury is significant. After all, if innate fear and anxiety are easily aroused even within the context of normative upbringing, can we ever be free of their negative effects? But this conclusion may be too deterministic. Instead, we need to ask ourselves what such findings mean to our psychological lives and adaptive behaviors. More specifically, once we understand, acknowledge, and accept the forces of fear and anxiety in our psyche, we can learn to live with them much more successfully.

DUALITY: THE GOOD NEWS

Fear-suffused unconscious self-states can indeed underlie and guide many of our feelings and defensive behaviors. In addition, even without a formal diagnosis of an anxiety disorder, most of us carry within us and occasionally enact emotional and behavioral patterns informed by old fears and other negative feelings. At the same time, in spite of the prevalence and reactivity of the fear system in our brain/mind/body, we are not defined by the fear system alone. We need to remember that an anxiety-informed state is just one state; most of us possess other more functional, optimistic, and relatively fear-free states that allow us to navigate the world.

We are familiar with how our moods shift, and the different feelings and thoughts that go with them. When we are in an anxious state, we often forget that we have access to other states that are not as frightened or given to triggered anxieties about failure and shame. Conversely, when we experience our more resilient, outgoing, and functional self-states, we often do not attend to the negative feelings that lie dormant in our darker side. These are the two most familiar psychological realms that we regularly inhabit. Of course, it's important to note that each of these states is far from being monolithic. There are many shades of emotions, feelings, and thoughts; we have varied conscious and unconscious behavioral patterns in each unique mingling of brain/mind networks. Indeed, we tend to fluctuate between various moods and the self-states that go with them. Even when experiencing a dark state, anxious, or depressed, it is useful to remember that lighter self-states exist as well. As we saw, one of the most important goals of psychotherapy is to strengthen a conscious dialogue between such internal states. Establishing a better integration through mindful awareness creates the necessary bridge between our injured selves and our more adaptive ones.

THE INTEGRATED SELF

In addition to exploring the many, many subtle, direct, and even dramatic ways in which old, entrenched fear-suffused behavioral patterns can inhibit us, I also wanted to emphasize the other self-states, the ones that are based on and express our more resilient and functional feelings and behaviors. This yin-yang psychological makeup, the back-and-forth journey between the two poles of who we are, seems to be universal. Throughout a single day, we may oscillate between these different feeling self-states. Depending on the environmental context and outside triggers, we may react with different moods and shifting internal monologues. Those different feeling states largely influence the interpretations and meanings we give to both external and internal stimuli.

As my experience with clients has taught me, inhabiting this yin-yang psychological experience is not necessarily the problem. Rather, it is our difficulty accepting our different selves and integrating them into one being that usually creates problems in life. Obviously, our different states are rarely equally balanced; as we have already realized, negative patterns tend to be stronger and more convincing than positive ones. But the level of dissociation or integration between them determines how we coexist with our more negative sides. The stronger the links are between the two modes of being, the more efficient is our emotional regulation.

A more integrated way of experiencing ourselves and the world would mean having the capacity to straddle both our anxious and resilient states at once (Bromberg, 1998, 2006, 2011). Even during a powerful catastrophizing state we might manage not to utterly believe its veracity and drown in it. We may be able, instead, to recruit more positive, reality-bound facts from the more resilient parts of our lives. We may be able to use reason and explore different perspectives. Ideally, the integration of our opposing psychological poles can teach our brain/mind/bodies to both automatically and deliberately remember our resilience.

It seems, then, the way to fully and successfully coexist with our anxious selves is to welcome them into the larger fabric of who we are. Doing this will lessen their demoralizing hold on us and will inevitably soften their internally leaning picture of the world. As adults, a beneficial coexistence may mean a perpetual tug-of-war between anxiety-suffused old internal maps of past experiences and conclusions and the facts surrounding us in the here and now in our current environment. I think that in part, psychological growth entails the ability to recognize these two realities: the internal pattern based on the past and the current one in which we are immersed. Of course, this differentiation can never be complete or absolute. The blending of the two realities, the past and the present, the unconscious and the conscious, is always there; it is a total expression of how the brain/mind works (see Chapter 1). But as we strive to become more conscious and accepting of our internal state, we need to always strive for the best possible approximation of this process as we can.

Indeed, the potential of many psychotherapeutic approaches to help us achieve this goal provides a hopeful dimension. Although there are many opportunities for the fear system to influence and shape our anxious and injured self-state, psychotherapy and mindfulness training can enhance the integration we want to achieve and the resultant acceptance of all different, at times conflicting, selves. An increased ability to identify, acknowledge, and internally communicate with an injured or anxious state in real-time will allow us to better integrate it into the larger picture of who we are. This acceptance does not mean defeat but rather continuous conscious efforts to coexist with negative self-states without being controlled by them or repeatedly and automatically enacting them.

Therapeutic and mindful approaches help us to become aware of our anxious selves, accept them, and simultaneously try to mitigate and change those elements that hurt us and hurt those we love. Some changes happen slowly, over time and outside our awareness, while others are quicker and benefit from more focused mindful attention. Through diverse techniques and interpersonal approaches, all psychotherapeutic modalities attempt to help clients deal with their difficult feelings, thoughts, and behaviors. Clients learn to identify and become aware of their difficulties; they learn to tolerate anxiety and to mindfully attend to behavioral patterns that don't work. Ultimately, painful feelings such as fear of failing and entrenched patterns of avoiding risks, especially those that leave us feeling exposed, become less damaging and debilitating. Chapter 15 addresses many of these techniques.

RESILIENCE

Just as the evolutionary presence of the fear system ensured survival, so did the capacity for resilience and moving forward despite threats and setbacks. Like the fear system, resilience guarantees our ability to adapt to a changing environment and cope with challenges (Moreno-Lopez et al., 2020). Obviously, the challenges to resilience are considerable under conditions of early adversity, abuse, and maltreatment. Thus, promoting resilient functioning in the face of adversity and trauma is one of the most important goals of any therapeutic approach and early intervention efforts (Feldman, 2020). Indeed, a growing body of work seeks to better understand the conditions under which resilience can be subjectively experienced and strengthened. Clearly, the more neuropsychological, developmental, social, and genetic factors involved in resilience are better understood and addressed, the more effective are the potential ways of cultivating it, especially in vulnerable populations.

Like most concepts that try to capture psychological states, resilience is dynamic in nature as well. Our resilience depends on the effects of the many external and interpersonal situations as well as how these factors interact with innate vulnerabilities and predispositions. Resilience may be evident in one life area but not in others. Individuals who are judged as successful by others, for example, may exhibit private, ongoing emotional and interpersonal difficulties, therefore failing to view themselves as successful. Conversely, in spite of the ability to form close bonds, some individuals may struggle to create a functional external life and thrive in that realm. Finally, self-reliance in the face of poverty and racial discrimination is especially challenging and constantly tested. Nevertheless, we often encounter people who have worked hard to overcome their own difficult past and the internal obstacles that such a past saddled them with.

And, indeed, many succeed. It is not that the difficulties of the past are erased or that their anxious states have disappeared. Rather, they have acquired the ability to recruit and experience more optimistic, hopeful, and balanced narratives that prevent them from totally succumbing to paralyzing negative states.

We saw throughout this book how negative self-narratives have a pernicious influence on our confidence and sense of self; the opposite seems to occur in states of resilience, which embody more hopeful and defiant narratives. Higher self-esteem, emotional regulation, and a positive outlook are linked to greater resilience in children (Gartland et al., 2019). The presence of a sense of self-efficacy, self-reliance, and personal autonomy help us acquire greater resilience after early adversities (Fritz et al., 2018). These resilience-promoting traits are the expression of complex interactions among neurobiological, genetic, cognitive, and social factors (Holmes et al., 2012; Ioannidis et al., 2020; Moreno-Lopez et al., 2020). Essentially, all these states are expressed in a pattern that embodies narratives that automatically provide optimism, self-confidence, and persistence.

Some explanations for resilience emphasize the importance of the early synchronicity between caregiver and infant. A healthy intersubjective dance leads to healthy shifts between frustration and dysregulation and then back to repair and calm (Feldman, 2020). This pattern of intersubjective behavior teaches a growing child that adverse situations and feelings happen. At the same time, subsequent efforts at repair from caregivers can provide evidence that experiences can also change. And as early intersubjective bonds are used to manage the child's stress, satisfying intersubjective synchronicity leads to greater resilience.

The few characteristics of resilience presented here in this final chapter demonstrate the difficulties of teasing out the specificity of the complex interactions between the fear system and resilience. There is an irony that the fear system was, in fact, our original resilience and survival system. But, in the modern world, it has now become a barrier to resilience. The good news is that resilience-promoting interventions are as important later in life as they are at the beginning; we can, in fact, relearn how to be resilient. Enhancing our capacity for resilience is coupled and entwined with the way we deal with our anxious selves, who are as ancient as our evolutionary past.

Another way to develop resilience is to develop more adaptive emotional regulation. Indeed, learning to cope equally well with predictable and unpredictable, stressful internal and external situations is an important therapeutic goal.

And again, realizing in real time how important it is to be in the here and now and not just act on old, entrenched maps is an aspect of emotion regulation. The links between emotional regulation and resilience are not surprising.

In a healthy self-reinforcing cycle, enhanced resilience enables us to successfully tackle stress, disappointments, and failures without becoming crushed by them. This is an important point. Obviously, we have no ability to go back and change past events and experiences; however, we can change our internal relationship to them and the degree to which they pervasively inhabit our internal world. The therapeutic and mindful intervention processes that lead to both emotional regulation and resilience offer a powerful potential antidote to the effects of early fear, stress, and anxiety.

Clearly, understanding the factors involved in more resilient neuropsychological states allows us to develop effective interventions from early on, especially in communities and families that are more vulnerable due to external hardships. As the information presented in this book has shown, the enduring effects of our early years on the development of potentially debilitating difficulties later on is indisputable. It is also undeniable that the brain/mind's innate resilience and, moreover, its infinite capacity to learn and integrate new emotional and cognitive habits can be fully taken advantage of to mitigate our early lives. More educational efforts and resources should be directed toward parents of infants and children, both those identified as at risk and those for whom normative stress may have lasting effects.

As this book has shown, the emotional risks we are exposed to from the beginning of life exist for all of us. It is my goal here to provide a solid foundation for understanding the pervasive workings of the fear system and how we may begin to heal from our evolutionary and early childhood wounding. More importantly, it is my intention that this book provides hope that, no matter how deep the scars, we can all achieve healing and resilience.

REFERENCES

Abraham, E., Posner, J., Wickramaratne, P. J., Aw, N., van Dijk, M. T., Cha, J., M. M., & Talati, A. (2020). Concordance in parent and offspring cortico-basal ganglia white matter connectivity varies by parental history of major depressive disorder and early parental care. *Social Cognitive and Affective Neuroscience, 15*(8), 889–903.

Acevedo, B. P., Pospos, S., & Lavretsky, H. (2016). The neural mechanisms of meditative practices: Novel approaches for healthy aging. *Current Behavioral Neuroscience Report, 3*(4), 328–339.

Acevedo, B. P., Jaglellowicz, J. A., Marhenke, R., & Aron, A. (2017). Sensory processing: Sensitivity and childhood quality effects on neural responses to emotional, Stimuli. *Clinical Neuropsychiatry: Journal of Treatment Evaluation. 14*(6), 359–373.

Adams, E. K., Heissel, J. A., Zeiders, K., & al. (2015). Developmental histories of perceived racial. Discrimination and diurnal cortisol profiles in adulthood: A 20-year prospective study. *Psychoneuroendocrinology, 62,* December, 279–291.

Admon, R., Vaisvaser, S., Erlich, N., Lin, T., Shapira-Lichter, I., Fruchter, E., Gazit, T., & Hendler, T. (2018). The role of the amygdala in enhanced remembrance of negative episodes and acquired negativity of related neutral cues. *Biological Psychology, 139,* 17–24.

Adolphs, R., & Anderson, D. J. (2018). *The neuroscience of emotion: A new synthesis.* Princeton University Press.

Aktar, E., Majdandži, M., de Vente, W., & Bögels, S. M. (2013). The interplay between expressed parental anxiety and infant behavioural inhibition predicts infant avoidance in a social referencing paradigm. *Journal of Child Psychology and Psychiatry, 54*(2), 144–156.

Alberini, C. M. (2005). Mechanisms of memory stabilization: Are consolidation and reconsolidation similar or distinct processes? *Trends in Neurosciences,* *28*(1), 51–56.

Alberini, C. M., & Chen, D. Y. (2012). Memory enhancement: Consolidation, reconsolidation and insulin-like growth factor 2. *Trends in Neurosciences,* *35*(5), 274–283.

Aliyari, H., Sahraei, H., Daliri, M. R., Minaei-Bidgoli, B., Kazemi, M., Agaei, H., Mohammad, S., Seyed, H. S. A. M., Mohammad, H. M., Mohammad, M., & Dehghanimohammadabadi, Z. (2018). The beneficial or harmful effects of computer game stress on cognitive functions of players. *Basic and Clinical Neuroscience,* *9*(3), 177.

American Psychiatric Association. (2013). *Diagnostic and statistical manual of mental disorders* (5th ed.). American Psychiatric Association.

Anders, S. L., Shallcross, S. L., & Frazier, P. A. (2012). Beyond criterion A1: The effects of relational and non-relational traumatic events. *Journal of Trauma and Dissociation,* *13*(2), 134–151.

Anderson, C. A., Berkowitz, L., Donnerstein, E., Huesmann, L. R., Johnson, J. D., Linz, D., Malamuth, N. M., & Wartella, E. (2003). The influence of media violence on youth. *Psychological Science in the Public Interest,* *4*(3), 81–110.

Anderson, C. A., & Bushman, B. J. (2018). Media violence and the general aggression model. *Journal of Social Issues,* *74*(2), 386–413.

Anderson, C. A., Bushman, B. J., Bartholow, B. D., Cantor, J., Christakis, D., Coyne, S. M., Donnerstein, E., Brockmyer, J. F., Gentile, D. A., Green, C. S., Huesmann, R., Hummer, T., Krahé, B., Strasburger, V. C., Warburton, W., Wilson, B. J., & Ybarra, M. (2017). Screen violence and youth behavior. *Pediatrics,* *140*(Supplement 2), S142–S147.

Anderson, C. A., Shibuya, A., Ihori, N., Swing, E. L., Bushman, B. J., Sakamoto, A., Rothstein, H. R., & Saleem, M. (2010). Violent video game effects on aggression, empathy, and prosocial behavior in eastern and western countries: A meta-analytic review. *Psychological Bulletin,* *136*(2), 151.

Anderson, M., & Jiang, J. (2018). *Teens, social media and technology 2018.* Pew Research Center.

Andreasen, N. C., & Pierson, R. (2008). The role of the cerebellum in schizophrenia. *Biological Psychiatry,* *64,* 81–88.

Aron, L. (1989). Dreams, narrative and the psychoanalytic method. *Contemporary Psychoanalysis,* *25*(1), 108–127.

Ansermet, F., & Magistrett, I. P. (2004). *Biology of freedom: Neural plasticity, experience, and the unconscious* (S. Fairfield, trans.). Other Press.

Atzl, V. M., Narayan, A. J., Rivera, L. M., & Lieberman, A. F. (2019). Adverse childhood experiences and prenatal mental health: Type of ACEs and age of maltreatment onset. *Journal of Family Psychology, 33*(3), 304.

Aue, T., Guex, R., Chauvigné, L. A., & Okon-Singer, H. (2013). Varying expectancies and attention bias in phobic and non-phobic individuals. *Frontiers in Human Neuroscience, 7,* 418.

Aue, T., & Okon-Singer, H. (2015). Expectancy biases in fear and anxiety and their link to biases in attention. *Clinical Psychology Review, 42,* 83–95.

Bach, S. (2006). *Getting from here to there: Analytic love, analytic process.* Analytic Press.

Bachant, J. (2019). *Exploring the landscape of the mind: An introduction to psychodynamic therapy.* International Psychoanalytic Books.

Baddeley, A. (2012). Working memory: Theories, models, and controversies. *Annual Review of Psychology, 63,* 1–29.

Bargh, J. A. (2007). Bypassing the will: Toward demystifying the nonconscious control of social behavior. In R. R. Hassin, J. S. Uleman, & J. A. Bargh (Eds.), *The new unconscious* (pp. 37–61). Oxford University Press.

Bargh, J. A. (2014). Our unconscious mind. *Scientific American, 310,* 30–38.

Bar-Haim, Y., Lamy, D., Pergamin, L., Bakermans-Kranenburg, M. J., & Van Ijzendoorn, M. H. (2007). Threat-related attentional bias in anxious and nonanxious individuals: A meta-analytic study. *Psychological Bulletin, 133*(1), 1.

Bar-Haim, Y., & Pine, D. S. (2013). Cognitive training research and the search for a transformative, translational, developmental cognitive neuroscience. *Developmental Cognitive Neuroscience, 4,* 1.

Barrett, L. F. (2017a). *How emotions are made: The secret life of the brain.* Houghton Mifflin Harcourt.

Barrett, L. F. (2017b). The theory of constructed emotion: An active inference account of interoception and categorization. *Social Cognitive and Affective Neuroscience, 12*(1), 1–23.

Basu, A., Kim, H. H., Basaldua, R., Choi, K. W., Charron, L., Kelsall, N., Hernandez-Diaz, S., Wyszynski, D. F., & Koenen, K. C. (2021). A cross-national study of factors associated with women's perinatal mental health and wellbeing during the COVID-19 pandemic. *PloS One, 16*(4), e0249780.

Batalle, D., Hughes, E. J., Zhang, H., Tournier, J. D., Tusor, N., Aljabar, P., Wali, L., Alexander, D. C., Hajnal, J. V., Nosarti, C., Edwards, A. D., & Counsell,

S. J. (2017). Early development of structural networks and the impact of prematurity on brain connectivity. *Neuroimage, 149,* 379–392.

Bateman, A. W., & Fonagy, P. (2012). *Handbook of mentalizing in mental health practice.* American Psychiatric Publishing.

Batson, C. D. (2011). *Altruism in humans.* Oxford University Press.

Baumeister, H. (2017). Behavioural activation training for depression. *Lancet, 389*(10067), 366–367.

Baumeister, R. F., & Vohs, K. D. (2001). Narcissism as addiction to esteem. *Psychological Inquiry, 12,* 206–10.

Bazan, A. (2017). Alpha synchronization as a brain model for unconscious defense: An overview of the work of Howard Shevrin and his team. *International Journal of Psychoanalysis, 98*(5), 1443–1473.

Bechara, A., Tranel, D., Damasio, H., Adolphs, R., Rockland, C., & Damasio, A. R. (1995). Double dissociation of conditioning and declarative knowledge relative to the amygdala and hippocampus in humans. *Science, 269*(5227), 1115–1118.

Beck, A. T., Brown, G., Steer, R. A., Eidelson, J. I., & Riskind, J. H. (1987). Differentiating anxiety and depression: A test of the cognitive content-specificity hypothesis. *Journal of Abnormal Psychology, 96*(3), 179.

Beebe, B. (2010). Mother-infant research informs mother-infant treatment. *Clinical Social Work Journal,* 38, 17–36.

Beebe, B., Jaffe, J., Markese, S., Buck, K., Chen, H., Cohen, P., Bahrick, L., Andrews, H., & Feldstein, S. (2010). The origins of 12-month attachment: A microanalysis of 4-month mother-infant interaction. *Attachment and Human Development, 12,* 3–141.

Beebe, B., & Lachmann, F. (2002). Organizing principles of interaction from infant research and the lifespan prediction of attachment: Application to adult treatment. *Journal of Infant, Child, and Adolescent Psychotherapy, 2*(4), 61–89.

Björgvinsson, T., & Hart, J. (2006). Cognitive behavioral therapy promotes mentalizing. In J. G. Allen & P. Fonagy (Eds.), *Handbook of mentalization-based treatment* (pp. 157–170). Wiley.

Blakemore, S. J., & Mills, K. L. (2014). Is adolescence a sensitive period for sociocultural processing? *Annual Review of Psychology, 65,* 187–207.

Bolten, M., Nast, I., Skrundz, M., Stadler, C., Hellhammer, D. H., & Meinlschmidt, G. (2013). Prenatal programming of emotion regulation: Neonatal reactivity as a differential susceptibility factor moderating the outcome of prenatal cortisol levels. *Journal of Psychosomatic Research, 75*(4), 351–357.

Bos, P. A. (2017). The endocrinology of human caregiving and its intergenerational transmission. *Development and Psychopathology, 20(3)*, 971–999.

Bostan, A. C., & Strick, P. L. (2018). The basal ganglia and the cerebellum: Nodes in an integrated network. *Nature Reviews Neuroscience, 19,* 338–350.

Böthe, B., Lonza, A., Štulhofer, A., & Demetrovics, Z. (2020). Symptoms of problematic pornography use in a sample of treatment considering and treatment non-considering men: A network approach. *Journal of Sexual Medicine, 17*(10), 2016–2028.

Bouvette-Turcot, A. A., Unternaehrer, E., Gaudreau, H., Lydon, J. E., Steiner, M., Meaney, M. J., & MAVAN Research Team. (2017). The joint contribution of maternal history of early adversity and adulthood depression to socioeconomic status and potential relevance for offspring development. *Journal of Affective Disorders, 207,* 26–31.

Bowen, H. J., Kark, S. M., & Kensinger, E. A. (2018). NEVER forget: Negative emotional valence enhances recapitulation. *Psychonomic Bulletin and Review, 25*(3), 870–891.

Bowen, K. L., Morgan, J. E., Moore, S. C., & van Goozen, S. H. (2014). Young offenders' emotion recognition dysfunction across emotion intensities: Explaining variation using psychopathic traits, conduct disorder and offense severity. *Journal of Psychopathology and Behavioral Assessment, 36*(1), 60–73.

Bowins, B. (2004). Psychological defense mechanisms: A new perspective. *American Journal of Psychoanalysis, 64*(1), 1–26.

Bowlby, J. (1969). *Attachment and loss. Vol. I. Attachment.* Basic Books.

Bowlby, J. (1973). *Attachment and loss: Vol. II. Separation.* Basic Books.

Bowlby, J. (1982). *Attachment and loss: Vol. I. Attachment* (2nd ed.). Basic Books.

Boyes, M. E., Hasking, P. A., & Martin, G. (2016). Adverse life experience and Psychological distress in adolescence: Moderating and mediating effects of emotion regulation and rumination. *Stress & Health*, 11 March, doi.org/10.1002/smi.2635.

Braten, S. (2007). Altercentric infants and adults: On the origin and manifestation of participant perception of others' acts and utterances. In S. Braten (Ed.), *On being moved: From mirror neurons to empathy* (pp. 111–136). Benjamins.

Braten, S., & Trevarthen, C. (2007). Prologue: From infant intersubjectivity and participant movements to simulation and conversation in cultural common sense. In S. Braten (Ed.), *On being moved: From mirror neurons to empathy* (pp. 21–34). Benjamins.

Briggs-Gowan, M. J., Grasso, D., Bar-Haim, Y., Voss, J., McCarthy, K. J., Pine, D. S., & Wakschlag, L. S. (2016). Attention bias in the developmental unfolding of post-traumatic stress symptoms in young children at risk. *Journal of Child Psychology and Psychiatry, 57*(9), 1083–1091.

Britton, W. B., Shahar, B., Szepsenwol, O., & Jacobs, W. J. (2012). Mindfulness-based cognitive therapy improves emotional reactivity to social stress: Results from a randomized controlled trial. *Behavior Therapy, 43*(2), 365–380.

Bromberg, P. M. (1998). *Standing in the spaces: Essays on clinical process, trauma and dissociation.* Analytic Press.

Bromberg, P. M. (2006). *Awakening the dreamer: Clinical journeys.* Analytic Press.

Bromberg, P. M. (2009). Truth, human relatedness, and the analytic process: An interpersonal/relational perspective. *International Journal of Psychoanalysis, 90*(2), 347–361.

Bromberg, P. M. (2011). *The shadow of the tsunami and the growth of the relational mind.* Routledge.Brooker, R. J., Kiel, E. J., MacNamara, A., Nyman, T., John Henderson, N. A., Schmidt, L. A., & Van Lieshout, R. J. (2020). Maternal neural reactivity during pregnancy predicts infant temperament. *Infancy, 25*(1), 46–66.

Brosch, T., Scherer, K. R., Grandjean, D. M., & Sander, D. (2013). The impact of emotion on perception, attention, memory, and decision-making. *Swiss Medical Weekly, 143*, w13786.

Brosschot, J. F., Verkuil, B., & Thayer, J. F. (2016). The default response to uncertainty and the importance of perceived safety in anxiety and stress: An evolution-theoretical perspective. *Journal of Anxiety Disorders, 41*, 22–34.

Brown, K. W., & Ryan, R. M. (2004). Perils and promise in defining and measuring mindfulness: Observations from experience. *Clinical Psychology: Science and Practice, 11*(3), 242–248.

Brown, R., Copeland, W. E., Costello, J., Erkani, A., & Worthman, M. (2009). Family and community influences on educational outcomes among Appalachian youth. *Journal of Community Psychology, 37*(7), 295808.

Burke, C. A. (2010). Mindfulness-based approaches with children and adolescents: A preliminary review of current research in an emergent field. *Journal of Child and Family Studies, 19*(2), 133–144.

Bushman, B. J., & Huesmann, L. R. (2006). Short-term and long-term effects of violent media on aggression in children and adults. *Archives of Pediatrics and Adolescent Medicine, 160*(4), 348–352.

Calkins, S. D. (2011). Caregiving as coregulation: Psychobiological processes and child functioning. In A. Booth, S. M. McHale, & N. S. Lansdale (Eds.), *Biosocial foundations of family processes* (pp. 49–59). Springer.

Callaghan, B. L., Gee, D. G., Gabard-Durnam, L., Telzer, E. H., Humphreys, K. L., Goff, B., Shapiro, M., Flannery, J., Lumian, D. S., Fareri, D. S., Caldera, C., & Tottenham, N. (2019). Decreased amygdala reactivity to parent cues protects against anxiety following early adversity: An examination across 3 years. *Biological Psychiatry: Cognitive Neuroscience and Neuroimaging, 4*(7), 664–671. https://doi.org/10.1016/j.bpsc.2019.02.001

Callaghan, B. L., & Richardson, R. (2012). The effect of adverse rearing environments on persistent memories in young rats: Removing the brakes on infant fear memories. *Translational Psychiatry, 2*(7), e138–e138.

Callaghan, B. L., & Tottenham, N. (2016). The stress acceleration hypothesis: Effects of early-life adversity on emotion circuits and behavior. *Current Opinion in Behavioral Sciences, 7*, 76.

Cameron, D., Caroll, P., & Hamilton, K. (2018). Evaluation of an intervention promoting emotion regulation skills for adults with persisting distress due to adverse childhood experiences. *Child Abuse and Neglect, 79*. 423433.

Camras, L. A. (2019). Facial expressions across the life span. In V. LoBue, K. Pérez-Edgar, & K. Buss (Eds.), *Handbook of emotional development* (pp. 83–103). Springer.

Cantor, J., Byrne, S., Moyer-Gusé, E., & Riddle, K. (2010). Descriptions of media-induced fright reactions in a sample of US elementary school children. *Journal of Children and Media, 4*(1), 1–17.

Capistrano, C. G., Bianco, H., & Kim, P. (2016). Poverty and internalizing symptoms: The indirect effect of middle childhood poverty on internalizing symptoms via an emotional response inhibition pathway. *Frontiers in Psychology, 17*, https://doi.org/10. 3389

Cantor, J., & Riddle, K. (2014). Media and fear in children and adolescents. In D. Gentile (Ed.), *Media violence and children: A complete guide for parents and professionals* (2nd ed., pp. 179–207). Praeger.

Carnagey, N. L., Anderson, C. A., & Bushman, B. J. (2007). The effect of video game violence on physiological desensitization to real-life violence. *Journal of Experimental Social Psychology, 43*(3), 489–496.

Caron, C. (2021, February 17). "Nobody has openings": Mental health providers struggle to meet demand. *New York Times*.

Carter, R. T., Johnson, V. E., Roberson, K., Mazzula, S. L., Kirkinis, J., Sant-Barker, S. (2016). Race-based traumatic stress, racial identity statuses, and psychological functioning: An exploratory investigation. *Professional Psychology: Research and Practice, 48*(1), 3037.

Casey, B. J., Galvan, A., & Hare, T. A. (2005). Changes in cerebral functional organization during cognitive development. *Current Opinion in Neurobiology, 15*(2), 239–244.

Champagne, F. A., Francis, D. D., Mar, A., & Meaney, M. J. (2003). Variations in maternal care in the rat as a mediating influence for the effects of environment on development. *Physiology and Behavior, 79*(3), 359–371.

Chartrand, T. L., Maddux, W. W., & Lakin, J. L. (2007). Beyond the perception-behavior link: The ubiquitous utility of motivational moderators of nonconscious mimicry. In R. R. Hassin, J. S. Uleman, & J. A. Bargh (Eds.), *The new unconscious.* Oxford University Press.

Choi, K. R., Seng, J. S., Briggs, E. C., Munro-Kramer, M. L., Graham-Bermann, S. A., Lee, R. C., & Ford, J. D. (2017). The dissociative subtype of post-traumatic stress disorder (PTSD) among adolescents: Co-occurring PTSD, depersonalization/derealization, and other dissociation symptoms. *Journal of the American Academy of Child and Adolescent Psychiatry, 56*(12), 1062–1072.

Choi-Kain, L. W., & Gunderson, J. G. (2008). Mentalization: Ontogeny, assessment, and application in the treatment of borderline personality disorder. *American Journal of Psychiatry, 165*(9), 1127–1135.

Churchland, P. S. (2013). *Touching a nerve: The self as brain.* Norton.

Chused, J. F. (1998). The evocative power of enactment. In S. J. Ellman & M. Moskowitz (Eds.), *Enactment: Toward a new approach to the therapeutic relationship* (pp. 93–109). Aronson.

Cibich, M., Woodyatt, L., & Wenzel, M. (2016). Moving beyond "shame is bad": How a functional emotion can become problematic. *Social and Personality Psychology Compass, 10*(9), 471–483.

Cimpian, A., & Steinberg, O. D. (2014). The inherence heuristic across development: Systematic differences between children's and adults' explanations for everyday facts. *Cognitive Psychology, 75*, 130–154.

Clausi, S., Iacobacci, C., Lupo, M., Olivito, G., Molinari, M., & Leggio, M. (2017). The role of the cerebellum in unconscious and conscious processing of emotions: A review. *Applied Sciences, 7*(5), 521.

Clewett, D., DuBrow, S., & Davachi, L. (2019). Transcending time in the brain:

How event memories are constructed from experience. *Hippocampus, 29*(3), 162–183.

Cohen, E., & Shulman, C. (2019). Mothers and toddlers exposed to political violence: Severity of exposure, emotional availability, parenting stress, and toddlers' behavior problems. *Journal of Child and Adolescent Trauma, 12*, 131140.

Coleman-Jensen, A., Gregory, C., & Singh, A. (2015). Household food security in the United States in 2013. *USDA Economic Research Report,* 26 October, http://dx.doi.org/10.2139/ssrn.2504067

Coker, T. R., Elliott, M. N., Schwebel, D. C., Windle, M., Toomey, S. L., Tortolero, S. R., Hertz, M. F., Peskin, M. F., & Schuster, M. A. (2015). Media violence exposure and physical aggression in fifth-grade children. *Academic Pediatrics, 15*(1), 82–88.

Collier, K. M., Coyne, S. M., Rasmussen, E. E., Hawkins, A. J., Padilla-Walker, L. M., Erickson, S. E., & Memmott-Elison, M. K. (2016). Does parental mediation of media influence child outcomes? A meta-analysis on media time, aggression, substance use, and sexual behavior. *Developmental Psychology, 52*(5), 798.

Colombetti, G. (2010). Enaction, sense-making, and emotion. In J. Stewart, O. Gapenne, & E. A. DiPaolo (Eds.), *Enaction: Toward a new paradigm for cognitive science* (pp. 145–164). MIT Press.

Conway, A., McDonough, S. C., McKenzie, M. J., Follet, C., & Sameroff, A. (2013). Stress- related changes in toddlers and their mothers following the attack of September 11. *American Journal of Orthopsychiatry, 83*(4), 538–544.

Courtois, C. A. (2004). Complex trauma, complex reactions: Assessment and treatment. *Psychotherapy: Theory, Research, Practice, Training, 41*(4), 412.

Coyne, S. M., Warburton, W. A., Essig, L. W., & Stockdale, L. A. (2018). Violent video games, externalizing behavior, and prosocial behavior: A five-year longitudinal study during adolescence. *Developmental Psychology, 54*(10), 1868.

Cozolino, L. (2006). *The neuroscience of human relationships: Attachment and the developing brain.* New York: Norton.

Cramer, P. (1998a). Coping and defense mechanisms: What's the difference? *Journal of Personality, 66*(6), 919–946.

Cramer, P. (1998b). Defensiveness and defense mechanisms. *Journal of Personality, 66*(6), 879–894.

Cramer, P. (2006). *Protecting the self: Defense mechanisms in action.* Guilford.

Cramer, P. (2015). Defense mechanisms: 40 years of empirical research. *Journal of Personality Assessment, 97*(2), 114–122.

Creswell, J. D. (2017). Mindfulness interventions. *Annual Review of Psychology, 68*, 491–516.

Cristóbal-Narváez, P., Sheinbaum, T., Ballespí, S., Mitjavila, M., Myin-Germeys, I., Kwapil, T. R., & Barrantes-Vidal, N. (2016). Impact of adverse childhood experiences on psychotic-like symptoms and stress reactivity in daily life in nonclinical young adults. *PloS One, 11*(4), e0153557.

Cronholm, P. F., Forke, C. M., Wade, R., Bair-Merritt, M. H., Davis, M., Harkins-Schwarz, M., Pachter, L. M., & Fein, J. A. (2015). Adverse childhood experiences: Expanding the concept of adversity. *American Journal of Preventive Medicine, 49*(3), 354–361.

Damasio, A. R. (1999). *The feeling of what happens: Body and emotion in the making of consciousness.* Harcourt Brace.

Damasio, A. R. (2000). A second chance for emotion. In R. D. Lane & L. Nadel (Eds.), *Cognitive neuroscience of emotion* (pp. 12–23). Oxford University Press.

Damasio, A. R. (2010). *Self comes to mind: Constructing the conscious brain.* Vintage.

D'Andrea, W., Ford, J., Stolbach, B., Spinazzola, J., & van der Kolk, B. A. (2012). Understanding interpersonal trauma in children: Why we need a developmentally appropriate trauma diagnosis. *American Journal of Orthopsychiatry, 82*(2), 187.

Dahaene, S., & Changeux, J. P. (2011). Experimental and theoretical approaches to conscious processing. *Neuron, 70*, 200–227. Danese, A., & McEwen, B. S. (2012). Adverse childhood experiences, allostasis, allostatic load, and age-related disease. *Physiology & Behavior, 106*(1).

Dapretto, M., Davis, M. S., Pfeifer, J. H., Scott, A. A., Sigman, M., Bookheimer, S. Y., & Icoboni, M. (2006). Understanding emotions in others: Mirror neuron dysfunction in children with autism spectrum disorders. *Nature Neuroscience, 9*, 28–31.

Davidson, R. J., & Begley, S. (2012). *The emotional life of your brain.* Hudson Street.

Davis, M., & Whalen, P. J. (2001). The amygdala: Vigilance and emotion. *Molecular Psychiatry, 6*(1), 13–34.

Desmedt, A., Marighetto, A., & Piazza, P. V. (2015). Abnormal fear memory as a model for posttraumatic stress disorder. *Biological Psychiatry, 78*(5), 290–297.

Diano, M., Celeghin, A., Bagnis, A., & Tamietto, M. (2017). Amygdala response to emotional stimuli without awareness: Facts and interpretations. *Frontiers in Psychology, 7*, 2029.

Di Paolo, E., Rohde, M., & De Jaegher, H. (2010). Horizons for the enactive mind: Values, social interaction, and play. In J. Stewart, O. Gapenne, & E. A. Di Paolo (Eds.), *Enaction: Toward a new paradigm for cognitive science* (pp. 33–87). MIT Press.

DiPietro, J. A. (2012). Maternal stress in pregnancy: Considerations for fetal development. *Journal of Adolescent Health, 51*(2), S3–S8.

Dixon, M. L., Thiruchselvam, R., Todd, R., & Christoff, K. (2017). Emotion and the prefrontal cortex: An integrative review. *Psychological Bulletin, 143*(10), 1033.

Dollar, J. M., & Calkins, S. D. (2019). The development of anger. In V. LoBue, K. Pérez-Edgar, & K. Buss (Eds.), *Handbook of emotional development* (pp. 199–225). Springer.

Domash, L. (2020). *Imagination, creativity and spirituality in psychotherapy: Welcome to Wonderland.* Routledge.

Duffy, K. A., McLaughlin, K. A., & Green, P. A. (2018). Early life adversity and health-risk behaviors: Proposed psychological and neural mechanisms. *Annals of the New York Academy of Sciences, 1428*(1), 151–169.

Dudai, Y. (2011). The engram revisited: On the elusive permanence of memory. In S. Nalbantian, P. M. Matthews, & J. L. McClelland (Eds.), *The memory process: Neuroscientific and humanistic perspectives* (pp. 29–40). MIT Press.

Du Rocher Schudlich, T. D., White, C. R., Fleischhauer, E. A., & Fitzgerald, K. A. (2011). Observed infant reactions during live interparental conflict. *Journal of Marriage and Family, 73*(1), 221–235.

Eifert, G. H., & Forsyth, J. P. (2005). *Acceptance and commitment therapy for anxiety disorders: A practitioner's treatment guide to using mindfulness, acceptance, and values-based behavior change.* New Harbinger.

Eiland, L., Ramroop, J., Hill, M., Manley, J., & McEwen, B. S. (2012). Chronic juvenile stress produces dendritic architectural remodeling and modulates emotional behavior in male and female rats. *Psychoneuroendocrinology, 37*(1), 39–47.

Elson, M., & Ferguson, C. J. (2014). Twenty-five years of research on violence in digital games and aggression. *European Psychologist, 19*(1), 33–46.

Evans, G. W. (2016). Childhood poverty and adult psychological well-being. *Proceedings of the National Academy of Sciences of the United States of America, 113*(52), 1494914952.

Evans, G. W. (2004). The environment of childhood poverty. *American Psychologist, 59*(2), 7792.

Evans, G. W., & Schamberg, M. A. (2009). Childhood poverty, chronic stress, and adult working memory. *Proceedings of the National Academy of Sciences of the United States of America, 106*(16), 65456549.

Fareri, D. S., & Tottenham, N. (2016). Effects of early life stress on amygdala and striatal development. *Developmental Cognitive Neuroscience, 19*, 233–247.

Farina, B., & Imperatori, C. (2017). What if dissociation were a psychopathological dimension related to trauma? Authors' reply to diagnostic challenges leading to underdiagnosis of dissociative disorders. *Neuropsychiatric Disease and Treatment, 13*, 409–410.

Farina, B., Liotti, M., & Imperatori, C. (2019). The role of attachment trauma and disintegrative pathogenic processes in the traumatic-dissociative dimension. *Frontiers in Psychology, 10*, 933.

Farisco, M., Laureys, S., & Evers, K. (2017). The intrinsic activity of the brain and its relation to levels and disorders of consciousness. *Mind and Matter, 15*(2), 197–219.

Feldman, R. (2007). Parent-infant synchrony and the construction of shared timing: Physiological precursors, developmental outcomes, and risk conditions. *Journal of Child Psychology and Psychiatry, 48*(3–4), 329–354.

Feldman, R. (2012). Parent-infant synchrony: A biobehavioral model of mutual influences in the formation of affiliative bonds. *Monographs of the Society for Research in Child Development, 77*(2), 42–51.

Feldman, R. (2016). The neurobiology of mammalian parenting and the biosocial context of human caregiving. *Hormones and Behavior, 77*, 3–17.

Feldman, R. (2020). What is resilience: An affiliative neuroscience approach. *World Psychiatry, 19*(2), 132–150.

Fergus, T. A., Valentiner, D. P., McGrath, P. B., & Jencius, S. (2010). Shame- and guilt-proneness: Relationships with anxiety disorder symptoms in a clinical sample. *Journal of Anxiety Disorders, 24*(8), 811–815.

Ferguson, C. J. (2015). Do angry birds make for angry children? A meta-analysis of video game influences on children's and adolescents' aggression, mental health, prosocial behavior, and academic performance. *Perspectives on Psychological Science, 10*(5), 646–666.

Ferguson, C. J., Rueda, S. M., Cruz, A. M., Ferguson, D. E., Fritz, S., & Smith, S. M. (2008). Violent video games and aggression: Causal relationship or byproduct of family violence and intrinsic violence motivation? *Criminal Justice and Behavior, 35*(3), 311–332.

Fergusson, D. M., & Lynskey, M. T. (1996). Adolescent resiliency to family adversity. *Journal of Child Psychology and Psychiatry, 37*(3), 281–292.

Fernyhough, C. (2013). *Pieces of light: How the new science of memory illuminates the stories we tell about our pasts.* HarperCollins.

Field, A. P. (2006a). The behavioral inhibition system and the verbal information pathway to children's fears. *Journal of Abnormal Psychology, 115*(4), 742.

Field, A. P. (2006b). Watch out for the beast: Fear information and attentional bias in children. *Journal of Clinical Child and Adolescent Psychology, 35*(3), 431–439.

Field, A. P., & Lester, K. J. (2010). Is there room for "development" in developmental models of information processing biases to threat in children and adolescents? *Clinical Child and Family Psychology Review, 13*(4), 315–332.

Fonagy, P., & Bateman, A. (2006). Progress in the treatment of borderline personality disorder. *British Journal of Psychiatry, 188*(1), 1–3.

Fonagy, P., Gergely, G., Jurist, E. L., & Target, M. (2002). *Affect regulation, mentalization and the development of the self.* Other Press.

Fonagy, P., & Target, M. (1998). An interpersonal view of the infant. In A. Hurry (Ed.), *Psychoanalysis and developmental therapy* (pp. 3–31). Karnac.

Forbes, M. K., Fitzpatrick, S., Magson, N. R., & Rapee, R. M. (2019). Depression, anxiety, and peer victimization: Bidirectional relationships and associated outcomes transitioning from childhood to adolescence. *Journal of Youth and Adolescence, 48*(4), 692–702.

Forssman, L., Peltola, M. J., Yrttiaho, S., Puura, K., Mononen, N., Lehtimäki, T., & Leppänen, J. M. (2014). Regulatory variant of the TPH 2 gene and early life stress are associated with heightened attention to social signals of fear in infants. *Journal of Child Psychology and Psychiatry, 55*(7), 793–801.

Foulkes, L., & Blakemore, S. J. (2016). Is there heightened sensitivity to social reward in adolescence? *Current Opinion in Neurobiology, 40*, 81–85.

Fox, A. S., Lapate, R. C., Shackman, A. J., & Davidson, R. J. (Eds.). (2018). *The nature of emotion: Fundamental questions.* Oxford University Press.

Fox, A. S., Oler, J. A., Tromp, D. P., Fudge, J. L., & Kalin, N. H. (2015). Extending the amygdala in theories of threat processing. *Trends in Neurosciences, 38*(5), 319–329.

Fox, A. S., & Shackman, A. J. (2019). The central extended amygdala in fear and anxiety: Closing the gap between mechanistic and neuroimaging research. *Neuroscience Letters, 693*, 58–67.

Francis L., DePriest, K., & Gross, D. (2018). Child poverty, toxic stress, and social determinants of health: Screening and care coordination. *Online Journal of Issues in Nursing, 23*(3), 2.

Frederickson, J. J., Messina, I., & Grecucci, A. (2018). Dysregulated anxiety and dysregulating defenses: Toward an emotion regulation informed dynamic psychotherapy. *Frontiers in Psychology, 9*, 2054.

Freese, J. L., & Amaral, D. G. (2009). Neuroanatomy of the primate amygdala. In P. J. Whalen & E. A. Phelps (Eds.), *The human amygdala* (pp. 3–43). Guilford.

Freud, S. (1926). Inhibitions, symptoms and anxiety. In J. Strachey (Ed. and Trans.), *The standard edition of the complete psychological works of Sigmund Freud* (vol. 20, pp. 77–174). Hogarth.

Freud, S. (1959a). *Complete psychological works: Autobiographical study; inhibitions, symptoms and anxiety; law analysis and other works, 1925–26.* Hogarth.

Freud, S. (1959b). *The ego and the id.* Norton.

Fritz, J., de Graaff, A. M., Caisley, H., Van Harmelen, A. L., & Wilkinson, P. O. (2018). A systematic review of amenable resilience factors that moderate and/or mediate the relationship between childhood adversity and mental health in young people. *Frontiers in Psychiatry, 9*, 230.

Gabard-Durnam, L. J., Flannery, J., Goff, B., Gee, D. G., Humphreys, K. L., Telzer, E., Hare, T., & Tottenham, N. (2014). The development of human amygdala functional connectivity at rest from 4 to 23 years: A cross-sectional study. *Neuroimage, 95*, 193–207.

Gabard-Durnam, L. J., Gee, D. G., Goff, B., Flannery, J., Telzer, E., Humphreys, K. L., Lumian, D. S., Fareri, D. S., Caldera, C., & Tottenham, N. (2016). Stimulus-elicited connectivity influences resting-state connectivity years later in human development: A prospective study. *Journal of Neuroscience, 36*(17), 4771–4784.

Gabard-Durnam, L. J., & McLaughlin, K. A. (2019). Do sensitive periods exist for exposure to adversity? *Biological Psychiatry, 85*(10), 789.

Gabard-Durnam, L. J., O'Muircheartaigh, J., Dirks, H., Dean, III, D. C., Tottenham, N., & Deoni, S. (2018). Human amygdala functional network development: A cross-sectional study from 3 months to 5 years of age. *Developmental Cognitive Neuroscience, 34*, 63–74.

Gaffrey, M. S., Barch, D. M., & Luby, J. L. (2016). Amygdala reactivity to sad faces in preschool children: An early neural marker of persistent negative affect. *Developmental Cognitive Neuroscience, 17*, 94–100.

Gallese, V. (2006). Intentional attunement: Embodied simulation and its role in social cognition. In M. Mancia (Ed.), *Psychoanalysis and neuroscience* (pp. 269–301). Springer.

Gallese, V. (2008). Mirror neurons and the social nature of language: The neural exploitation hypothesis. *Social Neuroscience, 3,* 317–333.

Gallese, V. (2009). Mirror neurons, embodied simulation, and the neural basis of social identification. *Psychoanalytic Dialogues, 19,* 519–536.

Gámez-Guadix, M. (2014). Depressive symptoms and problematic internet use among adolescents: Analysis of the longitudinal relationships from the cognitive-behavioral model. *Cyberpsychology, Behavior, and Social Networking, 17*(11), 714–719.

Gartland, D., Riggs, E., Muyeen, S., Giallo, R., Afifi, T. O., MacMillan, H., Hermann, H., Bulford, E., & Brown, S. J. (2019). What factors are associated with resilient outcomes in children exposed to social adversity? A systematic review. *BMJ Open, 9*(4), e024870.

Gazzaniga, M. (2007). My brain made me do it. In W. Glannon (Ed.), *Defining right and wrong in brain science: Essential readings in neuroethics* (pp. 183–194). Dana Press.

Gazzaniga, M. S. (2008). *Human: The science behind what makes us unique.* Harper Collins.

Gazzaniga, M. S. (2009). *The cognitive neurosciences.* MIT Press.

Gazzaniga, M. S., Ivry, R. B., & Mangum, G. R. (2014). *Cognitive neuroscience: The biology of the mind* (4th ed.). Norton.

Gee, D. G., Gabard-Durnam, L. J., Flannery, J., Goff, B., Humphreys, K. L., Telzer, E. H., Hare, T. A., Bookheimer, S. Y., & Tottenham, N. (2013). Early developmental emergence of human amygdala-prefrontal connectivity after maternal deprivation. *Proceedings of the National Academy of Sciences, 110*(39), 15638–15643.

Gekker, M., Coutinho, E. S. F., Berger, W., da Luz, M. P., de Araújo, A. X. G., da Costa Pagotto, L. F. A., Marques-Portella, C., Figueira, I., & Mendlowicz, M. V. (2018). Early scars are forever: Childhood abuse in patients with adult-onset PTSD is associated with increased prevalence and severity of psychiatric comorbidity. *Psychiatry Research, 267,* 1–6.

Gendlin, E. T. (2012). Implicit precision. In Z. Radman (Ed.), *Knowing without thinking: Mind, action, cognition, and the phenomenon of the background* (pp. 141–166). Palgrave Macmillan.

Giannarelli, L., Wheaton, L., & Shantz, K. (2021, February 16). 2021 poverty projections. The Urban Institute. https://www.urban.org/research/publication/2021-poverty-projections

Ginot, E. (1997). The analyst use of self, self-disclosure, and enhanced integration. *Psychoanalytic Psychology*, 14, 365–381.

Ginot, E. (2001). The holding environment and intersubjectivity. *Psychoanalytic Quarterly, 70*, 417–446.

Ginot, E. (2007). Intersubjectivity and neuroscience: Understanding enactments and their therapeutic significance within emerging paradigms. *Psychoanalytic Psychology, 24*, 317–332.

Ginot, E. (2009). The empathic power of enactments: The link between neuropsychological processes and an expanded definition of empathy. *Psychoanalytic Psychology, 26*(3), 290–309.

Ginot, E. (2012). Self-narratives and dysregulated affective states: The neuropsychological links between self-narratives, attachment, affect, and cognition. *Psychoanalytic Psychology, 29,* 59–80.

Ginot, E. (2015). *The neuropsychology of the unconscious: Integrating brain and mind in psychotherapy.* Norton.

Goldman, A. I. (2006). *Simulating minds: The philosophy, psychology, and neuroscience of mind reading.* Oxford University Press.

Gomez, J., Hoffman, H. G., Bistricky, S. L., Gonzalez, M., Rosenberg, L., Sampaio, M., Garcia-Palacios, A., Navarro-Haro, M. V., Alhalabi, W., Rosenberg, M., Meyer, W. J., & Linehan, M. M. (2017). The use of virtual reality facilitates Dialectical Behavior Therapy® "Observing Sounds and Visuals" mindfulness skills training exercises for a Latino patient with severe burns: A case study. *Frontiers in Psychology, 8,* 1611.

Gonzalez-Gadea, M. L., Herrera, E., Parra, M., Gomez Mendez, P., Baez, S., Manes, F., & Ibanez, A. (2014). Emotion recognition and cognitive empathy deficits in adolescent offenders revealed by context-sensitive tasks. *Frontiers in Human Neuroscience, 8,* 850.

Goode, T. D., & Maren, S. (2017). Role of the bed nucleus of the stria terminalis in aversive learning and memory. *Learning and Memory, 24*(9), 480–491.

Goodman G. (2014). Mentalization: An interpersonal approach to mindfulness. In J. M. Stewart (Ed.), *Mindfulness, acceptance, and the psychodynamic evolution: Bringing values into treatment planning and enhancing psychodynamic work with Buddhist psychology* (pp. 111–132). Context Press.

Gouva, M., Mentis, M., Kotrotsiou, S., Paralikas, T., & Kotrotsiou, E. (2015). Shame and anxiety feelings of a Roma population in Greece. *Journal of Immigrant and Minority Health, 17*(6), 1765–1770.

Graham, A. M., Fisher, P. A., & Pfeifer, J. H. (2013). What sleeping babies hear: A functional MRI study of interparental conflict and infants' emotion processing. *Psychological Science, 24*(5), 782–789.

Graham, A. M., Pfeifer, J. H., Fisher, P. A., Carpenter, S., & Fair, D. A. (2015). Early life stress is associated with default system integrity and emotionality during infancy. *Journal of Child Psychology and Psychiatry, 56*(11), 1212–1222.

Granat, A., Gadassi, R., Gilboa-Schechtman, E., & Feldman, R. (2017). Maternal depression and anxiety, social synchrony, and infant regulation of negative and positive emotions. *Emotion, 17*(1), 11.

Grawe, K. (2007). *Neuropsychotherapy: How the neurosciences inform effective psychotherapy.* Analytic Press.

Greenfield, D. N. (1999). Virtual addiction: Sometimes new technology can create new problems. Center for Internet Studies @ Psychological Health Associates

Greenwald, A. G., & De Houwer, J. (2017). Unconscious conditioning: Demonstration of existence and difference from conscious conditioning. *Journal of Experimental Psychology: General, 146*(12), 1705.

Greitemeyer, T., & Mügge, D. O. (2014). Video games do affect social outcomes: A meta-analytic review of the effects of violent and prosocial video game play. *Personality and Social Psychology Bulletin, 40*(5), 578–589.

Gross, J. J. (Ed.). (2013). *Handbook of emotion regulation.* Guilford.

Grossmann, T., & Jessen, S. (2017). When in infancy does the "fear bias" develop? *Journal of Experimental Child Psychology, 153*, 149–154.

Guendelman, S., Medeiros, S., & Rampes, H. (2017). Mindfulness and emotion regulation: Insights from neurobiological, psychological, and clinical studies. *Frontiers in Psychology, 8*, 220.

Gunnar, M. R., Hostinar, C. E., Sanchez, M. M., Tottenham, N., & Sullivan, R. M. (2015). Parental buffering of fear and stress neurobiology: Reviewing parallels across rodent, monkey, and human models. *Social Neuroscience, 10*(5), 474–478.

Guo, H., & Shen, H. (2021). Media exposure to COVID-19 epidemic and threatening dream frequency: A moderated mediation model of anxiety and coping efficacy. *Dreaming, 31*(1), 1.

Gusnard, D. A., Akbrudak, R., Shulman, G. L., & Raichle, M. E. (2001). Medial prefrontal cortex and self-referential mental activity: Relation to default mode of brain function. *Proceedings of the National Academy of Sciences, USA, 98*, 4259–4264.

Gyurak, A., Gross, J. J., & Etkin, A. (2011). Explicit and implicit emotion regulation: A dual-process framework. *Cognition and Emotion, 25*(3), 400–412.

Habas, C., & Manto, M. (2018). Probing the neuroanatomy of the cerebellum using tractography. *Handbook of Clinical Neurology, 154*, 235–249.

Hair, N. L., Hanson, J., & Wolfe, G. L. (2015). Association of child poverty, brain development, and academic achievement. *JAMA Pediatrics, 169*(9), 822–829.

Halevi, G., Djalovski, A., Vengrober, A., & Feldman, R. (2016). Risk and resilience trajectories in war-exposed children across the first decade of life. *Journal of Child Psychology and psychiatry, 57*(10), 1183–1193.

Halevi, G., Djalovski, A., Kanat-Maymon, Y., Yirmiya, K., Zagoory-Sharon, O., Koren, L., & Feldman, R. (2017). The social transmission of risk: Maternal stress physiology, synchronous parenting, and well-being mediate the effects of war exposure on child psychopathology. *Journal of abnormal psychology, 126*(8), 1087–1103.

Halfon, N., Larson, K., Son, J., Lu, M., & Bethell, C. (2017). Income inequality and the differential effect of adverse childhood experiences in US children. *Academic Pediatrics, 17*(7), 570–578.

Hartmann, H. (1964). *Essays on ego psychology.* International Universities Press.

Hanson, J. L., Nacewicz, B. M., & Suttere, M. J. (2015). *Biological Psychiatry, 77*(4), 313–323.

Hasan, Y., Bègue, L., & Bushman, B. J. (2013). Violent video games stress people out and make them more aggressive. *Aggressive Behavior, 39*(1), 64–70.

Hasenkamp, W., Wilson-Mendenhall, C. D., Duncan, E., & Barsalou, L. W. (2012). Mind wandering and attention during focused meditation: A fine-grained temporal analysis of fluctuating cognitive states. *Neuroimage, 59*(1), 750–760.

Haslam, R. H., Illner, A., & Chuang, S. (2003). Functional brain imaging: Evaluation of the effects of violent media exposure. *Paediatrics and Child Health, 8*(5), 283–284.

Hassin, R. R., Uleman, J. S., & Bargh, J. A. (Eds.), 2007. *The new unconscious.* Oxford University Press. Hastings, P. D., Nuselovici, J. N., Utendale, W. T., Coutya, J., McShane, K. E., & Sullivan, C. (2008). Applying the polyvagal theory to children's emotion regulation: Social context, socialization, and adjustment. *Biological Psychology, 79*(3), 299–306.

Hatfield, E., Cacioppo, J. T., & Rapson, R. L. (1994). Emotional contagion. *Current Directions in Psychological Science, 2*(3), 96–100.

Hayden, M. C., Müllauer, P. K., Beyer, K. J., Gaugeler, R., Senft, B., Dehoust, M. C., & Andreas, S. (2021). Increasing mentalization to reduce maladaptive defense in patients with mental disorders. *Frontiers in Psychiatry, 12.*

Hayes, L. J., Goodman, S. H., & Carlson, E. (2013). Maternal antenatal depression and infant disorganized attachment at 12 months. *Attachment and Human Development, 15*(2), 133–153.

Hayes, S. C., & Wilson, K. G. (1994). Acceptance and commitment therapy: Altering the verbal support for experiential avoidance. *Behavior Analyst, 17*(2), 289–303.

Heard-Garris, N., Williams, D. R., & Davis, M. (2018). Structuring research to address discrimination as a factor in child and adolescent health. *JAMA Pediatrics, 172*(2), 910912.

Hearld, K. R., Budhwani, H., & Chavez-Yenter, D. (2015). Panic attacks in minority Americans: Then effects of alcohol abuse, tobacco smoking, and discrimination. *Journal of Affective Disorders, 174*(15), 106112.

Heberle, A. E., & Carter, A. S. (2020). Is poverty on young minds? Stereotype endorsement, disadvantage awareness, and social-emotional challenges in socioeconomically disadvantaged children. *Developmental Psychology, 56*(2), 336349.

Hebb, D. (1949). *The organization of behavior.* Wiley.

Hebb, D. O. (2005). *The organization of behavior: A neuropsychological theory.* Psychology Press.

Heggeness, M., Fields, J., Trejo, Y., & Schulzetenberg, A. (2021). *Tracking job losses for mothers of school-age children during a health crisis.* US Census Bureau.

Hendler, T., & Admon, R. (2016). Predisposing risk factors for PTSD: Brain biomarkers. In C. Marting, V. Preedy, & V. Patel (Eds.), *Comprehensive guide to post-traumatic stress disorders* (pp. 61–75). Springer International.

Herman, J. L. (1992). Complex PTSD: A syndrome in survivors of prolonged and repeated trauma. *Journal of Traumatic Stress, 5*(3), 377–391.

Hermans, H. J. M. (2004). The dialogical self: Between exchange and power. In H. J. M. Hermans & G. Dimaggio (Eds.), *The dialogical self in psychotherapy* (pp. 13–28). Brunner-Routlege.

Herzberg, M. P., & Gunner M. R. (2020). Early life stress and brain function:

Activity and connectivity associated with processing emotion and reward. *Neuroimage*, 1 April, 116403. doi: 10.1016/j.neuroimage.2019.116493

Hoggard, L. S., Hill, L. K., Gray, D. L., & Sellers, R. M. (2015). Capturing the cardiac effects of racial discrimination: Do the effects "keep going"? *International Journal of Psychophysiology, 97*(2), 163170.

Holmes, A. J., Lee, P. H., Hollinshead, M. O., Bakst, L., Roffman, J. L., Smoller, J. W., & Buckner, R. L. (2012). Individual differences in amygdala-medial prefrontal anatomy link negative affect, impaired social functioning, and polygenic depression risk. *Journal of Neuroscience, 32*(50), 18087–18100.

Hope, E. C., Hoggard, L. S., & Thomas, A. (2015). Emerging into adulthood in the face of racial discrimination: Physiological, psychological, and sociopolitical consequences for African American youth. *Translational Issues in Psychological Sciences, 1*(4), 3342351.

Hopkins, J., Miller, J. L., Butler, K., Gibson, L., Hedrick, L., & Boyle, D. A. (2018). The relation between social support, anxiety and distress symptoms and maternal fetal attachment. *Journal of Reproductive and Infant Psychology, 36*(4), 381–392.

Horga, G., & Maia, T. V. (2012). Conscious and unconscious processes in cognitive control: A theoretical perspective and a novel empirical approach. *Frontiers in Human Neuroscience, 6*, 199.

Howell, B. R., McMurray, M. S., Guzman, D. B., Nair, G., Shi, Y., McCormack, K. M., Hu, X., Styner, M. A., & Sanchez, M. M. (2017). Maternal buffering beyond glucocorticoids: impact of early life stress on corticolimbic circuits that control infant responses to novelty. *Social Neuroscience, 12*(1), 50–64.

Hummel, A. C., Kiel, E. J., & Zvirblyte, S. (2016). Bidirectional effects of positive affect, warmth, and interactions between mothers with and without symptoms of depression and their toddlers. *Journal of Child and Family Studies, 25*(3), 781–789.

Iacoboni, M. (2008). *Mirroring people: The new science of how we connect with others.* Farrar, Straus and Giroux.

Iacoboni, M., Molnar-Szakacs, I., Gallese, V., Buccino, G., Mazziotta, J. C., & Rizzolatti, G. (2005). Grasping the intentions of others with one's own mirror neuron system. *PLoS Biology, 3*(3), e79.

Ioannidis, K., Askelund, A. D., Kievit, R. A., & Van Harmelen, A. L. (2020). The complex neurobiology of resilient functioning after childhood maltreatment. *BMC Medicine, 18*(1), 1–16.

Isobel, S., Goodyear, M., & Foster, K. (2019). Psychological trauma in the context of familial relationships: A concept analysis. *Trauma, Violence, and Abuse, 20*(4), 549–559.

Jaffe, J., Beebe, B., Feldstein, S., Crown, C. L., Jasnow, M. D., Rochat, P., & Stern, D. N. (2001). Rhythms of dialogue in infancy: Coordinated timing in development. *Monographs of the Society for Research in Child Development, 66*(2), i–viii, 1–132.

Javanbakht, A., Kim, P., Swain, J. E., & Liberzon, I. (2016). Sex specific effects of childhood poverty on neurocircuitry of processing of emotional cues: A neuroimaging study. *Behavioral Sciences, 6*(4), 28.

Jessen, S., & Grossmann, T. (2014). Unconscious discrimination of social cues from eye whites in infants. *Proceedings of the National Academy of Sciences, 111*(45), 16208–16213.

Jha, A. P., Stanley, E. A., Kiyonaga, A., Wong, L., & Gelfand, L. (2010). Examining the protective effects of mindfulness training on working memory capacity and affective experience. *Emotion, 10*(1), 54.

Johnson, D. C., & Casey, B. J. (2015). Extinction during memory reconsolidation blocks recovery of fear in adolescents. *Scientific Reports, 5*(1), 1–5.

Joinson, A. N. (2004). Self-esteem, interpersonal risk, and preference for e-mail to face-to-face communication. *CyberPsychology and Behavior, 7*(4), 472–478.

Jones, S. C., Lee, D. B., & Gaskin, A. L (2014). Emotional response profiles to racial discrimination: Does racial identity predict affective patterns? *Journal of Black Psychology.* https;// doi.org/10.1177/0095798413488628

Joseph, N. T., Peterson, L. M., Gordon, H., & Kamarck, Y. W. (2021). The burden of racial discrimination in daily-life moments: Increases in negative emotions and depletion of psychosocial resources among emerging adult African Americans. *Cultural Diversity and Ethnic Minority Psychology, 27*(2), 234244.

Jovanovic, T., & Ressler, K. J. (2010). How the neurocircuitry and genetics of fear inhibition may inform our understanding of PTSD. *American Journal of Psychiatry, 167*(6), 648–662.

Kabat-Zinn, J. (1990). *Full catastrophe living: Using the wisdom of your body and mind to face stress, pain and illness.* Delacorte.

Kabat-Zinn, J. (2005). Bringing mindfulness to medicine: An interview with Jon Kabat-Zinn, PhD. Interview by Karolyn Gazella. *Advances in Mind-Body Medicine, 21*(2), 22–27.

Kabat-Zinn, J., & Chapman-Waldrop, A. (1988). Compliance with an outpatient stress reduction program: Rates and predictors of program completion. *Journal of Behavioral Medicine*, *11*(4), 333–352.

Kagan, J. (1998). Biology and the child. In W. Damon & N. Eisenberg (Eds.), *Handbook of child psychology: Social, emotional, and personality development* (pp. 177–235). Wiley.

Kaiser, R. H., Clegg, R., Goer, F., Pechtel, P., Beltzer, M., Vitaliano, G., Olson, D. P., Teicher, M. H., & Pizzagalli, D. A. (2018). Childhood stress, grown-up brain networks: Corticolimbic correlates of threat-related early life stress and adult stress response. *Psychological Medicine*, *48*(7), 1157–1166.

Kalia, V., & Knauft, K. (2020). Emotion regulation strategies modulate the effects of adverse childhood experiences on perceived chronic stress with implications for cognitive flexibility. *PLOS ONE.* https://doi.org./10. 1371.

Kandel, E. R. (2001). The molecular biology of memory storage: A dialogue between genes and synapses. *Bioscience Reports*, 21, 565–611.

Kandola, A., Ashdown-Franks, G., Hendrikse, J., Sabiston, C. M., & Stubbs, B. (2019). Physical activity and depression: Towards understanding the antidepressant mechanisms of physical activity. *Neuroscience and Biobehavioral Reviews*, *107*, 525–539.

Kark, S. M., & Kensinger, E. A. (2015). Effect of emotional valence on retrieval-related recapitulation of encoding activity in the ventral visual stream. *Neuropsychologia*, *78*, 221–230.

Kark, S. M., & Kensinger, E. A. (2019a). Physiological arousal and visuocortical connectivity predict subsequent vividness of negative memories. *NeuroReport*, *30*(12), 800.

Kark, S. M., & Kensinger, E. A. (2019b). Post-encoding amygdala-visuosensory coupling is associated with negative memory bias in healthy young adults. *Journal of Neuroscience*, *39*(16), 3130–3143.

Kelson, J., Rollin, A., Ridout, B., & Campbell, A. (2019). Internet-delivered acceptance and commitment therapy for anxiety treatment: Systematic review. *Journal of Medical Internet Research*, *21*(1), e12530.

Kensinger, E. A., & Ford, J. H. (2020). Retrieval of emotional events from memory. *Annual Review of Psychology*, 71, 251–272.

Kernberg, O. F. (1975). *Borderline conditions and pathological narcissism.* Aronson.

Kernberg, O. F. (1997). Pathological narcissism and narcissistic personality disorder: Theoretical background and diagnostic classification. In E. F. Ronningstam

(Ed.), *Disorders of narcissism: Diagnostic, clinical, and empirical implications* (pp. 29–51). American Psychiatric Press.

Kernberg, O. F. (2007). The almost untreatable narcissistic patient. *Journal of the American Psychoapnalytic Association, 55*, 503–540.

Kessler, R. C., Berglunl., D. P., Demler, O., Jin, R., Merikangas, K. R., & Walters, E. E. (2005). Lifetime prevalence and age-of-onset distributions of DSM-IV disorders in the National Comorbidity Survey Replication. *Archives of General Psychiatry, 62*(6), 593–602.

Kessler, R. C., Petukhova, M., Sampson, N. A., Zaslavsky, A. M., & Wittchen, H. U. (2012). Twelve month and lifetime prevalence and lifetime morbid risk of anxiety and mood disorders in the United States. *International Journal of Methods in Psychiatric Research, 21*(3), 169–184.

Kiel, E. J., & Kalomiris, A. E. (2019). Emotional development and anxiety. In V. LoBue, K. Pérez-Edgar, & K. Buss (Eds.), *Handbook of emotional development* (pp. 65–693). Springer.

Kilford, E. J., Foulkes, L., & Potter , R. (2015). Affective bias and current, past and future adolescent depression: A familial high risk study. *Journal of Affective Disorder, 174*, March, 265271.

Killingsworth, M. A., & Gilbert, D. T. (2010). A wandering mind is an unhappy mind. *Science, 330*(6006), 932–932.

Kirkinis, K., Pieterse, A. L., Martin, C., Agiliga, A., Brownell, A. (2021). Racism, racial discrimination, and trauma: A systematic review of the social science literature. *Ethnicity & Health, 26*(3), 392412.

Klass, P. (2020, August 24). Young adults' pandemic mental health risks. *New York Times.*

Kohut, H. (1971). *The analysis of the self: A systematic approach to the psychoanalytic treatment of narcissistic personality disorders.* International Universities Press.

Konijn, E. A., Nije Bijvank, M., & Bushman, B. J. (2007). I wish I were a warrior: The role of wishful identification in the effects of violent video games on aggression in adolescent boys. *Developmental Psychology, 43*(4), 1038.

Korn, C. W., Vunder, J., Miró, J., Fuentemilla, L., Hurlemann, R., & Bach, D. R. (2017). Amygdala lesions reduce anxiety-like behavior in a human benzodiazepine-sensitive approach-avoidance conflict test. *Biological Psychiatry, 82*(7), 522–531.

Kotov, R., Perlman, G., Gámez, W., & Watson, D. (2015). The structure and short-term stability of the emotional disorders: A dimensional approach. *Psychological Medicine, 45*(8), 1687–1698.

Koziol, L. F. (2014). *The myth of executive functioning: Missing elements in conceptualization, evaluation and assessment.* Springer.

Koziol, L. F., & Budding, D. E. (2010). *Subcortical structures and cognition: Implications for neuropsychological assessment.* Springer.

Kragel, P. A., & LaBar, K. S. (2016). Decoding the nature of emotion in the brain. *Trends in Cognitive Sciences, 20*(6), 444–455.

Kral, T. R., Schuyler, B. S., Mumford, J. A., Rosenkranz, M. A., Lutz, A., & Davidson, R. J. (2018). Impact of short- and long-term mindfulness meditation training on amygdala reactivity to emotional stimuli. *Neuroimage, 181,* 301–313.

Kühn, S., Kugler, D., Schmalen, K., Weichenberger, M., Witt, C., & Gallinat, J. (2018). The myth of blunted gamers: No evidence for desensitization in empathy for pain after a violent video game intervention in a longitudinal fMRI study on non-gamers. *Neurosignals, 26*(1), 22–30.

Kühn, S., Kugler, D. T., Schmalen, K., Weichenberger, M., Witt, C., & Gallinat, J. (2019). Does playing violent video games cause aggression? A longitudinal intervention study. *Molecular Psychiatry, 24*(8), 1220–1234.

Lambert, H. K., King, K. M., Monahan, K. C., & McLaughlin, K. A. (2017). Differential associations of threat and deprivation with emotion regulation and cognitive control in adolescence. *Development and Psychopathology, 29*(3), 929–940.

Lane, R. D. (2008). Neural substrates of implicit and explicit emotional processes: A unifying framework for psychosomatic medicine. *Psychosomatic Medicine, 70,* 214–231.

Lane, R. D., Ryan, L., Nadel, L., & Greenberg, L. (2014). Memory reconsolidation, emotional arousal and the process of change in psychotherapy: New insights from brain science. *Behavioral Brain Sciences, 15,* 1–80.

Lang, P. J., McTeague, L. M., & Bradley, M. M. (2016). RDoC, DSM, and the reflex physiology of fear: A biodimensional analysis of the anxiety disorders spectrum. *Psychophysiology, 53*(3), 336–347.

Lanius, R. A., Williamson, P. C., Bluhm, R. L., Densmore, M., Boksman, K., Neufeld, R. W., Gati, J. S., & Menon, R. S. (2005). Functional connectivity of dissociative responses in posttraumatic stress disorder: A functional magnetic resonance imaging investigation. *Biological Psychiatry, 57*(8), 873–884.

Lapate, R. C., & Shackman, A. J. (2018). Afterword: What is an emotion? In

A. S. Fox, R. C. Lapate, A. J. Shackman, & R. J. Davidson (Eds.), *The nature of emotion: Fundamental questions* (2nd ed.). Oxford University Press.

Laurent, H., Laurent, S., Hertz, R., Egan-Wright, D., & Granger, D. A. (2013). Sex-specific effects of mindfulness on romantic partners' cortisol responses to conflict and relations with psychological adjustment. *Psychoneuroendocrinology, 38*(12), 2905–2913.

Lebow, M. A., & Chen, A. (2016). Overshadowed by the amygdala: The bed nucleus of the stria terminalis emerges as key to psychiatric disorders. *Molecular Psychiatry, 21*(4), 450–463.

LeDoux, J. (2000). Emotion circuits in the brain. *Annual Review of Neuroscience, 23*(1), 155–184.

LeDoux, J. (2002). *Synaptic self: How our brains become who we are.* Viking.

LeDoux, J. (2014). Coming to terms with fear. *Proceedings of the National Academy of Sciences, 111*, 2871–2878.

LeDoux, J. (2015). *Anxious: Using the brain to understand and treat fear and anxiety.* Penguin.

LeDoux, J. (2016). Coming full circle: From psychology to neuroscience and back. In R. Sternberg, S. Fiske, & D. Foss (Eds.), *Scientists making a difference: One hundred eminent behavioral and brain scientists talk about their most important contributions* (pp. 28–31). Cambridge University Press.

LeDoux, J., & Doyere, V. (2011). Emotional memory processing: Synaptic connectivity. In S. Nalbantian, P. M. Matthews, & J. A. McClelland (Eds.), *The memory process: Neuroscientific and humanistic perspectives* (pp. 153–171). MIT Press.

LeDoux, J., & Schiller, D. (2009). The human amygdala: Insight from other animals. In P. J. Whalen & E. A. Phelps (Eds.), *The human amygdala* (pp. 43–60). Guilford.

Lee, D. B., Peckins, M. K., Heinze, J. E., Miller, A. L., Assari, S., & Zimmerman, M. A. (2018). Psychological pathways from racial discrimination to cortisol in African American males and females, *Journal of Behavioral Medicine, 41*, 208–220.

Leeb, R. T., Price, S., Sliwa, S., Kimball, A., Szucs, L., Caruso, E., Godfred-Cato, S., & Lozier, M. (2020). COVID-19 trends among school-aged children—United States, March 1–September 19, 2020. *Morbidity and Mortality Weekly Report, 69*(39), 1410.

Leerkes, E. M., & Bailes, L. G. (2019). Emotional development within the family context. In V. LoBue, K. Pérez-Edgar, & K. Buss (Eds.), *Handbook of emotional development* (pp. 627–661). Springer.

Lenzi, D., Trentini, C., Pantano, P., Macaluso, E., Lenzi, G. L., & Ammaniti, M. (2008). Attachment models affect brain responses in areas related to emotions and empathy in nulliparous women. *Human Brain Mapping, 34*(6), 1399–1414.

Leppänen, J. M., Cataldo, J. K., Bosquet Enlow, M., & Nelson, C. A. (2018). Early development of attention to threat-related facial expressions. *PloS One, 13*(5), e0197424.

Leppänen, J. M., & Nelson, C. A. (2012). Early development of fear processing. *Current Directions in Psychological Science, 21*(3), 200–204.

Leung, L. (2011). Loneliness, social support, and preference for online social interaction: The mediating effects of identity experimentation online among children and adolescents. *Chinese Journal of Communication, 4*(4), 381–399.

Levine, D. S., Himle, J. A., Abelson, J. M., Matsuko, N., Dhawan, N., & Taylor, J. R. (2014). Discrimination and social anxiety disorders among African-Americans, Caribbean blacks, and non-Hispanic whites. *The Journal of Nervous and Mental Disease, 202*(3), 224–230.

Levinson, C. A., Byrne, M., & Rodebaugh, T. L. (2016). Shame and guilt as shared vulnerability factors: Shame, but not guilt, prospectively predicts both social anxiety and bulimic symptoms. *Eating Behaviors, 22*, 188–193.

Levinson, C. A., Kaplan, S. C., & Rodebaugh, T. L. (2014). *Personality: Understanding the socially anxious temperament*. Wiley.

Levy, J., Goldstein, A., & Feldman, R. (2017). Perception of social synchrony induces mother-child gamma coupling in the social brain. *Social Cognitive and Affective Neuroscience, 12*(7), 1036–1046.

Lewis, M. D. (2005). Bridging emotion theory and neurobiology through dynamic system modeling. *Behavioral and Brain Science, 28*, 169–194.

Lewis, M. (2019). The self-conscious emotions and the role of shame in psycho-pathology. In V. LoBue, K. Pérez-Edgar, & K. Buss (Eds.), *Handbook of emotional development* (pp. 311–350). Springer.

Lewis, M. D., & Todd, R. (2004). Toward a neuropsychological model of internal dialogue: Implications for theory and clinical practice. In H. J. M. Hermans & G. Dimaggio (Eds.), *The dialogical self in psychotherapy* (pp. 43–59). Brunner-Routledge.

Lewis, M. D., & Todd, M. (2007). The development of self-regulation: Toward the integration of cognition and emotion. *Cognitive Development*, *22*, 405–430.

Li, Y., Hou, X., Wei, D., Du, X., Zhang, Q., Liu, G., & Qiu, J. (2017). Long-term effects of acute stress on the prefrontal-limbic system in the healthy adult. *PLoS One*, *12*(1), e0168315.

Libet, B. (1985). Unconscious cerebral initiative and the role of conscious will in voluntary actions. *Behavioral and Brain Sciences*, *8*, 529–566.

Libet, M., Alberts, W. W., Wright, E. W., & Feinstein, B. (1967). Responses of human somatosensory cortex to stimuli below threshold for conscious sensation. *Science*, *158*, 1597–1600.

Lindquist, K. A., Satpute, A. B., Wager, T. D., Weber, J., & Barrett, L. F. (2016). The brain basis of positive and negative affect: Evidence from a meta-analysis of the human neuroimaging literature. *Cerebral Cortex*, *26*(5), 1910–1922.

Linehan, M. M. (2018). *Cognitive-behavioral treatment of borderline personality disorder*. Guilford.

Liotti, G., & Farina, B. (2016). Painful incoherence: The self in borderline personality disorder. In M. Kyrios, R. Moulding, M. Nedeljkovic, S. S. Bhar, G. Doron, & M. Mikulincer (Eds.), *The self in understanding and treating psychological disorders* (pp. 169–178). Cambridge University Press.

Lissak, G. (2018). Adverse physiological and psychological effects of screen time on children and adolescents: Literature review and case study. *Environmental Research*, *164*, 149–157.

Loftus, E. E. (1996). *Eyewitness testimony*. Harvard University Press.

Lyons-Ruth, K. (2003). Dissociation and the parent-infant dialogue: A longitudinal perspective from attachment research. *Journal of the American Psychoanalytic Association*, *51*, 883–911.

Lyons-Ruth, K., & Jacobvitz, D. (2016). Attachment disorganization from infancy to adulthood: Neurobiological correlates, parenting contexts, and pathways to disorder. In J. Cassidy & P. Shaver (Eds.), *Handbook of attachment: Theory, research, and clinical applications* (3nd ed., pp. 667–695). Guilford.

Madan, A., Mrug, S., & Wright, R. A. (2014). The effects of media violence on anxiety in late adolescence. *Journal of Youth and Adolescence*, *43*(1), 116–126.

Malone, J. C., Cohen, S., Liu, S. R., Vaillant, G. E., & Waldinger, R. J. (2013). Adaptive midlife defense mechanisms and late-life health. *Personality and Individual Differences*, *55*(2), 85–89.

Mammen, M. A., Busuito, A., Moore, G. A., Quigley, K. M., & Doheny, K. K. (2017). Physiological functioning moderates infants' sensory sensitivity in higher conflict families. *Developmental Psychobiology, 59*(5), 628–638.

Maras, D., Flament, M. F., Murray, M., Buchholz, A., Henderson, K. A., Obeid, N., & Goldfield, G. S. (2015). Screen time is associated with depression and anxiety in Canadian youth. *Preventive Medicine, 73*, 133–138.

Margolis, A. E., Lee, S. H., Peterson, B. S., & Beebe, B. (2019). Profiles of infant communicative behavior. *Developmental Psychology, 55*(8), 1594.

María-Ríos, C. E., & Morrow, J. D. (2020). Mechanisms of shared vulnerability to post-traumatic stress disorder and substance use disorders. *Frontiers in Behavioral Neuroscience, 14*, 6.

Mariotti, E. C., Waugh, M. H., McClain, C. M., Beevers, L. G., Clemence, A. J., Lewis, K. C., Miller, R., Mulay, A. L., Ridenour, J. M., Huprich, S. K., Pitman, S. R., & Meehan, K. B. (2021). Assessing self-definition and relatedness in level of personality functioning. *Journal of Personality Disorders*, 1–24.

Marsh, A. A., & Blair, R. J. R. (2008). Deficits in facial affect recognition among antisocial populations: A meta-analysis. *Neuroscience and Biobehavioral Reviews, 32*(3), 454–465.

Martin-Joy, J. S., Malone, J. C., Cui, X. J., Johansen, P. Ø., Hill, K. P., Rahman, M. O., Waldinger, R. J., & Vaillant, G. E. (2017). Development of adaptive coping from mid to late life: A 70-year longitudinal study of defense maturity and its psychosocial correlates. *Journal of Nervous and Mental Disease, 205*(9), 685–691.

Marusak, H. A., Elrahal, F., Peters, C. A., Kundu, P., Lombardo, M. V., Calhoun, V. D., Goldberg, E. K., Cohen, C., Taub, J. W., & Rabinak, C. A. (2018). Mindfulness and dynamic functional neural connectivity in children and adolescents. *Behavioural Brain Research, 336*, 211–218.

Mathews, V., Wang, Y., Kalnin, A. J., Mosier, K. M., Dunn, D. W., & Kronenberger, W. G. (2006, November 29). Violent video games leave teenagers emotionally aroused. *Science Daily.*

McCarthy, G., & Taylor, A. (1999). Avoidant/ambivalent attachment style as a mediator between abusive childhood experiences and adult relationship difficulties. *Journal of Child Psychology and Psychiatry and Allied Disciplines, 40*(3), 465–477.

McCoy, C. R., Glover, M. E., Flynn, L. T., Simmons, R. K., Cohen, J. L., Ptacek, T., Lefkowitz, E. J., Jackson, N. L., Akil, H., Wu, X., & Clinton, S. M. (2019).

Altered DNA methylation in the developing brains of rats genetically prone to high versus low anxiety. *Journal of Neuroscience, 39*(16), 3144–3158.

McEwen, B. S. (2012). Brain on stress: How the social environment gets under the skin. *Proceedings of the National Academy of Sciences of the United states of America. 109*(2), 17180–17185.

McEwen, B., Bowles, N., Gray, J., Hill, M., Hunter, R., Karatsoreos, I., & Nasca, C. (2015). Mechanisms of stress in the brain. *Nature Neuroscience, 18,* 1353–1363.

McGilchrist, I. (2009). *The master and his emissary: The divided brain and the making of the Western world.* Yale University Press.

McGrath, J. J., McLaughlin, K. A., Saha, S., Aguilar-Gaxiola, S., Al-Hamzawi, A., Alonso, J., . . . & Kessler, R. C. (2017). The association between childhood adversities and subsequent first onset of psychotic experiences: A cross-national analysis of 23 998 respondents from 17 countries. *Psychological Medicine, 47*(7), 1230–1245.

McLaughlin, K. A. (2016). Future directions in childhood adversity and youth psychopathology. *Journal of Clinical Child and Adolescent Psychology, 45*(3), 361–382.

McLaughlin, K. A., & Sheridan, M. A. (2016). Beyond cumulative risk: A dimensional approach to childhood adversity. *Current Directions in Psychological Science, 25*(4), 239–245.

McLaughlin, K. A., Weissman, D., & Bitrán, D. (2019). Childhood adversity and neural development: A systematic review. *Annual Review of Developmental Psychology, 1,* 277–312.

Meroda, K. J. (2021). *The analyst's vulnerability: Impact on theory and practice.* Routledge.

Meroda, K. J. (2010). *Psychoanalytic techniques: Working with emotion in the therapeutic relationship.* Guilford.

Merz, E. C., Tottenham, N., & Noble, K. G. (2018). Socioeconomic status, amygdala volume, and internalizing symptoms in children and adolescents. *Journal of Clinical Child & Adolescent Psychology. 47*(2), 312–323.

Miedzobrodzka, E., Buczny, J., Konijn, E. A., & Krabbendam, L. C. (2021, May 21). Insensitive players? A relationship between violent video game exposure and recognition of negative emotions. *Frontiers in Psychology, 12.*

Milad, M. R., & Quirk, G. J. (2012). Fear extinction as a model for translational neuroscience: Ten years of progress. *Annual Review of Psychology, 63,* 129–151.

Miles, O. W., & Maren, S. (2019). Role of the bed nucleus of the stria terminalis in PTDD: Insight from preclinical models. *Frontiers in Behavioral Neuroscience*. Doi 10.3389/fnbeh.2019.00068.

Miranda, B., & Louzã, M. R. (2015). The physician's quality of life: Relationship with ego defense mechanisms and object relations. *Comprehensive Psychiatry*, *63*, 22–29.

Mitchell, R., Hanna, D., Brennan, K., Curran, D., McDermott, B., Ryan, M., Craig, K., McCullough, E., Wallace, P., & Dyer, K. F. (2020). Alienation appraisals mediate the relationships between childhood trauma and multiple markers of posttraumatic stress. *Journal of Child and Adolescent Trauma*, *13*(1), 11–19.

Milojevich, H. M., Levine, L., Cathcart, E. J., & Quaz, J. A. (2018). The role of maltreatment in the development of coping strategies. *Journal of Applied Developmental Psychology, 54*, January–February, 23–32.

Mischkowski, D., Stavish, C. M., Palacios-Barrios, E. E., Banker, L. A., Dildine, T. C., & Atlas, L. Y. (2021). Dispositional mindfulness and acute heat pain: Comparing stimulus-evoked pain with summary pain assessment. *Psychosomatic Medicine*, *83*(6), 539–548.

Mobbs, D., Hagan, C. C., Dalgleish, T., Silston, B., & Prévost, C. (2015). The ecology of human fear: Survival optimization and the nervous system. *Frontiers in Neuroscience*, *9*, 55.

Montagner, R., Mogg, K., Bradley, B. P., Pine, D. S., Czykiel, M. S., Miguel, E. C., Rodhe, L. A., Manfro, G. G., & Salum, G. A. (2016). Attentional bias to threat in children at-risk for emotional disorders: Role of gender and type of maternal emotional disorder. *European Child and Adolescent Psychiatry*, *25*(7), 735–742.

Moore, G. A. (2009). Infants' and mothers' vagal reactivity in response to anger. *Journal of Child Psychology and Psychiatry*, *50*(11), 1392–1400.

Morales, S., Brown, K. M., Taber-Thomas, B. C., LoBue, V., Buss, K. A., & Pérez-Edgar, K. E. (2017). Maternal anxiety predicts attentional bias towards threat in infancy. *Emotion*, *17*(5), 874.

Morales, S., & Fox, N. A. (2019). A neuroscience perspective on emotional development. In V. LoBue, K. Pérez-Edgar, & K. Buss (Eds.), *Handbook of Emotional Development* (pp. 57–81). Springer.

Moreno-López, L., Ioannidis, K., Askelund, A. D., Smith, A. J., Schueler, K., & Van Harmelen, A. L. (2020). The resilient emotional brain: A scoping review of the medial prefrontal cortex and limbic structure and function in resilient adults with a history of childhood maltreatment. *Biological Psychiatry: Cognitive Neuroscience and Neuroimaging, 5*(4), 392–402.

Mouzon, D. M., Taylor, R. A., Woodward, A. T., & Chatters L. M. (2017). Everyday racial discrimination, everyday non-racial discrimination, and physical health among African-Americans. *Journal of Ethnic & Cultural Diversity in Social Work, 26*(1–2), 68–80.

Mu, Y., Guo, C., & Han, S. (2016). Oxytocin enhances inter-brain synchrony during social coordination in male adults. *Social Cognitive and Affective Neuroscience, 11*(12), 1882–1893.

Muller, J. N., Moroco, A., Loloi, J., Portolese, A., Wakefield, B. H., King, T. S., & Olympia, R. (2020). Violence depicted in superhero-based films stratified by protagonist/antagonist and gender. *Cureus, 12*(2).

Muris, P., Meesters, C., & van Asseldonk, M. (2018). Shame on me! Self-conscious emotions and big five personality traits and their relations to anxiety disorder symptoms in young, non-clinical adolescents. *Child Psychiatry and Human Development, 49*(2), 268–278.

Nava, E., Romano, D., Grassi, M., & Turati, C. (2016). Skin conductance reveals the early development of the unconscious processing of emotions. *Cortex, 84,* 124–131.

Nevarez, M. D., Morrill, M. I., & Waldinger, R. J. (2018). Thriving in midlife: The roles of childhood nurturance and adult defense mechanisms. *Journal of Research in Personality, 74,* 35–41.

Nevis, B. G. (2020). *Applying personality-informed treatment strategies to clinical practice: A theoretical and practical guide.* Routledge.

Noble, K. G., & Giebler, M. (2020). The neuroscience of socioeconomic inequity. *Current Opinion in Behavioral Science. 36,* December 2020, 23–28.

Nolen-Hoeksema, S., Wisco, B. E., & Lyubomirsky, S. (2008). Rethinking rumination. *Perspectives on Psychological Science, 3*(5), 400–424.

Ochsner, K. N., & Gross, J. J. (2005). The cognitive control of emotion. *Trends in Cognitive Science, 9,* 408–409.

Ochsner, K. N., Ray, R. R., Hughes, B., McRae, K., Cooper, J. C., Weber, J., Gabrieli, J. D. E., & Gross, J. J. (2009). Bottom-up and top-down processes in emotion generation: Common and distinct neural mechanisms. *Psychological Science, 20*(11), 1322–1331.

Oexle, N., Rüsch, N., Viering, S., Wyss, C., Seifritz, E., Xu, Z., & Kawohl, W.

(2017). Self-stigma and suicidality: A longitudinal study. *European Archives of Psychiatry and Clinical Neuroscience, 267*(4), 359–361.

Ohman, A. (2009). Human fear conditioning and the amygdala. In P. J. Whalen & E. A. Phelps (Eds.), *The human amygdala* (pp. 118–154). Guilford.

Okon-Singer, H. (2018). The role of attention bias to threat in anxiety: Mechanisms, modulators and open questions. *Current Opinion in Behavioral Sciences, 19*, 26–30.

Okon-Singer, H., Hendler, T., Pessoa, L., & Shackman, A. J. (2015). The neurobiology of emotion-cognition interactions: Fundamental questions and strategies for future research. *Frontiers in Human Neuroscience, 9*, 58.

Olds, D. D. (2006). Identification: Biological and perspectives. *Journal of the American Psychoanalytic Association, 54*, 17–46.

Opendak, M., Gould, E., & Sullivan, R. (2017). Early life adversity during the infant sensitive period for attachment: Programming of behavioral neurobiology of threat processing and social behavior. *Developmental Cognitive Neuroscience, 25*, 145–159.

Opendak, M., Robinson-Drummer, P., Blomkvist, A., Zanca, R. M., Wood, K., Jacobs, L., Chan, S., Tan, S., Woo, J., Venkataraman, G., Kirschner, E., Lundström, J. N., Wilson, D. A., Serrano, P. A., & Sullivan, R. M. (2019). Neurobiology of maternal regulation of infant fear: The role of mesolimbic dopamine and its disruption by maltreatment. *Neuropsychopharmacology, 44*(7), 1247–1257.

Orben, A., Tomova, L., & Blakemore, S. J. (2020). The effects of social deprivation on adolescent development and mental health. *Lancet Child and Adolescent Health, 4*(8), 634–640.

Ortner, C. N., Kilner, S. J., & Zelazo, P. D. (2007). Mindfulness meditation and reduced emotional interference on a cognitive task. *Motivation and Emotion, 31*(4), 271–283.

Pachter, L. M., Caldwell, C. H., Jackson, J. S., & Bernstein, B. (2018). Discrimination and mental health in a representative sample of African-American and Afro-Caribbean youth. *Journal of Racial and Ethnic Health Disparities, 6*, 831–837.

Pakenham, K. I., Landi, G., Boccolini, G., Furlani, A., Grandi, S., & Tossani, E. (2020). The moderating roles of psychological flexibility and inflexibility on the mental health impacts of COVID-19 pandemic and lockdown in Italy. *Journal of Contextual Behavioral Science, 17*, 109–118.

Panfil, A. L., Frandes, M., Nirestean, A., Hurmuz, M., Lungeanu, D., Crista-novici, M., Lemeti, L., Isac, A., Papava, I., & Bredicean, C. (2020). Inter-relation between defensive mechanisms and coping strategies in psychiatry trainees in Romania: A multicenter study. *Annals of General Psychiatry, 19*(1), 1–9.

Panksepp, J., & Biven, L. (2012). *Archeology of mind: The neuroevolutionary origins of human emotion.* Norton.

Papousek, M., & Papousek, H. (1990). Excessive infant crying and intuitive parental care: Buffering support and its failures in parent-infant interaction. *Early Child Development and Care, 65*(1), 117–126.

Pat-Horenczyk, R., Cohen, S., Ziv, Y., Achituv, M., Assulin,-Peretz, L., Blanchard, T. R., Schiff, M., & Brom, D. (2015). Emotion regulation in mothers and young children faced with trauma. *Infant Mental Health Journal, 36*(3), 337348.

Pattwell, S. S., & Bath, K. G. (2017). Emotional learning, stress, and develop-ment: An ever-changing landscape shaped by early-life experience. *Neurobiol-ogy of Learning and Memory, 143,* 36–48.

Pattwell, S., Liston, J., Deisseroth, K., & Lee, F. (2017). Role of bdnf in regulat-ing sensitive periods for fear regulation. *Biological Psychiatry, 81*(10), S9–S10.

Pavlov, I. P. (1927). *Conditioned reflexes: An investigation of the physiological activity of the cerebral cortex.* Oxford University Press.

Pavlova, N. M., McCallum, M., & Jillian, L. V. (2017). Remembering the hurt of childhood: A psychological review and call for future research. *Canadian Psychology, 58*(1), 5868.

Pérez-Edgar, K. (2019). Through the looking glass: Temperament and emotion as separate and interwoven constructs. In V. LoBue, K. Pérez-Edgar, & K. Buss (Eds.), *Handbook of emotional development* (pp. 139–168). Springer.

Perusini, J. N., & Fanselow, M. S. (2015). Neurobehavioral perspectives on the distinction between fear and anxiety. *Learning and Memory, 22*(9), 417–425.

Pessoa, L. (2008). On the relationship between emotion and cognition. *Nature Reviews Neuroscience, 9*(2), 148–158.

Pessoa, L. (2014). Understanding brain networks and brain organization. *Physics of Life Reviews, 11*(3), 400–435.

Pessoa, L. (2015). Précis on the cognitive-emotional brain. *Behavioral and Brain Sciences, 38,* e71.

Pessoa, L. (2016). Beyond disjoint brain networks: Overlapping networks for cognition and emotion. *Behavioral and Brain Sciences, 39,* e129.

Pessoa, L. (2017). A network model of the emotional brain. *Trends in Cognitive Science, 21*(5), 357–371.

Pessoa, L. (2018). Understanding emotion with brain networks. *Current Opinion in Behavioral Sciences, 19,* 19–25.

Pessoa, L., & Adolphs, R. (2010). Emotion processing and the amygdala: From a "low road" to "many roads" of evaluating biological significance. *Nature Reviews Neuroscience, 11,* 773–782.

Pessoa, L., & Hof, P. (2015). From Paul Broca's great limbic lobe to the limbic system. *Comparative Neurobiology, 523*(17), 2495–2500.

Phelps, E. A. (2006). Emotion and cognition: Insights from studies of the human amygdala. *Annual Review of Psychology, 57,* 27–53.

Phelps, E. A. (2009). The human amygdala and the control of fear. In P. J. Whalen & E. A. Phelps (Eds.), *The human amygdala* (pp. 204–219). Guilford.

Phelps, E. A., & Sharot, T. (2008). How (and why) emotion enhances the subjective sense of recollection. *Current Directions in Psychological Science, 17*(2), 147–152.

Pietrini, P., Guazzelli, M., Basso, G., Jaffe, K., & Grafman, J. (2000). Neural correlates of imaginal aggressive behavior assessed by positron emission tomography in healthy subjects. *American Journal of Psychiatry, 157*(11), 1772–1781.

Pollack, A., Watt, D. F., & Panksepp, J. (2000). The feelings of what happens: Body and emotion in the making of consciousness (a review). *Neuro-Psychoanalysis, 2,* 81–88.

Polman, H., de Castro, B. O., & van Aken, M. A. (2008). Experimental study of the differential effects of playing versus watching violent video games on children's aggressive behavior. *Aggressive Behavior: Official Journal of the International Society for Research on Aggression, 34*(3), 256–264.

Palanco-Roman, L., Danies, A., & Anglin, D. M. (2016). Racial discrimination as race-based trauma, coping strategies, and dissociative symptoms among emerging adults. *Psychological trauma: research, practice, and policy, 8*(5), 609617.

Porcerelli, J. H., Huth-Bocks, A., Huprich, S. K., & Richardson, L. (2016). Defense mechanisms of pregnant mothers predict attachment security, social-emotional competence, and behavior problems in their toddlers. *American Journal of Psychiatry, 173*(2), 138–146.

Porges, S. W. (2001). The polyvagal theory: Phylogenetic substrates of a social nervous system. *International Journal of Psychophysiology, 42*(2), 123–146.

Porges, S. W. (2007). The polyvagal perspective. *Biological Psychology, 74*(2), 116–143.

Porter, A. M., & Goolkasian, P. (2019). Video games and stress: How stress appraisals and game content affect cardiovascular and emotion outcomes. *Frontiers in Psychology, 10*, 967.

Posner, J., Cha, J., Roy, A. K., Peterson, B. S., Bansal, R., Gustafsson, H. C., Raffanello, E., Gingrich, J., & Monk, C. (2016). Alterations in amygdala-prefrontal circuits in infants exposed to prenatal maternal depression. *Translational Psychiatry, 6*(11), e935–e935.

Prasad, S., & Mishra, R. (2019). The nature of unconscious attention to subliminal cues. *Vision, 3,* 38.

Rachel, J., Mazza S. E., Lambert, J., & Cote, S. M. (2017). Early adolescence behavior problems and timing of poverty during childhood: A comparison of lifecourse models. *Social Science and Medicine, 177*, 35–42.

Raichle, M. E., MacLeod, A. M., Snyder, A. Z., Powers, W. J., Gusnard, D. A., & Shulman, G. L. (2001). A default mode of brain function. *Proceedings of the National Academy of Sciences, 98*, 676–682.

Ramachandran, V. S. (2011). *The tell-tale brain: Unlocking the mystery of human nature.* Norton.

Ramírez-Barrantes, R., Arancibia, M., Stojanova, J., Aspé-Sánchez, M., Córdova, C., & Henríquez, R. A. (2019). Default mode network, meditation, and age-associated brain changes: What can we learn from the impact of mental training on well-being as a psychotherapeutic approach? *Neural Plasticity, 3*, 1–15.

Reid, R. J., Coleman, K., Johnson, E. A., Fishman, P. A., Hsu, C., Soman, M. P., Trescott, C., Erikson, M., & Larson, E. B. (2010). The group health medical home at year two: Cost savings, higher patient satisfaction, and less burnout for providers. *Health Affairs, 29*(5), 835–843.

Repacholi, B. M., & Meltzoff, A. N. (2007). Emotional eavesdropping: Infants selectively respond to indirect emotional signals. *Child Development, 78*(2), 503–521.

Reynold, A. J., & Temple J. A. (2008). Cost-effective early childhood development programs from preschool to first grade. *Annual Review of Clinical Psychology, 4*, 109–139.

Richardson, H., & Saxe, R. (2020a). Development of predictive responses in theory of mind brain regions. *Developmental Science, 23*(1), e12863.

Richardson, H., & Saxe, R. (2020b). Early signatures of and developmental change in brain regions for theory of mind. In B. Chen & K. Y. Kwan (Eds.), *Neural circuit and cognitive development* (pp. 467–484). Academic Press.

Rizzolati, G., Fogassi, L., & Gallese, V. (2002). Motor and cognitive functions of the ventral premotor cortex. *Current Opinion in Neurobiology, 12*, 149–154.

Ruba, A. L., Johnson, K. M., Harris, L. T., & Wilbourn, M. P. (2017). Developmental changes in infants' categorization of anger and disgust facial expressions. *Developmental Psychology, 53*(10), 1826.

Russell, G., & Lightman, S. (2019). The human stress response. *Nature Reviews Endocrinology, 15*, 525–534. https://doi.org/1o.1038

Rubin, D. C. (2006). The basic systems model of episodic memory. *Perspectives on Psychological Science, 1*, 277–311.

Rüsch, N., Lieb, K., Göttler, I., Hermann, C., Schramm, E., Richter, H., Jacob, G. A., Corrigan, P. W., & Bohus, M. (2007). Shame and implicit self-concept in women with borderline personality disorder. *American Journal of Psychiatry, 164*(3), 500–508.

Sandstrom, M. J., & Cramer, P. (2003). Defense mechanisms and psychological adjustment in childhood. *Journal of Nervous and Mental Disease, 191*(8), 487–495.

Sar, V. (2011). Developmental trauma, complex PTSD, and the current proposal of DSM-5. *European Journal of Psychotraumatology, 2*(1), 5622.

Sar, V. (2017). Parallel-distinct structures of internal world and external reality: Disavowing and re-claiming the self-identity in the aftermath of trauma-generated dissociation. *Frontiers in Psychology, 8*, 216.

Satterthwaite, T. D., Xia, C. H., & Bassett, D. S. (2018). Personalized neuroscience: Common and individual-specific features in functional brain networks. *Neuron, 98*(2), 243–245.

Saxe, R. (2010). The right temporo-parietal junction: A specific brain region for thinking about thoughts. In G. Leslie (Ed.), *Handbook of theory of mind* (pp. 1–35). Taylor and Francis.

Saxe, R. (2018). Seeing other minds in 3D. *Trends in Cognitive Sciences, 22*(3), 193–195.

Saxe, R., & Houlihan, S. D. (2017). Formalizing emotion concepts within a Bayesian model of theory of mind. *Current Opinion in Psychology, 17*, 15–21.

Schaefer, M., & Northoff, G. (2017). Who am I: The conscious and the unconscious self. *Frontiers in Human Neuroscience, 17.*

Schäfer, J., Zvielli, A., Höfler, M., Wittchen, H. U., & Bernstein, A. (2018). Trauma, attentional dysregulation, and the development of posttraumatic stress: An investigation of risk pathways. *Behaviour Research and Therapy, 102,* 60–66.

Schiller, D., Levy, I., Niv, Y., LeDoux, J. E., & Phelps, E. A. (2008). From fear to safety and back: Reversal of fear in the human brain. *Journal of Neuroscience, 28*(45), 11517–11525.

Schore, A. N. (2003). *Affect regulation and the repair of the self.* Norton.

Schore, A. N. (2012). *The science of the art of psychotherapy.* Norton.

Sebastian, C. L., Tan, G. C., Roiser, J. P., Viding, E., Dumontheil, I., & Blakemore, S. J. (2011). Developmental influences on the neural bases of responses to social rejection: Implications of social neuroscience for education. *Neuroimage, 57*(3), 686–694.

Schmid, M., Peterman, F., & Fegert, J. M. (2013). Developmental trauma disorder: Pros and cons of including formal criteria in the psychiatric diagnostic system. *BMC Psychiatry, 13*(3). https://doi.org/10.1186/1471 -244X-13-3

Shackman, A. J., & Fox, A. S. (2016). Contributions of the central extended amygdala to fear and anxiety. *Journal of Neuroscience, 36*(31), 8050–8063.

Shackman, J. E., Shackman, A. J., & Pollak, S. D. (2007). Physical abuse amplifies attention to threat and increases anxiety in children. *Emotion, 7*(4), 838.

Shackman, A. J., Stockbridge, M. D., LeMay, E. P., & Fox, A. S. (2018). The psychological and neurobiological bases of dispositional negativity. In A. S. Fox, R. C. Lapate, A. J. Shackman, & R. J. Davidson (Eds.), *The nature of emotion: Fundamental questions* (2nd ed.). Oxford University Press.

Shackman, A. J., & Wager, T. D. (2019). The emotional brain: Fundamental questions and strategies for future research. *Neuroscience Letters, 693,* 68–74.

Shalev, L., Paz, R., & Avidan, G. (2018). Visual aversive learning compromises sensory discrimination. *Journal of Neuroscience, 38*(11), 2766–2779.

Sheets-Johnstone, M. (2010). Thinking in movement: Further analysis and validations. In J. Stewart, O. Gapenne, & E. A. DiPaolo (Eds.), *Enaction: Toward a new paradigm for cognitive science* (pp. 165–182). MIT Press.

Sheridan, M. A., Sarsour, K., Jutte, D., D'Esposito, W., & Bpyce, T. (2012). *Plos One.* https://doi.org/10.1371

Siegel, D. J. (2007). *The mindful brain: Reflection and attunement in the cultivation of well-being.* Norton.

Siegel, D. J. (2021). *Becoming aware: A 21-day mindfulness program for reducing anxiety and cultivating calm.* Penguin Random House.

Sigurdsson, T., Doyère, V., Cain, C. K., & LeDoux, J. E. (2007). Long-term potentiation in the amygdala: A cellular mechanism of fear learning and memory. *Neuropharmacology, 52*(1), 215–227.

Silvers, J. A., Insel, C., Powers, A., Franz, P., Helion, C., Martin, R. E., Weber, J., Mischel, W., Casey, B. J., & Ochsner, K. N. (2017). vlPFC-vmPFC-amygdala interactions underlie age-related differences in cognitive regulation of emotion. *Cerebral Cortex, 27*(7), 3502–3514.

Silvers, J. A., Lumian, D. S., Gabard-Durnam, L., Gee, D. G., Goff, B., Fareri, D. S., Caldera, C., Flannery, J., Telzer, E. H., Humphreys, K. L., & Tottenham, N. (2016). Previous institutionalization is followed by broader amygdala-hippocampal-PFC network connectivity during aversive learning in human development. *Journal of Neuroscience, 36*(24), 6420–6430.

Sladky, R., Geissberger, N., Pfabigan, D., Kraus, C., Tik, M., Woletz, M., Paul, K., Vanicek, T., Auer, B., Kranz, C., Lamm, C., Lanzenberger, R., & Windischberger, C. (2018). Unsmoothed functional MRI of the human amygdala and bed nucleus of the stria terminalis during processing of emotional faces. *Neuroimage, 168,* 383–391.

Smith, S., Duff, E., Groves, A., Nichols, T. E., Jbabdi, S., Westlye, L. T., Tamnes, C. K., Engvig, A., Walhovd, K. B., Fjell, A. M., Johansen-Berg, H., & Douaud, G. (2019). Structural variability in the human brain reflects fine-grained functional architecture at the population level. *Journal of Neuroscience, 39*(31), 6136–6149.

Solms, M., & Zellner, M. R. (2012a). Freudian drive theory today. In A. Fotopoulo, D. Plaff, & M. A. Conway (Eds.), *From the couch to the lab: Trends in psychodynamic neuroscience* (pp. 49–63). Oxford University Press.

Solms, M., & Zellner, M. R. (2012b). The Freudian unconscious today. In A. Fotopoulo, D. Plaff, & M. A. Conway (Eds.), *From the couch to the lab: Trends in psychodynamic neuroscience* (pp. 209–218). Oxford University Press.

Spada, M. M., Langston, B., Nikčević, A. V., & Moneta, G. B. (2008). The role of metacognitions in problematic internet use. *Computers in Human Behavior, 24*(5), 2325–2335.

Spinazzola, J., van der Kolk, B., & Ford, J. D. (2018). When nowhere is safe:

Trauma history antecedents of posttraumatic stress disorder and developmental trauma disorder in childhood. *Journal of Traumatic Stress, 31*(5), 631–642.

Stankovi, S. (2015). Virtual reality and virtual environments in 10 lectures. *Synthesis Lectures on Image, Video, and Multimedia Processing, 18*(3), 1–197.

Stern, D. N. (1985). *The interpersonal world of the infant: A view from psychoanalysis and developmental psychology.* Basic Books.

Stewart, J., Gappene, O., & DiPaolo, A. (Eds.). (2010). *Enaction: Toward a new paradigm for cognitive science.* MIT Press.

Sullivan, H. S. (Ed.). (1953). *The interpersonal theory of psychiatry.* Routledge.

Swain, J., Hancock, K., Hainsworth, C., & Bowman, J. (2013). Acceptance and commitment therapy in the treatment of anxiety: A systematic review. *Clinical Psychology Review, 33*(8), 965–978.

Swartz, J. R., Carrasco, M., Wiggins, J. L., Thomason, M. E., & Monk, C. S. (2014). Age-related changes in the structure and function of prefrontal cortex–amygdala circuitry in children and adolescents: A multi-modal imaging approach. *Neuroimage, 86,* 212–220.

Sznycer, D., Tooby, J., Cosmides, L., Porat, R., Shalvi, S., & Halperin, E. (2016). Shame closely tracks the threat of devaluation by others, even across cultures. *Proceedings of the National Academy of Sciences, 113*(10), 2625–2630.

Szycik, G. R., Mohammadi, B., Münte, T. F., & Te Wildt, B. T. (2017). Lack of evidence that neural empathic responses are blunted in excessive users of violent video games: An fMRI study. *Frontiers in Psychology, 8,* 174.

Tambini, A., Rimmele, U., Phelps, E. A., & Davachi, L. (2017). Emotional brain states carry over and enhance future memory formation. *Nature Neuroscience, 20*(2), 271–278.

Tang, H., Mai, X., Wang, S., Zhu, C., Krueger, F., & Liu, C. (2016). Interpersonal brain synchronization in the right temporo-parietal junction during face-to-face economic exchange. *Social Cognitive and Affective Neuroscience, 11*(1), 23–32.

Tarder-Stoll, H., Jayakumar, M., Dimsdale-Zucker, H. R., Günseli, E., & Aly, M. (2020). Dynamic internal states shape memory retrieval. *Neuropsychologia, 138,* 107328.

Taschereau-Dumouchel, V., Cortese, A., Chiba, T., Knotts, J. D., Kawato, M., & Lau, H. (2018). Towards an unconscious neural reinforcement intervention for common fears. *Proceedings of the National Academy of Sciences, 115*(13), 3470–3475.

Taylor, R. L., Cooper, S. R., & Jackson, J. J. (2020). Assessment of neighborhood poverty, cognitive functions, and prefrontal and hippocampal volumes in children. JAMA Network Open, 3(11), e2023774.

The Children's Defense Fund. (n.d.). Child poverty. https://www.childrensdefense .org/policy/policy-priorities/child-poverty/

Teychenne, M., Costigan, S. A., & Parker, K. (2015). The association between sedentary behaviour and risk of anxiety: A systematic review. BMC Public Health, 15(1), 1–8.

Thijssen, S., Muetzel, R. L., Bakermans-Kranenburg, M. J., Jaddoe, V. W., Tiemeier, H., Verhulst, F. C., White, T., & Van Ijzendoorn, M. H. (2017). Insensitive parenting may accelerate the development of the amygdala–medial prefrontal cortex circuit. Development and Psychopathology, 29(2), 505–518.

Todd, R. M., & Anderson, A. K. (2013). Salience, state, and expression: The influence of specific aspects of emotion on attention and perception. In K. N. Ochsner & S. Kosslyn (Eds.), The Oxford handbook of cognitive neuroscience (Vol. 2, pp. 11–31). Oxford University Press.

Todd, R. M., Cunningham, W. A., Anderson, A. K., & Thompson, E. (2012). Affect-biased attention as emotion regulation. Trends in Cognitive Sciences, 16(7), 365–372.

Todd, R. M., Evans, J. W., Morris, D., Lewis, M. D., & Taylor, M. J. (2011). The changing face of emotion: Age-related patterns of amygdala activation to salient faces. Social Cognitive and Affective Neuroscience, 6(1), 12–23.

Todd, R. M., & Manaligod, M. G. (2018). Implicit guidance of attention: The priority state space framework. Cortex, 102, 121–138.

Todd, R. M., Miskovic, V., Chikazoe, J., & Anderson, A. K. (2020). Emotional objectivity: Neural representations of emotions and their interaction with cognition. Annual Review of Psychology, 71, 25–48.

Todd, R. M., & Phelps, E. A. (2016). Attending to the world without an amygdala. In D. Amaral & R. Adolphs (Eds.), Living without an amygdala (p. 364). Guilford.

Tooby, J., & Cosmides, L. (2008). The evolutionary psychology of the emotions and their relationship to internal regulatory variables. In M. Lewis, J. M. Haviland-Jones, & L. F. Barrett (Eds.), Handbook of emotions (pp. 114–137). Guilford.

Torrisi, S., Alvarez, G. M., Gorka, A. X., Fuchs, B., Geraci, M., Grillon, C., & Ernst, M. (2019). Resting-state connectivity of the bed nucleus of the stria terminalis and the central nucleus of the amygdala in clinical anxiety. *Journal of Psychiatry and Neuroscience, 44*(5), 313.

Tottenham, N. (2012a). Human amygdala development in the absence of species-expected caregiving. *Developmental Psychobiology, 54*(6), 598–611.

Tottenham, N. (2012b). Risk and developmental heterogeneity in previously institutionalized children. *Journal of Adolescent Health, 51*(2), S29–S33.

Tottenham, N. (2014). The importance of early experiences for neuro-affective development. In S. L. Andersen & D. S. Pine (Eds.), *The neurobiology of childhood* (Vol. 16, pp. 109–129). Springer.

Tottenham, N. (2017, July). The brain's emotional development. *Cerebrum.*

Tottenham, N. (2019). Development of emotion regulation neurobiology and the fundamental role of early experiences. *Biological Psychiatry, 85*(10), S38.

Tottenham, N. (2020). Early adversity and the neotenous human brain. *Biological Psychiatry, 87*(4), 350–358.

Tottenham, N., & Gabard-Durnam, L. J. (2017). The developing amygdala: A student of the world and a teacher of the cortex. *Current Opinions in Psychology, 17,* 55–60.

Tottenham, N., Hare, T. A., Millner, A., Gilhooly, T., Zevin, J. D., & Casey, B. J. (2011). Elevated amygdala response to faces following early deprivation. *Developmental Science, 14*(2), 190–204. https://doi.org/10.1111/j.1467-7687 .2010.00971.x

Trecanni, G., Musazzi, L., & Perego, C. (2014). Stress and corticosterone increase the readily releasable pool of glutamate vesicles in synaptic terminals of prefrontal and frontal cortex. *Molecular Psychiatry, 19,* 433443. https://doi.org/10.1038

Tronick, E. (2007). *The neurobehavioral and social-emotional development of infants and children.* Norton.

Tronick, E. Z., & Cohn, J. F. (1989). Infant-mother face-to-face interaction: Age and gender differences in coordination and the occurrence of miscoordination. *Child Development, 60*(1), 85–92.

Troy, A. S., & Mauss, I. B. (2011). Resilience in the face of stress: Emotion regulation as a protective factor. In S. M. Southwick, B. T. Lita, D. Charney, & M. J. Friedman (Eds.), *Resilience and Mental Health: Challenges Across the Lifespan* (pp. 30–44). Cambridge University Press.

Tsuchiya, N., & Adolphs, R. (2007). Emotion and consciousness. *Trends in Cognitive Science, 11,* 158–167.

Tucker, C. J., Finkelhor, D., Turner, H., & Shattuck, A. (2013). Association of sibling aggression with child and adolescent mental health. *Pediatrics*, *132*(1), 79–84.

Uchida, S., Yamagata, H., Seki, T., & Watanabe, Y. (2018). Epigenetic mechanisms of major depression: Targetting neuronal plasticity. *Psychiatry and Clinical Neuroscience*. *72*(4), 212–227.

Uddin, L. Q., & Karlsgodt, K. H. (2018). Future directions for examination of brain networks in neurodevelopmental disorders. *Journal of Clinical Child and Adolescent Psychology*, *47*(3), 483–497.

USDHHS. (2017). *Child maltreatment 2015* [Data set]. US Department of Health and Human Services. https://www.acf.hhs.gov/cb/data-research/child-maltreatment

Vaisvaser, S., Lin, T., Admon, R., Podlipsky, I., Greenman, Y., Stern, N., Fruchter, E., Wald, I., Pine, D. S., Tarrasch, R., Bar-Haim, Y., & Hendler, T. (2013). Neural traces of stress: Cortisol related sustained enhancement of amygdala-hippocampal functional connectivity. *Frontiers in Human Neuroscience*, *7*, 313.

Vajda, A., Láng, A., & Péley, B. (2014). Investigation of the compulsive and impulsive behavioral addictions among adolescents. *Psychiatria Hungarica: A Magyar Pszichiatriai Tarsasag tudomanyos folyoirata*, *29*(2), 152–157.

van der Kolk, B. A. (2005). Developmental trauma disorder: Toward a rational diagnosis for children with complex trauma histories. *Psychiatric Annals*, *35*(5), 401–408.

van der Kolk, B. A. (2015). *The body keeps the score: Brain, mind and body in the healing of trauma*. Penguin.van der Kolk, B. A., Ford, J. D., & Spinazzola, J. (2019). Comorbidity of developmental trauma disorder (DTD) and posttraumatic stress disorder: Findings from the DTD field trial. *European Journal of Psychotraumatology*, *10*(1), 1562841.

van der Kolk, B. A., & McFarlane, A. C. (Eds.). (1996). *Traumatic stress: The effects of overwhelming experience on mind, body, and society*. Guilford.

van Huijstee, J., & Vermetten, E. (2017). The dissociative subtype of posttraumatic stress disorder: Research update on clinical and neurobiological features. *Behavioral Neurobiology of PTSD*, 229–248.

Volling, B. L., Gonzalez, R., Oh, W., Song, J. H., Yu, T., Rosenberg, L., Kuo, P., Thomason, E., Sayfer, P., & Stevenson, M. M. (2017). *Developmental trajectories of children's adjustment across the transition to siblinghood: Pre-birth predictors and sibling outcomes at one year*. Wiley.

Vonderwalde, I. (2019). DNA methylation within the amygdala early in life increases susceptibility for depression and anxiety disorders. *Journal of Neuroscience, 39*(45), 8828–8830.

Wadsworth, M. E., Evans, G. W., Grant, K., Carter, J. S., & Duffy, S. (2016). Poverty and the development of psychopathology. In D. Cicchett (Ed.), *Developmental Psychopathology: Risk, Resilience, and Intervention* (pp. 136179). Wiley.

Waldeck, D., Tyndall, I., Riva, P., & Chmiel, N. (2017). How do we cope with ostracism? Psychological flexibility moderates the relationship between everyday ostracism experiences and psychological distress. *Journal of Contextual Behavioral Science, 6*(4), 425–432.

Waldinger, R. (2017). *The cross-border connection.* Harvard University Press.

Watson, J. C., & Greenberg, L. S. (2011). Empathic resonance: A neuroscience perspective. In J. Decety & W. Ickes (Eds.), *The social neuroscience of empathy* (pp. 125–138). MIT Press.

Wegner, D. M. (2007). Who is the controller of controlled processes? In R. R. Hassin, J. S. Uleman, & J. A. Bargh (Eds.), *The new unconscious* (pp. 19–37). Oxford University Press.

Wehry, A. M., Beesdo-Baum, K., Hennelly, M. M., Connolly, S. D., & Strawn, J. R. (2015). Assessment and treatment of anxiety disorders in children and adolescents. *Current Psychiatry Reports, 17*(7), 52.

Whalen, P. J., Shin, L. M., McInerney, S. C., Fischer, H., Wright, C. I., & Rauch, S. L. (2001). A functional MRI study of human amygdala responses to facial expressions of fear versus anger. *Emotion, 1*(1), 70–83.

Whiteman, S. D., Solmeyer, A. R., & McHale, S. M. (2015). Sibling relationships and adolescent adjustment: Longitudinal associations in two-parent African American families. *Journal of Youth and Adolescence, 44*(11), 2042–2053.

Whittle, N., Fadok, J., MacPherson, K. P., Nguyen, R., Botta, P., Wolff, S. B., Müller, C., Herry, C., Tovote, P., Holmes, A., Singewald, N., Lüthi, A., & Ciocchi, S. (2021). Central amygdala micro-circuits mediate fear extinction. *Nature Communications, 12*(1), 1–11.

Wilson, B. J. (2008). Media and children's aggression, fear, and altruism. *Future of Children, 18*(1), 87–118.

Winnicott, D. W. (1969). The use of an object. *International Journal of Psychoanalysis, 50*, 711–716.

Yassa, M. A., Hazlett, R. L., Stark, C. E., & Hoehn-Saric, R. (2012). Functional MRI of the amygdala and bed nucleus of the stria terminalis during conditions of uncertainty in generalized anxiety disorder. *Journal of Psychiatric Research, 46*, 1045–1052.

Yehuda, R., Engel, S. M., Seckl, J., Maecus, S. M., & Berkowitz, G. S. (2005). Transgenerational effects of posttraumatic stress disorder in babies of mothers exposed to World Trade Center attacks. *Journal of Clinical Endocrinology and Metabolism, 90*, 4115–4118.

Yochman, A., & Pat-Horenczyk, R. (2020). Sensory modulation in children exposed to continuous traumatic stress. *Journal of Child & Adolescent Trauma, 13*, 93102.

Zachar, P., & Ellis, R. D. (2012). *Categorical versus dimensional models of affect: A seminar on the theories of Panksepp and Russell.* Benjamins.

Zaidan, H., Leshem, M., & Glaisler-Salomon, I. (2013). Prereproductive stress to female rats alters corticotropin releasing factor type 1 expression in ova and behavior and brain corticotropin releasing factor type 1 in offspring. *Biological Psychiatry, 74*, 680–687.

Zanarini, M. C., Weingeroff, J. L., & Frankenburg, F. R. (2009). Defense mechanisms associated with borderline personality disorder. *Journal of Personality Disorders, 23*(2), 113–121.

Zavos, H. M., Rijsdijk, F. V., Gregory, A. M., & Eley, T. C. (2010). Genetic influences on the cognitive biases associated with anxiety and depression symptoms in adolescents. *Journal of Affective Disorders, 124*(1–2), 45–53.

Zvyagintsev, M., Klasen, M., Weber, R., Sarkheil, P., Esposito, F., Mathiak, K. A., Schwenzer, M., & Mathiak, K. (2016). Violence-related content in video game may lead to functional connectivity changes in brain networks as revealed by fMRI-ICA in young men. *Neuroscience, 320*, 247–258.

INDEX

Note: Italicized page locators refer to figures.

ABOUT THE AUTHOR

Efrat Ginot has been practicing psychotherapy and psychoanalysis for over 35 years in New York City. She has also taught and supervised other psychotherapists and is a graduate of the New York University Postdoctoral Program for Psychotherapy and Psychoanalysis.

Her published books and papers integrate psychoanalytic thinking and neuropsychological research in new and original ways, advancing our understanding of psychodynamics and psychotherapeutic processes. In 2002 she received the Gradiva Award for best article reexamining the concept of the Holding Environment.

Her book *The Neuropsychology of the Unconscious: Integrating Brain and Mind in Psychotherapy* received the Gradiva Award for Best Book in 2016.

Her book *Our Anxious Selves: Neuropsychological Processes and their Enduring Influence on Who We Are* focuses on the oversized role that fear and anxiety play in our lives. Dr. Ginot has given lectures and workshops in the US and abroad. She is also a painter.